MW00810813

THE RISE AND FALL OF THE CTHULHU MYTHOS

THE RISE AND FALL OF THE CTHULHU MYTHOS

S. T. JOSHI

MYTHOS BOOKS

Mythos Books, LLC
351 Lake Ridge Road
Poplar Bluff, MO 63901–2177

www. mythosbooks.com

Published by Mythos Books LLC 2008

FIRST EDITION

ISBN 0-9789911-8-4

Contents

Preface

THIS BOOK BEGAN as an expansion of a 15,000-word essay on the Cthulhu Mythos that I wrote for *Icons of Horror and the Supernatural* (Greenwood Press, 2006). I found that in the space allotted to me I was able to treat neither the fundamental issues pertaining to the Mythos nor certain individual works in the depth or detail they deserved; hence I decided to expand the book to make it a full-fledged study of the entire phenomenon of the Cthulhu Mythos. There has, of course, not been such a study since Lin Carter's popular work, *Lovecraft: A Look Behind the "Cthulhu Mythos"* (1972)—a work that, by even the most charitable standard, cannot be said to have been written with scholarly rigour. What is more, not only have a great many new stories and novels of the Cthulhu Mythos been written in the past three or four decades, but a wealth of new documentary evidence—especially letters by Lovecraft and other important figures in the early development of the Mythos—have come to light, and the burgeoning scholarly literature on Lovecraft has probed his life, work, and thought with admirable perspicacity. As a result, the tools are now available for a much more accurate and detailed account of the evolution of this curious subgenre of horror literature.

I myself have long been publicly known as being generally hostile to contributions to the Cthulhu Mythos by writers other than Lovecraft—and even to some of Lovecraft's own Mythos tales. I wish to make clear here that I do not believe this stance to be taken *à priori,* but as a result of my judgment that most of these contributions are inferior when gauged by abstract aesthetic standards. It should be evident from this treatise that I do find some Mythos contributions to be intrinsically meritorious, whether or not they depart from Lovecraft's own stated goals and purposes in fiction writing. Indeed, I welcome the work of writers who make innovative and ingenious departures from Lovecraft's style, themes, and worldview, since I cannot see any advantage in merely mimicking his own manner without adding something new and fresh.

It is, of course, impossible for any human being, within a reasonable time frame, to read all the multifarious contributions to the Cthulhu Mythos from 1926 to the present day—contributions that take the form of stories, novellas, novels, works appearing in online venues, and so forth. Chris Jarocha-Ernst's *A Cthulhu Mythos Bibliography and Concordance* (1999) lists 2631 works by Lovecraft and others, although this number seems substantially inflated by numerous items that are only tangentially related to Lovecraft's conceptions. In this study, I have paid particular attention to the earliest Mythos writings—by Lovecraft and his immediate colleagues—but have had to be much more selective when dealing with what I believe to be the most significant or noteworthy works by later hands. Many of the tales and novels that I have determined to be of minimal literary merit have been passed over in merciful silence, since I see little reason to engage in the condemnation of works that in any case have achieved, or will shortly achieve, the oblivion they deserve.

In the text and notes I use the following abbreviations for works by Lovecraft:

AT	*The Ancient Track: Complete Poetical Works* (2001)
CB	*Commonplace Book* (1987; 2 vols.)
CE	*Collected Essays* (2004–06; 5 vols.)
D	*Dagon and Other Macabre Tales* (1986)
DH	*The Dunwich Horror and Others* (1984)
LB	*Letters to Robert Bloch* (1993)
M	*At the Mountains of Madness and Other Novels* (1985)
HM	*The Horror in the Museum and Other Revisions* (1989)
MW	*Miscellaneous Writings* (1995)
SL	*Selected Letters* (1965–76; 5 vols.)

When referring to works by other authors, I include page citations within the text, and the reader can refer to the bibliography to ascertain which editions of these works I have used for citation. I use the abbreviation JHL to refer to manuscripts in the H. P. Lovecraft Papers, John Hay Library, Brown University.

Over the thirty years in which I have been involved with the study of Lovecraft, I have benefited from the advice and assistance of many individuals, notably Dirk W. Mosig, Donald R. Burleson, David E.

Schultz, Marc A. Michaud, Will Murray, and (in spite of my disagreements with him on the scope and direction of the Mythos) Robert M. Price. For this volume, I have received particular assistance from Peter Cannon, Scott Connors, Stefan Dziemianowicz, John D. Haefele, Rob Latham, and W. H. Pugmire.

—S. T. J.

Introduction

THE SO-CALLED CTHULHU MYTHOS seemed, for a time, destined to overwhelm the work of its own putative creator, H. P. Lovecraft (1890–1937). Even today, the Mythos is proliferating in a bewildering array of media, from role-playing games to card games to interactive games to even a Tarot deck, and of course "tales of the Cthulhu Mythos" continue to appear in large numbers in both print and online venues. But, possibly because of the (one hopes temporary) demise of Robert M. Price's lively *Crypt of Cthulhu* and its companion journals (such as *Chronicles of the Cthulhu Codex*) and the decline in output of Chaosium's Cthulhu Mythos volumes, the Mythos is not quite the behemoth it was a decade or so ago. What is more, Lovecraft's own reputation has risen exponentially in both popular and critical circles with such volumes as my three annotated editions from Penguin Classics and, preeminently, the volume of Lovecraft's *Tales* (2005) from the Library of America—the culmination of a decades-long quest by leading scholars to give Lovecraft a firm place in the canon of American literature.

Nevertheless, there are no doubt many who confuse Lovecraft's own writings with the many imitations that purport to pay homage to his memory—or, rather, who believe that these imitations ought to be uniformly welcomed as part of a phenomenon called the "Cthulhu Mythos" that is broader than Lovecraft's own work. The dominant trend of Lovecraft scholarship since the 1970s, however, has striven to draw a clear distinction between Lovecraft's own work and work by other hands—even those of his contemporaries, and in particular those of his self-styled disciples or followers. Stanley C. Sargent, one of the more talented of those followers, has written with apparent resentment that "the very scholars who have gone to such great lengths to ensure Lovecraft receives the literary recognition he deserves tend to dismiss all or nearly all contemporary attempts to continue Lovecraft's legacy,"[1] and he goes on to quote a rather uncharitable remark of my own on the subject. But if these scholars are in reality *uniformly* dismissive of such "contemporary attempts," then they have committed an aesthetic and methodological error. While there is validity in making a distinction—largely in order to clarify the scope of Lovecraft's achievement—between what Lovecraft wrote (both in its specifics and in its broader philosophical ramifications) and what others have written in imitation of or homage to him, there is no justification for a blanket condemnation of the latter without analysing in detail its virtues and drawbacks.

As I myself have frequently been characterised as being uniformly dismissive in this manner (in spite of my frequently declared admiration of some of the Mythos work of such writers as Ramsey Campbell, Karl Edward Wagner, and Stanley C. Sargent himself), I felt it was incumbent upon me to specify my approbation and my disapproval of Mythos work by both Lovecraft himself and his numerous successors—with the important caveat, stated repeatedly throughout this book, that my praise or blame does not stem from the given work's departure (or lack of departure) from Lovecraft's own conceptions, but from its possession or lack of possession of intrinsic literary merits as determined by relatively common and widely accepted critical principles: a skilful and effective prose style, competence in the execution of the plot, the display of vivid, realistic, non-stereotypical characters, and, perhaps most significantly, the presence of a vital and distinctive message about human life and the cosmos above and beyond its surface events. These features are found in the best of Lovecraft's own work, so it would seem logical to expect them to be present in the work of those of his imitators who claim to be engaging upon something more than merely a literary game.

The phenomenon of literary imitation has perhaps not been studied to the degree it deserves. In some senses, there is a latent paradox in the whole proceeding. If a work does nothing but evoke recollections of the original it is mimicking, can it have any independent aesthetic value? If it departs too markedly from the original in style, conception, or theme, can it even be considered an imitation? What, indeed, is the purpose of imitation? Lovecraft himself, wittingly or unwittingly, imitated some of his favourite writers from time to time, most notably Edgar Allan Poe, Lord Dunsany, and (to a much less obvious degree) Arthur Machen and Algernon Blackwood. But in the great majority of cases, these imitations were the product of his literary apprenticeship, and in his mature fiction-writing phase he had absorbed these and other influences so that his work, while leaving traces of his predecessors, remained emphatically his own. We can see precisely the same scenario at work in the career of the leading contemporary horror writer, Ramsey Campbell, who began with a volume of frank Lovecraft imitations, *The Inhabitant of the Lake and Less Welcome Tenants* (1964), but then proceeded to find his own voice in work of striking brilliance and originality—but in which echoes of such writers as Lovecraft, Robert Aickman, and others are nonetheless faintly present.

There is hardly any question that imitation is, by and large, the province of literary neophytes. What is more, some writers inspire imitation far more than others. C. L. Moore wrote in a letter to Lovecraft: "No one can imitate Dunsany, and probably everyone who's ever read him has tried."[2] The remark is much more pertinent to Lovecraft. No doubt some of the more flamboyant surface features of Lovecraft's tales—his seemingly florid prose style, the bizarre monsters he places on stage, and, perhaps more broadly, the entire universe of horror he evokes in story after story—have been fatally tempting to young writers, most of whom fail to grasp the aesthetic and philosophical substance underlying the lurid exterior. It is perhaps understandable that devotees would seek to replicate Lovecraft's effects by replicating only that lurid exterior rather than the substance beneath.

Whether they are aware of it or not, Lovecraft's imitators are really seeking to use Lovecraft's work as a kind of literary crutch. The mere citation of the name "Innsmouth," for example, evokes an entire realm of sinister horror without the author having to do the hard work of creating it on his own. I do not mean to suggest that there is anything duplicitous in this procedure, for it frequently occurs unconsciously or with the best of intentions—the intention, namely, of associating oneself with work that has been found to be intensely powerful, moving, and evocative. Nevertheless, the end result is that the imitator does little beyond producing a kind of tepid rewriting of Lovecraft's own stories. This has occurred in the work of such presumably professional writers as August Derleth and Brian Lumley, at a time when they were far beyond the level of apprentices.

It is for this reason that I will maintain, in the course of this book, that many of the best "imitations" of Lovecraft are, paradoxically, precisely those that expand upon or transcend his own conceptions. It is only when this occurs that the work gains an independent aesthetic value—or, at least, has the potential to do so, if it has other literary virtues that raise it above the level of hackwork. There is no aesthetic value in merely copying another writer, even if that copying occurs on the level of deeper philosophical resonance as opposed to obvious surface features. An author who, for example, does not really have a genuine sense of "cosmicism" cannot convey Lovecraftian cosmicism convincingly even by the sedulous mimicry of Lovecraftian vocabulary. The result will not ring true, and the work's hollowness will be patent to all.

Those scholars who have not merely segregated the work of Lovecraft's imitators from Lovecraft's own work, but have denied that there even is any such phenomenon as the "Cthulhu Mythos" even in Lovecraft's own writing, appear to have carried their zeal for purification a bit too far. David E. Schultz, in a provocative article called "Who Needs the 'Cthulhu Mythos'?," exhibited such a distaste for August Derleth's perversions of Lovecraft's conceptions that he proposed discarding both the term and the conception entirely. If this seems like an extreme procedure (throwing the baby out with the bathwater), Schultz's reasons for doing so—as far as Lovecraft's own work is concerned—are compelling:

> . . . the pseudomythological elements to which Lovecraft referred were only part of the fictional background of his stories. They were never the subject of his stories, but rather part of the background against which the main action occurred. That is to say, Lovecraft did not write *about* Cthulhu, Yog-Sothoth, the *Necronomicon,* or any of the other places or creatures or books found in his stories. The subject of his stories was typically the small place that man occupies in an uncaring cosmos, and his fictional creatures were only part of the means by which he sought to demonstrate that.[3]

All this is well taken, and the upshot is that there is, and should be, a legitimate distinction between Lovecraft's own creations—in the broadest sense of the term, referring not merely to the pseudomythological elements (Cthulhu, the *Necronomicon,* and the like)—and those of his contemporaries or successors. In this book I will refer to the former as the Lovecraft Mythos and the latter as the Cthulhu Mythos.

In this sense I am fully in agreement with Schultz in asserting that the Cthulhu Mythos can be almost entirely dispensed with if the purpose is to study Lovecraft's own creations as an aesthetic or philosophical unity. I say "almost" because, as is evident to even the most superficial reader, Lovecraft's work was itself at least (and probably at most) minimally influenced by his own contemporaries' attempts to add to or elaborate upon his pseudomythological conceptions.

If, however, one were to suggest (and I do not maintain that Schultz does so—he simply does not address the point) that there are *no* interrelations of plot elements in Lovecraft's tales, then one would definitely be in error. There manifestly *is* something going on in Lovecraft's stories (mostly the ones from his last decade of writing) that is markedly different from the stories of his earlier career, and from the work of the great majority of his predecessors in the realm of horror fiction. Whether we think of his evolving pseudomythological references as merely a kind of joke (as John D. Haefele does when, somewhat misleadingly, he maintains that "neither Lovecraft nor Derleth took the Cthulhu Mythos very seriously"[4]—ignoring the serious philosophical issues Lovecraft was treating in his fiction, in which the elements of the Lovecraft Mythos were tools toward their conveyance) or as something more weighty, we have to acknowledge that Lovecraft himself began the procedure of linking his stories within a mythic framework, so that each individual story built upon the rest and the result was more than the sum of its parts.

I myself have come to believe that the pseudomythological elements are *plot devices* designed to convey the various philosophical, aesthetic, cultural, and even political themes that Lovecraft was seeking to convey in his tales. In this sense it may not be quite accurate to say that Lovecraft never wrote "about" Cthulhu and the rest; "The Call of Cthulhu" really is largely "about" Cthulhu, at least on a surface level: we are given much information (possibly unreliable) about the nature and origin of this entity, and toward the end we see a glimpse of him through the eyes of the hapless Norwegian who encountered him. It might be better to say that "The Call of Cthulhu" is not *only* about Cthulhu; Cthulhu serves as a symbol for the vast, unknowable cosmos in which all human history and aspirations are as nothing.

There is now little doubt that Lovecraft's work as a whole is an aesthetic and philosophical unity, although in this regard we may have been more influenced by Lovecraft's own commentary rather than by a rigorous examination of the stories themselves. Schultz makes a point of quoting Lovecraft's celebrated statement of 1927:

> Now all my tales are based on the fundamental premise that common human laws and interests and emotions have no validity or significance in the cosmos-at-large. To me there is nothing but puerility in a tale in which the human form—and the local human passions and conditions and standards—are depicted as native to other worlds or other universes. To achieve the essence of real externality, whether of time or space or dimension, one must forget that such things as organic life, good and evil, love and hate, and all such local attributes of a negligible and temporary race called mankind, have any existence at all. Only the human scenes and characters must have human qualities. *These* must be handled with unsparing *realism,* (*not* catch-penny *romanticism*) but when we cross the line to the boundless and hideous unknown—the shadow-haunted *Outside*—we must remember to leave our humanity and terrestrialism at the threshold. (*SL* 2.150)

All this sounds very impressive, but I wonder whether "all" Lovecraft's tales do in fact adhere to this schema. I will, in fact, maintain that "The Dunwich Horror" flatly fails to do so, and that for this and other reasons it is an aesthetically inferior tale. Nevertheless, some acknowledgment must be given to Lovecraft's stated purpose, even if he himself was unable in every instance to embody it in his fiction.

To the extent, then, that the various components of the Lovecraft Mythos are worth chronicling or categorising, even if only as possibly frivolous or insignificant plot devices, it seems to me that they fall into four broad categories:

1) *A fictional New England topography.* Lovecraft began his career with very generalised New England settings (e.g., "The Tomb" [1917]) or with tales set more or less nebulously in Providence (e.g., "From Beyond" [1920]). But beginning with "The Terrible Old Man" (1920), an entire array of imaginary New England cities—Arkham, Kingsport, Dunwich, Innsmouth—and accompanying topographical landmarks such as the Miskatonic River begin to be developed, with each successive tale building upon its predecessor and resulting in a richly complex fictional geography analogous to, say, Thomas Hardy's Wessex or William Faulkner's Yoknapatawpha County. We will find that many of

these locales—especially the cities—will undergo significant modification or alteration from story to story, as Lovecraft never felt bound by his previous work in fashioning elements for a subsequent tale.

2) *A growing library of imaginary "forbidden" books.* These books—chief among them the *Necronomicon* of Abdul Alhazred—are cited with increasing frequency in tales by Lovecraft (and, especially, by others), to such a degree that, even within Lovecraft's lifetime, the practice began to develop some signs of mechanical triteness. Nevertheless, in its original or pure conception the notion that certain rare and obscure books held cosmic secrets too dangerous (more from a psychological than a physical perspective) for profane eyes was a powerful one, and it was one that would naturally have appealed to the bookish Lovecraft.

3) *A diverse array of extraterrestrial "gods" or entities.* This, of course, is the essential core of the Cthulhu (as distinguished from the Lovecraft) Mythos, as each successive writer has felt it incumbent to invent some new outlandish god with an unpronounceable name, hideous outward form, and immense powers, usually devoted to the destruction of the human race. For Lovecraft, it would appear that these "gods" (who, in later tales, cease to be gods at all but become simply extraterrestrial aliens) are symbols—sometimes representing the unknowability of an infinite cosmos, sometimes the inexorable forces of chaos and entropy, and sometimes still other features of his complex and evolving philosophy. On occasion, in letters, Lovecraft would speak flippantly of these entities, for of course there was a certain spirit of fun involved in the concoction of these synthetic monsters, but the underlying seriousness of their creation is evident in the tales themselves.

4) *A sense of cosmicism.* This may perhaps not be a "plot device" in any meaningful sense, but is perhaps more an umbrella term that is meant to subsume or encapsulate all the other plot devices. We have seen that Lovecraft himself enunciated this principle of cosmicism as the defining and unifying element in his work. It may not be immediately obvious how, for example, the creation of an imaginary New England topography fosters cosmicism in his tales, but this plot device is so frequently and exhaustively used in the tales of the Lovecraft Mythos that it is worth singling out as a separate phenomenon; possibly Lovecraft felt that the transition from the mundane to the cosmic could be

achieved more satisfactorily with the use of a fictitious but rigorously realistic topographical milieu.

A fifth element, which is by no means restricted to Lovecraft's Mythos tales, may be worth identifying—that of the scholarly narrator or protagonist. This element figures in tales that have few or no pseudo-mythological elements (e.g., "The Shunned House," *The Case of Charles Dexter Ward*), but it certainly becomes a characteristic feature of the Mythos tales, and has also been seized upon by other writers who have chosen not to use several of the other plot devices cited above. It is of interest how few of these protagonists are affiliated with orthodox institutions of learning; they tend to be, as Lovecraft himself was, "gentlemen narrators" (as R. Boerem has noted[5]) who pursue their researches largely for their own interest, although they quickly develop a sense of urgency when they come to realise the cosmic stakes involved. Even Nathaniel Wingate Peaslee of "The Shadow out of Time," an orthodox professor of economics, gradually shifts to the study of psychology and archaeology as he explores the mysteries of the Great Race. The use of such figures in Lovecraft's tales is by no means surprising, for it helps to facilitate the peculiarly intellectual nature of his aesthetic agenda—the conveyance of terror at the thought of human insignificance in a boundless cosmos.

It may be worth pausing to consider the question of what tales "belong to" or are a "part of" or "utilise" the Lovecraft Mythos. Schultz makes the keen point that "In the nearly fifty years that the term ['Cthulhu Mythos'] has been in existence, there has been no consensus as to what stories are part of the 'Mythos', nor has there been a clear idea of why some stories should belong to it and others should not, especially in the case of the work of Lovecraft himself."[6] To be sure, the disputes among August Derleth, Lin Carter, and others as to what tales do or do not "belong" to the Mythos now seem pedantic and irrelevant; but it may still be worth identifying, purely for the purposes of certain types of analysis, which tales utilise the pseudomythological background more intensively than others. As Dirk W. Mosig observed, "in some of the tales elements of the [Lovecraft Mythos] are of pivotal importance, while in others they assume a marginal role, or are absent."[7] Making such a distinction need do no harm to our understanding of the overall unity of Lovecraft's work, and is analogous to thematic studies that isolate certain tales for the purpose of tracing the use of that theme (e.g., the theme of hereditary degeneration) over the course of Lovecraft's career. I do not here intend to make any definitive list of "tales of the Lovecraft Mythos," but my ensuing analysis should make it evident that I regard some tales as of "pivotal importance" and others as less so.

The broader issue of why Lovecraft even devised these particular plot elements to convey his literary message is impossible to treat in a small space. We may begin by noting the apparent paradox of the resolutely atheistic Lovecraft creating a series of stories in which "gods" appear to play a prominent role. But is this a paradox? Lovecraft knew enough of anthropology to understand what the purpose of a religion or a mythology is; it is, in Milton's celebrated words, "to justify the ways of God to men" (*Paradise Lost* 1.26). The majority of human religions explicitly or implicitly establish an intimate connexion between God or the gods and the human race; we are the focus of their attention, even if the gods on occasion do terrible things (for example, wiping out an entire city or people for some perceived sin or wrong). But Lovecraft found that, by the creation of what David E. Schultz has called an "antimythology,"[8] he could most powerfully convey the atheistic message that we are in fact insignificant atoms lost in the vortices of a boundless cosmos; the "gods" (really symbols of cosmic outsideness) care little for us and destroy us as heedlessly as we would destroy a colony of ants. Schultz goes on to say:

> The new antimythology was an ideal means by which Lovecraft could infuse his stories with a sense of the cosmic or otherworldly. The notion of gods and forbidden books known only by scholars or a small cult of followers and revealed to be authentic, not mythological, gave power to Lovecraft's fictional themes. In early stories, characters are alienated from their race; in later stories, the entire race is alienated as a whole from the cosmoc. The insignificance (real or perceived) of individuals is easy for us to comprehend. Lovecraft's ability to depict the insignificance of the entire population of a planet ushers us into the presence of cosmic horror.[9]

This conception is worth exploring in considerable detail, but I do not have the space to do so here.

Given that my discussion focuses very largely on the Mythos elements in Lovecraft's tales, I have not left myself sufficient room for an analysis of the actual literary merits of those tales. In one sense, this is a serious omission, for it is exactly my contention that Lovecraft's tales—whether "Mythos" or otherwise—have aesthetic virtues transcending the various plot devices he uses to convey his themes and conceptions, so that a failure to specify those virtues would blunt the thrust of my overall argument, especially since I repeatedly maintain that many of the tales of his imitators lack these virtues. All I can say in my defence is that I have treated Lovecraft's tales in more literary and philosophical detail elsewhere,[10] and that a repetition of my arguments here would make this book longer than it has any right to be. I will, at any rate, discuss the literary virtues and failings of Lovecraft's imitators in considerably greater detail.

The bulk of this book is, of course, devoted to a study of "additions" or elaborations of the Cthulhu (rarely the Lovecraft) Mythos by other hands. I think that the mere existence of this phenomenon has not received the consideration it deserves. There is really no parallel in the entire history of literature for such enduring and wide-ranging attempts to imitate or develop a single writer's conceptions. The parallels with Sherlock Holmes imitations by writers other than Sir Arthur Conan Doyle break down quickly, since we are there dealing chiefly with an individual literary character and only secondarily with broader conceptual or thematic elements; in any case, the rigid control over such imitations that the Conan Doyle estate was able to effect, through its legitimate ownership of the copyright to the stories and therefore to the character of Sherlock Holmes, prevented the dissemination of these imitations beyond a select circle of chosen writers. August Derleth, now widely acknowledged as the true founder of the Cthulhu Mythos, occasionally attempted to assert copyright control over the Mythos, but the claim was obviously fallacious and could not be enforced.

These imitations, of course, began during Lovecraft's lifetime, and it is at this point that we must take great care in our use of terminology to designate the phenomenon. It has carelessly been said that Lovecraft "approved" or "encouraged" or even "orchestrated" the elaboration of his Mythos by other hands—especially such colleagues as August Derleth, Donald Wandrei, Clark Ashton Smith, Frank Belknap Long,

Robert E. Howard, Robert Bloch, Henry Kuttner, and Fritz Leiber—but this is a highly misleading characterisation of what actually transpired. There was very little he could do to prevent anyone—a close colleague or a stranger—from writing and publishing Cthulhu Mythos stories; and his mild-mannered, courteous, and collegial temperament would have prevented him from condemning or criticising even those contributions that in all probability did not suit his tastes or that violated the aesthetic principles he himself had embodied in his own stories.

The critical passage that many defenders of the Cthulhu Mythos use to justify their additions, or to claim that Lovecraft "approved" them (at least on the part of his contemporaries), is found in a letter to August Derleth: "The more these synthetic daemons [Cthulhu and Yog-Sothoth] are mutually written up by different authors, the better they become as general background-material! I *like* to have others use my Azathoths & Nyarlathoteps—& return I shall use Klarkash-Ton's Tsathoggua, your monk Clithanus, & Howard's Bran."[11] I shall study this passage in greater detail later (see Chapter VI); for now we can say that the first sentence would seem substantially more important than the second, especially as regards the term "background-material." For it was exactly as background-material that the earliest Mythos writers, notably Smith and Howard, used Lovecraft's various creations—just as Lovecraft himself used Smith's Tsathoggua and *Book of Eibon*, Howard's Bran and Valusia, Long's Hounds of Tindalos, and even Derleth's Tcho-Tcho people in his own tales. Once again, to use Schultz's formulation, neither Lovecraft nor Smith nor Howard actually wrote *about* the various elements they borrowed from each other; they employed them merely as "background-material." It was only Derleth who wrote *about* these elements, making them the focal point of the story and having no broader aesthetic or philosophical purpose than to expound the Mythos and set up a scenario whereby the Mythos "gods" and other entities go through a series of plausible or implausible actions whose significance does not extend beyond the surface events.

In this sense, the great majority of subsequent writers of the Mythos have unwittingly followed Derleth rather than Lovecraft. The obvious reason for this, to put it bluntly, is that these writers are, for the most part, deficient in literary talent: they have nothing to convey in their tales beyond a purportedly horrific or exciting sequence of events using the Mythos elements as if they were mechanical pieces on a board game. All such Mythos writing is merely a "parlour game," as Maurice Lévy rightly termed it,[12] and it has exactly the aesthetic value that most parlour games have. It is only the exceptional writer—Ramsey Campbell (following his juvenile imitations), Colin Wilson, Fred Chappell, William Browning Spencer, and a very few others—who have been able to infuse their Mythos tales with the aesthetic substance to justify their existence as independent literary creations; it is no accident that it is exactly these writers who have departed most significantly from mere imitation of Lovecraft's style or manner or content, using Mythos elements as a springboard for their own (not Lovecraft's) ideas and conceptions.

As Steven J. Mariconda has pointed out in a trenchant article,[13] Mythos writing from the 1920s to the 1940s was carried on very largely, if not exclusively, in the pages of *Weird Tales*. Not only did nearly all Lovecraft's own major tales—with the significant exceptions of "The Colour out of Space," *At the Mountains of Madness,* and "The Shadow out of Time"—appear in the magazine, but so did most of the Mythos additions of Smith, Howard, Long, Derleth, and others. It was in the pages of *Weird Tales* that readers (as exhibited in the magazine's letter column, "The Eyrie") began noticing that several writers were drawing upon what seemed to be a little-known and esoteric mythology, and began wondering whether such imaginary tomes as the *Necronomicon* or *De Vermis Mysteriis* were real and could be consulted. In a very real sense, the Cthulhu Mythos, in its first two or three decades, could well be called the *Weird Tales* Mythos. Even today, the majority of Mythos work appears in the pages of a few small-press publishers—Chaosium, Fedogan & Bremer, Mythos Books—or magazines, notably *Crypt of Cthulhu, Chronicles of the Cthulhu Codex,* and some online venues. What this seems to suggest is that hard-core Mythos writing is chiefly intended for a devoted coterie of readers who can be expected to be familiar with even the most obscure or recondite references to gods, books, and other paraphernalia; but the celebrity of Lovecraft and of the Mythos in general has allowed it to expand well beyond the small press and into the realm of mainstream publishing and media.

Now that Lovecraft has become a figure of world literature, the extent to which he and his work are cited in novels and tales by writers high and low has grown exponentially. We find references to him and his creations in the work of such writers as Jorge Luis Borges, Paul Theroux, Thomas Pynchon, and Gore Vidal. Even within the narrow fields of supernatural fiction or science fiction, Lovecraft continues to be a dominant presence. This makes it logistically difficult to encompass the entire range of Lovecraft imitations or elaborations in a single treatise, and I have therefore had to be selective in my purview. My focus is very strictly on the Lovecraft and/or Cthulhu Mythos—that is, on novels and tales that utilise several of what I have identified as the core components of the Mythos, not merely one or two. I have had to exclude a wide array of works, some of which have considerable literary merits in their own right—such things as treatments of Lovecraft as a fictional character (where Mythos elements are otherwise not present), imitations of Lovecraft's non-Mythos work, parodies, and so forth. In some cases, of course, the line cannot be drawn very precisely, and individual judgments will differ as to whether a given work does in fact incorporate a sufficient number of Mythos elements to qualify for discussion. The treatment of Lovecraft's posthumous reputation—both in the realm of criticism and in the realm of creative writing, not to mention the multi-faceted realms of media adaptations—will have to be saved for another day.

Perhaps some words on my criteria of judgment may be in order. I have striven for as much objectivity and lack of presupposition as possible, and, in spite of outward appearances, I do not believe I have conducted this exercise with an ingrained prejudice against Mythos writing by writers other than Lovecraft. I generally condemn those writers who have done nothing but retell Lovecraft's own tales (usually badly) or done nothing to elaborate upon his conceptions; but I do not always praise those who *do* elaborate upon his conceptions, for some elaborations (say, by Derleth and his followers) prove to be, from a purely aesthetic perspective, imaginatively impoverished and hackneyed. I think all creative artists should recognise the extreme difficulty of taking another writer's conceptions and building upon them. It is as if one were involved in an athletic competition wearing someone else's uniform— one that may or may not fit very well, and that may hamper one from performing up to one's capabilities. If most Mythos writing is apprentice work, as it appears to be, then it is not surprising that it is endowed with the aesthetic failings to which most apprentice work—Lovecraft's own emphatically included—is liable.

I.

Anticipations (1917–26)

THE TASK OF HUNTING out "anticipations" of the Lovecraft Mythos in Lovecraft's writings prior to "The Call of Cthulhu" (1926) is, conceptually, a highly problematical exercise, for this use of hindsight to trace a specific theme or motif in Lovecraft's fiction can easily create a kind of "inevitability effect," whereby Lovecraft is seen inexorably to be heading toward the creation of the Mythos from the very outset of his literary career. In fact, it is plain that he had no idea of evolving anything like the Mythos when he began his mature fiction-writing career in 1917, and that even after "The Call of Cthulhu" his development of what later came to be called the Cthulhu Mythos was halting and improvisational at best. Accordingly, in the tracing of anticipations of the "gods," places, books, and other elements of the Lovecraft Mythos in Lovecraft's pre-1926 fiction, it needs to be kept in mind that Lovecraft had no thought of evolving the Mythos and was motivated by very different concerns as a fiction writer; and when, by the mid- to late 1920s, he appears to have come to some understanding that his tales were cohering into some kind of rough unity (a unity more of theme and philosophical orientation than of plot elements), he seems to have decided to pluck certain random features of his prior work and reinterpret them in light of his burgeoning pseudomythology. As a result, these tales—or the features within them that were so plucked—took on a somewhat different aspect or focus from what they had when originally written.

With these caveats borne in mind, we can examine Lovecraft's pre-1926 fiction to see what elements might have anticipated the Lovecraft Mythos.

"Dagon" (written in July 1917) would seem to stand out preeminently in this regard, although we may have reason to think otherwise after we examine the story. The second tale (after "The Tomb" [June

1917]) written following Lovecraft's nine-year hiatus of fiction-writing (in 1908 he had destroyed all but two of the stories he had written in the preceding five years or so, preserving only "The Beast in the Cave" [1905] and "The Alchemist" [1908]), it appears to feature a "god" that Lovecraft utilised in several later tales, notably "The Shadow over Innsmouth" (1931). In what sense, then, does the figure of Dagon in "Dagon" anticipate its later usages?

The very mention of the entity—or, rather, the affixing of the name Dagon to the creature that the narrator encounters after the land mass arises in the Pacific—is problematical. The narrator states that, after his experience, he "sought out a celebrated ethnologist, and amused him with peculiar questions regarding the ancient Philistine legend of Dagon, the Fish-God; but soon perceiving that he was hopelessly conventional, I did not press my inquiries" (*D* 19). The narrator is wrong on one point: Dagon was not in fact a fish-god of the Philistines. The error, however, is not Lovecraft's, for the name Dagon (in reality a weather god or vegetation deity) was thought by early biblical scholars to coincide with the Semitic *dag on* ("fish of sadness"). Dagon makes his most vivid appearance in Judges 16:23–31, where Samson destroys the Temple of Dagon in Gaza. It is said there: "The lords of the Philistines assembled to offer a great sacrifice to their god Dagon, and to rejoice and say, 'Our god has delivered into our hands Samson our enemy'" (Judges 16:23).

Lovecraft, however, is not stating explicitly that the creature encountered by the narrator in the Pacific is identical to Dagon; the mention of "legends" suggests that, in the narrator's eyes, the Philistine legend of Dagon was derived from some ancient encounter with the underwater creature. This would be in consonance with much of the rest of Lovecraft's fiction, including some of the central tales of the Lovecraft Mythos, in which it is hinted that many elements of human myth and legendry are dim recollections of human encounters with such hideous entities as Cthulhu or Yog-Sothoth. And yet, a careful reading of the story may lead us to think that there is really no vital connexion between the sea-creature and Dagon at all. Note the narrator's one fleeting glimpse of the entity:

> Then suddenly I saw it. With only a slight churning to mark its
> rise to the surface, the thing slid into view above the dark waters. Vast,

Polyphemus-like, and loathsome, it darted like a stupendous monster of nightmares to the monolith, about which it flung its gigantic scaly arms, the while it bowed its hideous head and gave vent to certain measured sounds. (*D* 18)

This is clearly an act of *worship*. What is the object of its worship? The monolith contained "both inscriptions and crude sculptures" (*D* 17), and the latter depict some quasi-human creatures (albeit with "webbed hands and feet, shockingly wide and flappy lips, glassy, bulging eyes, and other features less pleasant to recall" [*D* 18]) in the act of "paying homage at some monolithic shrine which appeared to be under the waves as well" (*D* 18)—but Lovecraft does not specify *to whom* these creatures are paying homage. The suggestion is that the monster seen by the narrator is not the *object of worship*, but *one of the worshippers*. In other words, the monster is not Dagon himself (or the prototype of Dagon), but is the worshipper of Dagon (or the prototype of Dagon). The monster is, in fact, one of an entire race of creatures (perhaps the only surviving one), all of them of immense size. This is the point of the narrator's remark: "Curiously enough, they seemed to have been chiselled [on the monolith] badly out of proportion with their scenic background; for one of the creatures was shewn in the act of killing a whale represented as but little larger than himself" (*D* 18). What this means is that the inhabitants of the underworld civilisation are *all* nearly the size of whales. (Robert M. Price has made the grotesque suggestion that, at the conclusion of the tale, the narrator actually sees the monster walking down the streets of San Francisco from his hotel room; but Lovecraft makes clear in a letter that this was a hallucination.[1])

The end result of all this is that we do not actually know anything about the physical or other attributes of the "god" (let us call him Dagon, even if he is only Dagon's prototype) that the monster worships. Lovecraft does not describe Dagon on the monolith seen by the narrator. However, the fact that the narrator later asks an ethnologist about "Dagon, the Fish-God" might suggest that Dagon is a still larger version of the monster whom the narrator encounters.

It should also be noted that, although "Dagon" is considerably more "cosmic" than the conventional "The Tomb," there is no suggestion of the extraterrestriality of any of the entities mentioned or hinted at in the story. The monster is itself merely a product of some underwater civilisation, portions of which have been fortuitously brought to the surface by the earthquake described earlier in the story. In this sense, the parallel to Cthulhu breaks down, for of course Cthulhu is only "imprisoned" in the underwater city of R'lyeh, and his ultimate origin was from the remote depths of space.

Nevertheless, the parallels in plot elements, and even in certain usages of language, between "Dagon" and "The Call of Cthulhu" are striking—to such a degree that, as David E. Schultz has pointed out, the latter is a "'cosmic' rewrite" of the former.[2] The resemblances are patent: the sudden emergence of a sunken land mass in the Pacific as a result of an earthquake; the brief but cataclysmic glimpse of the entity; the use of similar language in describing the entity (in "The Call of Cthulhu" it is stated: ". . . the titan Thing from the stars slavered and gibbered like Polypheme cursing the fleeing ship of Odysseus" [DH 153]); and the concluding philosophical reflexions about the perilous state of humanity in the wake of the creature's mere existence (in "Dagon": "I dream of a day when they [the creatures from the sea] may rise above the billows to drag down in their reeking talons the remnants of puny, war-exhausted mankind" [D 19]; in "The Call of Cthulhu": "Loathsomeness waits and dreams in the deep, and decay spreads over the tottering cities of men" [DH 154]).

But the most significant parallel between the two stories, and the chief point of resemblance between "Dagon" and the major tales of the Lovecraft Mythos, is Lovecraft's quite radical suggestion that we are dealing not (as with the great majority of previous works of supernatural fiction) with a single monstrous entity, but with an entire civilisation lurking beneath the waves—a kind of *counter-civilisation* that is only waiting its chance to overthrow "the remnants of puny, war-exhausted mankind." This is the true source of the (modified) cosmicism of the story; as Matthew H. Onderdonk noted:

> In "Dagon" we have the most concise and perhaps the best expression of the whole Lovecraftian credo. The account is factual and circumstantial, the idea of a submarine upheaval in the ocean's floor is plausible. That such an eventuation might produce evidence of a lost race does not seem impossible. . . . Over it all hangs the awareness of the terrible and acknowledged antiquity of the earth and man's tenuous sinecure thereon.[3]

That opening sentence may be a bit of an exaggeration, but Onderdonk's point is well taken.

The "forbidden book" theme enters Lovecraft's fiction in his very next tale, "Polaris" (1918), although rather tangentially. We find here a casual mention of the "long hours I gave each day to the study of the Pnakotic manuscripts and the wisdom of the Zobnarian Fathers" (*D* 22). Later, after hearing the spirit of the Pole Star whisper a curious poem to him, the narrator remarks: "Vainly did I struggle with my drowsiness, seeking to connect these strange words with some lore of the skies which I had learnt from the Pnakotic manuscripts" (*D* 23). That is all we learn, in this story, of these fugitive documents.

The Pnakotic Manuscripts (Lovecraft was careful to leave the title unitalicised, since it is a manuscript and not a printed work) make an appearance in nine subsequent Lovecraft stories and revisions, perhaps most strikingly in *The Dream-Quest of Unknown Kadath* (1926–27) and "The Shadow out of Time" (1934–35). Lovecraft was clearly taken with the idea of a *prehuman* document (as the Manuscripts are later described). Here, of course, they are merely *prehistoric*. For what has happened in this tale is that the mind of the narrator has been seized by a remote ancestor, 26,000 years in the past, and thrust into that ancestor's body. Upon his return to his own body, he is plagued by the fact that, partly through his own (i.e., his ancestor's) derelictions, he allowed the city of Olathoë, in the land of Lomar, to be overrun by the Inutos.

It should be made clear that the narrator is not in fact dreaming, but has had an access of ancestral memory. This point is worth noting when we come to study the *Dream-Quest*. For now, we can quickly take a look at the mention of the Pnakotic Manuscripts in another early story, "The Other Gods" (1921). There it is stated that Barzai the Wise was "deeply learned in the seven cryptical books of Hsan, and familiar with the Pnakotic Manuscripts" (*D* 128; this is the first time that the word "manuscripts" is capitalised), and later: "Now it is told in the mouldy Pnakotic Manuscripts that Sansu found naught but wordless ice and rock when he climbed Hatheg-Kla in the youth of the world" (*D* 131). The fact that "The Other Gods" also takes place in a prehistoric world (not a dream-world) may lend some weight to the word "mouldy": if the Manuscripts are already mouldy at this early date, perhaps they are prehuman after all. It is not clear what kind of entity

Sansu was—he could be human, but he could also be something else. The comment in "Polaris" that the Manuscripts contain some "lore of the skies" is not entirely helpful; perhaps it is meant to suggest some kind of treatise about cosmic entities. If that is the case, then Barzai's interest in the text would be understandable, since he is seeking information about the gods atop Hatheg-Kla. (These are, of course, merely the "gods of earth" [D 131], and the fact that he is startled to discover that Hatheg-Kla also holds "the *other* gods . . . the gods of the outer hells that guard the feeble gods of earth" [D 131] suggests that the Pnakotic Manuscripts contain nothing about these more baleful entities.)

The forbidden book theme is developed in "The Statement of Randolph Carter" (1919), where Harley Warren has a whole shelf of "strange, rare books on forbidden subjects"; the narrator describes them: "Most, I believe, are in Arabic; and the fiend-inspired book which brought on the end—the book which he carried in his pocket out of the world—was written in characters whose like I never saw elsewhere" (M 300). George Wetzel ought to have known better than to have stated that this book is "undoubtedly . . . the first mention in the Mythos" of the *Necronomicon*.[4] If the narrator knew Arabic and yet confessed that this book was in characters he had not seen elsewhere (and by implication the characters could not be English or Greek), then surely this is *not* the *Necronomicon*, for that book (as later stories make clear) exists only in Arabic (as *Al Azif*), Greek, Latin, and English. It is, in fact, stated later in the story that the book "came to him [Warren] from India" (M 300).

And yet, Wetzel may have been right in a broader sense, for this brief mention may in fact have been the nucleus of Lovecraft's concept of the *Necronomicon*. Warren's purpose in examining the underground tomb off the Gainesville pike is to test "his theory, *why certain corpses never decay, but rest firm and fat in their tombs for a thousand years*" (M 300), and this theory was clearly derived from his reading of the book from India. This approximate idea is expressed in an actual citation from the *Necronomicon* in "The Festival" (1923): "For it is of old rumour that the soul of the devil-bought hastes not from his charnel clay, but fats and instructs *the very worm that gnaws*" (D 216). So clearly both the *Necronomicon* (at this stage) and the book from India have something to do with corpses (hence the *necro-* stem, meaning "the dead") and with their ability (through sorcery?) to continue their existence in the grave without decaying.

"The Picture in the House" (December 1920) deals with a real book—Pigafetta's *Regnum Congo*—although Lovecraft's description of it makes it sound far weirder than it is. (He never saw this book at first hand, instead relying on a none too accurate description of it in an essay by Thomas Henry Huxley.[5]) Abdul Alhazred is first cited in "The Nameless City" (January 1921), where his "unexplainable couplet," "That is not dead which can eternal lie, / And with strange aeons even death may die" (*D* 98–99), is supplied. Here again the notion of bodily survival after death appears to be suggested. It is now widely known that the name Abdul Alhazred (a linguistic abomination in Arabic, since it contains a reduplicated article: Abd*ul Al*hazred) was coined during Lovecraft's juvenile *Arabian Nights* phase, possibly as early as the age of five. He states that "a certain elder—the family lawyer, as it happens"[6] may either have coined the name or "criticise[d] the choice I had otherwise made." (The family lawyer was one Albert A. Baker.) It should be stressed that the title *Necronomicon* is nowhere mentioned in "The Nameless City." Even though, in "History of the *Necronomicon*" (1927), Lovecraft describes Alhazred as "a mad poet of Sanaá, in Yemen" (*MW* 52), there is little evidence aside from the couplet that Alhazred wrote any extensive amount of poetry or that the *Necronomicon*—of which Alhazred is explicitly made the author in "The Hound" (September 1922)—contained much in the way of poetry. Indeed, if we assume that the couplet did in fact appear in the *Necronomicon*, the mere fact that Lovecraft so frequently singles it out as a "couplet" suggests that it is a stand-alone insertion into a largely prose text, rather than an extract from a longer versified work.

In "The Nameless City" it is written that "It was of this place [the nameless city in Arabia] that Abdul Alhazred the mad poet dreamed on the night before he sang his unexplainable couplet" (*D* 98). This information could only have come from text surrounding the couplet in Alhazred's book (whatever it was at this time). The couplet is cited again later in the story (*D* 109), and other esoteric works are also cited:

> In the darkness there flashed before my mind fragments of my cherished treasury of daemoniac lore; sentences from Alhazred the mad Arab, paragraphs from the apocryphal nightmares of Damascius,

and infamous lines from the delirious *Image du Monde* of Gauthier de Metz. I repeated queer extracts, and muttered of Afrasiab and the daemons that floated with him down the Oxus; later chanting over and over again a phrase from one of Lord Dunsany's tales—"the unreverberate blackness of the abyss". (*D* 103)

All these are (more or less) real. Damascius is mentioned in entry 121 of Lovecraft's commonplace book:

Photius tells of a (lost) writer named Damascius, who wrote
"Incredible Fictions"
"Tales of Daemons"
"Marvellous Stories of Appearances from the Dead". (*CB* 1.7)

Unfortunately, we do not know where Lovecraft derived this information. Photius' *Bibliotheca* (codex 130) mentions the works of Damascius (see *CB* 2.42), but how Lovecraft could have seen this text, or any discussion of it, remains unclear. Gauthier de Metz's *Image du Monde* is mentioned in the very next entry in the commonplace book: "Horrible things whispered in the lines of Gauthier de Metz (13th cen.) 'Image du Monde'" (*CB* 1.7). Lovecraft probably got this tidbit from S. Baring-Gould's *Curious Myths of the Middle Ages*, a book he owned and which clearly influenced "The Rats in the Walls" among others. Interestingly, in the first appearance of "The Nameless City" (*Wolverine*, November 1921), there was no mention of Gauthier de Metz; Lovecraft had written instead, "paragraphs from Poe and Baudelaire, and thoughts from the venerable Ambrose Bierce" (see *CB* 2.43). Lovecraft no doubt found this a bit tame, and when he revised the story (no earlier than the summer of 1923, when he first read Baring-Gould) he inserted the mention of Gauthier. The mention of Afrasiab is taken from Poe's "The Premature Burial." The sentence from Lord Dunsany occurs at the very end of the story "The Probable Adventure of the Three Literary Men," which Lovecraft admitted had actually inspired the story (see *SL* 1.122).

Finally, we come to "The Hound," where we learn that the two decadent protagonists come upon a curious amulet from the tomb of an undecaying corpse (note that theme again) in Holland: "we recognised it as the thing hinted of in the forbidden *Necronomicon* of the mad Arab Abdul Alhazred; the ghastly soul-symbol of the corpse-eating cult of inaccessible Leng, in Central Asia" (*D* 174). This is, chronologically, the first mention of the *Necronomicon* in Lovecraft's fiction. Later we learn that the protagonists "read much in Alhazred's *Necronomicon* about its [the amulet's] properties, and about the relation of ghouls' souls to the objects it symbolised" (*D* 174).

It is in "The Festival" (late 1923) that an actual (prose) citation from the *Necronomicon* occurs. I have already quoted a portion of it above. The narrator has discovered the book among a number of esoteric works he has found in a home in Kingsport, where he has come to celebrate a festival of which he knows little:

> . . . when I sat down to read I saw that the books were hoary and mouldy, and that they included old Morryster's wild *Marvells of Science,* the terrible *Saducismus Triumphatus* of Joseph Glanvil, published in 1681, the shocking *Daemonolatreia* of Remigius, printed in 1595 at Lyons, and worst of all, the unmentionable *Necronomicon* of the mad Arab Abdul Alhazred, in Olaus Wormius' forbidden Latin translation; a book which I had never seen, but of which I had heard monstrous things whispered. (*D* 211)

Here again all works except the *Necronomicon* itself are real—or, rather, are not Lovecraft's invention. Morryster's *Marvells of Science* is cited Ambrose Bierce's "The Man and the Snake," which Lovecraft first read in 1919. *Saducismus Triumphatus* is a defence of witchcraft belief. It is not known how Lovecraft came to learn of this volume: Poe cites Glanvil (or Glanvill) by name in "Ligeia" and "A Descent into the Maelström"; possibly Lovecraft consulted an annotated edition that cited Glanvill's book. The *Daemonolatreia* by Remigius (Nicholas Remy) is a real work, and we do not know how Lovecraft learned of it: Montague Summers's English translation dates only to 1930. The mention of Olaus Wormius here is one of only two citations in Lovecraft's fiction, the other occurring in "The Dunwich Horror" (1928).

Later in "The Festival" it is stated that the leader of the underground ceremony at one point "held above his head that abhorrent *Necronomicon* he had taken with him" (*D* 214); and at the very end of the story the narrator, now in a hospital, asks the doctors to let him consult a copy of the book, and thereby supplies the quotation that both concludes the story and presumably explains the events of the story. It is not entirely clear how it does so. The phrase quoted earlier ("For it is of old rumour . . .") suggests that the leader of the ceremony is in fact a preternaturally aged individual (as hinted by the narrator's glimpse of a watch borne by the leader, which "had been buried with my great-great-great-great-grandfather in 1698" [*D* 215]) who has prolonged his life by sorcery. Another quotation—"Great holes secretly are digged where earth's pores ought to suffice, and things have learnt to walk that ought to crawl" (*D* 216)—appears to refer to the underground tunnels that, in a memorable phrase, have made Kingsport "maggoty with subterraneous evil" (*D* 213) as well as to the hideous creatures encountered by the narrator underground ("a horde of tame, trained, hybrid winged things that no sound eye could ever wholly grasp, or sound brain ever wholly remember" [*D* 215]).

From these fleeting hints we can come up with some idea of what the *Necronomicon* was at this juncture. Clearly, as stated before, the notion of the anomalous properties of the dead (perhaps of dead sorcerers or "ghouls") is a central theme in the work. This point is worth emphasising not only because the title itself suggests it, but because, at this time in his career, Lovecraft had not in fact devised the notion of extraterrestrial "gods" or entities—except very fleetingly in a few stories we shall study later. Therefore, the *Necronomicon* at this moment was not at all the "cosmic" document that it would become later, when it tells of Cthulhu, Yog-Sothoth, and the rest. If anything, the persistent theme of bodily survival through sorcery is virtually all we know of the contents of the *Necronomicon* prior to 1926.

Much nonsense has been written in regard to the etymology of the Greek word "Necronomikon." Lovecraft himself started the absurdity by stating in a late letter: "The name *Necronomicon* (*nekros*, corpse; *nomos*, law; *eikōn*, image = An Image [or Picture] of the Law of the Dead) occurred to me in the course of a dream, although the etymology is perfectly sound" (*SL* 5.418). Unfortunately, for Lovecraft, who never progressed beyond the first six books of Xenophon's *Anabasis*, his etymology is almost entirely unsound. The last portion of it is particularly erroneous, since *-ikon* is nothing more than a neuter adjectival suffix and has nothing to do with *eikōn* (image).

There is more controversy over the *-nom* part of the term. The idea that it relates to *onoma* (name), leading some to translate the title as "The Book of Dead Names," can be ruled out immediately. Wetzel was a little closer to the truth when he drew a parallel between *Necronomicon* and *Astronomicon*, a poem on the stars by the Latin writer Manilius.[7] The etymology of *Necronomicon* has to be determined by analogy with such words as *astronomikos*, and by consultation of any one of several standard works on Greek etymology (for example, Emile Boisacq's *Dictionnaire étymologique de la langue grecque* [1919]) we learn that *astronomikos* is derived from *astron* (star) and *nemo*, a verb initially meaning "to divide" (as in a plot of land) and secondarily meaning "to consider." So the simple "meaning" of *Necronomicon* is "Book considering [or classifying] the dead."

This etymology, which I enunciated more than a quarter-century ago, has been attacked from time to time. There are those who still believe that *-nom* has to do with *nomos* (law, custom) or *nomikos* (relating to the law or [of an individual] learned in the law), so that the title would translate to "Book on the Laws of the Dead." But *nomos* (hence *nomikos*) is itself derived from *nemo*. Joan C. Stanley, in her entertaining work of pseudo-scholarship, *Ex Libris Miskatonici* (1993), contests my derivation, remarking: "A cursory examination of any Greek grammar will show that the verb can be neither conjugated nor inflected in any manner or in any dialect to allow for such an assertion."[8] I fear this is nonsense. In the first place, a *verb* cannot be inflected (this pertains only to nouns, adjectives, and pronouns). Secondly, no one is asserting that the *-nom-* stem is "conjugated" from *nemo;* but every Greek etymological dictionary *does* assert that *-nom-* is etymologically derived from *nemo*.

Robert M. Price, fresh from his study of deconstruction and other avant-garde modes of literary analysis, rattles off a succession of derivations—"Lovecraft ('Image of the Law of the Dead'), George Wetzel ('Book of the Names of the Dead'), Manly Bannister ('Book of the Laws of the Dead'), Colin Wilson ('Book of Dead Names'), S. T. Joshi ('Book Concerning the Dead'), and Pierre de Caprona ('Knower of the Laws of Death')"—and dismisses them all, claiming: "there *is* no meaning in that line of self-referring signifiers. Like the poem according to New Critical doctrine, the word 'Necronomicon' should not *mean* but simply *be*."[9] All this sounds clever, but in reality there are *two* things that the word "Necronomicon" means: what it actually means by the laws of Greek etymology ("Book considering [or classifying] the dead") and what Lovecraft *thought* it meant ("Image [or Picture] of the Laws of the

Dead"). It is, however, of interest to see that both these meanings have a distinctly uncosmic implication, relating merely to matters of life and death (whether of human beings or of other entities). Lovecraft later adapted the *Necronomicon* to convey far broader hints as to the nature of the universe and of humanity's place therein.

The broader question of where Lovecraft got the idea of imaginary books of "forbidden" knowledge is difficult to treat in short compass. One can point to the glancing mention, in "Supernatural Horror in Literature," of the "dramatic paraphernalia" of the old Gothic novels, one of which is the citation of "mouldy hidden manuscripts" (*D* 375). These manuscripts are, however, chiefly documents by human hands telling of their own adventures (such as the lengthy narrative of Monçada in Maturin's *Melmoth the Wanderer*), so the parallel to Lovecraft's own imaginary books is tangential at best. Donald R. Burleson cites a passage from Hawthorne's *American Notebooks*, dated October 17, 1835—"An old volume in a large library,—every one to be afraid to unclasp and open it, because it was said to be a book of magic"[10]—that he believes may be a source for the *Necronomicon*. Lovecraft certainly read Hawthorne very thoroughly, and his citation of an "unwritten plot" by Hawthorne, taken from the *American Notebooks*, in entry 46 of the commonplace book suggests that he had read the passage in question no later than 1921. (Schultz believes that an earlier entry, #42, is also derived from the *American Notebooks*, and this entry is the nucleus of "The Outsider" [1921].) Hawthorne is indeed one possible source; but consider this passage:

> Our books—the books which, for years, had formed no small portion of the mental existence of the invalid—were, as might be supposed, in strict keeping with this character of phantasm. We pored together over such works as the Ververt et Chartreuse of Gresset; the Belphegor of Machiavelli; the Heaven and Hell of Swedenborg; the Subterranean Voyage of Nicholas Klimm by Holberg; the Chiromancy of Robert Flud, of Jean D'Indaginé, and of De la Chambre; the Journey into the Blue Distance of Tieck; and the City of the sun of Campanella. One favorite volume was a small octavo edition of the *Directorium Inquisitorum*, by the Dominican Eymeric de Gironne; and there were passages in Pomponius Mela, about the old African Satyrs and Œgipans, over which Usher would sit dreaming for hours. His chief delight, however, was found in the perusal of an exceedingly rare

and curious book in quarto Gothic—the manual of a forgotten church—the *Vigiliae Mortuorum secundum Chorum Ecclesiae Maguntinae.*[11]

This is, of course, from Poe's "The Fall of the House of Usher." T. O. Mabbott notes that "The books mentioned as in the library of Roderick Usher are all—save *The Mad Trist*, which is integral to the action— actual books."[12] (Mabbott refers to a later sentence in the story: "The antique volume which I had taken up was the 'Mad Trist' of Sir Launcelot Canning . . ."[13]) This catalogue of titles is precisely analogous to those already cited in "The Nameless City" and "The Festival": Lovecraft's books are also for the most part real (or, if not real, not invented by himself), and the imaginary ones are exactly those that are "integral to the action."

It is, of course, understandable that a bookish individual like Lovecraft, who from a very early age saw in books a pathway to realms of unimagined wonder and terror, would be inclined to devise treatises of "forbidden lore" in tales early and late. What it suggests, in a broader thematic sense, is the peculiar power of words themselves—all apart from what the words signify—to have a *direct* impact or influence upon physical events. It is not surprising, therefore, that incantations are used throughout the tales of the Lovecraft Mythos, early and late.

It is also worth pondering the very notion of "forbidden" knowledge. Forbidden from what? The idea might strike us as superficially similar to the Catholic church's *Index Expurgatorius,* a list of books that Catholics are prohibited from reading because they are deemed threatening to orthodoxy; but clearly Lovecraft has a much wider implication in mind. These texts are "forbidden" because they reveal truths about humanity and its relation to the cosmos that could be both psychologically and physically threatening, jeopardising even our fleeting and tenuous position on this microscopic inkblot of a planet, lost in the vortices of space and time.

The third theme that I have defined as central to the Lovecraft Mythos—the imaginary place, specifically the collocation of imaginary cities in New England—is introduced in "The Terrible Old Man" (early 1920), which takes place in Kingsport. While "The Tomb" has a generalised New England setting, no specific cities or other landmarks are mentioned. "Beyond the Wall of Sleep" (1919) takes place in upstate

New York, a locale Lovecraft had not then visited and would not visit for years. "The Statement of Randolph Carter" is a bit of a puzzle. In recounting the dream that inspired the story, Lovecraft tells his fellow members of the Gallomo (the Midwesterners Alfred Galpin and Maurice W. Moe) about the "very ancient cemetery" that is the setting for the dream (and the story), adding: "I suppose no Wisconsinite can picture such a thing—but we have them in New-England" (*SL* 1.94). This does not definitively place the dream in New England, but the implication is surely there. But when Lovecraft came to write the story, he has the protagonists walking "together . . . on the Gainsville [*sic*] pike, walking toward Big Cypress Swamp" (*M* 299). When I prepared my corrected editions of Lovecraft's tales for Arkham House, I was persuaded by James Turner to emend "Gainsville" to "Gainesville," in the belief that Lovecraft meant to refer to the city in Florida. This would appear to make some sense: certainly there are few cypress swamps in New England; but conversely, there are probably not very many "very ancient cemeteries" in Florida. In any event, no other place name is cited in "The Statement of Randolph Carter." (In "Through the Gates of the Silver Key" it is remarked that Harley Warren is a "South Carolina mystic" [*M* 422], thereby perhaps lending some support to a southern setting of the story.)

But the Kingsport of "The Terrible Old Man" is very clearly in New England, both topographically and culturally. Even though the three immigrants who prove to be the victims of the story—Angelo Ricci, Joe Czanek, and Manuel Silva—represent the three dominant immigrant groups in Providence (Italian, Polish, and Portuguese), they are widely dispersed in the rest of New England as well; and the double-edged satire implicit in the reference to "that new and heterogeneous alien stock which lies outside the charmed circle of New England life and traditions" (*DH* 273) briskly portrays the social prejudice that old-time New Englanders (like Lovecraft) directed toward the unprecedented influx of foreigners from southern and eastern Europe in the 1890–1920 period.

At all events, the one thing to remember is that the Kingsport of "The Terrible Old Man" is a purely imaginary construct. The town was not associated with Marblehead, Mass., until "The Festival," written nearly a year after Lovecraft first visited that haven of colonial antiquity in December 1922. It may seem uncanny that there is in fact a Water Street in Marblehead, as mentioned in "The Terrible Old Man" (*DH* 272), but the coincidence is not particularly notable, since many coastal towns have Water Streets. All that we can conclude from this early story is that the town is in fact a seaport, analogous both in function and in name to Newburyport (which Lovecraft would first visit in 1923 and later use as the model for Innsmouth) and Newport, R.I. There has been some random speculation as to the origin of the name "Kingsport," but it would seem nothing more than a demonstration of Lovecraft's Anglophilia. Knowing of the prevalence of royal names prior to the Revolution, Lovecraft was probably having a bit of fun envisioning a city that—unlike Brown University, which felt it prudent to change its name from King's College after the United States' secession from England—retained its nomenclatural allegiance to Great Britain.

Arkham receives its first citation in "The Picture in the House." Here we have a bicyclist who had been spending some time "amongst the people of the Miskatonic Valley in quest of certain genealogical data" and was seeking to find "the shortest cut to Arkham" (*DH* 117). This is the first mention of the word Miskatonic in Lovecraft's fiction. Now that Will Murray's theory that Arkham had initially been placed inland has been demolished,[14] there is no reason to think that Arkham here is anywhere except on the coast, as in later stories. Whether it is at this point a fictional version of Salem is not entirely clear. The only other mention of the town in the story occurs when the preternaturally aged inhabitant of the ramshackle house croaks: "I hain't seed many folks 'long this rud sence they tuk off the Arkham stage" (*DH* 120). I am not interested in debating where Lovecraft derived the terms Arkham and Miskatonic. In the absence of documentary evidence from Lovecraft's letters, we can only conjecture. I have my doubts as to Robert Marten's theory that Arkham comes from the tiny village of Arkwright in Rhode Island.[15] "Miskatonic" seems pretty obviously based upon Housatonic, a river (and valley) in central Massachusetts extending down into Connecticut; but the location of the Housatonic need have no bearing on Lovecraft's placement (if, indeed, he had a definite placement in mind at this stage) of the Miskatonic Valley. (The Miskatonic River is not explicitly mentioned until "The Silver Key" [1926]; Miskatonic University is first cited in "Herbert West—Reanimator" [1921–22].)

Innsmouth is, curiously enough, mentioned in the Dunsanian story "Celephaïs" (November 1920), in a throwaway line: ". . . below the cliffs at Innsmouth the channel tides played mockingly with the body of a tramp who had stumbled through the half-deserted village at dawn" (*D* 89). This Innsmouth, of course, is in England, since the "tramp" in question is Kuranes, who was "alone among the indifferent millions of London" (*D* 83). Innsmouth would not be transferred to New England until its citation in several sonnets of *Fungi from Yuggoth* (1929–30).

Lovecraft gradually begins linking his imaginary towns in stories of the early 1920s. "Herbert West—Reanimator" does not contain much helpful data aside from the creation of Miskatonic University, specifically the medical school where Herbert West and his sidekick, the narrator of the story, are enrolled. Sefton Asylum—the institution where the reanimated Dr. Halsey is placed—is of some interest. Is this simply the name of the institution, or does it suggest that there is a nearby town called Sefton? The matter is unclear, since the name never recurs in any other Lovecraft tale. Still more interesting is the citation of "the neighbouring town of Bolton" (*D* 142). Now Bolton is a real town in east-central Massachusetts, but Lovecraft's description of it seems off the mark. It was (and is) a small agricultural community, but Lovecraft's mention of a "Bolton Worsted Mills" (*D* 144, 150) would suggest that it is an industrial community (he explicitly refers to it in "Herbert West" as a "factory town" [*D* 144]), which it manifestly is not. I remain unconvinced by Robert Marten's conjecture[16] that Lovecraft meant to coin an imaginary town and was unaware of the existence a real Bolton. My feeling is that simply changed the character of the (real) Bolton to suit his fictional purposes. Surely he was not bound to reproduce accurately the nature of a town that almost none of his readers was likely to have heard of. And once again, we need not assume that Lovecraft's Bolton is to be placed exactly (or even approximately) where the real Bolton is situated.

"The Unnamable" (September 1923) is of interest in supplying an implicit link between Arkham and Salem. The opening of the story finds Randolph Carter and Joel Manton sitting "on a dilapidated seventeenth-century tomb in the late afternoon of an autumn day at the old burying-ground in Arkham" (*D* 200); nearby is a tree "whose trunk has nearly engulfed an ancient, illegible slab." Now exactly such a tree-engulfed slab can be found in the Charter Street Burying Ground in Salem; I saw it myself years ago. (Recent visitors to the site state that the slab is no longer there.) Lovecraft himself states as much in a letter: "There is actually an ancient slab half engulfed by a giant willow in the middle of the Charter St. Burying Ground in Salem" (*SL* 2.139). The tale is otherwise an effective evocation of the lurking horrors of ancient New England (the core of the plot is taken from a passage in Cotton Mather's *Magnalia Christi Americana*).

As for "The Festival," its transformation of Marblehead into Kingsport is remarkable: while one can virtually duplicate the narrator's walk through the town in present-day Marblehead, Lovecraft's exquisite prose-poetry infuses the locale with an historic profundity that has a certain cosmicism of its own. There is some little controversy over exactly which real church (if any) Lovecraft had in mind for the tale; it was formerly believed that St. Michael's Episcopal Church (appropriately in Frog Lane) was the fane in question, but recent research by Donovan Loucks makes it clear that Lovecraft was alluding to one of the two Congregational churches in Marblehead.[17] Arkham is mentioned glancingly, most notably when the narrator subsequently finds himself in "St. Mary's Hospital in Arkham" (*D* 216). (The hospital had first been cited in "The Unnamable" [*D* 207].)

It can be seen from these early stories that Lovecraft is slowly heading toward envisioning an entire fictional New England topography constellated with imaginary towns of varying sorts—university towns, small villages or hamlets, factory towns, seaports—but the full flowering of this conception would only occur in the major tales of the Lovecraft Mythos. The important thing to remember is that Lovecraft never felt bound by previous data when elaborating upon his fictitious topography: consistency from one story to the next was not paramount in his mind, especially if the potential for more powerful imaginative exploitation of the theme required a deviation from a prior scenario. This point holds true for all aspects of the Lovecraft Mythos—places, "gods," and books alike.

The most problematical of the "anticipations" of the Lovecraft Mythos prior to 1926 is in the domain of extraterrestrial "gods" or entities. If there is any *plot* element that distinctively sets off the Lovecraft Mythos from the rest of Lovecraft's work, and indeed from the great majority of previous (and subsequent) horror literature, it is in the use of these extraterrestrial entities. It is his chief means of conveying cosmicism in his stories, and so it is important to trace the roots of the conception with care.

We have seen that the entity in "Dagon," whether he is in fact a god himself or merely the worshipper of a god that was the prototype of the historical Dagon, is by no means extraterrestrial. The first suggestion of a supramundane entity in Lovecraft is found in "Beyond the Wall of Sleep" (early 1919). This story tells of a crude backwoods denizen whose mind is possessed by some kind of cosmic being whose nature and attributes are not specified in detail. As this being speaks to the narrator through the latter's "cosmic 'radio'" (D 32), he states:

> "You and I have drifted to the worlds that reel about the red Arcturus, and dwelt in the bodies of the insect-philosophers that crawl proudly over the fourth moon of Jupiter. . . . We shall meet again—perhaps in the shining mists of Orion's Sword, perhaps on a bleak plateau in prehistoric Asia. Perhaps in unremembered dreams tonight; perhaps in some other form an aeon hence, when the solar system shall have been swept away." (D 34–35)

Here we have a very impressive demonstration of the fusion of the cosmicism of space and the cosmicism of time. The story is otherwise quite poor, but one can see why Lovecraft might have found highly suggestive kernels of thought and imagery in it that he would use in other, later works—notably "The Shadow out of Time."

There is, of course, no suggestion in "Beyond the Wall of Sleep" that the cosmic being is a "god" of any kind; indeed, the being suggests that there are perhaps an infinite number of such entities, and that even human beings can become "cosmic" entities "in the freedom of dreamless sleep" (D 34). Very different is Nyarlathotep in the prose-poem "Nyarlathotep" (December 1920), who seems every inch the "god" here, as he does in most of his appearances in Lovecraft's subsequent fiction. The fact that he appears in approximately human form (he "looked like a Pharaoh" [MW 32]) should not deceive us as to his superhuman qualities. Indeed, if we take his own word for it, he emerged "out of the blackness of twenty-seven centuries, and . . . heard messages from places not on this planet" (MW 32). The first part of the sentence seems to suggest a terrestrial origin (i.e., the 22nd dynasty of

Egypt, 945–712 B.C.E.), but the subsequent events of the tale manifestly imply that Nyarlathotep has some kind of influence upon the fate of the entire universe. The name Nyarlathotep, of course, has an Egyptian cast (the stem *-hotep* means "is pleased"), but this does not necessarily imply that Nyarlathotep is himself somehow an Egyptian entity; for, as Lovecraft states in regard to some of his other coined names, it could simply be that an Egyptian was the first to set down the name, doing so in a manner that reflected his own linguistic background. Nyarlathotep's "actual" name, and attributes, remain a mystery.

It is well known that the prose-poem is a fairly close transcript of a dream that Lovecraft had some weeks earlier. In the dream Samuel Loveman told Lovecraft to see Nyarlathotep if he came to Providence:

> I had never heard the name NYARLATHOTEP before, but seemed to understand the allusion. Nyarlathotep was a kind of itinerant showman or lecturer who held forth in publick halls & aroused widespread fear & discussion with his exhibitions. These exhibitions consisted of two parts—first, a horrible—possibly prophetic—cinema reel; & later some extraordinary experiments with scientific & electrical apparatus.[18]

The story makes it clear that Nyarlathotep is a kind of harbinger of universal chaos—and as such he fittingly becomes, in later tales, the "messenger" of the nuclear chaos Azathoth. The degree to which this conception of Nyarlathotep remains consistent in the rest of Lovecraft's work—and, indeed, the degree to which Lovecraft had a coherent idea of what Nyarlathotep stands for—will be discussed in later chapters.

We can deal briefly with "The Crawling Chaos" (1920/21), Lovecraft's second collaboration (following "The Green Meadow" [1918/19]) with Winifred V. Jackson. The title is manifestly taken from the fragmentary opening sentence of prose-poem ("Nyarlathotep . . . the crawling chaos . . ." [*MW* 32]). Lovecraft later admitted that "I took the title C. C. from my Nyarlathotep sketch . . . because I liked the sound of it."[19] This does not make it sound as if the idea of Nyarlathotep has much to do with "The Crawling Chaos," and sure enough it doesn't. The name Nyarlathotep is not mentioned anywhere, and the only connexion to the prose-poem is the general sense of cosmic decay, expressed powerfully at the end:

As the cloud of steam from the Plutonic gulf finally concealed the entire surface from my sight, all the firmament shrieked at a sudden agony of mad reverberations which shook the trembling aether. In one delirious flash and burst it happened; one blinding, deafening holocaust of fire, smoke, and thunder that dissolved the wan moon as it sped outward to the void.

And when the smoke cleared away, and I sought to look upon the earth, I beheld against the background of cold, humorous stars only the dying sun and the pale mournful planets searching for their sister. (*HM* 15)

Turning now to the fragment "Azathoth" (June 1922), which Lovecraft initially conceived as a full-scale novel but of which he wrote only about 500 words before abandoning it, we find that the entity of the title is not mentioned anywhere in the fragment. If, as many have maintained, the fragment is a kind of anticipation of *The Dream-Quest of Unknown Kadath*, we may conjecture that the "man who travelled out of life on a quest into the spaces whither the world's dreams had fled" (*D* 357) was to have undertaken a quest to confront Azathoth somewhere in the voids of space (or of the dream-world), just as Randolph Carter seeks to confront Nyarlathotep and demand the return of the "sunset city" of his dreams. Nothing in Lovecraft's letters of this period provides any clues as to his conception of Azathoth at this time—if, indeed, he had a coherent conception.

Possibly the name can provide clues. Whereas the name Nyarlathotep (which, as we have seen, came to Lovecraft in a dream) is clearly derived from Egyptian roots, Azathoth is meant to suggest Arabic roots. (R. H. Barlow, however, appears to suggest that the name also came to Lovecraft in a dream.[20]) No doubt Lovecraft was aware of the word *azoth*, an adaptation of an Arabic word meaning "the mercury," and conceived by mediaeval alchemists as the primary seed of all metals. I am not suggesting that this alchemical conception has anything do with Lovecraft's idea of Azathoth; I believe that he was only attempting to devise an Arabic-sounding name. In his contemporaneous discussions of the *Azathoth* novel Lovecraft does indeed suggest that it was to have been a kind of *Arabian Nights* story (albeit with dreamlike elements).[21] There is no reason to think that Azathoth was at this time anything like what he became later—the "boundless daemon-sultan

Azathoth, . . . who gnaws hungrily in inconceivable, unlighted chambers beyond time amidst the muffled, maddening beating of vile drums and the thin, monotonous whine of accursed flutes" (*M* 308), as *The Dream-Quest of Unknown Kadath* memorably phrases it. Even Azathoth's apparent control of dreams is a characteristic that can only be inferred from the existing fragment—and, perhaps, from the conjecture (and it is only that) that Lovecraft elaborated upon this conception in the *Dream-Quest.*

There are no other stories prior to "The Call of Cthulhu" that suggest the incursion of extraterrestrial "gods" or entities into the human realm. But we must now consider an entire category of tales that we have discussed only tangentially up to now: Lovecraft's "Dunsanian" stories. His provocative statement, in "Some Notes on a Nonentity" (1933), that it was Dunsany "from whom I got the idea of the artificial pantheon and myth-background represented by 'Cthulhu', 'Yog-Sothoth', 'Yuggoth', etc." (*CE* 5.209–10) has apparently been met with either stony silence or a scratching of the head by most scholars, who understandably have difficulty associating the ethereal, pagan gods of Dunsany's Pegāna pantheon (as found in *The Gods of Pegāna* [1905], *Time and the Gods* [1906], and a few scattered later tales) and the ferocious and titanic entities of Lovecraft's pseudomythology, at least as exhibited in his major tales. But I think that a quite literal interpretation of Lovecraft's remark can provide some clarification.

The phrase "artificial pantheon" points to Lovecraft's creation of an ersatz theogony created from his imagination, rather than from existing myth or folklore. Dunsany's own evocative coinage of names for his gods—Yoharneth-Lahai, Hlo-hlo, and the like—functions in exactly the same manner as Lovecraft's, suggesting dim echoes of classical, Semitic, or Oriental myth in such a way as to imply that those myths themselves were offshoots of an earlier mythology. But whereas many of Dunsany's gods are clearly symbols for natural forces (Slid is described as the "soul of the sea"), the gods of Lovecraft's pantheon are far less clearly defined in terms of their nature and attributes.

What becomes evident, in studying the dozen or so "Dunsanian" tales that he wrote in the 1919–21 period, is that Lovecraft is slowly and somewhat blunderingly working his way toward introducing his (initially Dunsanian) "gods" into the real world, thrusting them out of the poetic dream-world (or the remote past) and into diurnal reality.

It is striking, for one who maintained that Dunsany's "point of view is the most truly cosmic of any held in the literature of any period" (*D* 429), how *uncosmic* Lovecraft's own imitations are. Perhaps this is not so strange after all, for the breathtakingly cosmic nature of Dunsany's original creation—the entire universe and all the worlds in it are merely the dreams of the creator-god Māna-Yood-Sushāī—is difficult to duplicate. Moreover, Dunsany's cosmicism is chiefly expressed only in those first two volumes and rarely thereafter; the secret to the effectiveness of much of his work is its sly intermingling of fantasy and reality, as in such tales as "The Kith of the Elf-Folk" or "The Coronation of Mr. Thomas Shap." When Lovecraft said in early 1920 that "The flight of imagination, and the delineation of pastoral or natural beauty, can be accomplished as well in prose as in verse—often better. It is this lesson which the incomparable Dunsany hath taught me" (*SL* 1.110), he was acknowledging that his "Dunsanian studies" were effecting a broadening of his fictional palette and allowing him to express ideas and conceptions in an overtly philosophical manner (as in "The White Ship") in a way that could not be accomplished in the kind of Poe-esque supernatural horror he had been writing up to that point.

Accordingly, the only truly "cosmic" Dunsanian story in the Lovecraft canon is "The Other Gods" (written August 14, 1921). Although no actual gods are named here, the story may have some significance for the Lovecraft Mythos in its suggestion that there are "other" gods that stand behind the "gods of earth" (*D* 131)—by which Lovecraft could well have meant the standard gods of the earth's many religions, who (as his later fiction suggests) are merely clumsy symbols for the overpoweringly cosmic entities (Azathoth, Yog-Sothoth, etc.) who in reality dominate the universe. *The Dream-Quest of Unknown Kadath* is, in part, an extensive elaboration of this idea.

Lovecraft, of course, resurrects many place-names from the Dunsanian tales in the major tales of the Lovecraft Mythos, but in large part this seems merely a kind of in-joke. Few of these names—Lomar, Olathoë, and the like—have much significance in the real-world stories, nor even in the grand synthesis of the Dunsanian stories that occurs in the *Dream-Quest*. This kind of name-dropping does not suggest (as

George T. Wetzel believed) that Lovecraft's stories "should actually be considered not as separate works but rather the different chapters of a very lengthy novel,"[22] but rather that Lovecraft liked to have a bit of fun, even if he was the only person to "get" the joke.

And yet, there is a very real sense in which the stories Lovecraft wrote from 1926 until his death all built upon one another, and it is these stories that we must now examine.

II.

The Lovecraft Mythos: Phase I (1926–30)

LOVECRAFT'S DIARY ENTRY for August 12–13, 1925, written while he was living alone in Brooklyn, contains the laconic note: "write out story plot—'The Call of Cthulhu'" (*CE* 5.165). The 1925 diary was designed as a kind of *aide-mémoire* in writing letters to his aunts in Providence. The corresponding letter to Lillian D. Clark (August 13, 1925) tells of his "recovered creativeness of mood" (he had written "He" on August 11) and speaks of a "pilgrimage whose capricious oddity lent it the piquancy which dispels dulness." And then:

> Thence I went home—but not to bed, for I had much to write. A new story plot—perhaps a short novel—had occurred to my awakening faculties, & it was imperative to get it down in skeletonic detail whilst it was fresh. This, of course, was a matter of hours, since I adopted my complete development scheme in full. The writing itself will now be a relatively simple matter—it's to be called "The Call of Cthulhu", & I'll send you a copy as soon as it is written & typed . . . This new thing—if it turns out as long as I expect from a mere survey of the ground—ought to bring in a very decent sized cheque—it'll be in three or four parts.[1]

This tells us several things of importance. Bypassing the pathetic attempt to display his ability to rake in the shekels (at a period when his lack of a regular income was causing severe hardship both to himself and to his fragile marriage with Sonia Greene), we see that both the title and a detailed synopsis had been evolved at this time. The "complete development scheme" is not entirely clear, but I suspect it has to do with Lovecraft's later recommendation (found in "Notes on Writing Weird Fiction") of drawing up *two* synopses for a story—one relating events in order of chronological occurrence, the other in order of narration (see *CE* 2.176). Indeed, the events in "The Call of Cthulhu" are told in a markedly unchronological manner, leaping from the present (the "winter of 1926–27" [*DH* 126]) back to the American Archaeological Society gathering of 1908 (the real heart of the narrative, as far as the Lovecraft Mythos is concerned), and then back to the spring of 1925, with the narrative of the sailor Johansen. This chronological disjunction surely goes back to the synopsis of 1925, and may also have something to do with Lovecraft's otherwise curious comment that the finished story was *"cumbrous*—undeniably *cumbrous" (SL* 2.217).

The story did not in fact come to "short novel" length, but at 12,000 words it was the longest tale Lovecraft had written up to that point, exceeding "The Shunned House" (10,840 words). Moreover, it was not written for the better part of a year: its actual composition dates to the summer of 1926, months after Lovecraft's return to Providence in April. Lovecraft had confessed that he found the atmosphere of New York increasingly uncongenial, causing his pen to dry up; he seemed to require the emotional and aesthetic stimulus of his return to Providence to rekindle his creative fires. Indeed, "The Call of Cthulhu" was the first of an unprecedented series of novels and tales— amounting to some 150,000 words—that Lovecraft wrote in a period of eight or nine months.

In all the thousands of pages of correspondence I have read, I have never found any explanation of how Lovecraft originated the name Cthulhu. Did he simply sit down at a typewriter and peck the keys at random? Whereas other terms such as Azathoth, Yog-Sothoth, and Yuggoth are designed to suggest an Arabic origin—not that the entities themselves are Arabic, but that the Arab Abdul Alhazred interpreted these presumably extraterrestrial names through his own language, as the Romans devised the name *Jupiter* from *Zeus pater* (Zeus the father)—Cthulhu is clearly meant to be not merely non-English, but nonhuman. As Lovecraft explains in a late letter where he specifies the pronunciation of the name (*Khlûl'-hloo*): "My rather careful devising of this name was a sort of protest against the silly and childish habit of most weird and science-fiction writers, of having *utterly non-human entities* use a nomenclature *of thoroughly human character;* as if alien-organed beings could possibly have languages based on *human* vocal organs" (*SL* 5.11). (The "rather careful" comment presumably destroys my hypothesis about Lovecraft's random pecking at the typewriter, but he never truly elaborates upon this point.)

If the origin of the name is in doubt, so are numerous other features of the narrative. "The Call of Cthulhu" is a far more ambiguous story than many commentators (and imitators) have realised. In many ways, the nature and characteristics of the entity Cthulhu remain unclear. Consider, for example, the upshot of the archaeological meeting of 1908. When Inspector Legrasse relates his account of the degenerate worshippers in Louisiana, other scholars have their own stories to tell of similar events: a Professor William Channing Webb states that he had encountered, "high up on the West Greenland coast," a "singular tribe or cult of degenerate Esquimaux whose religion, a curious form of devil-worship, chilled him with its deliberate bloodthirstiness and repulsiveness" (DH 135). But exactly who or what do these Greenlanders— or, for that matter, the Louisianans—worship? Webb tells of a "supreme elder devil or tornasuk" and says that the Greenlanders also had a "very crude bas-relief of stone" (DH 135) similar to that brought in by Legrasse, which in turn is similar to the one fashioned by Henry Anthony Wilcox of Providence in his dreams.

Does this mean that the Greenlanders and the Louisianans are both worshipping Cthulhu? But how could either of these groups have caught sight of Cthulhu, if the latter is immured in his underwater city of R'lyeh deep in the Pacific? Cthulhu could presumably have influenced their dreams, as he seems to have the capability of doing; but what of the fact that one man, Joseph D. Galvez, interviewed later by the narrator tells a wild story of hearing, while the Louisiana degenerates are being rounded up, "the faint beating of great wings, and . . . a glimpse of shining eyes and a mountainous white [my emphasis] bulk beyond the remotest trees" (DH 138)? Cthulhu, when actually seen by Johansen, is described as "the green, sticky spawn of the stars" (DH 152). So clearly the entity in Louisiana is not itself Cthulhu. Then who is he?

I believe the answer is supplied by old Castro, whose narrative supplies the fundamental facts about the origin of Cthulhu. He first notes that "They worshipped . . . the Great Old Ones who lived ages before there were any men, and who came to the young world out of the sky. Those Old Ones were gone now, inside he earth and under the sea; but their dead bodies had told their secrets in dreams to the first men, who formed a cult which had never died." Castro goes on to say: "No man had ever seen the Old Ones. The carven idol was great Cthulhu, but none might say whether or not the others were precisely like him" (*DH* 139). In other words, the Louisiana entity is one of the Great Old Ones, who is not "precisely like" Cthulhu. Presumably other members of the Great Old Ones (who, let us recall, had come "from the stars, and brought Their images with Them" [*DH* 140]) are buried elsewhere in the dim corners of the earth—perhaps, say, in Greenland. It is odd, though, that Lovecraft does not devote much attention to these other Great Old Ones in "The Call of Cthulhu." Even though the narrator later refers to "the sunken, star-born Old Ones and their coming reign; their faithful cult *and their mastery of dreams*" (*DH* 147; Lovecraft's emphasis), the focus of the tale is squarely on Cthulhu.

It should also be emphasised that Castro's narrative must itself be taken with a grain of salt. There is no reason to believe—and Lovecraft does not wish us to believe—that what Castro says is "true" in every particular. It is by no means clear how Castro came by his information about Cthulhu and the Great Old Ones; all that is said is that he himself "claimed to have sailed to strange ports and talked with undying leaders of the cult in the mountains of China" (*DH* 140), but there is no independent verification of this. In any case, when Castro states that "Some day he [Cthulhu] would call, when the stars were ready, and the secret cult would always be waiting to liberate him" (*DH* 139), he appears to be radically magnifying the relation of the human worshippers to Cthulhu, who does not appear to need their aid to "liberate" himself. A later comment by Castro ("That cult would never die till the stars came right again, and the secret priests would take great Cthulhu from His tomb to revive His subjects and resume His rule of earth" [*DH* 141]) points in the same direction.

Cthulhu's momentary "liberation," as narrated by Johansen, is similarly fraught with ambiguities. Castro had mentioned that "When the stars were right, They [the Great Old Ones] could plunge from world to world through the sky; but when the stars were wrong, They could not live" (*DH* 140). So what happens when Cthulhu finally does emerge from the deep? The narrator explicitly states that "The stars were right again, and what an age-old cult had failed to do by design, a band of innocent sailors had done by accident" (*DH* 152). So the stars are now right, and R'lyeh (or, as the narrator suggests, a tiny portion of it) rises from the waves, releasing Cthulhu; but the earthquake that occurs at this very juncture fortuitously sends Cthulhu and R'lyeh back to the deep. In a reversal of the scenario in "Dagon," it is not that an earthquake forces a sunken land-mass to the surface, but that it sends it back down into the depths of the ocean. And yet, the comment about the "innocent sailors" is peculiar: surely their accidental opening of the "monstrously carven portal" (*DH* 152) was not by itself sufficient to release Cthulhu.

In any event, Lovecraft in this story begins unifying the scattered hints in previous stories in regard to the various elements that would become the Lovecraft Mythos. One critical passage reads as follows: "No book had ever really hinted of it [the Cthulhu cult], though the deathless Chinamen said that there were double meanings in the *Necronomicon* of the mad Arab Abdul Alhazred which the initiated might read as they chose" (*DH* 141), after which follows the "much-discussed couplet," "That is not dead . . ." At the risk of sounding monotonous, this sentence is itself ambiguous. In the first place, note the extreme narrative *distance* of the passage: this is the narrator paraphrasing an account by his uncle who is paraphrasing an account by Inspector Legrasse who is paraphrasing the account of old Castro who is relating the words of "deathless Chinamen." And what does the fact that there are "double meanings" in the *Necronomicon* really mean? Can it be that Cthulhu and the Great Old Ones are not actually cited by name in that text? Up to this point, aside from the couplet, no actual passage from the *Necronomicon* has been quoted aside from the paragraph at the very end of "The Festival," where no entities are mentioned; and the fact that the couplet itself is said to be prime evidence of the book's "double meanings" suggests that that couplet specifically refers (or, rather, alludes) to Cthulhu in his dead-but-dreaming state in R'lyeh.

One other point may be worth stressing. The narrator's description of Wilcox's bas-relief of Cthulhu ("If I say that my somewhat extravagant imagination yielded simultaneous pictures of an octopus, a dragon, and a human caricature, I shall not be unfaithful to the spirit of the thing" [*DH* 127]) recapitulates the *hybridity* evident in several of Lovecraft's previous entities, from the marine creatures carved on the monolith in "Dagon" ("they were damnably human in general outline despite webbed hands and feet, shockingly wide and flabby lips, glassy, bulging eyes, and other features less pleasant to recall" [*D* 18]) and the strange monsters under the church in "The Festival" ("They were not altogether crows, nor moles, nor buzzards, nor ants, nor vampire bats, nor decomposed human beings" [*D* 215]). I don't believe that the vague resemblance of all these entities to earthly creatures is at all meant to suggest that Cthulhu and the Great Old Ones are themselves somehow of earthly origin; rather, the various carvings of Cthulhu and his spawn (which, as Castro and others emphasise, are only approximations) are attempts by human imaginations to depict entirely alien entities. There is no question of Cthulhu's extraterrestrial origin; that much—and his power to influence dreams and his ability to recombine disparate parts of himself (confirming Castro's comment that "These Great Old Ones . . . were not composed altogether of flesh and blood. They had shape . . . but that shape was not made of matter" [*DH* 140])—are about all we really know about Cthulhu in "The Call of Cthulhu." The story is really more about the widely dispersed Cthulhu cult than it is about the entity they worship.

From a literary perspective, it is difficult to overstate the brilliance of "The Call of Cthulhu." It is exponentially superior to anything Lovecraft had previously written, and it is—far more than "Dagon," "Beyond the Wall of Sleep," or "The Music of Erich Zann"—the first truly *cosmic* story Lovecraft had written. It is the first of his tales that features all or most of the elements I have identified as essential to the Lovecraft Mythos, with the possible exception of the imaginary New England topography (the tale begins in Providence, and there are no mentions of Arkham, Kingsport, etc.). It is quite conceivable that, had Lovecraft written no further stories, the Cthulhu Mythos might still have come into being.

The brilliance of "The Call of Cthulhu" manifests itself in at least two ways—one technical and one philosophical. By "technical" I refer to the enormously skilful craftsmanship of the tale—its deliberately fragmented narration (embodying the inadvertent "piecing together of dissociated knowledge" [*DH* 125] mentioned in the story's celebrated first paragraph), its gradual but inexorable progression to a cataclysmic climax, its use of scientific verisimilitude to overcome the reader's initial scepticism in regard to the outlandish events it relates, and its remarkable skill in the use of language, alternating between scientific precision and evocative flamboyance. From a purely aesthetic perspective, the tale stands not only close to the pinnacle of Lovecraft's own corpus but head and shoulders above the work of all but his most eminent predecessors and contemporaries.

But it is its depth of philosophical substance that truly sets "The Call of Cthulhu" apart from Lovecraft's earlier work and, sadly, from the great majority of tales by his self-styled imitators. What we have here as an exquisite melding of cosmic horror—it is very clear that the fate not merely of the world but of the universe is involved, and that the human race and the entire history of earthly life on this planet is of risible insignificance in the light of Cthulhu's mere existence—and a peculiarly intimate, if intellectual, psychological horror, whereby the hapless narrator who has performed the unwitting "piecing together" faces a bleak life of emotional devastation because of his harrowing realisation of what Cthulhu is and is capable of ("I have looked upon all that the universe has to hold of horror, and even the skies of spring and the flowers of summer must ever afterward be poison to me" [*DH* 154]). No matter how hackneyed and formulaic Cthulhu has become in the hands of later writers, "The Call of Cthulhu" continues to evoke enormously powerful and complex emotions upon the sensitive reader, and its rich texture rewards repeated reading and analysis.

Two stories not ordinarily considered to contribute to the Lovecraft Mythos—"The Strange High House in the Mist" (written on November 9, 1926) and *The Dream-Quest of Unknown Kadath* (Autumn 1926–January 22, 1927)—may be considered here. The fact that the former is set in Kingsport is the least interesting thing about it. Far from being an evocation of Marblehead, the story is set in an imprecise New England topography that owes much to Lovecraft's imagination. He himself admitted that he had no specific locale in mind when writing the tale, stating that memories of the "titan cliffs of Magnolia" (*SL* 2.164)—a coastal area in Massachusetts that he had visited with Sonia Greene in 1922—in part prompted the setting. More significant is what Thomas Olney learns after he makes the arduous trip to visit the mysterious occupant of the house. This person tells Olney a variety of things, among which is this: "Years of the Titans were recalled, but the host grew timid when he spoke of the dim first age of chaos before the gods or even the Elder Ones were born, and when only *the other gods* came to dance on the peak of Hatheg-Kla in the stony desert near Ulthar, beyond the river Skai" (*D* 282). On the whole, this passage seems to be derived from "The Other Gods." It is, however, not clear who the Elder Ones are; they were mentioned in an equally inexplicable phrase earlier in the story ("When tales fly thick in the grottoes of tritons, and conches in seaweed cities blow wild tunes learned from the Elder Ones" [*D* 277]), a phrase that is exactly repeated at the end of the story (*D* 286).

Let us recall, however, that by the time "The Strange High House in the Mist" was written, Lovecraft was already at work on *The Dream-Quest of Unknown Kadath*, and there is good reason to believe that he had worked out the details—or, at any rate, the overall direction—of that short novel in advance. In that work, Randolph Carter is seeking to plead with the Great Ones (i.e., "the mild gods of earth" [*M* 407]) on Kadath for the restoration of the sunset city of his dreams. A critical passage in that novel occurs when Carter discusses his quest with Kuranes (resurrected from "Celephaïs"); the latter tells him:

> Kuranes did not know where Kadath was, or the marvellous sunset city; but he did know that the Great Ones were very dangerous creatures to seek out, and that the Other Gods had strange ways of protecting them from impertinent curiosity. He had learned much of the Other Gods in distant parts of space, especially in that region where form does not exist, and coloured gases study the innermost secrets. The violet gas S'ngac had told him never to approach the central void where the daemon-sultan Azathoth gnaws hungrily in the dark. Altogether, it was not well to meddle with the Elder Ones; and if they persistently denied all access to the marvellous sunset city, it were better not to seek that city. (*M* 255–56)

If any sense can be made of this, it is that the mild gods of earth are equivalent to the Great Ones and the Elder Ones, and that Nyarlathotep and Azathoth are among the Other Gods. This point appears to be confirmed by Nyarlathotep's comment to Carter: "Remember the Other Gods; they are great and mindless and terrible, and lurk in the outer voids" (*M* 403)—a comment that evokes Lovecraft's standard descriptions of Azathoth as mindless and lurking in the voids of chaos. I mention all this because it would seem that August Derleth derived his

notion of the (beneficent) Elder Gods as counterweights to the (evil)
Old Ones from these two stories—which, by a wonderful paradox, he
then determined did not "belong" to the Cthulhu Mythos!

Nyarlathotep, as is obvious, is a major presence in the *Dream-Quest*.
It is he who is constantly attempting to thwart Randolph Carter in his
quest for the sunset city; and at the end, when he tells Carter that that
city is only "the sum of what you have seen and loved in youth" (*M*
400), he has supplied Carter with the means to recover that city—but
this too is only a ruse: "Only to taunt had Nyarlathotep marked out the
way to safety and the marvellous sunset city; only to mock had that
black messenger revealed the secret of those truant gods whose steps
he could so easily lead back at will" (*M* 404). This comment tells us that
the Elder Ones are entirely under the control of Nyarlathotep, so that
they could hardly form any kind of countervailing cosmic force opposed to the Old Ones (a term that had not yet been mentioned in any
Lovecraft story, except as a short form of "Great Old Ones") or the
Other Gods. Nevertheless, Carter's apparent prowess as a dreamer
manages to thwart Nyarlathotep's plans. The precise manner in which
he does so is significant. As he is flying atop the shantak bird and
headed "toward those inconceivable, unlighted chambers beyond Time
wherein black Azathoth gnaws shapeless and ravenous" (*M* 404), Carter
realises that he is simply dreaming, and that all he need do is wake up to
return to the sunset city. He does so amidst cosmic cataclysm ("Aeons
reeled, universes died and were born again" [*M* 406]), but ultimately he
achieves his goal. We then learn that "Out of the void S'ngac the violet
gas had pointed the way, and archaic Nodens was bellowing his guid-
ance from unhinted deeps" (*M* 406). This sentence, added almost casually at the end of Carter's escape from Nyarlathotep, does not warrant
Robert M. Price's comment that "Randolph Carter is saved by exactly
the sort of *deus-ex-machina* intervention of 'hoary Nodens' to deliver him
from the clutches of Nyarlathotep"[2] as occurs in Derleth's stories of
the Elder Gods vs. the Old Ones. Carter's "delivery" is largely of his
own doing, and it appears that Nodens is merely acting as a kind of
cosmic cheerleader.

Nodens was first mentioned in "The Strange High House in the
Mist," in a passage about the "Mighty Ones" (= Elder Ones?): "Tri-
dent-bearing Neptune was there, and sportive tritons and fanstastic ne-

reids, and upon dolphins' backs was balanced a vast crenulate shell wherein rode the grey and awful form of primal Nodens, Lord of the Great Abyss" (*D* 283). He appears earlier in the *Dream-Quest*, where it is stated that the night-gaunts are creatures "whom even the Great Ones fear, and who own not Nyarlathotep but hoary Nodens as their lord" (*M* 372). It is well known that Nodens (or Nodons) was an actual god—a Celtic god of healing. Lovecraft no doubt was taken with the mention of him in Arthur Machen's "The Great God Pan" (1894), where a Roman inscription is translated as follows: "To the great Nodens (the god of the Great Deep or Abyss) Flavius Senilis has erected this pillar on account of the marriage he saw beneath the shade."[3] Nodens is not mentioned in any other stories by Lovecraft, and it is unclear whether he is even a member of the Elder Ones (the gods of earth), since the latter are explicitly stated to be "mild," whereas Nodens seems quite otherwise.

The importance of these two stories, however, is that they show Lovecraft slowly drawing his "gods" out of their Dunsanian land of dream or imagination and into the real world. Even the Other Gods are not quite as ferocious in the dream-world as they are in the real world; as Maurice Lévy has commented:

> The deities themselves no longer have that horrible aspect, those madness-inducing forms, which characterized them when they manifested themselves in the Waking World. . . . In the Land of Deeper Slumber it is not only possible to see the gods face to face, but even more to stand up to them; and Carter without too much trouble succeeds in foiling the ultimate ruse of the Crawling Chaos.[4]

Lovecraft had, of course, already made this transition in "The Call of Cthulhu," and the uniquely terrifying atmosphere of the tales of this first phase of the Lovecraft Mythos chiefly resides in the sense of human powerlessness in the face of the awesome Dunsanian gods that have been extracted from the realm of myth and dream and into that of waking, present-day reality.

In a broad thematic sense, *The Case of Charles Dexter Ward* (January–March 1, 1927) is a pendant to the *Dream-Quest;* for just as Randolph Carter learns that the sunset city he yearns for is the sum of the memories of his youth in New England, so does Charles Dexter Ward learn that it is Old Providence that "had brought him into being, and which had drawn him back toward marvels and secrets whose boundaries no prophet might fix" (*M* 165). In relation to the Lovecraft Mythos, its role is only tangential. The cryptic mentions of Yog-Sothoth—there are seven of them in the novel—constitute the first citations of that entity in Lovecraft. The first occurs when Joseph Curwen, now revived in the twentieth century, writes to a colleague: "I last Night strucke on yᵉ Wordes that bringe up YOGGE-SOTHOTHE, and sawe for yᵉ first Time that fface spoke of by Ibn Schacabao in yᵉ ———" (*M* 151). The passage is no doubt meant to be deliberately inscrutable, although the mention of Ibn Schacabao is designed to evoke the *Necronomicon* passage at the end of "The Festival" ("Wisely did Ibn Schacabao say, that happy is the tomb where no wizard hath lain, and happy the town at night whose wizards are all ashes" [*D* 216]). Accordingly, it can be assumed that the blank space left by Curwen is an allusion to the *Necronomicon*. A bit later, Ward himself is overheard shouting an incantation ("Yi-nash-Yog-Sothoth-he-lgeb-fi-throdog" [*M* 171]); this is a phonetic rendering of the incantation in the "ascending node" that Dr. Willett later finds on documents in the secret basement of Ward/Curwen's Pawtuxet bunga-low (*M* 205). Can this formula be the "Wordes" that Curwen was using to "bringe up" Yog-Sothoth? Possibly, but when Willett utters them he actually evokes the creature whose "essential saltes" are left in a vessel in the basement—the creature who later writes Willett a message in Saxon minuscules. Curwen had scribbled on a note: "Rais'd *Yog-Sothoth* thrice and was yᵉ nexte Day deliver'd" (*M* 215), another cryptic utterance. Suf-fice it to say that Lovecraft has intentionally left Yog-Sothoth undefined in this story; whether he knew at this time that he would resurrect him elsewhere cannot be known.

Some clues as to Yog-Sothoth's role, however, may be derived from studying exactly what Joseph Curwen and his cohorts were trying to do. The third-person narrator, apparently reflecting the thought processes of Dr. Willett as he penetrates further into Curwen's myster-ies, concludes at one point:

> What these horrible creatures . . . were doing or trying to do seemed fairly clear from their letters and from every bit of light both old and new which had filtered in upon the case. They were robbing the tombs of all the ages, including those of the world's wisest and greatest men, in the hope of recovering from the bygone ashes some vestige of the

consciousness and lore which had once animated and informed them. (*M* 199)

If this was all that Curwen was aiming for, then there would be little reason to believe that the novel has any meaningful relation to the Lovecraft Mythos; but there seems to be a bit more than this. For we read further: "What forces 'outside the spheres' had reached him [Ward] from Joseph Curwen's day and turned his mind on forbidden things?" (*M* 199). The phrase in quotation marks appears (more or less) in a letter that Curwen had written around 1750—the very letter in which Yog-Sothoth is mentioned for the first time. Curwen writes of a particular psalm in the *Liber Damnatus* (a fictitious work never cited elsewhere by Lovecraft): "This Uerse repeate eache Roodemas and Hallow's Eue; and ye Thing will breede in yᵉ Outside Spheres" (*M* 151). It is, of course, unclear—probably deliberately so—what this "Thing" is; it is not Yog-Sothoth himself, but perhaps some cosmic entity under his control. At any rate, this summoning clearly goes well beyond the raising up of the "essential saltes" of human beings to tap their brainpower.

The *Necronomicon* may be involved somehow. In Curwen's time a visitor, John Merritt, had been surprised to discover that a volume in Curwen's library, "conspicuously labelled as the *Qanoon-e-Islam*," was in fact "the forbidden *Necronomicon* of the mad Arab Abdul Alhazred, of which he had heard such monstrous things whispered some years previously after the exposure of nameless rites at the strange little fishing village of Kingsport, in the Province of the Massachusetts-Bay" (*M* 121). (This is the only mention of Lovecraft's imaginary New England topography in this novel.) In the same letter of 1750 Curwen writes: "I am foll'g out what Borellus saith, and haue Helpe in Abdool Al-Hazred his VII. Booke" (*M* 152). A letter to Curwen by Jedediah (actually Simon) Orne, cited earlier in the text, responds to this passage: "I have not yᵉ Chymicall art to followe Borellus, and owne my Selfe confounded by yᵉ VII. Booke of ye Necronomicon that you recommende" (*M* 138). I do not believe it is possible to make full sense of these hints; Lovecraft was apparently wishing to suggest—but no more than suggest—that Curwen and his band were involved in more cosmic activities than merely the resurrection of dead human bodies, but he deliberately left the matter vague and unresolved.

We now come to "The Colour out of Space" (March 1927). Several valiant souls, including August Derleth and Lin Carter, who have made carefully pondered lists of what stories do or do not "belong" to the Cthulhu Mythos have rigidly excluded "The Colour out of Space," although they have given no compelling reason—or, indeed, no reason at all—for doing so. The chief rationale is presumably that it fails to mention any of the standard "gods" of the Mythos. Well and good; but since it embodies—and does so with the highest possible artistry—two of the central traits of what I take to be the Lovecraft Mythos, namely the use of a fictitious New England topography and a cosmic perspective, I believe it is well worth studying here.

The opening sentence is celebrated: "West of Arkham the hills rise wild, and there are valleys with deep woods that no axe has ever cut" (*DH* 53). We are immediately placed within Lovecraft's evolving conception of an imaginary New England that is the haven of all manner of wonders and terrors. Arkham serves as a kind of touchstone in the story, as the "three professors from Miskatonic University" (*DH* 57) who come to Nahum Gardner's farm to examine the strange meteorite continually shuttle back and forth from Arkham to the remote countryside in a futile attempt to penetrate the mysteries of the strange visitor from space. We are here clearly dealing with some kind of extraterrestrial force or entity; but, in an exquisite example of artistic restraint, Lovecraft deliberately chooses not to provide definitive clues as to the nature—either physical or psychological—of the entity (entities?) inhabiting the meteorite. Even more than Cthulhu, these creatures are of a substance far different from anything known on earth or in the visible universe around us. The narrator believes that it might be a gas—

> but this gas obeyed laws that are not of our cosmos. This was no fruit of such worlds and suns as shine on the telescopes and photographic plates of our observatories. This was no breath from the skies whose motions and dimensions our astronomers measure or deem too vast to measure. It was just a colour out of space—a frightful messenger from unformed realms of infinity beyond all Nature as we know it; from realms whose mere existence stuns the brain and numbs us with the black extra-cosmic gulfs it throws open before our frenzied eyes. (*DH* 81)

Even more significant, the precise goals or motivations of the entities in the meteorite remain forever inscrutable; they cannot possibly be declared "evil," even though they are highly harmful to all earth life, because we cannot penetrate into their minds or psyches to pass any kind of moral judgment upon them. It was only a few months later that Lovecraft made his celebrated manifesto that "common human laws and interests and emotions have no validity or significance in the vast cosmos-at-large" (*SL* 2.150), and "The Colour out of Space" embodies this message as potently and skilfully as any story in the Lovecraft canon.

It may be worth discussing the fragment "The Descendant" (not Lovecraft's title) here. R. H. Barlow dated it (on no evidence that I can ascertain) to 1926, but a date of early 1927 seems more likely. It was in April 1927 that Lovecraft noted "making a very careful study of *London* . . . in order to get background for tales involving richer antiquities than America can furnish."[5] The fragment begins: "In London there is a man who screams when the church bells ring" (*D* 358). It deals with one Lord Northam, who strives fervently "not to think," because of some unspecified past experience that destroyed his psychological equilibrium; but one day a young friend of his named Williams brings him a copy of "the infamous *Necronomicon* of the mad Arab Abdul Alhazred" (*D* 359). It is here that we learn that, according to a "bent old bookseller in Chandos Street," "only five copies [of the *Necronomicon*] were known to have survived the shocked edicts of the priests and lawgivers against it and that all of these were locked up with frightened care by custodians who had ventured to begin a reading of the hateful blackletter" (*D* 360). This rather perfervid passage has created some awkwardness in later Mythos writing, since copies of the *Necronomicon* appear to pop up with disconcerting regularity here, there, and everywhere—as it does in this very fragment, since Williams seems to find one fairly easily "at a Jew's shop in the squalid precincts of Clare Market" (*D* 360). This passage appears to be the source of the first few sonnets of the *Fungi from Yuggoth* cycle (1929–30), where similarly a character purchases the *Necronomicon* from an elderly bookseller; and by a curious coincidence, those sonnets were then themselves the source of the story fragment "The Book."

Lovecraft specifies that this is the Latin text, although Olaus Wormius is not cited as the translator (he had been so identified in "The Festival"). The effect upon Lord Northam is dramatic: he faints when he hears the title of the book. The sight of it apparently induces him to tell what had frightened him in the past; but we do not learn much of this before the fragment peters out. All we know is that Northam once travelled to "the desert of Araby to seek a Nameless City of faint report, which no man has ever beheld" (D 361–62), which, if nothing else, definitively incorporates "The Nameless City" into the Lovecraft Mythos. There is no indication of what direction this story would have taken, or whether any of the "gods" or other elements would have come into play. There is a glancing mention of the "Elder Sign" (D 361), first cited in the *Dream-Quest* ("the farmer and his wife would only make the Elder Sign and tell him the way to Nir and Ulthar" [M 311]).

It was in the fall of 1927 that Lovecraft apparently wrote "History of the *Necronomicon.*" In a letter of November 27, 1927, he tells Clark Ashton Smith that he has "drawn up some data on the celebrated & unmentionable *Necronomicon* of the mad Arab Abdul Alhazred" (*SL* 2.201); the manuscript is written on correspondence Lovecraft received from one William L. Bryant (director of the museum at Roger Williams Park in Providence) dated April 27, 1927. If this brief squib tells us anything, it is that Lovecraft meant to draw upon the *Necronomicon* in future works and was keen on maintaining some kind of consistency in his citations to it and to the various editions or translations that have been printed over the past several centuries. It is here that Lovecraft first makes the error of dating Olaus Wormius's Latin translation to 1228, when in fact Wormius (Ole Wurm, a Danish scholar) was born in 1588 and died in 1654.[6] It is also here that Lovecraft definitively states that Alhazred "worshipp[ed] unknown entities whom he called Yog-Sothoth and Cthulhu" (*MW* 52), something that had not been explicit before. The Arabic title, *Al Azif* (derived from Samuel Henley's notes to William Beckford's *Vathek*), is given here for the first time. There is a casual mention of "the artist R. U. Pickman" (*MW* 53), but this does not necessarily incorporate "Pickman's Model" (written in the fall of 1926) into the Lovecraft Mythos, for there is nothing in that story to link it with any central Mythos elements.

Strangely enough, Lovecraft now begins to infuse his revisions and ghost-written tales with Mythos elements. This is perhaps not entirely surprising, since he would write no work of original fiction between "The Colour out of Space" and "The Dunwich Horror" (summer

1928). In the meantime, his fictional pen was being exercised, after a fashion, in revisions. In the fall of 1927 he rewrote Adolphe de Castro's "A Sacrifice to Science" (1893) as "The Last Test." It is in this story that, oddly, the first mention of Shub-Niggurath occurs. Dr. Alfred Clarendon and the strange figure named Surama (who proves to be an Atlantean mage) have a tense argument at one point, during which Clarendon says:

> "Be careful, you ——! There are powers against your powers—I didn't go to China for nothing, and there are things in Alhazred's *Azif* which weren't known in Atlantis! We've both meddled in dangerous things, but you needn't think you know all my resources. How about the Nemesis of Flame? I talked in Yemen with an old man who had come back alive from the Crimson Desert—he had seen Irem, the City of Pillars, and had worshipped at the underground shrines of Nug and Yeb—Iä! Shub-Niggurath!" (*HM* 47)

This is all a bit cloudy, and is presumably meant to be. The main thrust of the story is that Surama has brought back from Atlantis a kind of fever that *"isn't of this earth!"* (*HM* 56). Clarendon states: "There were cults, you know—bands of evil priests in lands now buried under the sea. Atlantis was the hotbed. That was a terrible place" (*HM* 54). The story is pretty bad, and in fact has exactly the frenetic, hysterical tone of many later tales of the Cthulhu Mythos. We are here introduced to the entities Nug and Yeb, although it does not appear that Lovecraft had a very clear conception of them. The names sound rather Dunsanian, perhaps similar to the Ged that we find in Dunsany's story "The Sword and the Idol," in *A Dreamer's Tales* (1910). Will Murray has conjectured that the names are meant to evoke the Egyptian deities Nut and Geb.[7] They appear only in Lovecraft's revisions. The above passage also constitutes the first (and only) citation in Lovecraft's fiction of the *Necronomicon* under its Arabic name (*Al Azif*); clearly this tale was written shortly after Lovecraft's codification of the *Necronomicon* editions in "History of the *Necronomicon*." The "Nemesis of Flame" is unexplained and never recurs in any Lovecraft tale; it may have been derived from "The Nemesis of Fire," one of the stories in Algernon Blackwood's *John Silence—Physician Extraordinary* (1908). There is also a fleeting mention of Yog-Sothoth (Clarendon states: "once I heard an old man in China calling on Yog-Sothoth—" [*HM* 43]), but it amounts to nothing.

It is unclear whether, in ghostwriting "The Curse of Yig" (early 1928) for Zealia Bishop, Lovecraft was attempting to devise a new "god" for his Mythos. The first-person narrator states:

> It seems that Yig, the snake-god of the central plains tribes—presumably the primal source of the more southerly Quetzalcoatl or Kukulcan—was an odd, half-anthropomorphic devil of highly arbitrary and capricious nature. He was not wholly evil, and was usually quite well-disposed toward those who gave proper respect to him and his children, the serpents; but in the autumn he became abnormally ravenous, and had to be driven away by means of suitable rites. That was why the tom-toms in the Pawnee, Wichita, and Caddo country pounded ceaselessly week in and week out in August, September, and October; and why the medicine-men made strange noises with rattles and whistles curiously like those of the Aztecs and Mayas. (*HM* 83)

In the story, the curse of Yig is apparently manifested—but not in the expected way. When Walker Davis kills a rattlesnake, he is not in turn killed by snakes, and certainly not by Yig (who does not appear, at least literally, in the story). Instead, snakes surround the bed of Walker's wife, Audrey, and she ends up killing Walker in the mistaken belief that he is Yig. Nine months later she gives birth to a hideous half-human, half-snake creature:

> The moving object was almost of human size, and entirely devoid of clothing. It was absolutely hairless, and its tawny-looking back seemed subtly squamous in the dim, ghoulish light. Around the shoulders it was rather speckled and brownish, and the head was very curiously flat. As it looked up to hiss at me I saw that the beady little black eyes were damnably anthropoid, but I could not bear to study them long. (*HM* 82)

It is evident that Yig has mated with Audrey. This is the first instance we have of one of the Lovecraftian "gods" begetting hybrid offspring from human beings—a dominant theme in "The Dunwich Horror" (written only a few months later) and "The Shadow over Innsmouth." Lovecraft had broached the subject in *The Dream-Quest of Unknown Kadath:* "It is known that in disguise the younger among the Great Ones often espouse the daughters of men, so that around the borders of the cold waste wherein stands Kadath the peasants must all bear their blood" (*M* 313). This conception—probably derived from the many stories of gods' interbreeding with humans in Greek mythology—is presented in the *Dream-Quest* as productive of awe (the hybrid offspring "would have queer lofty thoughts misunderstood by their fellows, and would sing of far places and gardens so unlike any known even in dreamland that common folk would call them fools" [*M* 313]), but in the real-world stories it is productive only of horror.

"The Curse of Yig" is an effective little horror tale; it is cleverly executed, and it benefits from the fact that the "god" of the title never actually appears, but is manifested only in his offspring. Lovecraft did not deliberately set out to create the entity in the given locale (Oklahoma); it was Zealia Bishop's insistence that a tale be set there (her own native region) that impelled Lovecraft to devise a myth or legend that could plausibly be thought to have emerged from the area in question.

Of "The Dunwich Horror" (written in the summer of 1928) it is difficult to speak in small compass. Even more than "The Call of Cthulhu," this story, for good or ill (mostly ill), made the Cthulhu Mythos—as distinct from the Lovecraft Mythos—possible. There is no need to rehearse the plot of this well-known tale. The central issue of the narrative is the cosmic entity Yog-Sothoth's mating with Lavinia Whateley, the albino daughter of Old Whateley, who gives birth to the "dark, goatish-looking" (*DH* 159) Wilbur (and his invisible twin). This scenario is almost certainly derived from Arthur Machen's "The Great God Pan," in which the strange woman Helen Vaughan is the offspring of the mating of Pan with a woman in a scientific experiment; the invisibility of Wilbur's twin is taken from such earlier stories of invisible monsters as Ambrose Bierce's "The Damned Thing" and Algernon Blackwood's "The Wendigo." A number of other literary influences—ranging from Anthony M. Rud's story "Ooze" (*Weird Tales*, March 1923) to Harper Williams's *The Thing in the Woods* (1924)—make the story a tissue of borrowings.

One question arises immediately: how and why did Yog-Sothoth choose Lavinia as his mate? Did Old Whateley, who has a reputation as a sorcerer practising black magic, summon the entity (as, apparently, Joseph Curwen did in *The Case of Charles Dexter Ward*)? There is no evidence of this, even though Old Whateley states when Wilbur is born:

"Ye needn't think the only folks is the folks hereabouts. Lavinny's read some, an' has seed some things the most o' ye only tell abaout. I calc'late her man is as good a husban' as ye kin find this side of Aylesbury; an' ef ye knowed as much abaout the hills as I dew, ye wouldn't ast no better church weddin' nor her'n" (*DH* 160). This doesn't tell us much; does the mention of "the hills" imply that there is some property about them that lured Yog-Sothoth there? At any rate, Old Whateley never claims to have effected the unorthodox union by his own actions.

There is, of course, some reason to wonder why so apparently powerful an entity as Yog-Sothoth would choose this backwoods albino as the Mary to usher in a new age of terror. Indeed, both the nature of Yog-Sothoth and his purpose in producing the two hybrid entities in the story are by no means clear. Even if we assume that Yog-Sothoth is, physically, only an infinitely larger version of the invisible creature—ropy tentacles and the like—we get no closer to his motivations. Why, in fact, does he even need Wilbur and the twin to carry out his plans? Dr. Henry Armitage, the valiant old librarian who foils the plot, speaks at one point of

> some plan for the extirpation of the entire human race and all animal and vegetable life from the earth by some terrible elder race of beings from another dimension. He would shout that the world was in danger, since the Elder Things wished to strip it and drag it away from the solar system and cosmos of matter into some other plane or phase of entity from which it had once fallen, vigintillions of aeons ago. (*DH* 185)

This would seem to suggest that Yog-Sothoth is not acting alone, even though no other cosmic entity figures in the story. This point is apparently confirmed by the passage from the *Necronomicon* (the lengthiest single passage from that text in Lovecraft's work) cited earlier in the story:

> The Old Ones were, the Old Ones are, and the Old Ones shall be. Not in the spaces we know, but *between* them, They walk serene and primal, undimensioned and to us unseen. *Yog-Sothoth* knows the gate. *Yog-Sothoth* is the gate. *Yog-Sothoth* is the key and guardian of the gate. Past, present, future, all are one in *Yog-Sothoth*. He knows where the Old Ones broke through of old, and where They shall break through again. . . . By Their smell can men sometimes know Them near, but of

Their semblance can no man know, *saving only in the features of those They have begotten on mankind* . . . Great Cthulhu is Their cousin, yet can he spy Them only dimly. *Iä! Shub-Niggurath!* . . . They wait patient and potent, for here shall They reign again. (*DH* 170)

This passage—which sounds rather like a combination of Lord Dunsany and Friedrich Nietzsche—is frustratingly ambiguous. It does not clarify whether Yog-Sothoth is one of the Old Ones (presumably equivalent to the Elder Things in the passage quoted above) or somehow separate; and it seems to suggest that Cthulhu is not an Old One, but only a "cousin" of the Old Ones (and, hence, that the Great Old Ones in "The Call of Cthulhu" are not equivalent to the Old Ones as cited here, but would be equivalent to the "Cthulhu spawn" cited in that tale). But these are small points. The idea of the Old Ones begetting offspring on mankind—taken, as I have just suggested, from the *Dream-Quest* but transferred to the real world—is obviously meant to account for Wilbur's (and his twin's) existence; but it does not explain *why* the Old Ones need these hybrid offspring to effect their purposes. The only clue we have is in the passage of Wilbur's diary that Armitage decodes: "They from the air told me at Sabbat that it will be years before I can clear off the earth, and I guess grandfather will be dead then, so I shall have to learn all the angles of the planes and all the formulas between the Yr and the Nhhngr. They from outside will help, but they cannot take body without human blood" (*DH* 184). So it appears that the Old Ones, being more or less non-material (at least, not material in any sense we can understand), require human flesh to effect their purposes on earth.

One of the many problems with the story, on a purely aesthetic level, is that the death of Wilbur (when a guard dog kills him as he tries to steal the *Necronomicon* from the Miskatonic University library) collapses the Old Ones' plans, so that the depredations of the invisible twin—who breaks out of the Whateley home, presumably because Wilbur has not fed him, and goes on a rampage in the town of Dunwich—only end up producing a certain amount of unfortunate damage, but are otherwise pretty harmless. In effect, the cosmic threat is already over, and the tale suffers a letdown as a result. Armitage, speaking pompously to the townspeople as they are tracking down the monster, states: "It's a frightful thing to have alive, but it isn't as bad as what

Wilbur would have let in he'd lived longer. You'll never know what the world has escaped. Now we've only this one thing to fight, and it can't multiply. It can, though, do a lot of harm; so we mustn't hesitate to rid the community of it" (*DH* 191). Armitage sounds as if he is speaking of some kind of annoying pest or nuisance.

The real flaw in the story is that, unlike "The Call of Cthulhu" and, preeminently, "The Colour out of Space," Lovecraft has attempted to make a shoot-'em-up action story, with brave good guys (Armitage and the human race in general) battling and defeating the bad guys (the Old Ones and their sundry cohorts or disciples). This naïve morality is explicitly in discord with Lovecraft's own stated motivations in story writing, as he had uttered just a year before: "To achieve the essence of real externality, whether of time or space or dimension, one must forget that such things as organic life, *good and evil* [my emphasis], love and hate, and all such local attributes of a negligible and temporary race called mankind, have any existence at all" (*SL* 2.150).

In order to avoid this conclusion, Donald R. Burleson has postulated that the story is in fact a parody. Keenly pointing out that it is Wilbur (and his twin) who comprise the true "heroes" of the tale (although they are tragic heroes) by fulfilling the eight stages of the hero myth-cycle, and noting that Armitage's "victory" over the Whateleys is likely to be (in cosmic terms) ludicrously short-lived (given the *Necronomicon* passage clearly stating that the Old Ones will one day triumph and clear off the earth), Burleson goes on to say that the tale thereby "ceases to be a 'good versus evil' story that fits only awkwardly into the Lovecraft canon."[8] I find this convincing—up to a point. But if Burleson is suggesting that the story was meant, in effect, to ridicule the crude tastes of *Weird Tales* readers (and, for that matter, the editor, Farnsworth Wright), then I must respectfully disagree. Although Armitage is in fact a pompous buffoon, he is clearly modelled upon the figure of Dr. Willett in *The Case of Charles Dexter Ward,* who is manifestly the "hero" or saviour of that tale. And in spite of such painfully melo-dramatic utterances as *"But what, in God's name, can we do?"* (*DH* 185), Armitage is a man clearly after Lovecraft's heart; he tells August Derleth that, as he was writing the story, "[I] found myself psychologically identifying with one of the characters (an aged scholar who finally combats the menace) toward the end."[9] How Lovecraft could have identified with such bombast as "We have no business calling in such things from outside, and only very wicked people and very wicked cults ever try to" (*DH* 197) is beyond my understanding.

What I think has happened is that Lovecraft, already shaken by *Weird Tales'* rejection of several stories ("The Shunned House," "Cool Air," "The Call of Cthulhu"), was responding unconsciously to the magazine's demands for explicitness and what he elsewhere referred to scornfully as the "humanocentric pose" (*MW* 155). Lovecraft spoke frequently in later years about how "that ass Wright got me into the habit of obvious writing with his never-ending complaints against the indefiniteness of my early stuff" (*SL* 3.395), and "The Dunwich Horror" (with, perhaps, a predecessor in the equally bad "The Horror at Red Hook") appears to be an instance of it.

A number of scholars have attempted to defend the aesthetic merits of the story. Some, like Robert M. Price, express unabashed enthusiasm for the story in spite (or because?) of its apparent aesthetic failings. Price has recently noted that "The Dunwich Horror" is "my favorite story by H. P. Lovecraft,"[10] and he then criticises scholars such as Dirk W. Mosig, Donald R. Burleson, and myself for disparaging the tale. Mosig, in Price's view, was "setting forth his own systematic philosophy of Lovecraft's fiction and criticizing not only Derleth (explicitly) but even Lovecraft (implicitly) for failing to stick to it. It is amusing to note how Mosig's successors have had to resort to dismissing Lovecraft's own 'The Dunwich Horror' as irony ('He can't have meant it!— or my theory's shot to hell!')."[11] Well, that's not quite what is going on. There is nothing wrong with putting forth what Lovecraft himself claimed to be his theory of weird fiction ("To achieve the essence of real externality . . ." as quoted above) and demonstrating (what is in fact the case) that "The Dunwich Horror" does not adhere to it. One does not, in fact, even need to appeal to Lovecraft's own theory to demonstrate that, on purely aesthetic terms, "The Dunwich Horror" is a failure. For all the validity of Burleson's views regarding the true "heroes" of the story, the tale does emphatically portray a good-versus-evil schema that is inherently naïve and conventional. Very few major works of literature adopt this moral dichotomy successfully, because it does not in fact correspond to the moral environment of real life.

In an engaging and half-satirical article, "Why 'The Dunwich Horror' Is So Great,"[12] Charles Hoffman puts forth several additional arguments. He first states that, given Lovecraft's assertion that "good" and "evil" are merely human attributes, Old Whateley can be considered "evil" in human terms (but not Yog-Sothoth or the Whateley twins). This distinction between the human and the otherworldly seems a bit strained, and Old Whateley would himself wish to be allied with the latter and not the former. Hoffman then remarks, in rebuttal to my assertion that Armitage is a "buffoon," that Lovecraft "would *never* portray an elderly scholar as a joke." He never would have *intended* to; but in this instance, he ended up (unintentionally) doing so. Hoffman asserts that Armitage's various utterances (regarded as pompous and bombastic by myself and others) are largely spoken to ignorant yokels who wouldn't understand him if he expressed himself in other ways; but no writer is obliged to carry realism to such a length that he (or his character) ends up sounding foolish and ridiculous. Hoffman's chief argument for the merit of the story is as follows: "'The Dunwich Horror' is so great because in it we find the most emphatic placement of *myth* in the Lovecraft *mythos*. It belies the notion that HPL was actually a science fiction writer slumming in the horror genre." But I don't know anyone who holds such a view: it is evident that Lovecraft's chief virtue, both intrinsically and historically, is the melding of horror and science-fiction tropes into an unclassifiable amalgam. And Hoffman's observation that "The Dunwich Horror" has "tremendous popular appeal" and has *"accessibility"* (an echo of Peter Cannon's earlier argument that the story might have worked well as a popular novel[13]) is a dubious compliment indeed. Stephen King's work is certainly accessible, but that in itself does not confer any aesthetic value upon it; indeed, rather the reverse.

The story, of course, is not a total loss. Its evocation of the landscape of backwoods New England is striking, although perhaps it is not quite as subtle as that in "The Colour out of Space." As Donald R. Burleson has pointed out,[14] the setting is a fusion of impressions derived from the area around Athol (where his friend W. Paul Cook lived) and Wilbraham, Massachusetts (where Lovecraft stayed with Edith Miniter for two weeks in the summer of 1928, just prior to writing the story). Dunwich makes its one and only appearance in this tale; the name is not even mentioned anywhere else in the Lovecraft corpus except fleetingly in the poem "The Ancient Track" (1929): "There was the milestone that I knew— / 'Two miles to Dunwich' . . ." (*AT* 63). The name Dunwich has led to some speculation, some believing that it derives from a town on the eastern coast of England that ended up underwater as a result of the erosion of the shoreline. The name is mentioned in Arthur Machen's short novel *The Terror* (1917), and I suspect that is where Lovecraft found the name. Whether he pronounced it in the British manner (*Dun´-nich*) is unknown.

Indeed, one of the most interesting comments Lovecraft makes about the story is that it "belongs to the Arkham cycle" (*SL* 2.246). Lovecraft never explains this laconic phrase, nor does he (to my knowledge) ever use it again. What it suggests is that Arkham is a kind of focal point for horrors that radiate out from it, as in Kingsport, Dunwich, and (later) Innsmouth. All these towns have relations of various sorts to Arkham; and, although Arkham itself can on occasion be portrayed as "witch-haunted" or such, it seems on the whole a haven of sanity as compared with these other locales. If this conjecture is plausible, it suggests that—at this juncture at any rate—Lovecraft is giving greater weight to his invented topography than to his invented theogony. This may be because that topography is, on the whole, a more vital and real presence in the stories in question than the "gods," who with rare exceptions are kept in the background and appear only fleetingly.

It is possible—although by no means certain—that around this time Lovecraft devised another imaginary New England town, one that he never used in a story: Foxfield. Among the Lovecraft papers at Arkham House is a hand-drawn "Plan of Foxfield—for possible fictional use."[15] On this map, an arrow pointing west indicates the direction in which "Aylesbury-Dunwich" lie, and an arrow pointing southeast indicates a "new road" to Arkham. A road pointing north leads to "Belton" (not Bolton), another "new" town never used in a story. This would suggest that Foxfield lies between Dunwich and Arkham, more toward eastern than central Massachusetts. Beyond that, we can say little; but at least the map must postdate "The Dunwich Horror."

The overall contribution of "The Dunwich Horror" to the Lovecraft Mythos is to make explicit, perhaps for the first time, that Alhazred's *Necronomicon* is a kind of guide to the Old Ones. In the passage in question, it is clear that Alhazred is, as it were, on the side of Yog-Sothoth and his cohorts. This, and the fact that it contains spells for conjuring up these dreaded entities, make the book (as Robert M. Price has pointed out) a grimoire as opposed to a demonology.[16] A grimoire is a book "containing recipes and prescriptions for spells." A demonology (and recall that Lovecraft referred to Alhazred as "the old Arab daemonologist" in "The Hound" [D 174]) is "a guidebook to heretical beliefs," in which the author "hates and fears the horrors he relates." This schema seems to work for the *Necronomicon* passage cited at the end of "The Festival" (even though in that tale the book is also used in the course of the underground ceremony by the townspeople), but in "The Dunwich Horror" Alhazred has "gone over to the enemy." This conception appears to have emerged explicitly in "History of the *Necronomicon*," where, as before cited, Alhazred is clearly said to have "worshipp[ed] unknown entities whom he called Yog-Sothoth and Cthulhu" (*MW* 52).

It is worth repeating, however, that we really get a very dim view of the nature and properties of Yog-Sothoth. As Charles Hoffman points out, Yog-Sothoth is indeed a mythic and deific figure (although Lovecraft never refers to him as a "god," and Armitage only alludes to this entity and his cohorts as "some terrible race of beings from another dimension" [DH 185]); but the precise meaning of "*Yog-Sothoth* knows the gate. *Yog-Sothoth* is the gate. *Yog-Sothoth* is the key and guardian of the gate" (*DH* 170) remains (deliberately) unclear. Manifestly, Lovecraft wished to create a sense of mystery and awe around Yog-Sothoth; and even when (as we shall see in the next chapter) Lovecraft systematically "demythologises" the Old Ones, Yog-Sothoth remains a cosmic being of immense but nebulous powers.

But we should also keep in mind the very real possibility that the *Necronomicon* is *wrong* (or, at least, not fully informed) about the attributes of Yog-Sothoth and the Old Ones. As before, there is no reason to think that Alhazred is "correct" in what he has written about these entities. Given Lovecraft's general scepticism regarding religion and religious texts, he very likely wished us to regard the orotund utterances of the *Necronomicon* as dubious at best and flatly erroneous at worst. Remember that we never even *see* Yog-Sothoth, but only his invisible twin; and when that entity is made visible for an instant, Armitage concludes only that *"It was his [Wilbur's] twin brother, but it looked more like the father than he did"* (*DH* 198). (How exactly Armitage knows this—except by consultation of passages in the *Necronomicon* not cited in the story—is unclear.) But to "look like" someone is not to look *exactly* like that person; so even Yog-Sothoth's physical attributes remain vague. Again, this is by no means a flaw in the story: Lovecraft clearly wished to retain ambiguity on a number of points, for all that other features of the tale are perhaps excessively explicit and obvious.

After writing "The Dunwich Horror," Lovecraft took what proved to be a vacation from original fiction writing for about a year and a half—his next work was "The Whisperer in Darkness," begun in February 1930 and finished in September. In the interim he produced some more ghostwritten tales of varying degrees of significance in terms of his myth-cycle. Of little importance is "The Electric Executioner," written in 1929 for Adolphe de Castro. This story, set in Mexico, contains such flippant references as "Cthulhutl fhtaghn! Niguratl-Yig! Yog-Sototl" (*HM* 74), which are meant to show that Aztecs had some knowledge of these entities and adapted their names into their own language. A little more significant—but only a little—is "Medusa's Coil," written in the summer of 1930 for Zealia Bishop. Here it is suggested that Marceline, the exotic Frenchwoman whom Denis de Russy marries and brings back to his home in Missouri, is in fact a hybrid creature whose origin is far older and more sinister. As Antoine de Russy, Denis's father, explains in referring to a painting by Denis's friend Frank Marsh:

> "The minute I saw it I understood what—she—was, and what part she played in the frightful secret that has come down from the days of Cthulhu and the Elder Ones—the secret that was nearly wiped out when Atlantis sank, but that kept half alive in hidden traditions and allegorical myths and furtive, midnight cult-practices. For you know she was the real thing. It wasn't any fake. It would have been merciful if it had been a fake. It was the old, hideous shadow that philosophers never dared mention—the thing hinted at in the *Necronomicon* and symbolised in the Easter Island colossi." (*HM* 187)

(This passage seems to hark back to the one previously quoted from "The Last Test," in which Dr. Clarendon asserted that Altantis was a "terrible place.") What is the "real thing" that Marceline embodies? Perhaps a later passage, in which Antoine again refers to Marsh's painting, clarifies the point:

> "But the scene wasn't Egypt—it was *behind* Egypt; behind even Atlantis; behind fabled Mu, and myth-whispered Lemuria. It was the ultimate fountain-head of all horror on this earth, and the symbolism shewed only too clearly how integral a part of it Marceline was. I think it must have been the unmentionable R'lyeh, that was not built by any creatures of this planet—the thing Marsh and Denis used to talk about in the shadows with hushed voices. In the picture it appears that the whole scene is deep under water—though everybody seems to be breathing freely." (*HM* 193)

In effect, it appears that Marceline was "the thing from which the first dim legends of Medusa and the Gorgons had sprung" (*HM* 193)—a point we have seen made in earlier stories, going all the way back to "Dagon," whereby the hideous gods or entities from space were the origin of all human mythology. But the story does not follow through on this conception, for at the end it is revealed that Marceline was, "though in deceitfully slight proportion, . . . a negress" (*HM* 200). To a racist like Lovecraft, this would no doubt comprise the acme of horror; but how her negroid blood is to be reconciled with her origin in R'lyeh is by no means explained.

The most significant story by far written at this time is "The Mound" (December 1929–January 1930), ghostwritten for Zealia Bishop. Lovecraft makes no secret of the fact that this novelette—fully as long as "The Whisperer in Darkness"—is entirely his work: "the 're-vision' job I'm doing now is the composition of an original tale from a single paragraph of locale & subject orders—not even a plot germ" (*SL* 3.88). R. H. Barlow noted that the sole "plot" provided by Bishop consisted of the following: "There is an Indian mound near here, which is haunted by a headless ghost. Sometimes it is a woman."[17] From these two sentences Lovecraft weaved a 25,000-word tale of underground horror that, although perhaps not as polished as his own work, must be regarded as one of his signal achievements as a fiction writer. But our purpose is not to analyse the story from a purely literary perspective but to assess its contribution to the Lovecraft Mythos.

It is by now well known that its extensive citation of Tsathoggua derives from Clark Ashton Smith's "The Tale of Satampra Zeiros," the story that introduced that entity, and which Lovecraft read with enthusiasm in December 1929, just as he was beginning work on the story. He writes to Smith:

> I can see & feel & smell the jungle around immemorial Commoriom, which I am sure must lie buried today in glacial ice near Olathoë, in the land of Lomar! It is of this crux of elder horror, I am certain, that the mad Arab Abdul Alhazred was thinking when he—even he—left something unmention'd & signify'd by a row of stars in the surviving codex of his accursed & forbidden *Necronomicon!* (*SL* 3.87)

This whimsical fusion of his own fictive elements with Smith's is exactly what occurs in the story, for the sixteenth-century protagonist, Pánfilo de Zamacona, learns that a temple in the underground realm of K'n-yan was

> built in imitation of certain temples depicted in the vaults of Zin, to house a very terrible black toad-idol found in the red-litten world and called Tsathoggua in the Yothic manuscripts. It had been a potent and widely worshipped god, and after its adoption by the people of K'n-yan had lent its name to the city which was later to become dominant in that region. (*HM* 140)

That last phrase refers to Tsath, evidently the capital city of K'n-yan. The vaults of Zin had first been cited in the *Dream-Quest* ("the ghasts, those repulsive beings which die in the light, and which live in the vaults of Zin" [*M* 339]), and it is again interesting how a dream-world locale has now been transferred to the real world. This occurs again when it is said that "Between glacial ages they [the denizens of K'n-yan] had some remarkable surface civilisations, especially one at the South Pole near the mountain Kadath" (*HM* 131).

Much earlier in the text, one of the explorers of the mound had come back half-insane and babbled of the "children of Tulu" (*HM* 101). This variant spelling of Cthulhu is used extensively in the story; the "correct" spelling is used only once, when the narrator remarks:

> Of one thing I am really glad, and that is that I could not then identify the squatting octopus-headed thing which dominated most of the ornate cartouches [on the cylinder in which Zamacona's manuscript was

found], and which the manuscript called "Tulu". Recently I have associated it, and the legends in the manuscript connected with it, with
some new-found folklore of monstrous and unmentioned Cthulhu, a
horror which seeped down from the stars while the young earth was
still half-formed . . . (*HM* 114–15)

And yet, at one point it is stated that the "Old Ones" (here referring to
the quasi-human inhabitants of K'n-yan) had "come down from the
stars to the world when it was very young" (*HM* 118) and that they
"worshipped Yig, the great father of serpents, and Tulu, the octopus-
headed entity that had brought them down from the stars" (*HM* 119),
and still later that there were "temples to Great Tulu, a spirit of universal harmony anciently symbolised as the octopus-headed god who had
brought all men down from the stars" (*HM* 136). This remarkably benign characterisation of Cthulhu may be surprising, but presumably the
denizens of K'n-yan could not be expected to have a dim view of their
own god. Once again, there is no compelling reason to accept this account of the Old Ones' origin as gospel; indeed, it is earlier stated, in
regard to their extraterrestrial origin, that "All this, of course, was legend now; and one could not say how much truth was in it, or how
much worship was really due to the octopus-headed being Tulu who
had traditionally brought them hither and whom they still reverenced
for aesthetic reasons" (*HM* 131). Lovecraft is again presenting a sceptical anthropology of religion, in which these sorts of origin-myths are to
be regarded as possibly fabricated (the mention of "aesthetic reasons"
is a nod to George Santayana, the Spanish-American philosopher
who—at least in Lovecraft's judgment—advocated religious belief as an
aesthetic, as opposed to a metaphysical, gesture).

Finally, there is mention of "the temples of Yig, Tulu, Nug, Yeb,
and the Not-to-Be-Named One which lined the road at infrequent in-
tervals . . . One squat, black temple of Tsathoggua was encountered,
but it had been turned into a shrine of Shub-Niggurath, the All-Mother
and wife of the Not-to-Be-Named One" (*HM* 144). This passage, along
with an earlier one containing passing references to Azathoth and
Nyarlatotep (*HM* 103), causes "The Mound" to be the one Lovecraft
story in which *all* the chief gods of his pantheon are cited. But most of
these citations are merely glancing references, and even Tsathoggua and
Tulu do not in the end figure much in the actual progress of the narra-

tive. The description of Shub-Niggurath as an "All-Mother" is the one explicit indication that she is a kind of fertility figure—a claim often made by scholars, but on very thin evidence as far as Lovecraft's original stories are concerned. Who is the "Not-to-Be-Named One" of whom she is the wife? It appears to be Yog-Sothoth, if a much later letter can be adduced as evidence. In speaking jokingly to Willis Conover, Lovecraft notes that "Yog-Sothoth's wife is the hellish cloud-like entity Shub-Niggurath, in whose honour nameless cults hold the rite of the Goat with a Thousand Young" (*SL* 5.303). This passage itself has been taken by several scholars to mean that Shub-Niggurath cannot be *identical* to the Goat with a Thousand Young, although perhaps the goat itself is also a fertility symbol. In this same letter Lovecraft goes on to state that Nug and Yeb are the offspring of Shub-Niggurath and Yog-Sothoth. The phrase "Not-to-Be-Named One" appears to be an adaptation "high-priest not to be described" (*M* 370) whom Randolph Carter encounters to his horror in the *Dream-Quest*.

In the end, however, it does not appear as if any of the "gods" mentioned in "The Mound" have much to do with the central narrative, which involves the attempt of Zamacona to flee from K'n-yan, in the company of a woman he has met there, T'la-yub; they are foiled in the attempt, brought back by guards, apparently tortured in the city's amphitheatre, and then re-stationed at the mound entrance (T'la-yub is by this time a reanimated headless corpse). The essence of the story is not the presence of the Mythos gods, or even their supposed role in the origin of the mound denizens, but an exhaustive portrayal of their civilisation—a portrayal in which Lovecraft, becoming increasingly concerned over the trend of Western civilisation in the wake of the stock market crash a few months earlier, makes telling depictions of the gradual decadence of the race as it descends from a refined aestheticism into crude savagery and sadism.

"The Mound," rejected by *Weird Tales* apparently for excessive length, did not see print until years after Lovecraft's death; and, unlike his original stories, it was not circulated among Lovecraft's colleagues, so that its influence on the earlier contributions to the Mythos by other writers was minimal. This cannot be said for "The Whisperer in Darkness," which has exercised both a beneficent and deleterious influence upon subsequent Mythos writing.

This novella, even more powerfully than in "The Colour out of Space," evokes the wonder and terror of the New England landscape—in this case, Vermont, which Lovecraft had visited in 1927 and 1928, finding it a remarkable haven of unspoiled antiquity. The story actually incorporates whole paragraphs from the essay "Vermont—A First Impression" (1927), although they have been subtly altered to enhance their horrific implications. This, really, is the heart of the story, and all the Mythos elements are quite peripheral or subsidiary.

One of the most interesting elements is the citation of Yuggoth. That object had first been cited in the sonnet cycle *Fungi from Yuggoth* (December 27, 1929–January 4, 1930), specifically in sonnet IV ("Recognition"): "I knew this strange, grey world was not my own, / But Yuggoth, past the starry voids" (*AT* 66). Again, in sonnet XIV ("Star-Winds"): "This is the hour when moonstruck poets know / What fungi sprout in Yuggoth" (*AT* 70). (It is noteworthy that the metre in both poems forces one to accent *Yuggoth* on the first syllable.) Steven J. Mariconda—to whose brilliant analysis of the revision of "The Whisperer in Darkness" I will be heavily indebted in the following discussion[18]—may be a little captious in asserting these citations do not necessarily commit one to the view that Yuggoth is a planet: it is difficult to imagine what a "world" could be if not a planet. But the mention of "past the starry voids" certainly does not suggest that it is within our solar system—and yet, this is exactly what Lovecraft asserts in "The Whisperer in Darkness" when he identifies the planet with the newly discovered Pluto. We face, here, a chronological conundrum: Pluto, although discovered by C. W. Tombaugh in early January 1930, was not announced in print until mid-March; but Lovecraft had already begun writing the story on February 24. Mariconda, however, has shown (by consultation with the surviving autograph manuscript of the tale) that references to Yuggoth have been inserted into the early parts of the manuscript at a later stage, presumably after Lovecraft heard of the discovery, which electrified him: it was "a thing which excites me more than any other happening of recent times. . . . I think I shall suggest its being named *Yuggoth!*" (*SL* 3.136). Specifically, this passage—

> The blasphemies which appeared on Earth, it was hinted, came from the dark planet Yuggoth, at the rim of the solar system; but this was itself merely the populous outpost of a frightful interstellar race whose

ultimate source must lie far outside even the Einsteinian space-time continuum or greatest known cosmos. (*DH* 228)

—was added at a later time.

This makes one wonder whether the term "fungi from Yuggoth" as applied to the crustacean entities in the tale figures in the original draft—and, more pertinently, what its exact signification is. The first time this phrase is used (*"They were the hellish tracks of the living fungi from Yuggoth"* [*DH* 250]) occurs fairly late in the text, so it probably postdates Lovecraft's identification of Yuggoth with Pluto. But he manifestly wishes to make clear that the creatures' ultimate origin lay far further in space, since their anomalous physical qualities (they cannot be photographed with an ordinary camera) would not be plausible if their origin could be traced to within our own solar system.

The central query, as far as the Lovecraft (or, for that matter, the Cthulhu) Mythos is concerned, is the role of Nyarlathotep. He is clearly worshipped by the fungi, as Akeley's recording of one of their woodland rites makes clear:

. . . so from the wells of night to the gulfs of space, and from the gulfs of space to the wells of night, ever the praises of Great Cthulhu, of Tsathoggua, and of Him Who is not to be Named. Ever Their praises, and abundance to the Black Goat of the Woods. Iä! Shub-Niggurath! The Goat with a Thousand Young! . . . go out among men and find the ways thereof, that He in the Gulf may know. To Nyarlathotep, Mighty Messenger, must all things be told. And He shall put on the semblance of men, the waxen mask and the robe that hides, and come down from the world of Seven Suns to mock. . . . (*DH* 226)

So it would appear that the fungi worship Cthulhu, Tsathoggua, Yog-Sothoth (if he is equivalent to "Him Who is not to be Named"), Shub-Niggurath, and Nyarlathotep—but preeminently the last. He is the only one of these entities who actually figures in the narrative; but he does so in a way that is by no means clear.

The issue is: Who is the creature who pretends to be Akeley at the end of the story?—who, in other words, is the "whisperer in darkness"? The standard interpretation is that it is Nyarlathotep, because of the phrase "waxen mask and the robe that hides" in the above quotation. This presumably tallies with the "face and hands of Henry Wentworth

Akeley" (*DH* 271) that Wilmarth, at the very end of the story, says he found (along with a discarded dressing gown) on the chair where the "whisperer" had been speaking to him.[19] But if this is the case, then at this moment *Nyarlathotep is in the shape of the fungi from Yuggoth.* This is made clear by the disjointed conversation Wilmarth hears later in the night, when two buzzing voices—one of which "held an unmistakable note of authority" (*DH* 266)—are heard. If the voice in authority is Nyarlathotep, then at that moment he is one of the fungi, since their voices are said to be "a buzzing imitation of human speech" (*DH* 236).

There are, however—as Sam Gafford has noted in a perspicacious article[20]—some problems with this theory. Firstly, why would Nyarlathotep take this form? In his previous appearances in Lovecraft—specifically, the prose-poem "Nyarlathotep" and *The Dream-Quest of Unknown Kadath*—he has clearly been in the shape of a human being, resembling an antique Pharaoh. As a result of his apparently alien shape in "The Whisperer in Darkness," Nyarlathotep has often been referred to as a shapeshifter—but, as Robert M. Price has pointed out, "If Nyarlathotep is a shape-changer, why would he have to resort to the crude disguise of donning Akeley's face and hands?"[21] Why could he not just assume the form of Akeley? Lovecraft never in fact states or implies in any story or other document that Nyarlathotep is a shapeshifter. The comment that "He shall put on the semblance of men" could merely refer to his adopting a disguise.

Gafford believes that there is evidence to suggest that Nyarlathotep is in fact in human guise, and that he communicates with Wilmarth by telepathy. Gafford points out that the Akeley-figure's lips never move, and that Wilmarth "had been able to understand the speaker when wholly across the room" (*DH* 262). I am not convinced by this argument: the failure of the lips to move could merely be a result of the fact that the "mask" (i.e., the face of Akeley) does not fit very well on the head of Nyarlathotep, whether that be a human head or an alien head. And Wilmarth's ability to hear the speaker could be a result of the immense power that clearly radiates from Nyarlathotep. Gafford wants to deny that the "first buzzing voice" in the nighttime colloquy is Nyarlathotep. True, there is no definitive textual evidence of this, but who else would have "an unmistakable note of authority" than he? Wilmarth's mention of "that hideous repressed buzzing" (*DH* 271) must refer both to the voice of the pseudo-Akeley (hence clearly one of the fungi) and the latent power of that voice, which is attempting to suppress itself so that it can pass for human.

In the end, it may not be possible to resolve this issue, but I still believe there is more evidence than not that Nyarlathotep is in fact in the guise of the fungi in this story.

Many of the details of Nyarlathotep's nature and purposes seem adapted from sonnets XXI ("Nyarlathotep") and XXII ("Azathoth") of *Fungi from Yuggoth*. It is there that Nyarlathotep is first referred to as a Messenger ("'I am His Messenger,' the daemon said, / As in contempt he struck his Master's head" [*AT* 73])—disregarding the passing mention of Nyarlathotep as a "black messenger" (*D* 404) in *The Dream-Quest of Unknown Kadath*. In neither poem is Nyarlathotep physically described, although in the first it is suggested that he is of human shape; indeed, this sonnet is largely a versified condensation of the prose-poem "Nyarlathotep." Azathoth figures hazily in "The Whisperer in Darkness"; the most provocative mention is when Nyarlathotep (pretending to be Akeley) tells Wilmarth "of the monstrous nuclear chaos beyond angled space which the *Necronomicon* mercifully cloaked under the name of Azathoth" (*DH* 256). The first mention of Azathoth in the story appears in the celebrated catalogue of names that the actual Akeley had written about to Wilmarth in a letter. Wilmarth paraphrases Akeley's writing:

> I found myself faced by names and terms that I had heard elsewhere in the most hideous of connexions—Yuggoth, Great Cthulhu, Tsathoggua, Yog-Sothoth, R'lyeh, Nyarlathotep, Azathoth, Hastur, Yian, Leng, the Lake of Hali, Bethmoora, the Yellow Sign, L'mur-Kathulos, Bran, and the Magnum Innominandum—and was drawn back through nameless aeons and inconceivable dimensions to worlds of elder, outer entity at which the crazed author of the *Necronomicon* had only guessed in the vaguest way. (*DH* 223)

One almost wishes that Lovecraft had not written this passage, for it seems to have provided the impetus for later Mythos writers to spin out their own catalogues of meaningless names as if their mere citation could create horror. What Lovecraft is attempting here to do is to *tantalise* rather than to *terrify:* he is suggesting that there is an entire realm of existence behind or beyond common life about which we know little.

Of the "new" names in this formulation, Hastur and the Lake of Hali come from Ambrose Bierce; Bethmoora from Lord Dunsany; Yian and the Yellow Sign from Robert W. Chambers; the Magnum Innominandum (Latin for "The Great Not-to-Be-Named"—an "unknown, unnamable deity" worshipped by the hill tribes of ancient Spain) from Lovecraft's great "Roman dream" of 1927 (*SL* 2.190), which Frank Belknap Long would borrow for *The Horror from the Hills* (1931); L'mur-Kathlos adapted from Robert E. Howard's Kathulos in "Skull-Face" (*Weird Tales,* October–December 1929). The citation of Bran is very complex and will be dealt with in Chapter IV.

The most controversial citation is that of Hastur. It is now well known that the name, although invented by Bierce in "Haïta the Shepherd" (1891) as a god of the shepherds, was appropriated by Robert W. Chambers in several stories in *The King in Yellow* (1895), variously as a constellation ("When from Carcosa, the Hyades, Hastur, and Aldebaran . . .") or as a human figure ("Look. Here come Hastur and Raoul").[22] Chambers also frequently cites the Lake of Hali, so that this mention may also derive more directly from Chambers than from Bierce. Later writers of the Cthulhu Mythos, of course, made Hastur a major "god" of the pantheon, but Lovecraft's citation, as well as a later one in the same story ("There is a whole secret cult of evil men (a man of your mystical erudition will understand me when I link them with Hastur and the Yellow Sign) devoted to the purpose of tracking them down . . ." [*DH* 239]), does not make it clear whether Hastur is even an entity, much less a god. Lovecraft never uses the term in any subsequent tale.

Another passage is of some interest:

> I learned whence Cthulhu *first* came, and why half the great temporary stars of history had flared forth. I guessed—from hints which made even my informant pause timidly—the secret behind the Magellanic Clouds and globular nebulae, and the black truth veiled by the immemorial allegory of Tao. The nature of the Doels was plainly revealed, and I was told the essence (though not the source) of the Hounds of Tindalos. The legend of Yig, Father of Serpents, remained figurative no longer . . . (*DH* 256)

There are many points of interest here. Once again, this passage tantalises the reader with the suggestion of immense stores of knowledge sealed off from the common herd. In a sense, the passage might constitute a kind of counterargument to Lovecraft's celebrated opening sentence of "Supernatural Horror in Literature": "The oldest and strongest emotion of mankind is fear, and the oldest and strongest kind of fear is fear of the unknown." And yet, whereas *Wilmarth's* fears are enhanced by his knowledge of what Nyarlathotep (if it is he) has told him, readers' fears are augmented by the fact that they remain in ignorance— Lovecraft is having his cake and eating it too.

The reference to "whence Cthulhu *first* emerged" suggests that Wilmarth has learned the ultimate origin of that entity, prior to his immersion under the sea. In "The Call of Cthulhu" it was stated only that he and his spawn "came to the young world out of the sky" (*DH* 139). The mention of Doels and the Hounds of Tindalos was taken directly from Frank Belknap Long's "The Hounds of Tindalos" (1929), which, along with L'mur-Kathulos, might constitute the first borrowing of a Mythos element from a colleague rather than from a predecessor. This has led Will Murray to assert, in a provocative article,[23] that the only genuine tales of the Lovecraft Mythos are "The Call of Cthulhu," "The Colour out of Space," and "The Dunwich Horror," since "Nothing Lovecraft penned after 'The Dunwich Horror' was free from external influence, tampering, borrowings and reciprocal playfulness." There are some problems with that view: as we shall see in Chapter IV, "The Dunwich Horror" itself contains a borrowing from Long: John Dee's English translation of the *Necronomicon* (see *DH* 169), which Long had cited as the epigraph to "The Space-Eaters" (*Weird Tales*, July 1928), although it did not appear when the story was published (Lovecraft had, however, seen the story in ms.). Lovecraft subsequently altered the ms. of "History of the *Necronomicon*" to include the Dee reference. But Murray's contention that Lovecraft "lost what is perhaps a writer's most precious right—that of primacy over his own material" seems overdrawn: the mere swapping of such references, usually occurring in passing and having no central bearing on the fundamental theme or motif of the story, could hardly constitute "losing primacy" over one's material.

"The Whisperer in Darkness" does indeed contain an even more prominent borrowing, when the pseudo-Akeley tells Wilmarth:

> "You know they [the fungi] were here long before the fabulous epoch of Cthulhu was over, and remember all about sunken R'lyeh when it was above the waters. They've been inside the earth, too—there are

openings which human beings know nothing of—some of them in these very Vermont hills—and great worlds of unknown life down there; blue-litten K'n-yan, red-litten Yoth, and black, lightless N'kai. It's from N'kai that frightful Tsathoggua came—you know, the amorphous, toad-like god-creature mentioned in the Pnakotic Manuscripts and the *Necronomicon* and the Commoriom myth-cycle preserved by the Atlantean high-priest Klarkash-Ton." (*DH* 254)

All this is a trifle laboured, and even as an in-joke it seems rather lame; but it is clearly meant to borrow not only from himself (specifically "The Mound") but from Clark Ashton Smith. Because this citation of Tsathoggua, appearing when the story appeared in *Weird Tales* for August 1931, preceded the publication of Smith's "The Tale of Satampra Zeiros" (*Weird Tales*, December 1931), many believed that Lovecraft had invented the god and that Smith had borrowed from him. But again, it is a passing mention and has no bearing on the story.

The repeated citations of the *Necronomicon* are of great interest, because they make explicit what had only been hinted at in earlier stories: that Alhazred is in fact either in error in regard to the various "deities" or entities or other particulars of the Lovecraft Mythos, or is deliberately concealing them in a mask of symbol and allegory. The fact that Alhazred can only "guess" at the meaning of certain names or terms in a "vague way" definitively destroys the contention that we can find the "truth" about the "gods" by a direct consultation of the *Necronomicon* or other "forbidden" books.

Thematically, "The Whisperer in Darkness" is substantial but also flawed. In terms of the working out of the plot, it would appear that Wilmarth is far too gullible a character to be plausible. He is unable to detect numerous instances in which the aliens (and/or Nyarlathotep) have attempted to communicate with him pretending to be Akeley (on one occasion actually sending him a telegram with Akeley's name misspelled); and the final letter that the aliens write to him, carefully specifying that he bring all letters and other materials from Akeley "as consultative data" (*DH* 241)—an obvious attempt to make sure that Wilmarth brings up all the evidence he had obtained from Akeley so that, when it is taken from him, he will have nothing to show the authorities in making a case against the aliens—is something that a man of Wilmarth's intellect should have seen through. One of the story's first readers, Bernard Austin Dwyer, apparently voiced these criticisms to Lovecraft when hearing a draft of the story in the summer of 1930; and although Lovecraft did make attempts to mitigate Wilmarth's gullibility, Mariconda is correct in noting that "These attempts unfortunately come across as feeble afterthoughts."

More significantly, in terms of Lovecraft's stated aesthetic of weird fiction, the story again portrays the aliens as duplicitous, hostile to humanity, and in other ways conventionally "evil"—if, perhaps, not to the extent of the Whateley clan in "The Dunwich Horror." The fungi's engaging in rather comical shootouts with Akeley at his isolated farm come across as outtakes from a bad Western. In spite of the fact that, as the real Akeley tells Wilmarth in his first letter, "They could easily conquer the earth, but have not tried so far because they have not needed to. They would rather leave things as they are to save bother" (*DH* 218), they have a remarkably difficult time dealing with the lonely recluse and his pack of dogs in Vermont.

Nevertheless, the extraordinarily rich atmosphere of rustic horror—the true heart of the story—and the spectacularly cosmic implications of disembodied brains traversing the boundless universe and their ability to communicate with alien intelligences across the cosmos make "The Whisperer in Darkness" rank very high in Lovecraft's corpus. At one point Wilmarth becomes fired with a burning desire to probe the universe's secrets—"To shake off the maddening and wearying limitations of time and space and natural law—to be linked with the vast *outside*—to come close to the nighted and abysmal secrets of the infinite and the ultimate—surely such a thing was worth the risk of one's life, soul, and sanity!" (*DH* 243)—but in the end he draws back from the brink in horror. Perhaps, as we shall see in the next chapter, the Lovecraft of a few years later would have had Wilmarth take the plunge after all.

This first phase of the Lovecraft Mythos saw Lovecraft introduce his chief "gods," who figure importantly in four stories: Cthulhu ("The Call of Cthulhu"), Yog-Sothoth ("The Dunwich Horror"), and Nyarlathotep (*The Dream-Quest of Unknown Kadath* and "The Whisperer in Darkness"). And yet, even in these stories, they make very rare appearances on stage: indeed, only Cthulhu and (in the *Dream-Quest*) Nyarlathotep are actually seen by any characters whose words we can read.

In other cases, the "gods" remain largely offstage, their influence apparent only through their underlings or offspring. The cosmic element that is the chief feature of Lovecraft's writing is vividly apparent in "The Call of Cthulhu," "The Colour out of Space," and "The Whisperer in Darkness"; much less so in "The Dunwich Horror." What is more significant, of the eleven original stories Lovecraft wrote from the summer of 1926 to the end of 1930, six ("The Call of Cthulhu," *The Dream-Quest of Unknown Kadath*, "The Colour out of Space," "History of the *Necronomicon*," "The Dunwich Horror," "The Whisperer in Darkness") are centrally concerned with the Lovecraft Mythos, while three others ("The Strange High House in the Mist," "The Descendant," *The Case of Charles Dexter Ward*) are tangentially related; only "The Silver Key" and "Pickman's Model" are entirely unrelated to the Mythos. And, as we have seen, several important revisions (notably "The Curse of Yig" and "The Mound") add details to the Mythos.

It is therefore evident that Lovecraft himself—as his correspondence reveals—was beginning to become aware that there was an overall coherence in his fiction that extended beyond philosophical orientation and thematic unity and reached to the level of plot and motif, so that each new tale built upon its predecessors and was almost written with the expectation that the reader was familiar with those tales and could therefore understand their complex interlocking system of references. Perhaps, therefore, George T. Wetzel was only slightly exaggerating when he maintained that Lovecraft's stories are chapters of an immense novel. This period also saw the first "additions" to the Mythos by other writers, and Lovecraft's acknowledgement of those additions by references in his own tales.

But the Lovecraft Mythos would, in the final six years of Lovecraft's creative life, evolve in ways that even he probably did not envision. In part, this evolution was the result of his own philosophical development; but it was also the result of a surprising number of additions and borrowings of Mythos elements by his friends and colleagues. It is this development that we shall now discuss.

III.

The Lovecraft Mythos: Phase II (1931–36)

IN EARLY 1931, Lovecraft wrote a highly significant letter to Frank Belknap Long. The trigger for the discussion was Lovecraft's (and perhaps Long's) reading of Joseph Wood Krutch's *The Modern Temper* (1929), a rather lugubrious treatise that maintained that many former emotions that were the foundation of artistic creation—say, honor, class-consciousness, and especially love—had now become aesthetically unusable because modern science (especially the sciences of physics, biology, chemistry, and psychology) had shown these emotions to be anything but transcendent and cosmic, but instead mundane, artificial, and limited to specific eras and cultures. The query thus became: On what emotional bases can art now be established?

Lovecraft studied the question from the perspective of weird fiction. He wrote:

> Fantastic literature cannot be treated as a single unit, because it is a composite resting on widely divergent bases. I really agree that "Yog-Sothoth" is a basically immature conception, & unfitted for really serious literature. . . . But I consider the use of actual folk-myths as even more childish than the use of new artificial myths, since in employing the former one is forced to retain many blatant puerilities & contradictions of experience which could be subtilised or smoothed over if the supernaturalism were modelled to order for the given case. The only permanently artistic use of Yog-Sothothery, I think, is in symbolic or associative phantasy of the frankly poetic type; in which fixed dream-patterns of the natural organism are given an embodiment & crystallisation. (*SL* 293)

Great care must be taken in interpreting Lovecraft's remarks here. We should not assume that "Yog-Sothothery" is necessarily identical to our conceptions of the Cthulhu Mythos, or even the Lovecraft Mythos. Rather, the context appears to establish that Lovecraft was using the term to denote the Dunsanian poetic fantasy in which "gods" appear in a never-never land of the imagination, something akin to his own *Dream-Quest of Unknown Kadath*. This point appears to be clarified by a later statement:

> But there is another phase of cosmic phantasy (which may or may not include frank Yog-Sothothery) whose foundations appear to me as better grounded than those of ordinary oneiroscopy; personal limitation regarding the *sense of outsideness*. I refer to the aesthetic crystallisation of that burning & inextinguishable feeling of mixed wonder & oppression which the sensitive imagination experiences upon scaling itself & its restrictions against the vast & provocative abyss of the unknown. (*SL* 3.294)

In other words, cosmicism within a setting of (quasi-)supernatural realism—the kind of thing we have seen in "The Call of Cthulhu" and "The Colour out of Space." Lovecraft believed that no conceivable advances of science could ever destroy this sense of "outsideness"—the perception of human insignificance within the vast cosmos-at-large. But compositions based upon this idea must conform to the most advanced conceptions of present-day science, otherwise they will come across as obviously implausible, as conventional tales of ghosts and vampires do. This leads to the following conclusion:

> The time has come when the normal revolt against time, space, & matter must assume a form not overtly incompatible with what is known of reality—when it must be gratified by images forming *supplements* rather than *contradictions* of the visible & mensurable universe. And what, if not a form of *non-supernatural cosmic art*, is to pacify this sense of revolt—as well as gratify the cognate sense of curiosity? (*SL* 3.295–96)

The importance of this statement cannot be overemphasised. Not only does it outline Lovecraft's aesthetic path for the remainder of his life, it provides clues to show that even much of his earlier work was heading in this direction years before he ever made this utterance. It is highly interesting to see Lovecraft observing that "In 'The Colour out of Space' I began to get near it—though 'Dunwich' & the 'Whisperer' represent a relapse" (*SL* 3.296)—exactly the judgment of many leading Lovecraft scholars.

This letter, composed on February 27, 1931, was written at exactly the time when Lovecraft was writing what could well be the pinnacle of his aesthetic achievement—the short novel *At the Mountains of Madness* (February–March 22, 1931). It could be expected that the work would embody the principles Lovecraft has outlined, and it does just that. What we find in this novel is that creatures called the "Old Ones"— whom Lake, the scientist who first discovered their frozen remains, notes "reminds one of certain monsters of primal myth, especially fabled Elder Things in *Necronomicon*" (*M* 20), creatures who are "supposed to have created all earth-life as jest or mistake" (*M* 22)—came down from distant space millions of years ago, establishing colonies all over the world, but ultimately suffered a decline and retained only an immense city in the Antarctic, and were finally overthrown by the shoggoths, the hideous protoplasmic entities they had created as slave-labour.

The first difficulty we must face is exactly what relation these "Old Ones" have to creatures so designated in Lovecraft's earlier tales. It is a bit maddening that Lovecraft uses this term to denote an apparently wide array of entities, chiefly to emphasise their immense antiquity as compared with the human race. One important passage in the novel is the following:

> They [the Old Ones] were the makers and enslavers of that [earth] life, and above all doubt the originals of the fiendish elder myths which things like the Pnakotic Manuscripts and the *Necronomicon* affrightedly hint about. They were the Great Old Ones that had filtered down from the stars when earth was young—the beings whose substance an alien evolution had shaped, and whose powers were such as this planet had never bred. (*M* 59–60)

This sounds as if the Old Ones are perhaps equivalent to the Cthulhu spawn in "The Call of Cthulhu," but a later passage makes clear that, after the Old Ones had already established themselves on earth, "Another race—a land race of beings shaped like octopi and probably corresponding to the fabulous pre-human spawn of Cthulhu—soon began filtering down from cosmic infinity and precipitated a monstrous war which for a time drove the Old Ones wholly back to the sea" (*M* 66). So clearly the Cthulhu spawn are the enemies of the Old Ones. Could the *Necronomicon* passage in "The Dunwich Horror" be of help? Perhaps; but Alhazred's remark that "Great Cthulhu is Their cousin, yet can he spy Them only dimly" (*DH* 170) does not seem to reflect the precise relationship between Cthulhu and the Old Ones in *At the Mountains of Madness*. Moreover, the relation of the Old Ones to Yog-Sothoth is highly problematical in the story; the latter is not even mentioned except in passing, as part of Danforth's mad and fragmentary ravings at the end of the story (*M* 106).

What Lovecraft seems to be doing here is definitively "demythologising" his "gods" so that they become mere extraterrestrials. Robert M. Price, who first brought this development to our attention in an important article,[1] has gone on to observe in a later article that this tendency was in rudimentary existence all along, at least since "The Call of Cthulhu."[2] There is nothing in that story, nor in "The Colour out of Space" or "The Whisperer in Darkness," to suggest that the entities we have been accustomed to refer to as "gods" are in fact gods in any meaningful sense: the mere fact that certain human (or, as in "The Whisperer in Darkness," alien) sects worship them as gods (as the fungi clearly worship Nyarlathotep and others) does not make them gods in fact. Indeed, even "The Dunwich Horror" (*pace* Charles Hoffman) falls into this pattern. Hoffman criticises my use of the term "mere extraterrestrials" in referring to Cthulhu, Yog-Sothoth, and the like, but the metaphysical difference between an extraterrestrial entity, however powerful, and an actual god is so immense that the term "mere" is entirely justified.

Lovecraft here makes explicit what he has suggested in varying degrees all along—that the *Necronomicon* and other books of "forbidden" lore are actually mistaken about the true nature of the "gods" they write about. The passage quoted above states unequivocally that the Old Ones are the "originals" of "fiendish elder beings" that the *Necronomicon* is only "hinting about." Another passage—"These viscous masses were without doubt what Abdul Alhazred whispered about as the 'shoggoths' in his frightful *Necronomicon,* though even that mad Arab had not hinted that any existed on earth except in the dreams of those who had chewed a certain alkaloidal herb" (*M* 62)—again shows Alhazred to be in error. If he is in error, then the various cultists who look upon the *Necronomicon* and other tomes as embodying the "truth" about the "gods" are similarly in error.

The important point that the Old Ones had actually "created" all earth-life is a significant departure from previous stories. In "The Call of Cthulhu" the Great Old Ones had merely come down from the stars, and, after they went "inside the earth and under the sea," "had told their secrets in dreams to the first men, who had formed a cult which had never died" (*DH* 139). (Once again, however, this statement, by old Castro, may need to be taken with a grain of salt; but even Castro, who is intent on exaggerating the connexions between the Great Old Ones and their human devotees, makes no suggestion that the former created all life on earth.) There is similarly no such suggestion in the *Necronomicon* passage in "The Dunwich Horror." Lovecraft's motivation in *At the Mountains of Madness* is clearly to suggest a rather contemptible origin of our species, since at one point the protagonists, studying the bas-reliefs in the Old Ones' city, "see in some of the very last and most decadent sculptures a shambling primitive mammal, used sometimes for food and sometimes as an amusing buffoon by the land dwellers, whose vaguely simian and human foreshadowings were unmistakable" (*M* 65). This incredibly misanthropic conception does not in fact recur in later stories, although perhaps only because Lovecraft decided not to put these Old Ones on stage in later works except incidentally.

The shoggoths are of some minimal interest. The name was first cited in sonnet XX ("Night-Gaunts") of *Fungi from Yuggoth*: ". . . down the nether pits to that foul lake / Where the puffed shoggoths splash in doubtful sleep" (*AT* 72). What significance this citation has, in a sonnet about the night-gaunts, remains unclear. Will Murray has pointed out[3] that the nucleus of the idea of shoggoths may have come from a passage in "The Mound" (which, let us recall, was written exactly at the time *Fungi from Yuggoth* was being composed), where it is stated that "the beings of Yoth had possessed the art of synthetically creating life, and had made and destroyed several efficiently designed races of industrial and transportational animals in the course of their history" (*HM* 139). Later, when the men of K'n-yan had explored N'kai (which lies below Yoth), they had found "living things that oozed along stone channels and worshipped onyx and basalt images of Tsathoggua . . . they were amorphous lumps of viscous black slime that took temporary shapes for various purposes" (*HM* 141). These are unquestionably shoggoths, but Lovecraft does not give them a name here.

At the Mountains of Madness produces a grand synthesis of Love-craft's previous Mythos tales, including even several of his "Dun-sanian" tales—and in a much less flippant way than in "The Whisperer in Darkness" with its meaningless catalogue of names and terms. It has frequently been pointed out that Lovecraft is deliberately inconsistent with himself when he asserts that the Old Ones' city in the Antarctic is equivalent to Leng, which in "The Hound" he had placed in central Asia. Commentators seem less disturbed by the fact that Leng appears to be in the dream-world in *The Dream-Quest of Unknown Kadath*. In that work Leng is apparently near Kadath, which in "The Mound" has al-ready been taken out of the dream-world and placed in Antarctica ("at the South Pole near the mountain Kadath" [*HM* 131]). Lovecraft ex-plains the discontinuity by remarking: "Mythologists have placed Leng in Central Asia; but the racial memory of man—or of his predeces-sors—is long, and it may well be that certain tales have come down from lands and mountains and temples of horror earlier than Asia and earlier than any human world we know" (*M* 29).

Similarly, several cities from the Dunsanian tales are lodged firmly (as, in fact, they were in those tales as well) in the prehistory of the earth, as when Lovecraft states that "Here sprawled a palaeogean mega-lopolis compared with which the fabled Atlantis and Lemuria, Commo-riom and Uzuldaroum, and Olathoë in the land of Lomar are recent things of today—not even of yesterday; a megalopolis ranking with such whispered pre-human blasphemies as Valusia, R'lyeh, Ib in the land of Mnar, and the Nameless City of Arabia Deserta" (*M* 47). Of this catalogue of names, Commoriom and Uzuldaroum were invented by Clark Ashton Smith and Valusia by Robert E. Howard. "Ib in the land of Mnar" comes from Lovecraft's "The Doom That Came to Sar-nath" (1919), which is now retroactively hijacked into the Lovecraft Mythos. I do not believe the term "fabled" means that the locales in question are merely embodied in fable and not in reality; the term in-stead appears to suggest their extreme antiquity—an antiquity that, nevertheless, is a mere yesterday when compared to the Old Ones' city.

Lovecraft also makes numerous references to his previous story, "The Whisperer in Darkness," not only by dropping the name of Al-bert N. Wilmarth several times in the story, but by incorporating the fungi from Yuggoth in the prehistory of the earth. They are alluded to when the narrator, looking at the bas-reliefs, notes "a new invasion from outer space—this time by half-fungous, half-crustacean creatures from a planet identifiable as the remote and recently discovered Pluto" (*M* 68). (This itself, however, conflicts with "The Whisperer in Darkness," where it is clearly stated [*DH* 254] that the fungi from Yuggoth had arrived on earth before the Cthulhu spawn.) Indeed, Lovecraft goes on to say, in reference to the Cthulhu spawn and the fungi, that "It was curious to note from the pictured battles that both the Cthulhu spawn and the Mi-Go seem to have been composed of matter more widely different from that which we know than was the substance of the Old Ones" (*M* 68). This would add further evidence to the belief that the Old Ones are not identical to the Old Ones in the *Necronomicon* quotation in "The Dunwich Horror," where it is said: "Not in the spaces we know, but *between* them, They walk serene and primal, undimensioned and to us unseen" (*DH* 170).

It is difficult to convey the thematic and aesthetic richness of *At the Mountains of Madness*. It is Lovecraft's most concentrated expression of cosmicism—both the cosmicism of space and the cosmicism of time. In spite of his fondness for "The Colour out of Space," on at least one occasion Lovecraft unequivocally declared it his "best" story (*SL* 4.24). This comment was made some months after Farnsworth Wright rejected the story for *Weird Tales*, evidently on the basis of length and indivisibility into sections for serial publication. (Lovecraft had actually envisioned its division into two parts—six chapters in each part—in which each segment would have occupied a smaller space than "The Whisperer in Darkness," which ran uncut in a single issue of *Weird Tales*.[4]) It is rather harrowing to read Lovecraft writing late in life that the novel's "hostile reception by Wright and others to whom it was shown probably did more than anything else to end my effective fictional career" (*SL* 5.224). Lovecraft also faced the nearly simultaneous rejection of a collection of his stories by G. P. Putnam's Sons and the rejection of a batch of tales sent to Harry Bates of *Strange Tales*. The summer of 1931 was not a good period for Lovecraft as a fiction writer.

The strain shows in the composition of his next story, "The Shadow over Innsmouth" (November–December 3, 1931), although certainly not in the end result, for in its own way it is a triumph of regional atmosphere just as *At the Mountains of Madness* is a triumph of cosmicism. Lovecraft reports that the various rejections had caused him to undertake a reassessment of his whole approach to fiction writing, with the result that "I am using the new idea as a basis for what might be called laboratory experimentation—writing it out in different manners, one after the other, in an effort to determine the mood and tempo best suited to the theme" (*SL* 3.435). But, in the end, "All my recent experimenting came to naught. I tore up all the tentative versions & wrote the god damn thing the way I would have written it in the first place—producing 68 pages which I shall probably never bother to type" (*SL* 3.441). Fortunately, Lovecraft did type up the text; but he himself did not submit it anywhere. August Derleth submitted it twice to *Weird Tales*, but Wright rejected it both times—again on the grounds of length and of lack of divisibility. It finally appeared in a crude and typo-ridden edition from William L. Crawford's Visionary Press (1936).

But Lovecraft's disparaging remarks about the story should not blind us to its merits. It evokes the sinister decay of a backwoods New England town (in this case Innsmouth, based largely on Newburyport, Mass.) about as vividly as any tale in the Lovecraft canon. As mentioned earlier, the name Innsmouth was resurrected from "Celephaïs" (where it was set in England) by way of several *Fungi from Yuggoth* sonnets, where the setting appears to be New England. In "The Port" (VIII) the locale is explicitly tied to Arkham:

> Ten miles from Arkham I had struck the trail
> That rides the cliff-edge over Boynton Beach,
> And hoped that just at sunset I could reach
> The crest that looks on Innsmouth in the vale. (*AT* 67)

Boynton Beach is also imaginary, but Lovecraft never cites it elsewhere. In "The Bells" (XIX) there is a passing mention of how the narrator "thought of all the chimes my visions carried; / Of quiet Innsmouth, where the white gulls tarried / Around an ancient spire that once I knew" (*AT* 72), which is not very helpful.

I am not particularly concerned with the exact location (fictional or otherwise) of Innsmouth, or of its relation to other such (real) cities as Ipswich and Rowley. It would seem that Lovecraft's vivid depiction of this decaying seaport is largely his own creation, even if the tale as a whole owes something to Algernon Blackwood's "Ancient Sorceries," where the inhabitants an entire town transmogrify into cats at night, and to Robert W. Chambers's "The Harbor-Master" (1897—the first five chapters of the episodic novel *In Search of the Unknown* [1904]) and Irvin S. Cobb's "Fishhead" (1911), both of which deal with hybrid monsters from the sea. While there is certainly something of a racist undercurrent to the story—the hideous results of mating between human beings and the fish-frogs called the Deep Ones echoes Lovecraft's fears of the mingling of different human races—this element is largely submerged and does not affect our appreciation of Lovecraft's artistry in creating an atmosphere of clutching and cumulative horror. And, of course, the masterstroke of having the protagonist, who so ardently seeks to flee the monstrous creatures, prove to be genealogically related to them effects a brilliant union of external and internal horror.

Innsmouth does have some kind of relation—topographical or otherwise—to the other towns in Lovecraft's fictional New England. Kingsport is cited a few times, first on the narrator's bus ride from Arkham to Innsmouth. At one point he makes note of "where the Manuxet joins the sea just north of the long line of cliffs that culminates in Kingsport Head and veer off toward Cape Ann" (*DH* 315–16). Kingsport Head—first cited in *At the Mountains of Madness*, where a wireless station is located (*M* 8)—is apparently some kind of bluff or headland that looks out to sea. Cape Ann is an actual site, referring to the northern portion of the peninsula on which the towns of Gloucester and Rockport are situated, northeast of Salem (Arkham) but south of Newburyport (Innsmouth). Zadok Allen's passing reference to "some Kingsport fishermen" (*DH* 336) doesn't add much to our knowledge. It is of some significance that Arkham is presented as the town of relative normalcy in regard to aberrant Innsmouth. There is even a reference to "the queer ancient house of which so many legends are told" (*DH* 316), an obvious allusion to "The Strange High House in the Mist."

In regard to the Lovecraft Mythos, the one thing that strikes the reader is the degree to which Lovecraft explicitly establishes connexions between this tale and its predecessors, specifically the (then unpublished) *At the Mountains of Madness*. It is as if Lovecraft expected his readers to read his tales in order of composition, so that each successive story could add its cumulative weight to what went before. This is most readily evident in the apparent relations between the Deep Ones and the shoggoths. "Ever hear tell of a *shoggoth?*" Zadok Allen croaks to the narrator (*DH* 340). The narrator hasn't, but later, in a dream, "I saw a *shoggoth* for the first time, and the sight set me awake in a frenzy of screaming" (*DH* 367). It becomes clear that the Deep Ones and the shoggoths are or were allied against the Old Ones of *At the Mountains of Madness,* as Zadok speaks of "sarten signs as was used onct by the lost Old Ones, whoever they was" (*DH* 331). At the end the narrator comments: "The Deep Ones could never be destroyed, even though the palaeogean magic of the forgotten Old Ones might sometimes check them" (*DH* 367). This reference to magic is a bit anomalous, conflicting as it does with the "non-supernatural cosmic art" that Lovecraft had proclaimed as his aesthetic yardstick; but once again, we are not obliged to accept the narrator's words here as "true": they are manifestly the product of what the Deep Ones (specifically his ancestor Pth'thya-l'yi) told him. The narrator continues: "For the present they would rest; but some day, if they remembered, they would rise again for the tribute Great Cthulhu craved. It would be a city greater than Innsmouth next time" (*DH* 367). The same strictures apply to this remark, and all that can legitimately be derived from it is that the Deep Ones have a relation to both the shoggoths and to Cthulhu (whom they perhaps worship) against the barrel-shaped Old Ones of *At the Mountains of Madness,* and that they are planning a more extensive incursion upon human civilisation after their setback at Innsmouth, when federal agents blew up much of the town.

The exact origin of the Deep Ones is worth investigating. Their very name (although the term Deep Ones is cited only once in the story, in the passage quoted above) and their obvious comfort in water would bespeak an earthly origin, and nothing in Zadok's account refutes this conception. Indeed, Zadok at one point observes: "Seems that human folks has got a kind o' relation to sech water-beasts—that everything alive come aeout o' the water onct, an' only needs a little change to go back again" (*DH* 331). Not only is this an anticipation of the ending (where the seemingly human narrator, now realising his blood ties to the Deep Ones, prepares to go underwater to join them), but it flatly contradicts the account in *At the Mountains of Madness,* where the Old Ones had created all earth-life—including the human race—as a jest or mistake. Possibly there is no strict contradiction: the Old Ones had themselves flourished underwater, and it is conceivable that they had created various species at random in the water, and that by the normal process of evolution some of these species (including humans) had taken to land. But this would mean that the Deep Ones themselves were created by the Old Ones—something that "The Shadow over Innsmouth" never suggests.

The hybridity of the Deep Ones—and, much more so, the offspring of their matings with humans—is again an old theme in Lovecraft, and in a sense explicitly ties the story back to its ultimate origin, "Dagon," where it was mentioned that the undersea creatures "were damnably human in general outline despite webbed hands and feet, shockingly wide and flabby lips, glassy, bulging eyes, and other features less pleasant to recall" (*D* 18)—exactly like the Innsmouth denizens. Lovecraft tips his hand to the intimate connexion between the two stories by his citation of Dagon. "Dagon and Ashtoreth—Belial an' Beëlzebub," Zadok mutters at one point (*DH* 334), and later: "All in the band of the faithful—Order o' Dagon—an' the children shud never die, but go back to the Mother Hydra an' Father Dagon what we all come from onct" (*DH* 337)—as well as frequent citations of the cult, the Esoteric Order of Dagon. But again, Dagon (whatever he may be in either story) never makes an actual appearance, and he may be merely a kind of symbol or figurehead worshipped by the cult.

In spite of his apparent dismay at the overall progression of his writing, Lovecraft managed to produce another story only a few months after writing "The Shadow over Innsmouth": "The Dreams in the Witch House" (January–February 28, 1932). It is, however, not one of his stellar performances. Steven J. Mariconda has aptly deemed it "Lovecraft's Magnificent Failure—its uneven execution is not equal to its breathtaking conceptions, which are some of the most original in imaginative literature."[5] The "conceptions" Mariconda refers to are the spectacularly cosmic attempts to envision hyperspace (the fourth dimension), in which all objects appear as a stream of cubes and other geometrical shapes flying through infinity. But the defects of the story are a lamentably hackneyed prose style, almost a parody of Lovecraft's normally evocative prose ("Everything he saw was unspeakably menacing and horrible . . . he felt a stark, hideous fright" [*M* 267]) and some curious lapses in logic and plausibility. One of the most striking would seem to be the fact that Keziah Mason, a reputed witch of the seventeenth century who has stumbled upon the secret of traversing through space and time, is frightened by the conventional appearance of a crucifix that Walter Gilman thrusts into her face. Scott Connors, however, has recently suggested to me that this incident might be explained by appealing to the fact that Keziah herself appears to subscribe to conventional views as to the powers of witches, so that her fright at a crucifix could be *psychologically* plausible. But what are we to make of this passage, dealing with one of Gilman's dreams, where he finds himself on some high, balustraded terrace:

> . . . his oversensitive ears caught something behind him, and he looked back across the level terrace. Approaching him softly though without apparent furtiveness were five figures, two of which were the sinister old woman and the fanged, furry little animal. The other three were what sent him unconscious—for they were living entities about eight feet high, shaped precisely like the spiky images on the balustrade, and propelling themselves by a spider-like wriggling of their lower set of starfish-arms. (*M* 278)

In other words, the barrel-shaped entities from *At the Mountains of Madness*. What exactly are they doing here? Even if it is assumed that Gilman is not merely dreaming but having access to some actual realm of entity (a point emphasised by his bringing back one of the "spiky images" into his world after waking up), what is the point of dragging in a reference to these creatures? Has Gilman gone to the planet where they originated—and if so, why? What relation could Keziah and Brown Jenkin have to these Old Ones? The passage seems to have no other reason than to establish a connexion between this story and its predecessor—but it serves no aesthetic purpose, because the Old Ones have no meaningful role in the tale.

The role of Azathoth and Nyarlathotep is somewhat more significant, although also plagued with ambiguities. The "Black Man" that Gilman sees in his dreams is explicitly identified with Nyarlathotep toward the end: "There was the immemorial figure of the deputy or messenger of hidden and terrible powers—the 'Black Man' of the witch-cult, and the 'Nyarlathotep' of the *Necronomicon*" (*M* 286). Curiously enough, this very wording suggests that both the names "Black Man" and "Nyarlathotep" disguise a creature who may have another name entirely. In any event, the evident purpose of Keziah and Brown Jenkin is to drag Gilman to the throne of Azathoth to make him sign his name in a book there. Exactly what purpose this would serve is never clarified, but Gilman struggles hard to prevent this outcome:

> He must meet the Black Man, and go with them all to the throne of Azathoth at the centre of ultimate Chaos. That was what she [Keziah] said. He must sign in his own blood the book of Azathoth and take a new secret name now that his independent delvings had gone so far. What kept him from going with her and Brown Jenkin and the other to the throne of Chaos where the thin flutes pipe mindlessly was the fact that he had seen the name "Azathoth" in the *Necronomicon,* and knew it stood for a primal evil too horrible for description. (*M* 272–73)

But remember that previous Lovecraft stories had established that the *Necronomicon* is very likely in error in regard to fundamental facts about the universe; could it be in error here as well? This account is manifestly what Keziah has told Gilman, and she herself, as has already been suggested, is merely a creature of the primitive superstition of seventeenth-century witchcraft; she herself has taken on another name (Nahab) when she joined the witch-cult (*M* 264). So this is very likely her own (mistaken?) view of what she is to do and what is to happen.

What in fact happens is that, in Gilman's final dream in hyperspace, he stoutly resists Keziah's attempts to sacrifice an infant, but as he is throttling her Brown Jenkin manages to kill the infant and fill up a bowl with its blood. Once again, what purpose this serves is not made clear; for all that happens is that Gilman wakes up stone deaf. He has apparently managed to kill Keziah, so perhaps this has negated or interrupted the ceremony, whatever its intent. But by this time the idea of Gilman's signing Azathoth's book has apparently been forgotten.

"The Dreams in the Witch House" is confused in its overall direction and purpose. Lovecraft has made a valiant attempt to update the witchcraft legend by tying it to advanced mathematics, but the execution is flawed and clumsy. In regard to the Lovecraft Mythos (or, perhaps one should say, the Cthulhu Mythos), Lovecraft drops some names here and there—"the fragmentary *Book of Eibon*" (*M* 263), invented by Clark Ashton Smith, and "the suppressed *Unaussprechlichen Kulten* of von Junzt" (*M* 263), the joint invention of Robert E. Howard (who created von Junzt) and August Derleth and others (who devised

the [grammatically inaccurate] German title *Unaussprechlichen Kulten*)—
but they don't amount to much and have little bearing on the story. It is
of some interest to see Lovecraft depicting Arkham as a "changeless,
legend-haunted" (*M* 262) city, precisely analogous to its real-life analogue Salem, but far different from its relatively benign appearance in
recent stories. The tale seems, on the surface, more conventionally supernatural than other tales of this period, but careful study suggests that
it does not in fact depart significantly from Lovecraft's desideratum of
"non-supernatural cosmic art."

Lovecraft actually wrote many more revisions or ghostwritten tales
than original tales during the period 1931–36, and a number of these
feature central elements of his Mythos. To such a degree do these elements figure in the revisions that we can definitely speak of a "revision
mythos" in which certain "gods," books, and other components are
cited exclusively or largely in the revisions.[6] I have already noted that
Nug and Yeb are mentioned only in the revisions, although in a whimsical genealogy of his invented gods drawn up in a letter of April 27,
1933 (*SL* 4.183), they are designated as the direct offspring of Yog-
Sothoth and Shub-Niggurath; more surprisingly, Cthulhu is the offspring of Nug and Tsathoggua the offspring of Yeb—a point never
made in any original story or revision.

The five tales ghostwritten for Hazel Heald all appear to have been
written in the years 1932 and 1933, and therefore in the period between
the completion of "The Dreams in the Witch House" (February 1932)
and Lovecraft's next original tale, "The Thing on the Doorstep" (August 21–24, 1933). There is very little evidence as to Heald's contribution to these tales—"The Man of Stone," "The Horror in the
Museum," "Winged Death," "Out of the Aeons," and "The Horror in
the Burying-Ground"—but they all appear to have a thematic similarity
in that they focus on a living human brain trapped within a dead, alien,
or immobilised body. The least interesting, from a Mythos standpoint
(or, indeed, from any other standpoint), is "The Man of Stone," evidently the first of the Heald revisions. Here we learn of a Daniel "Mad
Dan" Morris, who stumbles upon an ancestral copy of the *Book of Eibon*
and finds in it a formula to turn any living creature into a stone statue.
Quite frankly, the horning in of the *Book of Eibon* into this story is quite

artificial. Even though Mad Dan threatens at one point to "use the secrets in the *Book* and call in certain Powers" (*HM* 208) and then thinks "of calling in the emanation of Yoth" (*HM* 209), whatever that is, he later admits that the formula "really depends more on plain chemistry than on the Outer Powers" and that "What it amounts to is a kind of petrification infinitely speeded up" (*HM* 209). Morris's various expostulations—"*Iä! Shub-Niggurath!* The Goat with a Thousand Young!" (*HM* 209); "*Iä R'lyeh!* Praise the Lord Tsathoggua!" (*HM* 211)—are merely formulaic, and even more implausible in that he apparently wrote them in a diary rather than uttering them *viva voce*.

"Winged Death" is even less relevant. A scientist, Thomas Slauenwite, has discovered a rare insect in South Africa whose bite is fatal unless treated with a certain drug; the natives call the insect the "devil-fly" because after killing its victim it purportedly takes over the deceased's soul or personality. Sure enough, Slauenwite's own soul enters the body of a devil-fly at the end of the story, and he tells of his dreadful fate by dipping his insect body into a bottle of ink and writing several sentences on the ceiling of a hotel room. This ridiculous story contains a fleeting mention of megaliths in Uganda that "used to be a haunt or outpost . . . of the evil gods Tsadogwa and Clulu" (*HM* 247), but nothing is made of this, and the tale proceeds without any further incorporation of Mythos elements.

"The Horror in the Museum" constitutes a most amusing parody of what would soon become the excesses of the Cthulhu Mythos. In this tale we are concerned, not with a mere statue or bas-relief of a cosmic god, but *the actual god himself*—in this case, Rhan-Tegoth, who is mercifully cited in no other tale. The curator of a waxworks museum in London, George Rogers, claims to have captured the deity on an expedition to Alaska. Rogers has devoted a corner of his museum to such creatures as "black, formless Tsathoggua, many-tentacled Cthulhu, proboscidian Chaugnar Faugn, and other rumoured blasphemies from forbidden books like the *Necronomicon*, the *Book of Eibon*, or the *Unaussprechlichen Kulten* of von Junzt" (*HM* 216). He shows his sceptical friend Stephen Jones a photograph of Rhan-Tegoth—

> The thing in the picture squatted or was balanced on what appeared to be a clever reproduction of the monstrously carved throne in the other curious photograph. . . . There was an almost globular

torso, with six long, sinuous limbs terminating in crab-like claws. From the upper end a subsidiary globe bulged forward bubble-like; its triangle of three staring, fishy eyes, its foot-long and evidently flexible proboscis, and a distended lateral system analogous to gills, suggesting that it was a head. Most of the body was covered with what first appeared to be fur, but which on closer examination proved to be a dense growth of dark, slender tentacles or sucking filaments, each tipped with a mouth suggesting the head of an asp. On the head and below the proboscis the tentacles tended to be longer and thicker, and marked with spiral stripes—suggesting the traditional serpent-locks of Medusa. (*HM* 224–25)

There is a bit more, but this should suffice. It appears that this description is a compound or selection from the various other "gods" Lovecraft has previously invented. What is more interesting is that he has, in this and other revisions, gone back to an older conception of the Mythos in which magic, incantations, and the like play a role—something that is largely excluded from the stories of the "Phase II" period. Earlier, Rogers tells how he came upon the entity: "'It all comes from that long ritual in the eighth Pnakotic fragment. When I got it figured out I saw it could have only one meaning. There were things in the north before the land of Lomar—before mankind existed—and this was one of them" (*HM* 221). Rogers's mysterious assistant, Orabona, has helped him to capture the deity. Although Orabona "knew enough of the Elder Lore to be properly frightened" at the sight of Rhan-Tegoth, that entity was motionless because "It needed the nourishment of sacrifice" (*HM* 221). So they manage to crate it up in a big box and bring it back to London. After giving it a sacrifice (a dog), Rogers exclaims: "I am the first priest of It's [*sic*] latter-day hierarchy. Iä! Shub-Niggurath! The Goat with a Thousand Young!" (*HM* 225). But of course, in the end Rogers himself turns out to be the next sacrifice to Rhan-Tegoth, and he ends up as a wax statue in his own museum.

"The Horror in the Museum" would be a very bad story if considered as a serious attempt at cosmic weird fiction; but it becomes evident that Lovecraft, to relieve the tedium of ghostwriting, is merely playing with his Mythos elements in a spirit of fun and self-parody. When Rogers, after challenging Jones to spend a night alone in the museum, comes there himself and shouts, "Fool! Spawn of Noth-Yidik and effluvium of K'thun! Son of the dogs that howl in the maelstrom of Azathoth!" (*HM* 234), it is difficult to resist a smile.

We do learn a few small details about the Mythos entities. Yog-Sothoth, who is also depicted in the museum, is shown to be "only a congeries of iridescent globes, yet stupendous in its malign suggestiveness" (*HM* 230). I'd pay much to know this is depicted in wax. But this description seems to conflict with the idea that he is made up of ropy tentacles, like his offspring in "The Dunwich Horror." In a late letter Lovecraft conveniently notes that "he assumes a variety of shapes—solid, liquid, and gaseous—at will" (*SL* 5.303).

Another figure in the museum is "Gnoph-keh, the hairy myth-thing of the Greenland ice, that walked sometimes on two legs, sometimes on four, and sometimes on six" (*HM* 230). It is well known that the Gnophkehs were first cited as a species in "Polaris" (1918)—"the hairy, long-armed, cannibal Gnophkehs" (*D* 22)—and then in *The Dream-Quest of Unknown Kadath* (*M* 310) and "The Mound" (*HM* 141). And since, in "Polaris," the land of Lomar is clearly in the frozen North, we can assume that Gnoph-keh is a kind of embodiment of the species. He is never cited in any other story.

"Out of the Aeons" is perhaps the most significant tale from a Mythos perspective, and it is a creditable piece of work. In a sense it reprises the atmosphere of the *Dream-Quest* and other of Lovecraft's Dunsanian tales, even though it is set in the distant past of the earth rather than in dreamland. We are here concerned with an ancient mummy housed in the Cabot Museum of Archaeology in Boston, with an accompanying scroll in indecipherable characters. The mummy and scroll remind the curator, Richard H. Johnson, of a passage in "the hellish and suppressed *Black Book* or *Nameless Cults* of von Junzt" (*HM* 271) dealing with the god Ghatanothoa. Somewhere on earth there is a place called K'naa, which was "a sacred place, since from its midst the bleak basalt cliffs of Mount Yaddith-Gho soared starkly into the sky, topped by a gigantic fortress of Cyclopean stone, infinitely older than mankind and built by the alien spawn of the dark planet Yuggoth, which had colonised the earth before the birth of terrestrial life" (*HM* 272). This is manifestly an adaptation of the onyx castle at the summit of Kadath in the cold waste. Let it pass that the idea of the Yuggoth spawn colonising the earth does not fit very well with *At the Mountains*

of Madness, where the barrel-shaped Old Ones created earth-life and the
Yuggoth spawn came at quite a later date. Lovecraft continues:

> The spawn of Yuggoth had perished aeons before, but had left
> behind them one monstrous and terrible living thing which could
> never die—their hellish god or patron daemon Ghatanothoa, which
> lowered and brooded eternally though unseen in the crypts beneath
> that fortress on Yaddith-Gho. . . . For no living thing could behold
> Ghatanothoa, or even a perfect graven image of Ghatanothoa,
> however small, without suffering a change more horrible than death
> itself. Sight of the god, or its image, as all the legends of the Yuggoth-
> spawn agreed, meant paralysis and petrifaction of a singularly shocking
> sort, in which the victim was turned to stone and leather on the
> outside, while the brain within remained perpetually alive—horribly
> fixed and prisoned through the ages, and maddeningly conscious of
> the passage of interminable epochs of helpless inaction till chance and
> time might complete the decay of the petrified shell and leave it
> exposed to die. (*HM* 272)

Needless to say, the mummy is that of "T'yog, High-Priest of Shub-
Niggurath and guardian of the copper temple of the Goat with a Thousand Young" (*HM* 273), who had sought to "deliver mankind from its
brooding menace" (*HM* 274) but failed in the attempt, so that his living
brain is now imprisoned within the mummified body.

In a broad sense, T'yog's quest parallels that of Randolph Carter in
the *Dream-Quest.* Like Carter, he

> thought long on the powers of the various gods, and had had strange
> dreams and revelations touching the life of this and earlier worlds. In
> the end he felt sure that the gods friendly to man could be arrayed
> against the hostile gods, and believed that Shub-Niggurath, Nug, and
> Yeb, as well as Yig the Serpent-god, were ready to take sides with man
> against the tyranny and presumption of Ghatanothoa. (*HM* 273)

This passage is really quite remarkable. This is the first and only time
when such gods as Shub-Niggurath, Nug, Yeb, and Yig are deemed
"friendly to man." More significantly, it is perhaps the only instance in
all Lovecraft's writing that some kind of breakdown of the gods as for
or against man is provided. (The *Dream-Quest* is not a legitimate antece-
dent in this regard: Nodens and S'ngac, whatever their actual roles in
foiling the plans of Nyarlathotep, seem to be rooting specifically for

Carter and not for the human race as a whole.) This is, as we shall see, the exact premise of the Derleth Mythos, but it does not appear as if Derleth himself ever attributed the origin of this conception to "Out of the Aeons"; rather, he maintained (erroneously) that it was implicit in Lovecraft's original writing.

Ghatanathoa is never cited in any subsequent Lovecraft story, either original or ghostwritten. Probably Lovecraft felt he had said all that he cared to say about this entity in "Out of the Aeons." This story, even more than its predecessors, clearly declares the various Mythos entities to be "gods" rather than mere extraterrestrials. Curiously, Lovecraft makes no attempt at describing the physical features (or any other characteristics) of Ghatanathoa, perhaps because "no human being . . . had ever seen" (*HM* 277) the entity. He makes a fleeting connexion with "The Whisperer in Darkness" by noting that T'yog's scroll was enclosed within a "carven cylinder of *lagh* metal—the metal brought by the Elder Ones from Yuggoth, and found in no mine of earth" (*HM* 274). Similarly, Swami Chandraputra (from "Through the Gates of the Silver Key") makes an appearance (*HM* 270).

"The Horror in the Burying-Ground" is apparently the last of the Heald revisions, and it too has an undercurrent of sly satire and parody. Its very opening sentence seems a kind of mockery of that of "The Dunwich Horror" ("When the state highway to Rutland is closed, travellers are forced to take the Stillwater road past Swamp Hollow" [*HM* 289]). Here again the idea is that of a living brain encased in an immobilised body—in this case, that of Henry Thorndike, the undertaker of Stillwater, who has designed a peculiar chemical compound that, when injected into a living person, will simulate death even though the person is alive and conscious. Naturally, Thorndike is inadvertently injected with his own formula and is buried alive. All kinds of flippant references to previous (original) Lovecraft stories occur here, from a "Mrs. Akeley's cat" (*HM* 291) to Fred and Darius Peck (reminiscent of Darius Peck in "In the Vault") to Elder Atwood (recalling Professor Atwood in *At the Mountains of Madness*). There are no actual Mythos references in the story.

We may as well discuss other, later revisions of relevance to the Mythos. There are in fact only two, "The Tree on the Hill" (May 1934), revised for Duane W. Rimel, and "The Diary of Alonzo Typer" (October

1935), revised for William Lumley. In the former, one Constantine Theunis, a rather bored writer of esoteric books, looks upon some photographs of a curious tree that his friend Single has taken. He recalls that Rudolf Yergler's *Chronicle of Nath* has mentioned a landscape of this sort, and believes that this tree—or, rather, the shadow that it casts—bodes ill for mankind unless a "Gem" can be found to hurl the shadow back to the cosmic realm from which it came. Theunis manages to turn the trick.

The story is divided into three parts, and the question is how much of it did Lovecraft write. There is general agreement that Lovecraft wrote the entire third section; but did he write the second? It is in this section that the *Chronicle of Yath* is cited; indeed, a lengthy quotation from it is given. My feeling is that the second section was largely written by Rimel; but Rimel has explicitly testified that Lovecraft both invented the title *Chronicle of Yath* and wrote the actual quotation from it that appears in this section.[7] The extract contains a mention of "Ka-Nefer the High-Priest" (*HM* 405). The "high-priest Ka-Nefer" was cited in entry 183 of the commonplace book (*CB* 1.11), and it is inconceivable that this imaginary Egyptian figure could have been devised independently by Rimel. (Whether Lovecraft adapted the name from the earlier "Nephren-Ka" in "The Outsider" [*DH* 52] and *The Case of Charles Dexter Ward* [*M* 197] cannot be determined.)

"The Diary of Alonzo Typer" is one of the saddest of Lovecraft's revisions—a dreadful tale that only gains respectability when compared with the nearly illiterate draft written by its original author.[8] We are taken to upstate New York—specifically, the Buffalo area, where Lumley resided—and introduced to Alonzo Typer, an occult investigator who is exploring the house of an old Dutch family, the van der Heyls. He eventually discovers that an "ancient forgotten One" is lurking beneath the house who will show Typer "the gateway I would enter, and give me the lost signs and words I shall need" (*HM* 316). In the end Typer is dragged off by the creature, writing in his diary to the bitter end.

What is interesting is that several of the more provocative citations are Lumley's, not Lovecraft's. Lovecraft has, of course, peppered the story with Mythos elements of his own, particularly the growing library of occult books. Hence we find mentions of the "Pnakotic Manuscripts [and] the Eltdown Shards" (*HM* 311), the latter borrowed from Richard F. Searight; and again: "There was a Greek *Necronomicon*, a Norman-

French *Livre d'Eibon,* and a first edition of old Ludvig Prinn's *De Vermis Mysteriis"* (*HM* 312–13). But the mention of the "Book of Hidden Things" (*HM* 319) is adapted from Lumley's *Book of Forbidden Things.* It is not clear that Lovecraft's version is an improvement. Yian-Ho, cited frequently in the story, is an intriguing case. It is cited in Lumley's draft, and he presumably borrowed it from "Through the Gates of the Silver Key" (1932–33; *Weird Tales,* July 1934), where it is mentioned that "he alone of living men had been to Yian-Ho" (*M* 435). We have seen that Yian is a term coined by Robert W. Chambers (in *The Maker of Moons* [1896]) and cited in "The Whisperer in Darkness." Lumley's draft states: "Yian Ho! that lost and hidden city wherein lurk secrets aeons-old!" There is nothing like this in "Through the Gates of the Silver Key," and Lovecraft has attempted to keep Lumley's language when he wrote in "The Diary of Alonzo Typer": "Yian-Ho, that lost and hidden city wherein brood aeon-old secrets, and of which dim memories older than the body lurk behind the minds of all men" (*HM* 314). Another Lumley invention was the "seven lost signs of terror" (capitalised in Lovecraft's version [*HM* 317]).

It is clear that Lovecraft did not put a great deal of creative effort into these revisions. Many of the scenarios in them are formulaic adaptations of motifs he had himself used in earlier stories (some of which were unpublished), and their diction is oftentimes flamboyant, careless, and reminiscent of Lovecraft's purple prose at its worst. Lovecraft frequently admitted that working on these revisions was helpful in keeping his own fictional pen in practice; but he wrote only three original stories—"The Thing on the Doorstep," "The Shadow out of Time," and "The Haunter of the Dark"—in the last five years of his life, and a case could be made that the time and effort spent on the revisions sapped whatever energy he might have had for working on his own tales. But for one who needed income wherever he could find it, the revisory work was an unfortunate necessity.

"Through the Gates of the Silver Key" (October 1932–April 1933) is neither a revision nor an original story, but a collaboration forced upon Lovecraft by E. Hoffmann Price, who was so taken with "The Silver Key" that he himself wrote an abysmal sequel to it, "The Lord of Illusion."[8] "The Silver Key" (1926), of course, is not a Mythos story except insofar as it features Randolph Carter, who has his celebrated encounter with Nyarlathotep in *The Dream-Quest of Unknown Kadath*. But the collaboration adds some interesting sidelights. Price had taken what was essentially a philosophical tale or allegory and tried to make a cosmic adventure story out of it; Lovecraft, while bending over backwards to preserve Price's overall conception, attempted to minimise the discontinuity between the original and the sequel, with indifferent success.

In this tale, Carter goes through various "gateways," led by one 'Umr at-Tawil, and encounters the Ancient Ones. He learns that there are "archetypes" for every entity in the universe and that each person's entire ancestry is nothing more than a facet of the single archetype. Carter finds that he is himself a facet of the "SUPREME ARCHE-TYPE" (*M* 444), who appears to be Yog-Sothoth. But when Carter attempts to return to earth, he apparently fails to manipulate the "angle of his consciousness-plane" (*M* 445) properly, and ends up in the form of the alien entity Zkauba the wizard. It is in this form (under a disguise) that he appears as the Swami Chandraputra at a meeting in New Orleans to determine the settling of Carter's estate.

Lovecraft has preserved several key passages from Price's draft. Early in the text there is a substantial quotation from the *Necronomicon* (*M* 430–31) that is largely adapted from Price's text. Much more significantly, a later passage—"He [Carter] wondered at the vast conceit of those who had babbled of the *malignant* Ancient Ones, as if They could pause from their everlasting dreams to wreak a wrath upon mankind. As well, he thought, might a mammoth pause to visit frantic vengeance on an angleworm" (*M* 433–34)—is also taken almost directly from Price's draft. It is, of course, not entirely clear who the Ancient Ones are—the term is not used anywhere else in Lovecraft—but they appear very much to be in line with the Old Ones as cited in the *Necronomicon* passage in "The Dunwich Horror" ("Not in the spaces we know, but *between* them, They walk serene and primal, undimensioned and to us unseen" [*DH* 170]), but without the sense of hostility with which Alhazred endowed them. Where he had stated, "They wait patient and potent, for here shall They reign again," in "Through the Gates of the Silver Key" the Ancient Ones *already* rule the cosmos, so there is no need for them to make any incursions upon the minuscule inkblot called the earth. This is cosmicism in its true sense, and the fact that

Lovecraft retained Price's wording here suggests that he agreed with his conception. (Price, however, does not mention Yog-Sothoth in his draft, so that the identification of the Supreme Archetype with Yog-Sothoth is Lovecraft's invention.)

"The Thing on the Doorstep" (August 21–24, 1933) was written a full year and a half after his last work of original fiction, "The Dreams in the Witch House." This was one of the blackest periods in Lovecraft's career, as he continued to be plagued with self-doubt about the merits of his work and reacted with increasing depression to each new rejection from *Weird Tales* or a book publisher. In the summer of 1933 Lovecraft undertook a kind of analytical survey of weird fiction, in an attempt to ascertain the sources of the effectiveness of some of the better works of weird fiction in literary history. The result was not only some very interesting (and curious) documents—notably "Notes on Writing Weird Fiction" and "Weird Story Plots" (plot synopses of two dozen or so celebrated tales of horror)—but "The Thing on the Doorstep."

The story is, however, among Lovecraft's poorer later efforts. For one thing, its attempt to meld the age-old theme of psychic possession or transference—derived, in this case, from H. B. Drake's *The Shadowy Thing* (1928; first published in England as *The Remedy* [1925]) and Barry Pain's *An Exchange of Souls* (1911)—with the Mythos is at best indifferently successful. Secondly, the prose is again excessively florid and overdone. And third, the core plot element (the psychic transference of mind between Edward and Asenath Derby) is so obvious that it generates no suspense in the reader.

The story does have its interest for the Lovecraft Mythos, however. We learn that Asenath Waite is of the Innsmouth Waites, and as a result that town resumes its place of honour as Lovecraft's weirdest community—a distinction that Arkham was about to assume in "The Dreams in the Witch House." One wonders whether there is something about the Innsmouth denizens—presumably those who are the product of miscegenation between humans and the Deep Ones—that in some way endows them with this ability for mind-transference. Asenath herself is in reality her father Ephraim Waite, who forcibly exchanged his decaying body with that of his own daughter when he was about to die. Note that Asenath was "the child of his [Ephraim's] old age by an unknown wife who always went veiled" (*DH* 280)—an obvious allusion to a Deep One. It does not, however, appear that all Innsmouthians are capable of mind-transference: it is specifically remarked of Ephraim that he "was known to have been a prodigious magical student in his day" (*DH* 280), so presumably he picked up his powers in that manner. Edward Derby quickly suspects Asenath of being Ephraim, remarking "He found it in the *Necronomicon*" (*DH* 289). Derby does not here explain what "it" is, but clearly it must be some kind of formula that facilitates mind-transference.

Once again Lovecraft makes deliberate attempts to connect this tale with some of its predecessors. When Derby, after a particularly harrowing excursion in Maine, is brought back to Arkham, he shouts, "The pit of the shoggoths!" (*DH* 287). The expression is repeated later (*DH* 296). It does not appear as if this is just an expostulation, for Derby goes on to say, "I saw a shoggoth—it changed shape" (*DH* 287). He in fact may be alluding to shoggoths when he informs the narrator, Daniel Upton: "I'll tell you something of the forbidden horrors she led me into—something of the age-old horrors that even now are festering in out-of-the-way corners with a few monstrous priests to keep them alive" (*DH* 295). So, even if very indirectly, "The Thing on the Doorstep" reemphasises the point made in "The Shadow over Innsmouth"—that the shoggoths are allied with the Deep Ones. (It is worth keeping in mind that, at the time this story was written, neither *At the Mountains of Madness*—where the shoggoths had been invented—nor "The Shadow over Innsmouth" had been published.)

But this story, even more than "The Dreams in the Witch House," resurrects the First Phase Mythos conception of competing forms of magic, such as we saw in *The Case of Charles Dexter Ward* and "The Dunwich Horror." The otherwise curious citation of "priests" in the above quotation underscores this point. Derby goes on to say that Asenath "would have got me [i.e., his body] for good at Hallowmass— they hold a Sabbat up there beyond Chesuncook, and the sacrifice would have clinched things" (*DH* 294). We are pretty far from the "non-supernatural cosmic art" of *At the Mountains of Madness*. Upton, at any rate, does not resort to magic spells of his own, using instead the blunter but perhaps ultimately ineffective counterweight of a revolver to destroy Derby's body. Derby, however, does make note of "certain occult defences I never told you about" (*DH* 293), and it is apparently these that allowed him to take Asenath by surprise and kill her (although, of course, that did not stop her mind from eventually leaving her body and usurping Derby's).

In spite of Lovecraft's peppering the word "cosmic" throughout the story ("some damnable, utterly accursed focus of unknown and malign cosmic forces" [*DH* 290]), "The Thing on the Doorstep" is singularly uncosmic in its overall orientation. It is by no means clear what Ephraim/Asenath could have accomplished once they gained full and irrevocable possession of Derby's body. Early in the story it is stated that Asenath's "crowning rage . . . was that she was not a man," because "Given a man's brain, she declared, she could not only equal but surpass her father in mastery of unknown forces" (*DH* 281). But what forces are these? Perhaps Lovecraft is being deliberately coy in failing to specify the matter, but on the whole "The Thing on the Doorstep" is merely a kind of supernaturalised domestic tragedy. It is no accident that the portrait of Asenath has something of Lovecraft's mother and something of his ex-wife, Sonia Greene, in it.

To proceed from this tale to Lovecraft's next work of original fiction—begun more than a year later—is to enter an entirely different universe. "The Shadow out of Time" (November 1934–February 22, 1935) is one of Lovecraft's towering achievements, and now that the story as he originally wrote it has been published,[9] we can read it in all its unvarnished brilliance. This was another tale that was very difficult in its genesis, and Lovecraft wrote either two or three entire drafts—including an initial draft of only 16 pages (*SL* 5.71)—before being satisfied with it. In reality, however, he was never satisfied with it—to such a degree that he never typed the story himself, but instead circulated the handwritten draft first to August Derleth and then to R. H. Barlow, who typed the text surreptitiously when Lovecraft was visiting him in Florida in the summer of 1935. Lovecraft did not even have a hand in its sale, as Donald Wandrei submitted it without Lovecraft's knowledge or permission to F. Orlin Tremaine of *Astounding Stories*, who accepted it without, apparently, reading it; it appeared in the June 1936 issue.

Of the cosmic sweep of this story it is difficult to speak without hyperbole. It ranks with *At the Mountains of Madness* as the pinnacle of Lovecraft's achievement in this regard. Although the text begins in

Arkham (where Nathaniel Wingate Peaslee is a professor of economics) and shifts to Australia, the scope of the tale encompasses the entire cosmos and reaches hundreds of millions of years into the past—and future. We are here concerned with a group or species called the Great Race—so called because "it alone had conquered the secret of time. It had learned all things that ever were known *or ever would be known* on the earth, through the power of its keener minds to project themselves into the past and future, and through gulfs of millions of years, and study the lore of every age" (48). It can be seen from this description that the premise is adapted from "The Thing on the Doorstep"—with the important distinction that the mind-transference takes place *over time*. And unlike that story, there is no suggestion that magic or spells have anything to do with this process.

It is not entirely clear whether the Great Race should be regarded as a feature of the Lovecraft Mythos. Unlike the Old Ones of *At the Mountains of Madness,* they have not been "demythologised" from previous "gods" of Lovecraft's earlier stories. There is no question that they are nothing but extraterrestrials—although of course the cone-shaped creatures that inhabited Australia 150,000,000 years ago were merely the temporary bodies that housed the minds of the Great Race at that particular juncture. Of course, the Great Race has encounters with other entities from Lovecraft's earlier tales; but it is difficult to fuse the cosmic histories in this story with that of *At the Mountains of Madness*—notably the sequence of the various aliens' arrivals on earth (barrel-shaped Old Ones, spawn of Cthulhu, and fungi from Yuggoth). There is perhaps no actual contradiction, but that is only because in "The Shadow out of Time" Lovecraft does not provide any specific dates, or even the order in which the various aliens came to earth. There is only passing mention of the Great Race's warfare against "reptilian and octopodic invaders" (the Cthulhu spawn?) as well as against the "winged, star-headed Old Ones who centred in the Antarctic" (60–61). The fungi from Yuggoth are not mentioned, and Lovecraft creates another alien species, the Elder Things, "a horrible elder race of half-polypous, utterly alien entities which had come through space from immeasurably distant universes and had dominated the earth and three other solar planets about six hundred million years ago" (61). This would place their arrival in the pre-Cambrian era, a time when the Old Ones of *At the Mountains of Madness* had already established colonies all over the earth. This is perhaps the best evidence that Lovecraft was heedless the details of prior tales when devising a new work.

For all the science-fictional bearing of the story, Lovecraft is intent on preserving at least a shadowy element of supernatural horror; he does this particularly by citing his various books of occult lore, although it is difficult to see how they truly figure in the narrative. One of the things that the Great Race mind does during the five years he occupies Peaslee's body is to consult these books: "There is tangible proof . . . that I went minutely through such things as the Comte d'Erlette's *Cultes des Goules*, Ludvig Prinn's *De Vermis Mysteriis*, the *Unaussprechlichen Kulten* of von Junzt, the surviving fragments of the puzzling *Book of Eibon*, and the dreaded *Necronomicon* of the mad Arab Abdul Alhazred" (38). But nothing is said of what was learned from these books. A later mention of a "note appended to von Junzt's *Unaussprechlichen Kulten*" (47) is equally unhelpful. Of course, in a sense Lovecraft is paying tribute to his friends' contributions here: *Cultes des Goules* and Ludvig Prinn was invented by Robert Bloch, *De Vermis Mysteriis* was Lovecraft's Latin version of Bloch's title *Mysteries of the Worm*, and the *Book of Eibon* was invented by Clark Ashton Smith (first cited by Lovecraft in "The Dreams in the Witch House" [*M* 263]). Somewhat less irrelevant is the mention of the Eltdown Shards: ". . . when the minds of the Great Race sped across the void from that obscure trans-galactic world known in the disturbing and debatable Eltdown Shards as Yith" (61–62). The Eltdown Shards had been invented by Richard F. Searight, who had affixed a quotation from them as an epigraph to "The Sealed Casket" (the epigraph was removed when the story appeared in *Weird Tales*, March 1935). Yith is Lovecraft's invention: he had created it when he revised Duane W. Rimel's sonnet cycle "Dreams of Yith" (*Fantasy Fan*, July and September 1934). Rimel's own title was "Dreams of Yid": in his naiveté he apparently did not know that "Yid" was an opprobrious term for a Jew.

Lovecraft tips his hat to his friends in another passage: "Of earthly minds there were some from the winged, star-headed, half-vegetable race of palaeogean Antarctica; one from the reptile people of fabled Valusia; three from the furry pre-human Hyperborean worshippers of Tsathoggua; one from the wholly abominable Tcho-Tchos . . ." (56). It is odd that he would cite the Old Ones in Antarctica as "earthly" minds, since their origin is so obviously extraterrestrial; but let that pass. Otherwise, we have allusions to Robert E. Howard, Clark Ashton Smith, and August Derleth. Derleth and Mark Schorer had created the Tcho-Tcho people in "The Lair of the Star-Spawn" (*Weird Tales*, August 1932); Lovecraft had first referred to them in "The Horror in the Museum" (*HM* 221). A later reference to "Crom-Ya, a Cimmerian chieftain of B.C. 15,000" (57) is another reference to Howard, as Conan and his Cimmerians worship the god Crom.

It should be evident, however, that these allusions and in-jokes are all fleeting and inconsequential, and have no bearing on the overall thrust of the narrative. The narrative's true concerns have to do with the immense gulfs of space and time suggested by the mental and physical voyagings of the Great Race, and the sense of existential disorientation evoked by the displacement of one's own mind into the body of an alien entity. This powerful message is by no means subverted, or even affected, by the passing references to Mythos elements that Lovecraft sprinkles along the way. Indeed, those elements come to seem increasingly irrelevant, so that they no longer serve even to aid in the conveyance of the cosmic message.

It is understandable that Lovecraft would lift central elements of "The Shadow out of Time" for his segment of the round-robin story "The Challenge from Beyond" (Lovecraft wrote his segment in August 1935): his tale was still lying in manuscript at this time, and he felt no compunction in borrowing from it for a composite story that was merely a *jeu d'esprit*. In doing so, however, Lovecraft creates certain awkwardnesses. George Campbell, coming upon a cube that appears to be drawing his mind into it, recalls an account of these cubes in "those debatable and disquieting clay fragments called the Eltdown Shards" (*MW* 75). Here Lovecraft invents a 1912 translation of the shards by the Reverend Arthur Brooke Winters-Hall; in this translation is an account of a race of wormlike creatures on an alien world "whose attainments and whose control of natural forces surpassed anything within the range of terrestrial imagination" (*MW* 76). These creatures use the cubes as a vehicle for mind-transference. One such cube had landed on earth "a hundred and fifty million years ago" (*MW* 77)—exactly the time of Peaslee's "dreams" of occupying the body of a member of the Great Race. The Great Race (never so called in "The Challenge from

Beyond") quickly deduce the nature of the cube and lock it away, so that their own minds are not sucked back through it.

Robert M. Price[10] detects several inconsistencies in the depiction of the Great Race in "The Shadow out of Time" and "The Challenge from Beyond," but a number of these are more apparent than real. First, Price notes the curious designation of the Great Race as "the ruling terrestrial species" (*MW* 77), with no reference to its origin on Yith. But Lovecraft need not be implying that the Great Race's *origin* is terrestrial; rather, it is clear that the origin of the *cone-shaped beings* at that time housing the *minds* of the Great Race *is* terrestrial: "The beings of a dying elder world, wise with the ultimate secrets, had looked ahead for a new world and species wherein they might have long life; and had sent their minds en masse into that future race best adapted to house them—the cone-shaped beings *that peopled our earth* [my emphasis] a billion years ago" (51). Price also points out that, in "The Challenge from Beyond," there is reference to "the great polar city" (*MW* 77) where the Great Race has kept the cube sent by the wormlike creatures—a city never cited or alluded to in "The Shadow out of Time." But it is never suggested in that story that the city in Australia where Peaslee's mind finds itself is the only one of the cone-shaped beings' habitations. Indeed, the expression "peopled our earth" suggests a much broader scope of colonisation.

Lovecraft's final original story, "The Haunter of the Dark" (November 5–9, 1935), is his swan song to the Lovecraft Mythos—and, perhaps, his unwitting introduction to the Cthulhu Mythos. Written immediately after he heard the good news of the double sale of *At the Mountains of Madness* and "The Shadow out of Time" to *Astounding Stories*, it is a direct sequel to "The Shambler from the Stars" (*Weird Tales*, September 1935), by Robert Bloch, to whom the tale is dedicated. Lovecraft picked up on the suggestion of B. M. Reynolds, the writer of a letter to the editor of *Weird Tales*, for such a sequel, since Bloch's tale had featured a character obviously based on Lovecraft who suffers a grisly end. As is well known, Lovecraft had given Bloch his permission to kill him off in this manner, with a formal letter to that effect dated April 30, 1935,[11] and signed by, among other entities, Friedrich von Junzt (this was the second time—following a letter to Bloch of mid-June 1933[12]—that Lovecraft had supplied von Junzt's first name; Howard had never done so, nor did Lovecraft himself in any stories or revisions, although he believed he had).

As far as the Mythos is concerned, the story contains one more catalogue of occult books: "He [Robert Blake] had himself read many of them—a Latin version of the abhorred *Necronomicon,* the sinister *Liber Ivonis,* the infamous *Cultes des Goules* of Comte d'Erlette, the *Unaussprechlichen Kulten* of von Junzt, and old Ludvig Prinn's hellish *De Vermis Mysteriis*" (*DH* 100). All this begins to sound a bit formulaic. *Liber Ivonis* is of some minimal interest, as it is Lovecraft's Latinised form of *Book of Eibon* (he cites a French version, *Livre d'Eibon,* invented by Clark Ashton Smith, in "The Diary of Alonzo Typer" [*HM* 313, 317]).

The central feature of the story, of course, is the strange entity confined in the belfry of the Starry Wisdom church in Providence, whom Blake at the end of the story declares to be "an avatar of Nyarlathotep, who in antique and shadowy Khem even took the form of man" (*DH* 114). What, exactly, does this mean? The term "avatar" originated in Hindu mythology, and as such it is defined by the *Oxford English Dictionary* as "The descent of a deity to the earth in an incarnate form." Lovecraft may be using the term in a more generalised sense, meaning "Manifestation in human form; incarnation." Of course, the entity itself does not take human form, but would seem to be merely a nebulous black mass—although if we are to believe Blake's final diary entries (especially the reference to "titan blur," "black wings," and "three-lobed burning eye" [*DH* 115]), the creature does have some specific physical characteristics. Does the fact that it is (presumably) killed by lightning mean that Nyarlathotep himself has died? Lovecraft does not answer the question. But the phrasing above suggests, perhaps for the first time, that Nyarlathotep can take many shapes. And it tallies with his appearance in human form in the prose-poem "Nyarlathotep" and in *The Dream-Quest of Unknown Kadath* ("Khem" being a synonym for Egypt).

Blake declares that the Haunter of the Dark is "awaked by gazing into the Shining Trapezohedron" (*DH* 106). It was fashioned on "dark Yuggoth, before ever the Old Ones brought it to earth" (*DH* 106). This is a bit vexing, for it appears that the term "Old Ones" is here being used to denote the fungi from Yuggoth. Later "it was treasured and placed in its curious box by the crinoid things of Antarctica" (*DH* 106)—i.e., the Old Ones of *At the Mountains of Madness.* The Pharaoh

Nephren-Ka is resurrected from "The Outsider" and *The Case of Charles Dexter Ward*. And there is a routine citation of Azathoth, "Lord of All Things, encircled by his flopping horde of mindless and amorphous dancers, and lulled by the thin monotonous piping of a daemoniac flute held in nameless paws" (*DH* 110). It may be worth pausing here to discuss Azathoth. So far as I can tell, he never actually appears in any Lovecraft story. The impression develops that he is merely a symbol for the mystery of an unknown and unknowable cosmos. But then, what to make of those dancers and pipers who seem constantly in his attendance? They too are probably symbols, designed to augment the sense of Azathoth's inscrutability.

"The Haunter of the Dark" is fair to middling Lovecraft. Although elegantly written and with a powerful sense of cumulative horror, it does not seem to broach broader thematic or philosophical issues as the greatest of his tales do. The various Mythos references come off somewhat in the manner of window-dressing. It hardly matters whether the Shining Trapezohedron was designed on Yuggoth or anywhere else, so long as its function in releasing the Haunter of the Dark is emphasised. Even the figure of Nyarlathotep—avatar or otherwise—is of little consequence. The critical issue in the story is the ability of this creature to meld its mind with that of Robert Blake, so that they die simultaneously from the bolt of lightning. That bolt may function in the same manner as the earthquake in "The Call of Cthulhu"—an accident of nature that by sheer happenstance prevents a monstrous creature from terrorising the earth. In that sense, "The Haunter of the Dark" fosters the notion of human insignificance that is the dominant theme of Lovecraft's overall work, although its expression of that notion is by no means as powerful as in other tales.

It should once again be stressed that very few of the central tales of the Lovecraft Mythos are actually "about" the Mythos. The various names and terms found in the story are simply devices to foster thematic concerns of a very different sort. These concerns—the insignificance of humanity in a boundless cosmos; the fragility of our control of even the tiny realm of the earth; the psychological effects of fear upon sensitive minds; the psychic isolation produced by knowledge of the true nature of the universe; the successive rise and fall of a multitude of civilisations, each with its heyday and its inevitable decline—are the true heart of Lovecraft's greatest stories, and in many of them the Mythos plays a relatively minor role. The transition from traditional supernaturalism to "non-supernatural cosmic art" is, while unsystematic in the latter period of Lovecraft's career, nonetheless triumphantly evident in such tales as *At the Mountains of Madness* and "The Shadow out of Time"; and it is unfortunate that the more conventional—and less meritorious—of Lovecraft's tales, from "The Dunwich Horror" to "The Dreams in the Witch House" to "The Thing on the Doorstep," were the ones that most succeeding writers of the Cthulhu Mythos drew upon for their own work. Had they chosen Lovecraft's better work to imitate, the Cthulhu Mythos might not be quite the travesty of Lovecraft's vision that it is.

IV.

Contemporaries (I)

THE DUST JACKET to Frank Belknap Long's *The Rim of the Unknown* (Arkham House, 1972), written by Donald Wandrei, states that "Long has the honor of being one of the six individuals designated by Lovecraft at his death with exclusive permission to make use of his Cthulhu mythos and his idea-book for literary purposes, a privilege that Long has used only sparingly."[1] This is, of course, entirely false: Lovecraft made no such designation. In a late essay, August Derleth maintained that "Eight other writers added considerably to the Cthulhu Mythos,"[2] but he does not specify who these were. Presumably they are Long, Derleth, Clark Ashton Smith, Robert E. Howard, Donald Wandrei, Robert Bloch, and perhaps Henry Kuttner and Fritz Leiber. At any rate, Long is, chronologically, the first, so we shall begin our discussion of the proliferation of the Cthulhu (as distinct from the Lovecraft) Mythos during Lovecraft's lifetime with Long.

Frank Belknap Long (1901–1994) began writing "The Space-Eaters" (*Weird Tales*, July 1928) around September 1927. He must have told Lovecraft about it (and about the fact that Lovecraft would be featured in the story as a character), for Lovecraft wrote a whimsical response at the time:

> As for your new novelette—look here, young man, you'd better be mighty careful how you treat your aged and dignified Grandpa as hero! You mustn't make me do anything cheerful or wholesome, & remember that only the direst of damnations can befit so inveterate a daemon of the cosmick abysses. And, young man, *don't forget that I am prodigiously lean*. I am *lean*—LEAN, I tell you! **Lean!** (*SL* 2.171–72)

That last comment reflects Lovecraft's mortification, during his New York period (1924–26), at his ballooning to nearly 200 pounds under his wife Sonia's culinary attentions. During the year and a quarter (1925–26) when he was living alone, he managed to lose more than fifty pounds and get back to his ideal weight of 144 or thereabouts. I cannot find any substantive comment by Lovecraft on the story, but no doubt he was flattered to be included as a character—even as a "hero"—in the tale. I regret to say, however, that "The Space-Eaters" is a wild, histrionic, and rather ridiculous story.

The celebrated epigraph from "John Dee's *Necronomicon*"—the first concrete "addition" to Lovecraft's mythos—was omitted from the *Weird Tales* appearance. I am not sure that its initial readers missed very much. Here it is: "The cross is not a passive agent. It protects the pure of heart, and it has often appeared in the air above our sabbats, confusing and dispersing the powers of Darkness" (60). Why the Arab Abdul Alhazred (even if he was an "indifferent Moslem" [*MW* 52]) would write in this manner about the Christian cross is not evident. Long had already cited John Dee in an earlier story, "The Were-Snake" (*Weird Tales*, September 1925), a tale that also cites Abdul Alhazred. "The Space-Eaters" as a whole is an attempt at Lovecraftian cosmicism—to "suggest a horror that is utterly unearthly; that makes itself felt in terms that have no counterpart on earth" (62)—but in so doing it lapses into bathos in its idea of monsters eating their way through space. (A later story basically on the same idea, but without Mythos trappings—"The Brain-Eaters" [*Weird Tales*, July 1932]—is not much better.) Since no Mythos "gods" or entities are mentioned in the tale, it is unclear what relation—if any—the space-eaters have to Cthulhu, Yog-Sothoth, et al. Indeed, this tale is (the epigraph from the *Necronomicon* notwithstanding) not so much a Mythos tale as one rather loosely inspired by Lovecraft's general conceptions—and, of course, it is one of the first tales in which Lovecraft figures as a character.

Many of the words put into the mouth of "Howard" (in his discussions with "Frank") are taken pretty directly from Lovecraft's letters to Long, or from Lovecraft's face-to-face discussions with Long in New York. The portrait of Lovecraft in this story is not, in fact, particularly flattering, and he comes across (unintentionally) as dogmatic, bombastic, and intolerant. Long's forays into cosmicism fall quite flat, even though he attempts to reflect what he believes to be Lovecraftian cosmic indifferentism when Howard explains why the space-eaters have not in fact conquered the earth, when they could so easily do so: "Perhaps they discovered that human brains were too trivial and absurd to bother with. Perhaps we ceased to amuse them" (86).

Considerably superior is "The Hounds of Tindalos" (*Weird Tales*, March 1929), which perhaps betrays the influence of Lovecraft's "Hypnos" and "The Call of Cthulhu" in various particulars, but which nonetheless remains a breathtakingly cosmic narrative. Halpin Chalmers, repudiating Einstein and other modern astrophysicists, declares that it is possible to go back through time; and he does just that, seeing a vast panorama of history:

> "I watch the migrations from Atlantis. I watch the migrations from Lemuria. I see the elder races—a strange horde of black dwarfs overwhelming Asia, and the Neanderthalers with lowered heads and bent knees ranging obscenely across Europe. I watch the Archaeans screaming into the Greek islands, and the crude beginnings of Hellenistic culture. I am in Athens and Pericles is young." (98)

In its latter sections the tale becomes acutely chilling when Chalmers unwittingly arouses the Hounds of Tindalos ("They are hungry and athirst!" [101]) who move through the angles of space to pursue him:

> "All the evil in the universe was concentrated in their lean, hungry bodies. Or had they bodies? I saw them only for a moment; I cannot be certain. *But I heard them breathe.* Indescribably for a moment I felt their breath upon my face. They turned toward me and I fled screaming. In a single moment I fled screaming through time. I fled down quintillions of years." (102)

It may be noted that the pseudo-Akeley's remark in "The Whisperer in Darkness"—"Do you know that Einstein is wrong, and that certain objects and forces *can* move with a velocity greater than that of light? With proper aid I expect to go backward and forward in time, and actually *see* and *feel* the earth of remote past and future epochs" (*DH* 253)—is clearly derived from Long's story. It could even be conjectured that the notion of a strange-angled room in "The Dreams in the Witch House" (1932) is taken from this work.

Lovecraft cites the Hounds of Tindalos in "The Whisperer in Darkness": "I was told the essence (though not the source) of the Hounds of Tindalos" (*DH* 256). Just before this Lovecraft has written:

"The nature of the Doels was plainly revealed" (*DH* 256), another reference to "The Hounds of Tindalos." Long is as coy as Lovecraft on the "nature" of the Doels, for the only citation of them occurs in a purported excerpt from Chalmers's *The Secret Watchers:* "In my room at night I have talked with the Doels. And in dreams I have seen their maker" (108). I trust we can mercifully put to rest the conjecture that the "Dholes" supposedly mentioned in *The Dream-Quest of Unknown Kadath* are the source of the Doels; the correct reading in that novel is "bholes" (see *M* 335). It is, of course, highly probable that Long derived his Doels from Arthur Machen's Dôls (cited in "The White People"). To compound the confusion, Lovecraft once (and only once) cites an esoteric work called the "Dhol chants" (no italics) in "The Horror in the Museum" (*HM* 217).

The Horror from the Hills (*Weird Tales,* January–February and March 1931), as is well known, incorporates Lovecraft's account of his great "Roman dream" of Halloween 1927 bodily into the text (it constitutes nearly the whole of chapter 5). This dream-account—which also exists in letters to Donald Wandrei (published as "The Very Old Folk") and Bernard Austin Dwyer (published in *SL* 2.189–97)—of course has no explicit Mythos elements in it, speaking only of peculiar creatures (*miri nigri*—"the strange dark folk") who infested the hills above the town of Pompelo in the Roman province of Hispania Citerior (Spain). The *miri nigri* worship an entity referred to by the Romans as the Magnum Innominandum (the great not-to-be-named), but in the dream neither the strange dark folk nor the Magnum Innominandum are actually seen.

Long's novel somewhat artificially incorporates this dream-fragment into its narrative. *The Horror from the Hills* picks up from "The Hounds of Tindalos" in introducing us to Algernon Harris, who succeeded "the late Halpin Chalmers" (8) as curator of the Manhattan Museum of Fine Arts. The tale opens with anthropologist Clark Ulman returning from an expedition having discovered a strange entity—Chaugnar Faugn, the elephant god of Tsang. This detail—as well as a later mention of "the desert plateau of Tsang" (15)—betrays a Lovecraft influence, as Lovecraft notes in a letter that Long's original title for the work was *The Elephant God of Leng.*[3]

The novel develops into a tolerably able weird/adventure story up to the time Harris and his colleagues, Dr. Imbert and Roger Little, rather absurdly pursue Chaugnar Faugn with an "entropy machine" that will presumably send it back into the dimension from which it came. Actually, the machine does not destroy Chaugnar, but casts it back in time, and there is always the possibility that it will return. That return (like that of Cthulhu) "will be presaged in dreams" (99), but for the time being humanity is safe.

What, then, is the relevance of the "Roman dream"? Little relates the dream after hearing Harris casually mention the name Chaugnar Faugn. Is, then, Long's elephant god to be equated with the Magnum Innominandum? That term is not used in *The Horror from the Hills*, but Long appears to establish a connexion by having Little remark: "That name—Chaugnar Faugn. I was certain that something, somewhere, bore it—that the ghastliness that took Publius Libo on the high hills was an actuality, but not, I had hoped, an actuality for us. Something long past, surely, a horror of the ancient world that would never return to . . ." (60–61).

These three stories are, in large part, the extent of Long's imitations of Lovecraft (and/or the Lovecraft Mythos) during Lovecraft's day. Thereafter, Long largely took to writing science fiction in an effort to establish himself in such markets as *Astounding* and, later, *Unknown*. Long would not return to the Lovecraft idiom for decades. In the sense that his three early Lovecraftian tales—and, indeed, his early stories generally—reflect Lovecraftian cosmicism, they can be considered authentic contributions to the Lovecraft Mythos. They are by no means as richly profound and meaningful as the best of Lovecraft's, and they are in fact inferior to several other Long stories that do not utilise Lovecraftian motifs (such as "The Man with a Thousand Legs" and "Second Night Out"), but they are able ventures nonetheless.

Clark Ashton Smith's role as an "imitator" of Lovecraft and as a "contributor" to the Cthulhu Mythos is highly problematical. We have seen that Smith himself created Tsathoggua first and that Lovecraft quickly co-opted the entity in "The Mound," "The Whisperer in Darkness," and "Out of the Aeons," although in none of these stories—save perhaps the last—does Tsathoggua figure much in the overall narrative. Lovecraft was clearly intent on merely alluding to Smith's own creation as a means of suggesting the existence of an entire body of eldritch myth unknown to the general public.

The question, however, is whether Smith (1893–1961), in creating Tsathoggua, the *Book of Eibon,* and certain other elements that are now regarded as "part" of the Cthulhu Mythos, was explicitly or even implicitly "imitating" Lovecraft. Some Smith scholars—notably Donald Sidney-Fryer—have violently repudiated such a suggestion; but perhaps a more nuanced approach is needed. There seems little doubt that Lovecraft was at least one influence—and perhaps a major one—in persuading Smith to resume fiction writing in 1929. Early in his career, around 1910, Smith had written a handful of stories, but then abandoned fiction for poetry for nearly two decades. When he came into contact with Lovecraft in 1922, he was still exclusively a poet (although he had written a number of prose-poems, some included in *Ebony and Crystal: Poems in Verse and Prose* [1922]). But he was immediately taken with Lovecraft's stories, manuscripts of which he continually borrowed over the next decade or more. It was Smith who, among others, encouraged Lovecraft to submit to *Weird Tales* when it was founded in 1923. Smith did produce "The Abominations of Yondo" and "Sadastor" (a short-short story or long prose-poem) in 1925, but then wrote no fiction until "The Last Incantation" (September 23, 1929), which initiated his incredible six-year run of fiction writing, during which he wrote more than 100 stories.

"The Tale of Satampra Zeiros" was written on November 16, 1929, and is therefore one of the earliest tales of Smith's resumption of fiction-writing. The dominant influence is clearly not Lovecraft, but Lord Dunsany, whose sardonic tales of tit-for-tat vengeance in *The Book of Wonder* (1912) were clearly the model for the story. (Sidney-Fryer, however, also denies any significant influence of Dunsany on Smith.[4]) The tale is set in Hyperborea, a fictitious realm of early human history corresponding roughly to Greenland. Tsathoggua is, amusingly enough, referred to as "one of the elder gods" (155): whether Derleth picked up the term from this story is unclear. Smith goes on to say that the god "receives no longer any worship from men, but before whose ashen altars, people say, the furtive and ferocious beasts of the jungle, the ape, the giant sloth, and the long-toothed tiger, have sometimes been seen to make obeisance and have been heard to howl or whine their inarticulate prayers" (155). This comment, and others like it in Smith's tales, may have inspired Lovecraft's remark in *At the Mountains of Madness* that

"A few daring mystics . . . have suggested that the devotees of Tsathoggua were as alien to mankind as Tsathoggua himself" (*M* 29).

Smith's own account of the sculptured image of Tsathoggua in the temple in Hyperborea has remained canonical: "He was very squat and pot-bellied, his head was more like that of a monstrous toad than a deity, and his whole body was covered with an imitation of short fur, giving somehow a vague suggestion of both the bat and the sloth. His sleepy lids were half-lowered over his globular eyes; and the tip of a queer tongue issued from his fat mouth" (156). In this tale, however, the god himself does not appear—nor does he in any of Smith's stories except one. What we do find, however, is a hideous black liquid that kills one of the thieves who has come to rob the temple of Tsathoggua and seriously injures the other one:

> . . . the bowl was filled with a sort of viscous and semi-liquescent substance, quite opaque and of a sooty color. . . . This ebullition increased rapidly, the center swelled as if with the action of a powerful yeast, and we watched in utter horror while an uncouth amorphous head with dull and bulging eyes arose gradually on an ever-lengthening neck, and stared us in the face with primordial malignity. Then two arms—if one would call them arms—likewise arose inch by inch, and we saw that the thing was not, as we had thought, a creature immersed in the liquid, but that the liquid itself had put forth this hideous neck and head, and was now forming these damnable arms, that groped toward us with tentacle-like appendages in lieu of claws or hand! (157)

A very effective and innovative passage—but is it in fact so innovative? Lovecraft had created something similar in his tale "He" (1925), in which the remains of ancient Indians are presented in a very analogous manner:

> . . . the door fell in pieces to admit a colossal, shapeless influx of inky substance starred with shining, malevolent eyes. It poured thickly, like a flood of oil bursting a rotten bulkhead, overturned a chair as it spread, and finally flowed under the table and across the room to where the blackened head with the eyes still glared at me. Around that head it closed, totally swallowing it up, and in another moment it had begun to recede; bearing away its invisible burden without touching me, and flowing again out of that black doorway and down the unseen stairs, which creaked as before, though in reverse order. (*D* 275)

The remarkable thing, however, is that, even if Smith was influenced by this passage in his tale, Lovecraft in turn may have been influenced by Smith in his depiction of the proto-shoggoths in "The Mound"—the very tale he was writing when he received the manuscript of "The Tale of Satampra Zeiros."

It is in "The Door to Saturn" (*Strange Tales*, January 1932; written July 25, 1930) that the wizard Eibon is introduced. In that story he is referred to as the "infamous heretic Eibon" (54), although this is only from the perspective of Morghi, "the high priest of the goddess Yhoundeh" (54), who hopes to eliminate his rival in some fashion. In this tale Tsathoggua is cited as Zhothaqquah, for reasons that are not entirely clear: it would be understandable if such a variant existed in another civilisation in which Tsathoggua was known or worshipped, but this is a tale of Hyperborea itself, so the variant seems inexplicable. Perhaps we are to assume that the name Tsathoggua (which, let us recall, was not worshipped by the actual denizens of Hyperborea but by some unspecified earlier race of creatures) has become corrupted over time. In any case, it is stated that Zhothaqquah "had come to Earth in former aeons from the planet Cykranosh (the name by which Saturn was called in Mhu Thulan), and Cykranosh itself had been merely a way-station in his travels from remoter worlds and systems" (57). Eibon manages to escape to Saturn to elude his persecutors. Like "The Tale of Satampra Zeiros," this story is whimsical and satirical in its narrative tone, very different from Lovecraft's erudite sobriety, and its setting in a half-fantastic realm largely of Smith's imagination also contrasts with Lovecraft's painstaking topographical realism. These are, of course, not criticisms of Smith's work, but they show how different in orientation he was from Lovecraft as a fiction writer.

The *Book of Eibon* is first cited in "The Holiness of Azédarac" (*Weird Tales*, November 1933; written May 19, 1931). Lovecraft read the story in manuscript no later than August 1931,[5] well before he wrote "The Dreams in the Witch House" (February 1932), where he repeats the citation. The story is set in Smith's mediaeval French realm of Averoigne. There are passing references to "Azazel and the Old Ones" and "Iog-Sotôt and Sodagui, those demons who are more ancient than the world" (3). Of the *Book of Eibon* itself it is said that it "contains the oldest incantations, and the secret, man-forgotten lore of Iog-Sotôt and Sodagui" (4), and later it is called "that primordial manual of sorcery" (5). But all these Mythos trappings have no role in the story, which is once again a satire—this time on religious piety. Brother Ambrose seeks to bring charges against Azédarac, the bishop of Ximes, for his practice of black magic, but is instead sent back in time by a potion; going forward in time by another potion given to him by a seductive woman he has met, he finds that he has gone by his own era some seventy years, at which time Azédarac has become a saint.

The same point can be made of another Smith story, "The Nameless Offspring" (*Strange Tales*, June 1932; written November 12–December 27, 1931), which actually contains an epigraph from the *Necronomicon* that is one of the more effective passages written by someone other than Lovecraft ("Many and multiform are the dim horrors of Earth, infesting her ways from the prime" [7], etc.). The only problem is that this citation, highly cosmic in its implications, has very little to do with the story, which is an effective but on the whole quite noncosmic story of a ghoul.

The one tale where Smith might be said to have directly imitated Lovecraft is "The Return of the Sorcerer" (*Strange Tales*, September 1931; written January 4, 1931), and it is one of his poorest. Here we have a citation from the Olaus Wormius Latin translation of the *Necronomicon* (58), which sounds substantially similar to the quotation in "The Festival." The story is nothing but an elementary revenant tale in which the dismembered corpse of the wizard Helman Carnby comes back to exact vengeance on his brother and murderer, John. Not only is the tale entirely lacking in cosmicism, but it shows what a handicap Smith generally worked under when he set a tale in the real world. As he had written to Lovecraft in a letter: "I am far happier when I can create *everything* in a story, including the milieu."[6] Smith did not have enough interest in or sympathy with the real world to portray it effectively.

We now come to "Ubbo-Sathla" (*Weird Tales*, July 1933; written February 15, 1932). As this tale has been enshrined in Derleth's *Tales of the Cthulhu Mythos* (1969), one can assume that it must have some relation to the (Lovecraft or Cthulhu) Mythos. But its relations are surprisingly tangential. It is a brilliant tale of regression, in which a man of the modern world, Paul Tregardis, somehow goes back in time to inhabit a succession of increasingly remote human and animal forms until he finally unites with Ubbo-Sathla, "a mass without head or members, spawning the gray, formless efts of the prime and the grisly prototypes of terrene life" (111), as the epigraph from the *Book of Eibon* has it. The *Necronomicon* is also cited, although to little purpose: it is stated merely that Tregardis had collated the *Book of Eibon* "with the frightful *Necronomicon* of the mad Arab, Abdul Alhazred. He had found many correspondences of the blackest and most appalling significance, together with much forbidden data that was either unknown to the Arab or omitted by him . . . or by his translators" (113).

In the sense that Ubbo-Sathla appears to be only the ultimate source of life on earth (the epigraph states: "And all earthly life, it is told, shall go back at last through the great circle of time to Ubbo-Sathla" [111]), the entity could be considered somewhat less cosmic than Yog-Sothoth, Nyarlathotep, or several others. But the spectacular reach of the story into the remotest depths of earthly life makes it cosmic enough for anyone's taste. But in what sense is it Lovecraftian? Can Smith be said to have been influenced by Lovecraft at all? His own cosmicism is certainly not derived from Lovecraft, for it is evident in his earliest poetry, written a decade before he ever encountered the Providence writer. True, Ubbo-Sathla is said to be a "formless, idiotic demiurge" (115), bringing Lovecraft's standard portrait of Azathoth to mind; but Smith could have devised this formulation without reference to any Lovecraft tale.

It is in "The Seven Geases" (*Weird Tales*, October 1934; written October 1, 1933) that Tsathoggua, not to mention several other baleful deities, actually make an appearance. But this story too is a satire. For we are here concerned with Lord Ralibar Vooz, "high magistrate of Commoriom" (131), who offends the sorcerer Ezdagor and is forced to experience a succession of "geases" (dooms), the first of which is an actual encounter with Tsathoggua. But that imposing god disdains the gift and sends Ralibar packing successively to Atlach-Nacha, Haon-Dor, the serpent-people, and so on and so forth. Abhoth ("the coeval of the oldest gods" [147]) may perhaps be an analogue of Azathoth, but the parallel is nebulous.

Remarkably, Smith stated in a letter that "such a tale as 'The Coming of the White Worm' might be regarded as a direct contribution to the Mythos."[7] Elsewhere Smith declared that the story "purports to be Chapter IX of *The Book of Eibon*,'[8] although this designation is found only on the typescript (now used as the basis of a variant text published in *Strange Shadows*) and did not appear when the tale was published in *Stirring Science Stories* (April 1941). It is not entirely clear why Smith thought this a "direct contribution" to the Mythos. The story concerns the warlock Evagh, who joins a band of other warlocks in accompanying an immense white worm as it floats along an immense iceberg. At one point Evagh "knelt then and prayed to the Old Ones, who dwell secretly in subterrene caverns, or abide under the sea or in the supermundane spaces" (68). It would appear that the worm, Rlim Shaikorth, is one of the Old Ones. As Rlim devours each of the warlocks in turn, Evagh feels he has no option but to kill the creature—which he does. Once again, as with other Smith tales, the atmosphere of the story is more reminiscent of Lovecraft's Dunsanian tales, and therefore sharply in contrast with the central narratives of the Lovecraft Mythos.

A much better case could be made for "The Beast of Averoigne" (published in altered form in *Weird Tales,* May 1933) as a contribution to the Mythos. Smith himself stated that the story "contain[s] suggestions drawn from the Lovecraftian cosmos."[9] Indeed, it proves to be a sly imitation of "The Dunwich Horror." The mediaeval French province is plagued by a creature that has come from a "flaming comet from ulterior space" (58) [shades of "The Colour out of Space"]. A sorcerer named Luc le Chaudronnier, taking hold of "the ring of Eibon" (58), combats the creature. He learns that "the Beast, . . . in its own proper form, was invisible and intangible to men, and could manifest itself only in a fashion supremely abominable" (58). He takes a "certain rare powder that had been recommended by the demon in the purple gem" (59)—not to make the entity visible (for it is not, strictly speaking, invisible, like Wilbur Whateley's twin), but to destroy it. The story is clever, but the remoteness of the setting robs it of the immediacy of effect that we find in Lovecraft's tales set in the contemporary world.

What we find, therefore, is that Smith only directly imitated Lovecraft in a single story, the mediocre "Return of the Sorcerer." Such of his inventions as Tsathoggua, the *Book of Eibon,* and other items were quickly adopted by Lovecraft and others—to such a degree that Smith himself, in a letter to August Derleth in early 1933, wrote: "It would seem that I am starting a mythology."[10] Lovecraft himself was very clear on the distinctness of Smith's "mythology" from his own; as he wrote to Robert E. Howard in 1930: "Clark Ashton Smith is launching another mock mythology revolving around the black, furry toad-god *Tsathoggua* . . . I am using Tsathoggua in several tales of my own and of revision-clients" (*SL* 3.166). As late as 1944 Smith was talking of "parallelisms between the Cthulhu Mythos and my own cycles,"[11] as if they were two logically separable phenomena.

Robert E. Howard (1906–1936) came into epistolary contact with Lovecraft in the summer of 1930. One of his earliest comments concerned Lovecraft's pseudomythology: "I have noted in your stories you refer to Cthulhu, Yog Sothoth, R'lyeh, Yuggoth, etc. Adolphe de Castro, I note, mentions these gods, places, or whatever they are, only the spelling is different, as Cthulutl, Yog Sototl. Both you and he, I believe, have used the phrase *fhtagn*."[12] This remark was inspired by a letter to the letter column of *Weird Tales*, "The Eyrie," by N. J. O'Neail, who noted: "I was very much interested in tracing the apparent connection between the characters of Kathulos, in Robert E. Howard's 'Skull-Face', and that of Cthulhu, in Mr. Lovecraft's 'The Call of Cthulhu'. Can you inform me whether there is any legend or tradition surrounding that character?"[13] Lovecraft clarified to Howard that all these citations constituted "a synthetic mythology of my own" (*SL* 3.166). Howard had noted that O'Neail had "wondered if I did not use some myth regarding this Cthulhu in 'Skull Face.' The name Kathulos might suggest that, but in reality I merely manufactured the name at random, not being aware at the time of any legendary character named Cthulhu—if indeed there is."[14] Howard may not have been entirely candid here. "Skull-Face" (*Weird Tales*, October, November, and December 1929) was apparently written sometime in 1928, probably after the publication of "The Call of Cthulhu" in *Weird Tales* (February 1928). In the novella, Kathulos is an Atlantean sorcerer, hence very different from Cthulhu; but the name could still have resonated with Howard and led unconsciously to the formulation of Kathulos. Howard wrote an enthusiastic letter about "The Call of Cthulhu," published in "The Eyrie" for May 1928.[15] Lovecraft, of course, returned the compliment by citing a "L'mur-Kathulos" in "The Whisperer in Darkness."

The citation of Bran in "Whisperer" is a matter of some perplexity. It has been assumed that this is a nod to Howard, and Lovecraft implies as much when, in a letter, he refers in passing to "Howard's Bran."[16] The first published mention of Bran in Howard is in "Kings of the Night" (*Weird Tales*, November 1930), which appeared after Lovecraft had completed his story. In Howard's tale, Bran Mak Morn, king of the Picts, teams up with King Kull to defeat the Romans in a battle. Did Lovecraft read this story in manuscript, therefore accounting for his citation of Bran in "Whisperer"? Apparently not; but consider this passage in a letter by Howard to Lovecraft: "Thank you very much for the kind things you said about the 'Bran-cult.' I notice the current Weird Tales announces my 'Kings of the Night' for next month's issue. I hope you like the story. Bran is one of the 'Kings'. I intend to take your advice about writing a series of tales dealing with Bran."[17] This letter is undated, but was apparently written in September 1930, while Lovecraft was wrapping up the final draft of "Whisperer." The comment "I hope you like the story" suggests that Lovecraft had not yet read it. The previous letters by both Howard and Lovecraft are missing, so the precise context of their discussion of the "Bran-cult" is not clear. But in any case, there was some kind of discussion, and Lovecraft appears to have added the term "Bran" in the celebrated "Whisperer" passage (*DH* 223) as a nod to Howard. Steven J. Mariconda has indicated that the term was indeed added in the autograph manuscript at a later date.[18]

Turning to Howard's own tales, we find only a single story that could be considered an "imitation" of Lovecraft, but numerous tales that drop Lovecraftian terms in passing. In almost every case these terms are irrelevant to the overall progression of the story. Consider "The Children of the Night" (*Weird Tales*, April–May 1931), of which Lin Carter, in his ingenuous naiveté, has remarked: "Oddly enough, the several indexes known to me which list 'all' the Cthulhu Mythos stories omit this yarn."[19] Carter should not have been surprised. In spite of passing references to the *Necronomicon*, von Junzt's *Nameless Cults* (the first such citation by Howard), "such nameless and ghastly gods and entities as Cthulhu, Yog-Sothoth, Tsathoggua, Gol-goroth, and the like" (175), and Lovecraft's "The Call of Cthulhu" itself, the story has nothing to do with any Lovecraftian conceptions, but is instead concerned with a man who, by hereditary memory, goes back in time into the body of a remote ancestor in Pictish times.

The one explicit Cthulhu Mythos story by Howard is "The Black Stone" (*Weird Tales*, November 1931). Here Howard creates the figure of "the mad poet" (10) Justin Geoffrey, who wrote a volume entitled *The People of the Monolith*. Lovecraft was taken with this invention, citing Geoffrey in "The Thing on the Doorstep" as a friend of Edward Derby, who at the age of eighteen wrote his own poetry volume, *Azathoth and Other Horrors*. Lovecraft, however, remarks that Geoffrey "died screaming in a madhouse in 1926 after a visit to a sinister, ill-regarded village in Hungary" (*DH* 277). This generally follows Howard's story, but the date of Geoffrey's death is an invention of Lovecraft. I believe that he was alluding to the suicide of George Sterling in 1926, and that Derby at this point is a stand-in for Sterling's pupil Clark Ashton Smith, who published *The Star-Treader and Other Poems* (1912) when he was nineteen.

In "The Black Stone" Howard provides bibliographical information on *Nameless Cults*. I need not go into the absurd discussions between Lovecraft, August Derleth, E. Hoffmann Price, and others as to the proper German title of this work; it was resolved to be *Unaussprechlichen Kulten*, although this is ungrammatical German (it should either be *Unaussprechliche Kulten* or *Die Unaussprechlichen Kulten*). This title was first cited in "The Dreams in the Witch House" (*M* 263). Lovecraft also inadvertently supplied von Junzt's first name, Friedrich. Howard had never mentioned von Junzt's first name, but in a letter to Robert Bloch (c. late June 1933), who had cited the first name as Conrad in a story, Lovecraft writes: ". . . you give Howard's von Junzt the praenomen of *Conrad*, whereas at least one printed allusion (which I put in a story I ghost-wrote for a revision-client!) establishes it as *Friedrich*. Howard himself, amusingly enough, did not give von Junzt a first name so far as I know. (Am I mistaken?)"[20] Lovecraft is mistaken—in so far as he did not in fact mention von Junzt's first name in any story, original or revision.

In any case, "The Black Stone" involves Geoffrey visiting the mysterious village of Stregoicavar ("witch-town") in Hungary and having a vision of a wild rite at the "black stone"—a monolith that is "octagonal in shape, some sixteen feet in height and about a foot and a half thick" (15). Eventually Geoffrey sees that "a huge monstrous toadlike thing squatted on the top of the monolith!" (23). Who is this entity? Robert M. Price wishes us to believe that this is Gol-Goroth, who is mentioned otherwise only in "The Children of the Night" (see the citation above) and "The Gods of Bal-Sagoth" (*Weird Tales*, October 1931), although in the latter story he is described merely as "a mighty form, sinister and abhorrent."[21] There is also no reason to think that a jewel cited in "The Thing on the Roof" (*Weird Tales*, February 1932) and described as being "in the shape of a toad" (65) refers to Gol-Goroth. (This story also refers to the Black Stone and a Temple of the Toad.) Indeed, given Howard's earlier citation of Tsathoggua (in "The Children of the Night"), it might be easiest to assume that Howard is in fact referring to Smith's god in both "The Black Stone" and "The Thing on the Roof." It is worth noting that the latter story is similarly quite un-Lovecraftian in theme, being merely a hackneyed supernatural revenge tale.

The Black Stone is worth pausing over. It may be thought to be an allusion to the "black stone" (*DH* 221) cited in "The Whisperer in Darkness," but one cannot be certain of the matter. This black stone is an object that Akeley wants to send to Wilmarth, as it contains hieroglyphs found in the *Necronomicon;* but the stone is described as "a somewhat irregularly carved surface of one by two feet" (*DH* 222), hence very different from Howard's looming monolith. Of course, Lovecraft himself is probably alluding to the "black seal" cited by Arthur Machen in "Novel of the Black Seal" (a segment of *The Three Impostors*), which is described as "a piece of dull, black stone, two inches long from the handle to the stamp, and the stamping end a rough hexagon an inch and a quarter in diameter."[22] Possibly Howard did borrow the term from Lovecraft (or directly from Machen), even though his object is of a very different sort.

"Dig Me No Grave" (*Weird Tales*, February 1937) contains passing references to Yog-Sothoth, Kathulos, and Yuggoth (75), but is otherwise merely a tale of a man who sells his soul to the devil for prolonged life. "People of the Dark" (*Strange Tales*, June 1932) is a reprise of "The Children of the Night," in which a man of the present day suddenly goes back in time and turns into Conan of Cimmeria (!). Here again the Black Stone, as well as a "Cavern of the Children of the Night" (152), are cited, although to no particular purpose. Finally, "Worms of the Earth" (*Weird Tales*, November 1932) refers to Dagon (a "witch-woman of Dagon-Moor" [186], "Dagon's Barrow" [189]), the Black Stone (189), and the "black secrets of R'lyeh" (198), but is otherwise another tale of Bran Mak

Morn battling the Romans. One small detail, however, is of interest. Bran's actual encounter with the eponymous worms of the earth—evidently the "little people" who have fled underground in the wake of advancing humanity—is depicted as follows: "The worms of the earth! Thousands of vermin digging like moles far below the castle, burrowing away the foundations—gods, the land must be honeycombed with tunnels and caverns—these creatures were even less human than he had thought—what ghastly shapes of darkness had he invoked to his aid?" (203). This proves to be nothing more than an imitation of a passage in "The Lurking Fear" (which had appeared in *Weird Tales* for June 1928): "'My God! . . . Molehills . . . the damned place must be honeycombed . . . how many . . . that night at the mansion . . .'" (*D* 197).

"The Fire of Asshurbanipal" (*Weird Tales*, December 1936) is perhaps Howard's most successful attempt to fuse his own swashbuckling, action-adventure style with the Lovecraftian idiom. Set in the Middle East, the tale seems to promise a more than glancing treatment of Lovecraft's motifs when the protagonists—the American Steve Clarney and some Arab compatriots—come upon an ancient deserted city and "believed it to be the ancient, ancient City of Evil spoken of in the *Necronomicon* of the mad Arab Alhazred—the city of the dead on which an ancient curse rested" (91). The curse in question refers to a doom that would be activated if a valuable gem is removed from the hand of a skeleton clutching it. An Arab tells of an ancient magician, Xuthltan, who cried out "on the forgotten gods, Cthulhu and Koth and Yog-Sothoth" (103), and laid the curse. Steve in fact takes up the gem, whereupon, from a "hideous black well," an "Invader from Outer Gulfs and far black reaches of cosmic being" (105) emerges. Steve later tells what he saw:

> "It was gigantic and black and shadowy; it was a hulking monstrosity that walked upright like a man, but it was a toad, too, and it was winged and tentacled. I saw only its back; if I'd seen the front of it—its face—I'd have undoubtedly lost my mind. The old Arab was right; God help us, it was the monster that Xuthltan called up out of the dark blind caverns of the earth to guard the Fire of Asshurbanipal!" (107–8)

All this is quite effective, and represents Howard's most able use of Lovecraftian motifs—but they are expressed in his own idiom, with fast-paced action and plenty of fisticuffs.

The mention of the god Koth may be worth pausing over. It is inconceivable that Howard was alluding to the "Tower of Koth" (*M* 340) cited in *The Dream-Quest of Unknown Kadath* and *The Case of Charles Dexter Ward*, for Howard could not have read these unpublished works. Howard in any case cites Koth elsewhere—although it seems that in other works it is a place, as in the Conan story "The Scarlet Citadel" (*Weird Tales*, January 1933): "He was the real ruler of Koth" (380). So Howard apparently invented Koth independently of Lovecraft.

While it is evident that Howard is attempting to link his stories, after a fashion, by repeated references to von Junzt, Justin Geoffrey, the Black Stone, and the like, his sole "Cthulhu Mythos" tale remains "The Black Stone"; and this tale does not rank high in his output. Consider Howard's lurid description of the entity sitting on top of the monolith as seen by Geoffrey:

> I saw its bloated, repulsive and unstable outline against the moonlight and set in what would have been the face of a natural creature, its huge, blinking eyes which reflected all the lust, abysmal greed, obscene cruelty and monstrous evil that has stalked the sons of men since their ancestors moved blind and hairless in the tree-tops. In those grisly eyes were mirrored all the unholy things and vile secrets that sleep in the cities under the sea, and that skulk from the light of day in the blackness of primordial caverns. And so that ghastly thing that the unhallowed ritual and sadism and blood had evoked from the silence of the hills, leered and blinked down on the bestial worshippers, who groveled in abhorrent abasement before it. (23)

This attempt to mimic Lovecraft's flamboyant rhetoric merely results in empty bombast and fustian. It is an unwitting parody of Lovecraft's idiom, because it is not natural to Howard's clipped, fast-paced prose. It is one more sign that Howard was not suited to being an imitator—whether of Lovecraft or anyone else. He may have used the elements of Lovecraft's pseudomythology as "background-material" exactly as Lovecraft wished, but these elements are oftentimes quite irrelevant to the stories in question and thereby come across as forced and meaningless.

The case of Donald Wandrei (1908–1987) is highly interesting. Although he became a correspondent of Lovecraft in late 1926, visited Lovecraft twice in Providence, helped August Derleth found Arkham

House in 1939, and wrote prolifically for the science fiction and horror pulps, not a single one of his stories contains an explicit reference to a Lovecraftian entity or term.

Early in his career Wandrei had written a story called "The Chuckler" (not published until its appearance in *Fantasy Magazine,* September 1934), which he described as "partly a definite answer to 'The Statement of Randolph Carter.'"[23] Lovecraft, for his part, said of it that "I'd tend to say that it is not so much a *sequel* to 'Randolph Carter' as something *suggested* by that yarn."[24] The story of course has no Mythos elements.

"The Tree-Men of M'bwa" (*Weird Tales,* February 1932) is often assumed to be a Mythos tale, although on what grounds is by no means clear. Surely the unusual name in the title is not meant to evoke such a name as R'lyeh; it is merely a coined name indicative of the African locale of the tale. M'bwa is a dead black man who "moves at the bidding of the master in the Whirling Flux" (55). This master is of "a different universe, a different dimension . . . He has communion with entities older than earth" (55). This is all pretty vague, and a later reference to the master as "the Evil Old One" (56) is scarcely less so. The tale grippingly depicts the transformation of human beings into trees by means of a drug or potion, but cannot be considered genuinely Lovecraftian in any meaningful sense. Lovecraft himself enjoyed the story ("I must congratulate you on the novel & original cosmic thrills, & the extremely effective climax, of The Tree-Men"[25]), but he certainly betrays no inkling that the story was a homage to his own work.

"Something from Above" (*Weird Tales,* September 1930), about a meteor that lands on earth, is pretty clearly influenced by "The Colour out of Space," but cannot qualify as a Mythos story. A later story, "The Fire Vampires" (*Weird Tales,* February 1933), can be even more quickly dismissed. Although featuring a character named "Ftaggua, Lord of Ktynga" (an inhabitant of a comet that is approaching the earth), the story otherwise has no relation to the Mythos in plot or theme.

Very different is *Dead Titans, Waken!,* the novel that Wandrei wrote between September 1929 and the end of 1931. Somewhat revised, it was published as *The Web of Easter Island* (1948). The early version of the novel has now surfaced and will one day be published,[26] so my discussion will concern this version, although as far as the Mythos is concerned the later version is substantially similar, so that my citations will be from the published text. As he began the work, Wandrei described it as "a story of age-old horror."[27] His most substantive comment appears in a letter of June 1930:

> At present I am hard at work on a novel, tentatively titled "Dead Titans Waken: A Mystery of Time and Spirit". As the title probably suggests, it is a romance of terror and horror, commencing near the locale of Stonehenge and concluding on Easter Island. This is the novel which I began in New York last summer, and which I mentioned to you at the time. The novel has great possibilities, if I can successfully achieve a rather stupendous feat in handling so long a work. I have many incentives to keep me at it—the sheer pleasure of creating, my father's failing health, necessity of improving my financial condition, and the interest of some three publishers who express their willingness to consider the novel when completed. With time, energy, and a little luck, I may be able to complete it by the early part of August.[28]

None of this betrays any suggestion that Wandrei was writing a "Lovecraftian" novel, but the influence of Lovecraft nevertheless hangs heavy over it. The incomprehensible gibberish uttered by various human characters—an echo of the speech of the titans—is clearly modelled upon the R'lyehian language introduced by Lovecraft in "The Call of Cthulhu" (1926). Indeed, if one removes the first three letters of the word "septhulchu" (10), one sees an elementary anagram of "Cthulhu." The origin of a later piece of gibberish ("k'tuhl" [30]) is too obvious for comment. Wandrei's use of the documentary style—filled with letters, diaries, newspaper clippings, and the like—also reflects Lovecraft's similar usage in "The Call of Cthulhu" and "The Whisperer in Darkness." In particular, the chapter dealing with bizarre manifestations occurring all over the world, as a result of the imminent awakening of the Titans, clearly evokes an identical (but much more condensed) passage in "The Call of Cthulhu" in which the rising of Cthulhu had similar world-wide ramifications ("Here was a nocturnal suicide in London . . ." [DH 132]). The very fact that the emergence of the Titans depends on the position of the stars ("When the stars are come to the positions prophesied and fixed in the pattern prescribed, then will the titans awaken and return" [127]) is a direct nod to "The Call of Cthulhu." There is a glancing reference to the possibility that the Titans are "the originators of the human virus on earth" (134). It is conceivable that this reflects an influence of *At the Mountains of Madness*, where a similar claim is made for the Old Ones in Antarctica. Wandrei read Lovecraft's novel in manuscript no later than July 1931,[29] in time for him to insert an allusion to it in his own work.

The critical issue, as far as the specifics of the Mythos are concerned, is: Who, or what, are the Titans, and in what sense are they related to the Great Old Ones or any other entities created by Lovecraft? Wandrei is deliberately evasive on the issue, and in effect puts forth the tacit assumption that his Titans are the sole rulers of the universe and have no relation to any Lovecraftian entities because the latter do not exist in his universe. In other words, Wandrei is not working in Lovecraft's shadow or making any kind of "addition" to Lovecraft's Mythos, but is devising a conception of the universe largely of his own invention, although infused with Lovecraftian motifs of cosmic indifferentism. Even the physical nature of the Titans remains in doubt. While on Easter Island, Graham sees them in a dream:

> His dream-self half-glimpsed the titans, of a different, more complex, and heightened order of existence, incomprehensible in either the completeness or the detail of their wholly alien, wholly inconceivable aspect, for by no human terms could they be analyzed, they who were outside the range of human senses, outside of time and space. And Graham's dream-self, dwarfed by these other-dimensional titans, trembled; trembled at the hue of living light that never was on sea or land; trembled at the flux of forces and energies and powers that pursued objectives of their own, independent of the titans; trembled at the shifting interchange of pure intelligence and wilful light and active operations of hyper-space and hyper-time; trembled at the soaring citadels of an architecture that adjusted itself automatically to the separate requirements of each inhabitant and each power, so that it simultaneously presented many shapes and occupied many facets of hyper-space and hyper-time; trembled most of all at the purposes beyond this outside universe, the ultimate goal of the titans which had created the dimensions on which their existence depended and would endure when the foundations and the strange spaces themselves had been consumed. (144–45)

Wandrei is here attempting to express the nearly inexpressible; and even if he is not entirely successful, his very attempt to envision utterly non-human and unearthly entities and forces is very much in line with the Lovecraft of "The Colour out of Space" and *At the Mountains of Madness*.

Dead Titans, Waken! is a meritorious work—crude in spots, but on the whole a compelling and spectacularly cosmic narrative, especially in its later portions, when the protagonist, Carter Graham, is sent millions of years into the future to continue his combating of the Titans' return. It has a fundamental seriousness of tone and purpose lacking in Long's *The Horror from the Hills*. It could stand, in fact, as the first genuine novel of the Lovecraft (as opposed to the Cthulhu) Mythos by someone other than Lovecraft. And Wandrei has achieved the feat without a single explicit reference to any Lovecraftian entity or place-name.

It should not be assumed, of course, that the cosmicism in the novel is a direct product of Wandrei's reading of Lovecraft. His early writing, both in prose and in poetry, shows that he himself was endowed with the cosmic spirit well before he encountered Lovecraft's work; it was, indeed, their congruence on this subject that led to the particularly close relationship between Wandrei, Smith, and Lovecraft. Lovecraft himself concluded as much, writing to Smith about "the cosmic quality": "You have it yourself to a supreme degree, & so have Wandrei & Bernard Dwyer" (*SL* 3.196). It was no doubt their harmony on this point that led Wandrei to be so impressed with "The Call of Cthulhu," *At the Mountains of Madness*, and other of Lovecraft's more "cosmic" works.

V.

Contemporaries (II)

I N THE COURSE OF THE 1930S, Lovecraft began to attract a cadre of associates and disciples somewhat younger than such colleagues as Long, Howard, Smith, Derleth, and Wandrei, although all these were also younger than he. In several instances Lovecraft went to considerable effort to tutor these youngsters (nearly all of them were teenagers when they first came into epistolary contact with Lovecraft) in the art of writing, and they were in turn significantly more influenced by his work, and more interested in "adding" to his pseudomythology, than the writers discussed in the previous chapter.

Robert Bloch (1917–1994) has never made any secret of his literary and personal debt to H. P. Lovecraft. Bloch corresponded with Lovecraft for the last four years of the latter's life and received invaluable assistance and advice from the elder writer in the craft of weird fiction. Only now, however, are we able to probe the details of this literary tutelage, with the nearly simultaneous publication of Lovecraft's *Letters to Robert Bloch* (1993) and an augmented edition of Bloch's collection of Lovecraftian pastiches, *Mysteries of the Worm* (1993). These documents make two things very evident: first, that Bloch—who first wrote to Lovecraft when he was sixteen, had his first story professionally published when he was seventeen, and died at the age of seventy-seven a revered figure in the field, just as Lovecraft had been—quickly evolved into a skilful writer in the Lovecraftian tradition; and second, that this apprentice work is both intrinsically valuable and of consuming interest for its foreshadowing of Bloch's later and more distinguished work in the realm of psychological suspense.

Bloch first came in touch with Lovecraft in April 1933, and his first object was to read as much of Lovecraft's work as he had not previously found in magazines. To this end he asked his correspondent to lend him many tales; Lovecraft did so, supplying a list of all the tales he had written up to that time, several of which were still unpublished. In his very first letter to Bloch, however, Lovecraft himself asked his young correspondent whether he had written any weird work (*LB* 7) and, if so, whether he might see samples of it. Bloch took up Lovecraft's offer in late April, sending him two short items, "The Gallows" and another work whose title is unknown.

Lovecraft's response to these pieces of juvenilia (which, along with a good many others Bloch sent to the Providence writer, do not survive) is typical: while praising them, he also gave helpful advice derived from his many years as both a critic and a practitioner of the weird tale:

> It was with the keenest interest & pleasure that I read your two brief horror-sketches; whose rhythm & atmospheric colouring convey a very genuine air of unholy immanence & nameless menace, & which strike me as promising in the very highest degree. I think you have managed to create a dark tension & apprehension of a sort all too seldom encountered in weird fiction, & believe that your gift for this atmosphere-weaving will serve you in good stead when you attempt longer & more intricately plotted pieces. . . . Of course, these productions are not free from the earmarks of youth. A critic might complain that the colouring is laid on too thickly—too much overt inculcation of horror as opposed to the *subtle, gradual suggestion of concealed horror* which actually raises fear to its highest pitch. In later work you will probably be less disposed to pile on great numbers of horrific words (an early & scarcely-conquered habit of my own), but will seek rather to select a *few* words—whose precise position in the text, & whose deep associative power, will make them in effect more terrible than any barrage of monstrous adjectives, malign nouns, & unhallowed verbs. (*LB* 10)

This is a litany that Lovecraft would repeat for at least another year; and although it took Bloch a little while to realise the wisdom of this caveat, he finally did so. Indeed, by the 1940s Bloch had already evolved the tight-lipped, blandly cynical style that would serve him well in his later crime fiction—fiction that, in its relentless emphasis on the psychology of aberrant individuals, is in many ways more potently horrifying than the adjective-choked supernaturalism of his early work.

And yet, Bloch was clearly fond of this thickly laid-on horror at this stage in his career, as indeed Lovecraft was at a corresponding age and

for some years after. One gauge of this tendency was Bloch's relative
fondness for the tales of Lovecraft's he was reading at this time. It is
understandable that he would express enthusiasm for "The Outsider,"
"The Hound," and "The Lurking Fear," but remain relatively cool toward *At the Mountains of Madness* and "The Shadow over Innsmouth"
(*LB* 20), where Lovecraft was attempting to rein in his adjectives and
write with more scientific precision and restrained suggestiveness. Although many of Bloch's own early tales do not survive, "The Laughter
of a Ghoul"—read by Lovecraft in June 1933 (*LB* 20) and published in
the *Fantasy Fan* for December 1934—seems representative of them:
"Slithering secrets dwelt within the archaic avenues of the vast and
sombre forest near my manor in the hills—secrets black and hideous,
haunting and unspeakable, such as demonian presences mumble nightly
in the aeon-dead abysses beyond the light of stars." What Lovecraft
probably liked about work of this kind—even though he also recognised that an overuse of fevered prose resulted in unintended humour—was precisely its "atmosphere-weaving," a quality he (correctly)
believed sadly lacking in most of the weird fiction published in the
pulps. He continually excoriated the brisk, "cheerful" style of the aver-
age pulp product, in which spectacular defiances of natural law were
regarded both by the characters and by the author with a bland casual-
ness that is fatal to convincingness. Overcoloured as Bloch's early tales
may have been, they at least were attempting to achieve an *emotional
preparation* for the supernatural.

Lovecraft read something entitled "The Feast" in late June 1933, remarking that it "forms a very clever union of the macabre & the comic"
(*LB* 21). It is not clear whether this is an early version of "The Feast in
the Abbey," but Lovecraft in any case read that story in September; indeed, he supplied the title, since Bloch had evidently sent it to Lovecraft
without one (*LB* 35). This is, of course, Bloch's first published story in
Weird Tales (it appeared in the January 1935 issue), although "The Secret
in the Tomb" (*Weird Tales*, May 1935) had been accepted earlier, in July
1934 (*LB* 50). Lovecraft read the latter tale as well, although apparently
not before its acceptance. He did, however, recommend some minor
corrections (*LB* 52), which Bloch seems to have made.

Both these stories evince a fascination with the mythical books of
the "Cthulhu Mythos" that would remain constant throughout Bloch's

early work. It was in these tales that Bloch devised Ludvig Prinn's *Mysteries of the Worm*, and Lovecraft mentions other titles that were cited in an earlier draft of "The Secret in the Tomb" but later excised (Mazonides' *Black Spell of Saboth*, Petrus Averonius' *Compendium Daemonum*). In "The Suicide in the Study" (*Weird Tales*, June 1935) we find other such titles as "the Black Rites of mad Luveh-Keraph, priest of Bast, or Comte d'Erlette's ghastly *Cultes des Goules*" (19). Luveh-Keraph scarcely requires elucidation, save to note that this coinage appears to be Bloch's invention, not Lovecraft's. Some have thought that Bloch merely abstracted this from one of Lovecraft's letters, which frequently include whimsical signatures of this sort; but in fact Lovecraft uses the "Luveh-Keraph" signature for the first time only in April 1935 (*LB* 65), a month after having read "The Suicide in the Study" (*LB* 61). In other words, he picked up the usage from Bloch's story, as a sort of wry acknowledgement.

There is not much to say about these early tales, save that they may be marginally better than most of the other material appearing in *Weird Tales*. If nothing else, the verve of their adjective-laden prose and lurid incidents is engaging. "The Secret in the Tomb" is a preposterous story about a man who battles a skeleton in his ancestral tomb. "The Feast in the Abbey" (not included in *Mysteries of the Worm*) tells of cannibalism in a mediaeval monastery. "The Suicide in the Study" is perhaps the most interesting of the lot: a reprise of the Jekyll/Hyde theme, it tells of a man who believes that the good and evil sides of every individual are *"co-existent"* (20) and seeks to bring up his evil side from the depths of his personality. The story is hampered by a conventional conception of what constitutes good and evil; but the evil side, when it finally emerges, presents a loathsome sight:

> Out of the darkness nightmare came; stark, staring nightmare—a monstrous, hairy figure; huge, grotesque, simian—a hideous travesty of all things human. It was black madness; slavering, mocking madness with little red eyes of wisdom old and evil; leering snout and yellow fangs of grimacing death. It was like a rotting, living skull upon the body of a black ape. It was grisly and wicked, troglodytic and wise. (22)

Here evil is pictured as simultaneously subhuman (the Darwinian beast) and somehow superhuman—"wise" and incapable of being controlled by our "good" side.

The early story of Bloch's that has brought him the greatest celebrity for its connexions with Lovecraft is "The Shambler from the Stars"
(*Weird Tales*, September 1935). Lovecraft mentions something called
"The Shambler in the Night" in a letter of November 1934 (*LB* 55);
this may be an early version of the story, although if so it is odd that
Lovecraft makes no mention in his letter of its central feature—the fact
that Lovecraft himself is a character in the story. We all know the story
of how "The Shambler from the Stars" was provisionally accepted by
Farnsworth Wright of *Weird Tales*, who felt that Bloch needed to get
Lovecraft's permission to kill him off (although Wright had evidently
not felt a similar need when, years before, Frank Belknap Long had
done the same to Lovecraft in "The Space-Eaters"), so that Lovecraft
wrote his whimsical letter to Bloch in late April 1935 authorising him
"to portray, murder, annihilate, disintegrate, transfigure, metamor-
phose, or otherwise manhandle the undersigned in the tale entitled
THE SHAMBLER FROM THE STARS" (*LB* 67).

The critical issue about the story is not that it is a "contribution" to
the "Cthulhu Mythos" but that, like Long's tale, it makes Lovecraft a
character and, accordingly, assists in the fostering of the Lovecraft legend—the legend of the gaunt, reclusive delver into occult mysteries. Of
course, he is never named, merely identified as a "mystic in New England" who was "a writer of notable brilliance and wide reputation
among the discriminating few" (26–27). But even more interesting,
perhaps, is how *Bloch himself* has become a character in his own story. In
its early parts Bloch presents a sort of objective assessment of his own
career as a writer up to that point, finding much dissatisfaction in it:

> I wanted to write a real story, not the stereotyped, ephemeral sort of
> tale I turned out for the magazines, but a real work of art. The creation
> of such a masterpiece became my ideal. I was not a good writer, but
> that was not entirely due to my errors in mechanical style. It was, I felt,
> the fault of my subject matter. Vampires, werewolves, ghouls, mytho-
> logical monsters—these things constituted material of little merit.
> Commonplace imagery, ordinary adjectival treatment, and a prosaically
> anthropocentric point of view were the chief detriments to the pro-
> duction of a really good weird tale. (26)

This paragraph could have come directly out of Lovecraft's writings on
the subject, such as "Notes on Writing Weird Fiction" (1933). That last

comment about point of view seems to derive from a letter by Lovecraft to Bloch in June 1933, in which he remarks how he had once (in
the "Eyrie" for March 1924) advised "having a story told from an un-
conventional & non-human angle," specifically a story "from the
ghoul's or werewolf's point of view" (*LB* 21); he goes on to remark that
H. Warner Munn had attempted to embody this conception in "The
Werewolf of Ponkert," but had botched the job because Munn's "sympathies were still with mankind—whereas I called for sympathies
wholly dissociated from mankind & perhaps violently hostile to it" (*LB*
21). This notion is not in fact present in "The Shambler from the
Stars," but does find its way into "The Dark Demon."

Lovecraft's avowed sequel to Bloch's story—"The Haunter of the
Dark," written in November 1935 and published in *Weird Tales* for December 1936—continues the fusion of the real and the imaginary in its
portrayal of character. Here the protagonist, Robert Blake, is said to
come (like Bloch) from Milwaukee (the address given in the story—620
East Knapp Street—was in fact Bloch's address), but the apartment he
occupies on a visit to Providence is transparently Lovecraft's own dwelling at 66 College Street. Then again, the titles of the stories Blake is said
to have written at this time—"The Burrower Beneath," "The Stairs in
the Crypt," "Shaggai," "In the Vale of Pnath," and "The Feaster from
the Stars" (*DH* 94)—form an exquisite union of elements found in both
Bloch's and Lovecraft's stories. In early March 1935 Lovecraft had wryly
remarked on Bloch's success in landing tales with titles like "The —— in
the ——";[1] he echoes them in the above list, although his own tales very
frequently have titles of this sort as well. At the end of "The Haunter of
the Dark" Robert Blake is left a glassy-eyed corpse staring through a window—a somewhat more tasteful demise than that of the victim of "The
Shambler from the Stars," who ends up torn to pieces by a nameless entity.

For "The Shambler from the Stars" Lovecraft devised the Latin title of *Mysteries of the Worm*—*De Vermis Mysteriis*—and claimed to have
modified the narrator's statement of his ignorance of Latin, "since
knowledge of elementary Latin is so universal" (*LB* 65). And yet, the
narrator's lack of knowledge of Latin is critical to the development of
the plot, since it is precisely because he finds a Latin copy of *De Vermis
Mysteriis*, which he is unable to read, that he feels the need to seek out
his New England correspondent and show him the work. (Bloch's defi-

ciencies in Latin make themselves all too evident in another title he devised, the nonsensical *Daemonolorum,* cited in "The Brood of Bubastis" [95] and elsewhere.)

"The Dark Demon" (*Weird Tales,* November 1936) is interesting in this context because it again displays Lovecraft as a character and, more important, becomes a parable for his early assistance to Bloch's literary development. Here the narrator testifies that he had come into contact with the writer Edgar Gordon, a "reclusive dreamer" (62) living in the same town. They develop a warm correspondence and also meet in person: "What Edgar Gordon did for me in the next three years can never adequately be told. His able assistance, friendly criticism and kind encouragement finally succeeded in making a writer of sorts out of me, and after that our mutual interest formed an added bond between us" (62). Lovecraft does not seem to have read this tale prior to publication (see *LB* 84), but he warmly commends it; he makes no mention of the above tribute, but no doubt he saw clearly its import and was heartened by it. Although Lovecraft himself is mentioned by name elsewhere in the story (62), Gordon becomes a transparent Lovecraft figure in his bizarre dreams and the very strange work he begins writing as a result of them: the "stories [were] in first-person, but the narrator was not a *human being*" (64). Gordon, when pressed by the narrator as to where he is getting his ideas, makes cloudy references to a "Dark One," remarking: "He isn't a destroyer—merely a superior intelligence who wishes to gain mental rapport with human minds, so as to enable certain—ah— exchanges between humanity and Those beyond" (66). This idea is unquestionably derived from Lovecraft's "The Whisperer in Darkness," in which aliens from the depths of space wish to take the brains of selected human beings on fantastic cosmic voyagings.

The mention of dreams is interesting, since in August 1933 Lovecraft, commenting with amazement on Bloch's claim that he dreamed only twice a year, related a hideous dream in which some mediaeval soldiers attempt to hunt down a monstrous entity but to their horror see it meld insidiously with the body of their leader. Bloch claimed to be working on a story based upon this dream (see *LB* 33), but apparently never completed it; it does not survive. He does, however, in "The Dark Demon" echo Lovecraft's scorn of conventional Freudian interpretations of dreams. Bloch's narrator remarks, "Gordon's fantasies were far from the ordinary Freudian sublimation or repression types" (63); Lovecraft in his letter had written: "I may add that all I know of dreams seems to contradict flatly the 'symbolism' theories of Freud. It may be that others, with less sheer phantasy filling their minds, have dreams of the Freudian sort; but it is very certain that I don't" (*LB* 31).

It is with "The Faceless God" (*Weird Tales*, May 1936) that Bloch begins his twofold fascination with Egypt and with the Lovecraftian "god" Nyarlathotep. One of Bloch's earliest enquiries to Lovecraft was an explanation of some of the invented names and terms that appear in his tales. In regard to one such query Lovecraft responds in May 1933: "'Nyarlathotep' is a horrible messenger of the evil gods to earth, who usually appears in human form" (*LB* 11–12). Bloch, who in his early days was attempting pictorial art, actually drew a picture of Nyarlathotep, which Lovecraft charitably says "just fits my conception" (*LB* 21).

It would be of interest to know which of Lovecraft's stories mentioning Nyarlathotep Bloch did in fact read. I see no evidence that he had at this time read the early prose-poem "Nyarlathotep" (1920), which had appeared only in amateur magazines; it is here that the connexion between Nyarlathotep and Egypt is explicitly made, and it is this connexion that Bloch develops. The prose-poem is in fact listed in the list of stories Lovecraft sent to Bloch in April 1933, but it is crossed off; and the subsequent letters do not suggest that Lovecraft ever lent it to Bloch. If Lovecraft had in fact sent the item, one imagines that he would not have had to "define" Nyarlathotep as he did in the letter in May. Nyarlathotep is glancingly mentioned in "The Rats in the Walls" (1923), extensively cited in *The Dream-Quest of Unknown Kadath* (1926–27) (which Bloch did not read), and glancingly cited in "The Whisperer in Darkness" (1930) and "The Dreams in the Witch House" (1932).

In fact, Bloch probably derived most of his information on Nyarlathotep from "The Haunter of the Dark," the story Lovecraft wrote in November 1935 and dedicated to Bloch. Toward the end of the tale the character Robert Blake writes in his diary: "What am I afraid of? Is it not an avatar of Nyarlathotep, who in antique and shadowy Khem even took the form of man?" (*DH* 114). Here is the Egyptian connexion that Bloch picked up on. "The Faceless God" tells the story of the attempts of an evil Dr Stugatche[2] to unearth a statue of Nyarlathotep buried in the sands of Egypt, only to meet a fittingly horrible end. I am not clear why Bloch conceived of Nyarlathotep as faceless—a detail that perhaps inadvertently recalls Lovecraft's night-gaunts.

Bloch notes that his Egyptological ("or Egyptillogical") tales were "conscious attempts to move away from Lovecraft's literary turf" (255). How successful Bloch was, in this early period, in these attempts is debatable. He perhaps had not read—or did not know of Lovecraft's hand in—"Under the Pyramids" (the story published in *Weird Tales* as "Imprisoned with the Pharaohs" and attributed to Harry Houdini), and of course Nyarlathotep's Egyptian connexion had indeed been established by Lovecraft. Such a story as "The Opener of the Way" (*Weird Tales*, October 1936), while still perhaps somewhat Lovecraftian in style, does not employ Lovecraft's pantheon of invented deities but seeks to invest horror in the real gods of Egypt (in this case Anubis). "The Brood of Bubastis" (*Weird Tales*, March 1937) is very similar: aside from insignificant references to *De Vermis Mysteriis*, this tale is nothing but a story of the cat-goddess Bubastis and involves the ingenious idea of an ancient Egyptian colony in England. Lovecraft read the story about two months before his death, noting: "Your Bubastis story is excellent, despite the dubious light in which it presents my beloved felidae" (*LB* 87).

"The Secret of Sebek" (*Weird Tales*, November 1937)—a story probably written just after Lovecraft's death—is an interesting case. The story is set in New Orleans and concerns the god Sebek, who has the head of a crocodile and the body of a man. A character sees such a figure in a costume ball and, thinking the man in disguise, attempts to pull off his crocodile mask—only to find that "I felt beneath my fingers, not a mask, but living flesh!" (129). The dominant influence on this story appears to be "Through the Gates of the Silver Key," which is likewise set in New Orleans and likewise concludes apocalyptically with a character who pulls off an actual mask from another character (Randolph Carter in the body of the extraterrestrial wizard Zkauba), finding a horribly alien countenance underneath. Again, only some random mentions of invented books make this a "Cthulhu Mythos" story.

"Fane of the Black Pharaoh" (*Weird Tales*, December 1937) is perhaps the most interesting of Bloch's Egyptian tales, both for its intrinsic effectiveness and for its connexions with Lovecraft. This is an entire story about the pharaoh Nephren-Ka. The name had been invented by Lovecraft and is first cited in the early story "The Outsider" (one of

Bloch's favourites): "Now I . . . play by day amongst the catacombs of Nephren-Ka in the sealed and unknown valley of Hadoth by the Nile" (*DH* 52). Lovecraft resurrects him in a single tantalising sentence in "The Haunter of the Dark": "The Pharaoh Nephren-Ka built around it [the Shining Trapezohedron] a temple with a windowless crypt, and did that which caused his name to be stricken from all monuments and records" (*DH* 106). Bloch elaborates upon this sentence, although departing somewhat from it. In "Fane of the Black Pharaoh" Nephren-Ka is rumoured to have been a worshipper of Nyarlathotep, and his "atrocious sacrifices" (134) caused him to be deposed. Then, hiding in a secret temple, Nephren-Ka is granted the gift of prophecy by Nyarlathotep and paints an enormous series of pictures of the years and centuries to come. A modern explorer learns just how much truth there is in this old fable.

"The Shadow from the Steeple" (*Weird Tales,* September 1950) simultaneously concludes the trilogy begun with "The Shambler from the Stars" and "The Haunter of the Dark" and is Bloch's final word about Nyarlathotep. As early as December 1936 Lovecraft wrote, ". . . I hope to see 'The Shadow in the Steeple' when you get it written" (*LB* 84); this is an early version of the story, as Bloch notes,[3] but for some reason he put it aside for many years before resuming it. The story as we have it was either written or revised around 1950, for it makes mention of Edmund Fiske's "fifteen-year quest" (183) to discover the truth about the death of Robert Blake.

As in "The Dark Demon," both Bloch and Lovecraft become characters in the story—the latter explicitly and by name. The narrator notes: "Blake had been a precocious adolescent interested in fantasy-writing, and as such became a member of the 'Lovecraft circle'—a group of writers maintaining correspondence with one another and with the late Howard Phillips Lovecraft, of Providence" (180). Later it is said that "another Milwaukee author" (181) had written a story about Nephren-Ka entitled "Fane of the Black Pharaoh"! With somewhat questionable taste, Bloch even incorporates Lovecraft's death into the fabric of the plot, noting that Fiske had intended in early 1937 to visit Lovecraft and query him about Blake's death, but that Lovecraft's own passing foiled these plans. Bloch has written on many occasions of the shock he felt at hearing of Lovecraft's death, and the narrator of "The Shadow from the Steeple" remarks that Lovecraft's "unexpected passing plunged Fiske into a period of mental despondency from which he was slow to recover" (185); but I still wonder whether it was proper for Bloch to make fictional use of both Lovecraft's life and his demise in this fashion. In any event, it transpires that Dr Dexter—the "superstitious" (*DH* 114) physician who had hurled the Shining Trapezohedron into the river after Blake's death—is Nyarlathotep himself, a clever twist on Lovecraft's premise. The story also effectively incorporates features from the sonnet "Nyarlathotep" from Lovecraft's *Fungi from Yuggoth*, which says that ". . . at last from inner Egypt came / The strange dark one to whom the fellahs bowed" and that "wild beasts followed him and licked his hands" (*AT* 72).

Bloch's Egyptian tales may have been an attempt to escape partially from Lovecraft's influence, but we have seen that they were only indifferently successful in that objective, although many of them are quite successful as stories. Bloch was so steeped in Lovecraft's work at this time that many borrowings may well have been unconscious. Hence something so slight as one character's observation in "The Grinning Ghoul" (*Weird Tales*, June 1936) that there is no dust on the stairs of a crypt (57) may be an echo of the similarly dust-free corridors of the ancient city in *At the Mountains of Madness*, swept clean by the passing of a shoggoth. "The Creeper in the Crypt" (*Weird Tales*, July 1937) is set in Arkham and makes clear allusions to Lovecraft's "The Dreams in the Witch House"; but it may also betray the influence of "The Shadow over Innsmouth" (the narrator, after his experiences, seeks aid from the federal government to suppress the horror), and also perhaps of "The Terrible Old Man," as the tale involves a Polish and an Italian criminal who kidnap a man only to undergo a loathsome fate in the cellar of an old house, just as in Lovecraft's story a Pole, a Portuguese, and an Italian seek to rob the Terrible Old Man but meet death at his hands instead.

"The Sorcerer's Jewel" (*Strange Stories*, February 1939) is clearly a variation on "The Haunter of the Dark" and its Shining Trapezohedron. A character refers to a "Star of Sechmet":

> "Very ancient, but not costly. Stolen from the crown of the Lioness-headed Goddess during a Roman invasion of Egypt. It was carried to Rome and placed in the vestal girdle of the High-Priestess of Diana. The barbarians took it, cut the jewel into a round stone. The black centuries swallowed it." (155)

This is precisely analogous to the "history" of the Trapezohedron, from remote antiquity to the present, provided by Lovecraft in "The Haunter of the Dark"—and it is in this passage that Lovecraft mentions Nephren-Ka. And, just as Blake, when looking into the Shining Trapezohedron, "saw processions of robed, hooded figures whose outlines were not human, and looked on endless leagues of desert lined with carved, sky-reaching monoliths" (*DH* 104), so a similar experience befalls a character in "The Sorcerer's Jewel": "A swirling as of parted mists. A dancing light. The fog was dispersing, and it seemed to be opening up—opening to a view that receded far into the distance. . . . At first only angles and angles, weaving and shifting in light that was of no color, yet phosphorescent. And out of the angles, a flat black plain that stretched upward, endlessly without horizon" (156–57).

But Bloch's early Lovecraftian tales may be of the greatest interest, at least as far as Bloch's own subsequent career is concerned, for the hints they provide of how he metamorphosed his writing from the florid supernaturalism of his youth to the psychological suspense of his maturity. At first glance, these two modes could not be more different; but in several tales of the late 1930s through the 1950s, Bloch shows how elements from both can be fused to produce a new amalgam.

The first thing Bloch had to do was to gain control of his style. Already by late 1934 Lovecraft is noting that "The tendency toward over-colouring so marked last year is waning rapidly, & your command of effective diction . . . is becoming more & more dependable" (*LB* 55). One of the stories that elicited this comment was "The Grinning Ghoul," and indeed it is one of the first of Bloch's stories that plays on the distinction between psychological and ontological horror. The protagonist is a "moderately successful practising psychiatrist" (51), one of whose patients is a professor who admits to having bizarre dreams. Naturally, the psychiatrist initially dispenses with the dreams as mere vagaries, but later learns that they have an all too real source.

Still more remarkable, and one of the finest stories of Bloch's early period, is the (until recently) uncollected tale "Black Bargain" (*Weird Tales*, May 1942). Here both the Lovecraftian idiom and the customary Lovecraftian setting have been abandoned totally, and the subtle incursion of horror into a very mundane environment produces potently chilling effects. A cynical and world-weary pharmacist supplies some odd drugs—aconite, belladonna, and the like—to a down-and-outer who comes into his store clutching a large black book in German black-letter. A few days later the customer returns, but he has been transformed: he is spruced up with new clothes and claims that he has been hired by a local chemical supply house. As the man, Fritz Gulther, and the pharmacist celebrate the former's good fortune at a bar, the pharmacist notices something anomalous about the man's shadow: its movements do not seem to coincide with Gulther's. Thinking himself merely drunk, the pharmacist attempts to put the incident out of his mind.

Gulther then offers the pharmacist a job at the chemical company as his assistant. Going there, the pharmacist finds in Gulther's office the book he had been carrying—it is, of course, *De Vermis Mysteriis*. Eventually he worms the truth out of Gulther: Gulther had uttered an incantation, made a sacrifice, and called up the Devil, who had offered him success on one condition: "'He told me that I'd have only one rival, and that this rival would be a part of myself. It would grow with my success'" (215). Sure enough, Gulther's shadow seems both to be growing and to be subsuming Gulther's own life-force. As Gulther begins to panic, the pharmacist suggests that they prepare a counter-incantation to reverse the effect; but when he returns to Gulther's office with chemicals he has brought from his pharmacy, he finds Gulther transformed:

> I sat. Gulther rested on the desk nonchalantly swinging his legs.
> "All that nervousness, that strain, has disappeared. But before I forget it, I'd like to apologize for telling you that crazy story about sorcery and my obsession. Matter of fact, I'd feel better about the whole thing in the future if you just forget that all this ever happened." (217)

The pharmacist, dazed, agrees, but he knows that something has gone wrong. In fact, the shadow has now totally usurped Gulther.

It is not the use of *De Vermis Mysteriis* that represents the Lovecraftian connexion in this fine, understated tale; instead, it is Gulther's concluding transformation. In effect, the shadow has taken possession of Gulther's body and ousted his own personality—in exactly the same way that, in "The Thing on the Doorstep" (1933), Asenath Waite ousts the personality of her husband Edward Derby from his body and casts it into her own body. The concluding scene in "Black Bargain" is very similar to a scene in Lovecraft's story where Derby's personality is evicted while he is being driven back to Arkham from Maine by the narrator, Daniel Upton. Asenath (in Derby's body) remarks: "'I hope you'll forget my attack back there, Upton. You know what my nerves are, and I guess you can excuse such things'" (*DH* 291).

Several years later Bloch wrote another powerful tale, "The Unspeakable Betrothal" (*Avon Fantasy Reader*, 1949)—whose title, Bloch has repeatedly insisted, is not his. Here too we encounter a prose style radically different from the adjective-riddled hyperbole of "The Feast in the Abbey," and Bloch effectively experiments with stream-of-consciousness in capturing the visions that plague a young girl both at night and by day:

> But everything kept going round and round, and when Aunt May walked past the bed she seemed to flatten out like a shadow, or one of the things, only she made a loud noise which was really the thunder outside and now she was sleeping really and truly even though she heard the thunder but the thunder wasn't real nothing was real except the things, that was it nothing was real any more but the things. (168)

These visions—which convince the girl's family and friends that she is psychologically aberrant—again prove to be based upon reality, and at the end she is transported into space by the entities have infiltrated her mind. Two years prior to the publication of this story, Bloch had written his first non-supernatural novel of psychological horror, *The Scarf* (1947); and the rest of his career would see an alteration between supernaturalism and psychological suspense, with intermittent fusions of the two. "The Unspeakable Betrothal" is such a fusion in its sensitive delineation of a psyche that has been rendered subtly non-human by outside sources. And yet, even here the influence of Lovecraft can be felt. "The Whisperer in Darkness" is very much in evidence in the "deep, buzzing voice" (166) that the girl hears, and also at the conclusion when nothing but the girl's face is left, as her body has been spirited away. Lovecraft himself, however, is not given enough credit for mingling supernatural and psychological horror: he did just that in "The Shadow over Innsmouth" and perhaps also in "The Shadow out of Time," and Bloch may well have found suggestive hints in both.

"Notebook Found in a Deserted House" (*Weird Tales*, May 1951) uses somewhat the same stylistic device as "The Unspeakable Betrothal" in its narration by an ill-educated boy rather than a learned omniscient narrator. This story does not feature much psychological analysis, and in its rather grotesque misconstrual of Lovecraft's shoggoth (here interpreted as some sort of tree spirit) it led the way to Ramsey Campbell's similar error in his juvenile story, "The Hollow in the Woods" (in *Ghostly Tales* [1957/58]). But, if nothing else, it shows how a tale of basically Lovecraftian conception can be adapted to a very different idiom. Here, again, however, perhaps Bloch was simply adapting Lovecraft's own extensive use of New England dialect in such tales as "The Picture in the House," "The Dunwich Horror," and "The Shadow over Innsmouth."

"Terror in Cut-Throat Cave" (*Fantastic*, June 1958) is of interest in combining the crime or adventure story with supernaturalism. The basic plot of the tale may have been conceived as early as 1933, for Lovecraft makes mention of one of Bloch's story plots as the "idea of finding a *Thing* in the hold of a long-sunken treasure-ship" (*LB* 26). This is, indeed, exactly the core of "Terror in Cut-Throat Cave," although by the time Bloch wrote it he had mastered the tough-guy style he would use to such powerful effect in *The Dead Beat* (1960), and his powers of characterisation render the three main figures crisply—Howard Lane, the jaded writer who seeks a thrill from searching for underwater treasure; Don Hanson, a lumbering giant who has eyes for nothing but money; Dena Drake, Don's mistreated companion, who stays with her brutal lover for lack of any other meaningful goal in her life. I am not certain why this story is in *Mysteries of the Worm:* there is no "Mythos" allusion of any kind in it, and Robert M. Price's suggestion that Hanson is "something of a modern Obed Marsh" (218) is unconvincing. And yet, there is one fascinating Lovecraftian connexion. Toward the end Lane's mind is taken over by the nameless submerged entity, and he writes: "For already I was a part of it and it was a part of me" (249). No reader can fail to recall Robert Blake's poignant reflexion of the fusion of his own mind with that of the avatar of Nyarlathotep in "The Haunter of the Dark": "I am it and it is I . . ." (*DH* 115). That one sentence in Bloch's story is enough to reveal his borrowing of a central feature of Lovecraft's tale for his own work.

Henry Kuttner (1914–1958) came in touch with Lovecraft in February 1936, and over the next year they exchanged about ten letters. Kuttner established himself in *Weird Tales* with the publication of "The Graveyard Rats" in the March 1936 issue, but he was a relative novice.

Over the next three years he wrote a dozen stories drawing upon Lovecraft's pseudomythology, some of which Lovecraft read and criticised.

Kuttner's chief "additions" to the Mythos, if they can be called that, are the *Book of Iod* and various baleful entities such as Iod and Nyogtha. Iod is first cited in "The Secret of Kralitz" (*Weird Tales*, October 1936), along with Yuggoth, Cthulhu, and Yog-Sothoth, and is described as "the Source, [who] is worshipped beyond the outer galaxies" (8). This is not very helpful, especially in that the story itself merely involves reanimation of the dead and therefore has no substantive relation to Lovecraft's mythology. The actual *Book of Iod* is first cited in "Bells of Horror" (*Strange Stories*, April 1939), where we learn that the Huntington Library has a translation of it by Johann Negus and that it itself is an "abhorrent and monstrous volume of ancient esoteric formulae about which curious legends still cling. Only a single copy of the original volume, written in the prehuman Ancient Tongue, is said to exist" (151). What language is meant by the "Ancient Tongue" can only be conjectured, as well as how the diligent Negus came to learn it in order to translate out of it. Presumably, the passage from the *Book of Iod* that follows, referring to "The Dark Silent One [who] dwelleth deep beneath the earth on the shore of the Western Ocean" (152), refers to Iod, making him some kind of sea creature. The tale, while attempting to draw upon the early history of California (its premise is a series of bells buried in California by Junipero Serra, one of the Spanish founders of the region), lapses into bathos when Kuttner attempts to incite fear in the reader by repetitions of the word "*Clang-g-g!*" throughout the story.

In a later story, however, "The Hunt" (*Strange Stories*, June 1939), we get an actual glimpse of Iod, who is called "the Hunter of Souls":

> It was not a homogeneous entity, this unholy specter, but it partook hideously of incongruous elements. Strange mineral and crystal formations sent their fierce glow through squamous, semitransparent flesh, and the whole was bathed in a viscid, crawling light that pulsed monstrously about the horror. A thin slime dripped from membranous flesh to the car's hood; and as this slime floated down, hideous, plant-like appendages writhed blindly in the air, making hungry little sucking sounds. (177)

For all the floridity of the writing, this is not an ineffective attempt to describe a creature of bizarre and anomalous properties.

For Nyogtha we have better information. In a passage from the *Necronomicon* cited in "The Salem Horror" (*Weird Tales*, May 1937), we find this:

> Men know him as the Dweller in Darkness, that brother of the Old Ones called Nyogtha, the Thing that should not be. He can be summoned to Earth's surface through certain secret caverns and fissures, and sorcerers have seen him in Syria and below the black tower of Leng; from the Thang Grotto of Tartary he has come ravening to bring terror and destruction among the pavilions of the great Khan. Only by the looped cross, the Vach-Viraj incantation and the Tikkoun elixir may he be driven back to the nighted caverns of hidden foulness where he dwelleth. (31)

This story is one on which Lovecraft extensively commented when he read it in manuscript in March 1936. Aside from correcting all manner of historical and topographical errors made by Kuttner about Salem, Massachusetts, a place he had never visited and knew little about, Lovecraft was concerned both about the motivation of the story and about the fact that "the colour is laid on too thickly—strange things come too rapidly in succession, & with too great abruptness."[4] It does not seem as if Kuttner has done much to address either of these flaws in his final draft. In the story, one Carson, a writer, pursues a rat down to the cellar of the house in Salem in which he is renting a room. He finds that he can work best while in this space (called the witch's room), but in so doing he has unwittingly unleashed the spirit (or perhaps the body) of Abigail Prinn, a witch who had died in 1692. Lovecraft had noted that the story was "a little *vaguely motivated.* Just *what* started the major phenomena at the particular time they did start? Surely Carson was not the first to occupy the old witch's room—& yet one can hardly imagine a repetition of this sort of phenomena every time someone lights a fire in the fireplace."[5] Kuttner has blunderingly tried to remedy this defect by stating that Carson had sat on a black stone in the centre of the room, which proves to be some kind of "focal point" that (in the words of Michael Leigh, an occultist who saves the day) can be "tuned to pick up certain malign vibrations the nature of which you could not comprehend!" (26).

The scenario just outlined makes it clear that "The Salem Horror" is only a slight variation of "The Dreams in the Witch House." Lovecraft appears to have been aware of this, as he commented: "I've largely forgotten my own 'Witch House', but I think I had my student-victim dabbling in mathematico-magical formulae of a rare kind, which eventually reached a dangerous parallelism with those of the bygone witch—hence placed the two in rapport."[6] In the end Leigh comes to the rescue with the muttering of a spell. Exactly how Nyogtha is even involved is never made clear. Leigh comments that Prinn "served strange gods" (31), but what her purpose is in returning from the dead, and where Nyogtha fits into the scheme, remains a mystery.

"The Salem Horror" is a very bad story—a confused, overwritten imitation of an already poor Lovecraft story, in which the self-important bombast of Michael Leigh destroys any atmosphere that Kuttner may have established.

Regrettably, Leigh returns in "The Black Kiss" (*Weird Tales*, June 1937), cowritten with Robert Bloch. Here the theme is mind-transference, probably derived from "The Thing on the Doorstep." This is Kuttner's first story set in California, and the use of a topography actually known to the author is certainly a step in the right direction. No Mythos names or terms are mentioned, as Graham Dean, the protagonist, finding his mind transferred into the body of a hideous sea-creature, actually kills his own body.

"The Invaders" (*Strange Stories*, February 1939) is also set in California and adopts a strikingly modern narrative tone. We are treated to an obvious portrait of Lovecraft in the depiction of the writer Michael Hayward:

> Very few writers could create the strange atmosphere of eldritch horror that Hayward put into his fantastic tales of mystery. He had imitators—all great writers have—but none attained the stark and dreadful illusion of reality with which he invested his oftentimes shocking fantasies. He went far beyond the bounds of human experience and familiar superstition, delving into uncanny fields of unearthliness. Blackwood's vampiric elementals, M. R. James' loathsome liches— even the black horror of de Maupassant's "Horla" and Bierce's "Damned Thing"—paled by comparison. (86)

A nice tribute. But the story is ultimately disappointing. Hayward has found a formula in *De Vermis Mysteriis* for a drug that incites ancestral memories; but unfortunately, this also has the effect of letting in certain gods hostile to mankind. As Hayward has written on a manuscript, in ancient times "there came to Earth certain beings from another dimension of space, inhuman, monstrous creatures which desired to wipe out all life from the planet." But there was "a tremendous conflict . . . in which the gods friendly to mankind were arrayed against the hostile invaders" (97). This unimaginative and morally simplistic utilisation of the Derleth Mythos leads to a predictable result: the horrible "invaders" are banished by a "Word of Power" (102) spoken by the narrator!

There is no need to discuss other of Kuttner's Mythos stories in detail. "Spawn of Dagon" (*Weird Tales*, July 1938) attempts to meld Lovecraftian cosmicism with sword-and-sorcery battle scenes. "The Frog" (*Strange Stories*, February 1939) regales us with a man being chased by a giant frog. "Hydra" (*Weird Tales*, April 1939) asserts that the apparently mythical creature Hydra is in fact an extraterrestrial being seeking to return to earth. Thankfully, we are saved by the intervention of another occultist, Kenneth Scott.

It can be seen that Kuttner has utilised, in almost every single instance, Lovecraft's earlier conceptions of the Mythos as an offshoot of black magic, with spells, incantations, and other occultist paraphernalia. Lovecraft's later conception of the Mythos as an instantiation of "non-supernatural cosmic art" has entirely escaped Kuttner, as it escaped August Derleth. From a purely literary perspective, not a single one of Kuttner's Mythos stories is particularly meritorious. They may well be apprentice work, but what Kuttner ultimately learned from his apprenticeship is that his own literary temperament was ill-suited to the Lovecraftian idiom—or, at any rate, to what he took the Lovecraftian idiom to be.

Fritz Leiber's apparently startling remark that H. P. Lovecraft was "the chiefest influence on my literary development after Shakespeare"[7] may perhaps be less puzzling if we interpret the statement absolutely literally; for Leiber's emphasis here may be on the word *development,* and if this is the case, then it suggests that Lovecraft's own work—as well as his brief but intense correspondence with Leiber (1910–1992) in 1936–37—provided Leiber with suggestions as to the improvement of the style, plotting, motivation, and conception of his early tales, and that these suggestions held Leiber in good stead throughout the subsequent course of his long and fruitful career. It is a truism that Leiber, perhaps

alone of Lovecraft's literary associates, did not imitate Lovecraft either
stylistically or thematically—except in the late work, "The Terror from
the Depths" (1976), commissioned for a volume of Cthulhu Mythos
pastiches (see chapter VIII)—but instead struck out on his own right
from the beginning of his career. This aesthetic independence has been
a major reason for the survival of Leiber's work while that of other,
more derivative writers has achieved merited oblivion; but that Lovecraft taught Leiber much about the craft of writing is evident both from
Leiber's several insightful critical essays on Lovecraft and from his early
tales, especially those gathered in his first collection, *Night's Black Agents*
(1947). (Leiber's essays on Lovecraft, along with Lovecraft's letters to
Leiber and tales by Leiber influenced by Lovecraft, are now gathered in
Fritz Leiber and H. P. Lovecraft: Writers of the Dark [2004].)

I do not have the space here to discuss Leiber's essays on Lovecraft, but a comment in one of them is of interest in the context of his
own work. "The 'Whisperer' Re-examined" (1964) is a sharp criticism
of "The Whisperer in Darkness" from the point of view of its deficient
characterisation: the protagonist, Albert N. Wilmarth, is too easily
"hoodwinked" (301) by the alien entities of the tale. This leads to a
more general criticism of Lovecraft:

> In "Notes on the Writing of Weird Fiction" Lovecraft summed up
> [his] limitation: "All that a wonder story can ever be is *a vivid picture of a
> certain type of human mood.*" This aesthetic dictum, while having some
> technical validity, breathes loneliness and can be very stultifying to the
> writer's urge to say things about the real world, set down insights into
> real people, speculate imaginatively, and get closer to his reader than
> merely sharing "a vague illusion of the strange reality of the unreal." (302)

This criticism is not entirely fair to Lovecraft—who was not interested
in the "real world" or in setting down insights into "real people," and
whose cosmic perspective was opposed to the vaunting of human beings against the awesome backdrop of the cosmos—but it points to
Leiber's own belief that fantasy, horror, and even cosmicism are not
incompatible with the portrayal of vital human characters with whom
the reader can identify.

In "My Correspondence with Lovecraft" Leiber tells the story of
his brief personal involvement with the Providence writer. He had been
profoundly moved by reading "The Colour out of Space" in *Amazing*

Stories (September 1927) and *At the Mountains of Madness* and "The Shadow out of Time" in 1936 issues of *Astounding Stories*. No doubt he read Lovecraft's other stories in *Weird Tales* as well, but the citation of the above three tales—Lovecraft's most "science-fictional" works—points to their focal influence upon Leiber's early work. Too shy to write to the great master of weird fiction, however, Leiber nonetheless came into contact with Lovecraft when his wife Jonquil wrote to him through *Weird Tales*. For a time Lovecraft was writing separate letters to both Fritz and Jonquil (as well as to Leiber's early collaborator Harry O. Fischer), although the duration of this correspondence was quite brief: perhaps no longer than the period from October 1936 to March 1937, when Lovecraft died at forty-six. Neither Fritz nor Jonquil could know that Lovecraft was already in the final stages of intestinal cancer; and it is poignant to read—given the near-certainty that bad diet was a significant cause of Lovecraft's illness and death—how Leiber and Fischer ruminated "that something must be done to provide Lovecraft with fresh vegetables" (294).

But that brief association was enough to effect some permanent changes in Leiber's work. Leiber had sent the typescript of his novelette, "Adept's Gambit" (rejected by *Weird Tales*), to Lovecraft; in response, Lovecraft on December 19, 1936, wrote a letter of twenty sheets, written on both sides of the page—perhaps 10,000 words in length—commenting in detail on points of style and historical accuracy in the tale, and supplying a copious reading-list of works on Greek and Roman history for any future historical fiction that Leiber might do. Leiber is right to call this lengthy epistle "crazily generous by hard-headed standards," and he goes on to say that it "influenced me permanently toward greater care in the polishing and final preparation of manuscripts" (293).

The version of "Adept's Gambit" published in *Night's Black Agents* is very likely quite different from what Leiber sent to Lovecraft, since Leiber confesses that the novelette went through "three or four recastings and rewritings"[8] after its initial rejections. One of these versions contained references to Lovecraft's Mythos, and Leiber was probably wise in excising them from the final draft. This draft, long thought to be lost, has recently surfaced, but it has yet to be published, and I have not had access to it. The existing text of "Adept's Gambit" does not bear much resemblance to Lovecraft's own work; indeed, in its picaresque narrative, its vivid character portrayals, and its liberal doses of humour and buffoonery it is about as far from the bulk of Lovecraft's dark, brooding, non-humanocentric work as can be imagined. Lovecraft himself was aware of the fact, remarking in his letter that "the style & manner of approach are almost antipodal to my own" (38). There is perhaps an accidental resemblance to Lovecraft's then-unpublished novel, *The Dream-Quest of Unknown Kadath*—Lovecraft remarks on the similarity himself ("This picaresque kind of writing has a strong fascination, & I once attempted it myself . . . in a long novelette" [43])—but of course Leiber could not actually have been influenced by that work.

If "Adept's Gambit" bears little resemblance to Lovecraft's work, another Fafhrd and Gray Mouser story is so dependent upon Lovecraftian conceptions that it can qualify as a pastiche, although even this tale is considerably more imaginative than other Lovecraft-derived works. "The Sunken Land" (1942) is a story in which Fafhrd catches a fish in whose mouth is found an object that is both a ring and a key. This object makes Fafhrd think of the legends of a land called Simorgya, whose inhabitants "'were mighty magicians, claiming power over wind and wave and the creatures below. Yet the sea gulped them down for all that'" (135). The ship on which Fafhrd and the Mouser are sailing is rammed by another ship, controlled by the evil Lavas Laerk, and after a fight with its crew Fafhrd is taken prisoner and made to serve as an oarsman. Lavas Laerk is seeking to attain the sunken land of Simorgya, and after a time he and his crew seem to do so, coming upon a vast mountain jutting out of the sea. But something seems to be wrong, and Fafhrd is the only one to be aware that "Simorgya had indeed sunk under the sea and only risen up yesterday—or yester-hour" (142). Lavas Laerk comes upon the treasure-house of Simorgya and his crew revels in the gold and jewels therein; but from behind a golden door a "strange, undulant blanketlike sea monster" (143) emerges and overwhelms Lavas Laerk's men, while Fafhrd escapes with the help of the Mouser, whose ship has arrived to rescue him. Simorgya then once again falls back into the sea.

This story is an amalgam of at least four different Lovecraft stories, although some of the borrowings are very slight. When the Mouser, seeing the ring for the first time, remarks that he "did not recognize the

style" (133), we think of the bizarre jewellery of the Innsmouth denizens of "The Shadow over Innsmouth," which "belonged to some set-
tled technique ... utterly remote from any—Eastern or Western,
ancient or modern—which [the narrator] had ever heard of or seen exemplified" (*DH* 311). Later, as Lavas Laerk's crew penetrate the treasure-house and note its eerie phosphorescence, we are perhaps meant to
recall Lovecraft's early tale, "The Temple" (1920), which involves a
German submarine commander who comes upon a similarly phosphorescent temple buried beneath the waves of the Atlantic. And that
"blanketlike" monster is perhaps akin to Lovecraft's protoplasmic
shoggoth from *At the Mountains of Madness*.

But clearly the predominant influence on this tale is "The Call of
Cthulhu," Lovecraft's prototypical account of a sunken continent that
suddenly rises up from the waves and from which the shapeless mon-
strosity Cthulhu momentarily emerges to wreak havoc on a hapless
crew of Norwegian sailors who come upon it by accident. Indeed, "The
Sunken Land" is largely a rewriting of "The Call of Cthulhu," transfer-
ring the setting from the real world of the South Pacific to an heroic
fantasy realm and including rather more fisticuffs and swordplay than
was Lovecraft's wont.

Another early Leiber tale—"Diary in the Snow," first published in
Night's Black Agents—is less obviously derivative but still owes its very
conception to Lovecraft. Here it transpires that a race of extraterrestrial
entities, dwelling in a world of bitter cold, discover the existence of
Earth and look with envy at its temperateness. As they dwell on a
planet enormously distant from earth, mind-exchange with the inhabitants of Earth is the only feasible way to effect their removal from their
world; and "Diary in the Snow" is the account of a writer in a remote
snowbound cottage who unwittingly serves as the conduit for the creatures' advent to this planet, unaware that the science-fiction tale he is
writing is in reality his subconscious mind's warning of how these entities are planning to usurp the human race.

There is, perhaps, no specific Lovecraft story which served as the
model for "Diary in the Snow," although the conceptions broached in
it are heavily Lovecraftian. The idea of mind-exchange over enormous
distances of space brings "The Shadow out of Time" to mind, and this
is perhaps the most direct influence. Lovecraft, of course, used mind-

exchange in a number of other tales, notably "The Thing on the Door-step" and "The Haunter of the Dark"; but only "The Shadow out of Time" involves mind-exchange over vast galactic spaces. Also, the sce-nario of the writer and his colleague being besieged by alien forces—for after a time they develop a dim awareness of the true state of affairs—recalls "The Whisperer in Darkness," where Henry Akeley finds him-self trapped in his lonely Vermont farmhouse as the fungi from Yug-goth seek to overwhelm him and take his mind on stupendous trans-cosmic voyages. One telling tip of the hat to Lovecraft is the narrator's description, at the outset, of the anomalous phenomena he notes around him as "a sense of strangeness, a delightful feeling of adventur-ous expectancy" (151). Lovecraft may well have used that latter phrase in a letter to Leiber, for it became a standard coinage in his own aes-thetic of the weird: "What has haunted my dreams for nearly forty years is *a strange sense of adventurous expectancy connected with landscape and architec-ture and sky-effects*" (*SL* 3.100).

Other early Leiber tales are influenced by Lovecraft in less signifi-cant ways; indeed, in some cases the resemblance may be accidental. "The Inheritance" also deals with personality-exchange and was per-haps influenced by "The Thing on the Doorstep." "The Man Who Never Grew Young" appears to reflect Lovecraft's fascination with time—recall his celebrated statement that "*Conflict with time* seems to me the most potent and fruitful theme in all human expression" ("Notes on Writing Weird Fiction" [*MW* 113])—in its depiction of a man who somehow travels backward through time. The influence of "The Shadow out of Time" may be conjectured, although the parallels are not very precise: Leiber's tale simply involves a man who himself is somehow doubling back upon the time-stream.

The uncollected tale "The Dead Man" (*Weird Tales*, November 1950) betrays—as Stefan Dziemianowicz has pointed out[9]—a peculiar influence of "The Thing on the Doorstep" in its use of a series of three knocks followed by two more as a cue to bring a patient out of a hyp-notic trance. Lovecraft used the identical three-and-two pattern as a se-cret code between two characters in his story.

A reading of *Night's Black Agents* makes clear the central lesson Leiber learned from Lovecraft: the need to update the horror tale to make it relevant to present-day concerns. Lovecraft, of course, did so by fusing horror and science fiction, replacing the fear of vampires, werewolves, and ghosts (all completely outmoded in the light of contemporary science) with that of the boundless cosmos. Antiquarian though he may have been, Lovecraft was keenly aware of such radical and potentially disturbing conceptions as Einsteinian space-time, the quantum theory, and Heisenberg's indeterminacy principle, and utilised them to give a distinctly modern cast to such stale conceptions as the vampire ("The Shunned House") and the witch ("The Dreams in the Witch House"), to say nothing of the possibility of extraterrestrial incursions in such tales as "The Colour out of Space," "The Whisperer in Darkness," *At the Mountains of Madness,* and "The Shadow out of Time."

Leiber went about it in a somewhat different way. In his belief that weird fiction must be made relevant to contemporary audiences by means of vividly realised human characters and realism of setting, Leiber melded supernatural horror with the very real horrors of urbanism ("Smoke Ghost," "The Hound"), crime ("The Automatic Pistol"), and the omnipresent anxiety of living in the modern world ("The Dreams of Albert Moreland"); anticipating in this regard the work of Ramsey Campbell and many other contemporary writers. In a few striking stories ("The Hill and the Hole," "A Bit of the Dark World") Leiber even attempts (successfully) to duplicate Lovecraft's harrowing cosmicism.

"Smoke Ghost" is Leiber's prototypical tale of the horror to be found in the city. The very title suggests a paradoxical union of the antiquated (a ghost) and the modern (smoke from factories). This ghost, however, in the eyes of the protagonist, Mr Wran, is "'a ghost from the world today, with the soot of the factories on its face and the pounding of machinery in its soul'" (109). The vista of slum roofs seen by Wran symbolises for him "certain disagreeable aspects of the frustrated, frightened century in which he lived" (112). When Wran's son sees the ghost and cries, "Black man, black man" (120), we are not to interpret the remark racially but as emblematic of the omnipresent filth—literal and moral—in modern society. We may also think of Leiber's discussion, in "A Literary Copernicus," of Nyarlathotep, who in "The Dreams in the Witch House" appears as the Black Man. In pondering what Nyarlathotep may "mean," Leiber conjectures that one possibility is that "Nyarlathotep stands for man's self-destructive intellectuality, his awful ability to see the universe for what it is and thereby kill in himself all naive and beautiful dreams" (286). This is not exactly what is going on in "Smoke Ghost," but Leiber may still have learned from Lovecraft how to use a symbol something like Nyarlathotep to convey his own views on the state of modern man.

Leiber's "The Hound" exactly mirrors the title of one of Lovecraft's early tales, but this duplication may be accidental, as Leiber's tale appears to owe nothing at all to Lovecraft's lurid and consciously self-parodic story. Leiber's "The Hound" is grimly potent, but again we are to see in the hound of the tale a symbol for the horrors of urbanism: "this thing . . . was part and parcel of the great sprawling cities and chaotic peoples of the Twentieth Century" (187). Later the narrator's friend, speaking of the relentless march of technology, points to the inability of the human spirit to keep pace:

> "Meanwhile, what's happening inside each of us? I'll tell you. All sorts of inhibited emotions are accumulating. Fear is accumulating. Horror is accumulating. A new kind of awe of the mysteries of the universe is accumulating. A psychological environment is forming, along with the physical one. . . . Our culture becomes ripe for infection. . . . our culture suddenly spawns a horde of demons. And, like germs, they have a peculiar affinity for our culture. They're unique. They fit in. You wouldn't find the same kind any other time or place." (190–91)

"The Automatic Pistol" is a somewhat slighter but piquant tale that effects a union of the gangster story and the supernatural tale. A criminal's gun is explicitly compared to a witch's familiar (133), making us recall perhaps how Lovecraft brought the tale of witchcraft up to date in "The Dreams in the Witch House" by the incorporation of Einsteinian physics. There the ratlike creature Brown Jenkin, the familiar of the witch Keziah Mason, appears in hyperspace as a "polyhedron of unknown colours and rapidly shifting surface angles" (*MM* 273). In these tales Leiber pioneers the modernisation of the weird tale; but he does so not as Lovecraft did—by attempting to make the supernatural plausible by appeals to advanced science—but by placing it in the frenetic urban milieu that holds so many of us in its tenacious grip. Nevertheless, it is likely that Leiber found in Lovecraft's tales some suggestive hints of how such a modernisation might be effected.

Three tales in *Night's Black Agents* feature the cosmicism and the very intellectualised, philosophical horror that lie at the core of Lovecraft's best work. In "The Dreams of Albert Moreland" the central character dreams that he is playing a chesslike game on some enormous gameboard, convinced that the fate of mankind depends on the outcome. The basic plot is strikingly similar to that of "The Dreams in the Witch House," in particular the tableau where a statuette from Moreland's dream-world is found in his room, a scene identical to one found in Lovecraft's tale, and a confirmation that the "dreams" in both tales bear some harrowing relationship to the "real" world. (Leiber could not know that a further similarity exists in the original title of Lovecraft's story—"The Dreams of Walter Gilman.") When Moreland fancies that "some cosmic beings, neither gods nor men, had created human life long ago as a jest or experiment or artistic form" (169), we are clearly meant to recall Lake's conjecture in *At the Mountains of Madness* that the Old Ones had created all earth life as "jest or mistake" (*MM* 22). But Leiber performs a brilliant union of social commentary and cosmicism by attributing the "omnipresent anxiety" that Moreland sees on "each passing face" as symptomatic of a broader evil:

> For once I seemed able to look behind the mask which every person wears and which is so characteristically pronounced in a congested city, and see what lay behind—the egotistical sensitivity, the smouldering irritation, the thwarted longing, the defeat . . . and, above all, the anxiety, too ill-defined and lacking in definite object to be called fear, but nonetheless infecting every thought and action, and making trivial things terrible. And it seemed to me that social, economic, and physiological factors, even Death and the War, were insufficient to explain such anxiety, and that it was in reality an upswelling from something dubious and horrible in the very constitution of the universe. (173)

Later Moreland believes that he is "getting perilously close to the innermost secrets of the universe and finding they were rotten and evil and sardonic" (175), a common theme in Lovecraft's work.

"The Hill and the Hole" speaks of some anomalous survey readings whereby a hill seems to be a pit, leading the narrator to reflect about "how little most people knew about the actual dimensions and boundaries of the world they lived in" (159). And later: "Once admit that the dimensions of a thing might not be real . . . and you cut the foundations from under the world" (165). Lovecraft speaks in "The Call of Cthulhu" of the geometry of R'lyeh being *"all wrong"* (*DH* 143) and of "an angle which was acute, but behaved as if it were obtuse" (*DH* 152), exactly the sort of reversal that we find in Leiber's tale. The fact that a surveyor's instrument confirms the anomalousness of the situation may point to the influence of "The Colour out of Space," where a spectroscope is applied to the meteorite and reveals "shining bands unlike any known colours of the normal spectrum" (*DH* 58). In both cases it is important that the weird phenomena not be discounted as a mere hallucination; and the utilisation of scientific instruments in perfect working order is the best means to suggest that some genuine bizarrerie actually exists.

"A Bit of the Dark World" (1962) is a later story added to the revised (1978) edition of *Night's Black Agents*, probably because Leiber considered it to be thematically similar to the Lovecraftian tales in the volume. There is, of course, a passing reference to "Mountains of Madness near the South Pole" (201), but the relationship is deeper than this. This tale consists largely of an intellectual discussion of the foundations of fear. Whereas one character speaks of mundane horrors—"'Nazi death camps, brain-washing, Black-Dahlia sex murders, race riots, stuff like that'"—another character counters: "'I'm talking about supernatural horror, which is almost the antithesis of even the worst human violence and cruelty. Hauntings, the suspension of scientific law, the intrusion of the utterly alien, the sense of something listening at the rim of the cosmos or scratching faintly at the other side of the sky'" (200), a very Lovecraftian formulation. Later a character has a cosmic experience very similar to those of Lovecraft's protagonists:

> I looked up at the heavens. There was no Milky Way yet, but there would be soon, the stars were flashing on so brightly and thickly at this smog-free distance from LA. I saw the Pole Star straight above the dark star-silhouetted summit-crag of the hillside across from me, and the Great Bear and Cassiopeia swinging from it. I felt the bigness of the atmosphere, I got a hint of the stupendous distance between me and the stars, and then—as if my vision could go out in all directions at will, piercing solidity as readily as the dark—I got a lasting, growing, wholly absorbing sense of the universe around me. (214)

The tale goes on to relate exactly such an "intrusion of the utterly alien," an entity as incomprehensible as the creature (or creatures) in "The Colour out of Space."

It can be seen from the above discussion that Leiber never wrote an explicitly "Cthulhu Mythos" tale in his early work, and indeed would not do so until "The Terror from the Depths" (1976). Instead, his work exhibits significant traces of Lovecraftian influence while remaining very much Leiber's own work. These tales are a model for the benefits of pastiche and the intelligent assimilation of literary influence—but of course this can only occur when a writer actually has something of his own to say. The great majority of Cthulhu Mythos pastichists have nothing to say, and one wishes they would acknowledge the fact by actually saying (or writing) nothing.

Before Lovecraft's death, several other writers tangentially associated with Lovecraft produced stories featuring light or heavy borrowings of his myth-cycle. The most curious example, perhaps, is "The House of the Worm" by Mearle Prout (*Weird Tales*, October 1933). Almost nothing is known about this author aside from the fact that he published three other stories in *Weird Tales* between 1937 and 1939. He is clearly not a correspondent of Lovecraft, and yet his story borrows from—indeed, lifts actual sentences from—"The Call of Cthulhu" and other Lovecraft stories.

The premise of the tale is the possibility of collective thought actually creating reality. The narrator and his friend, Fred, discuss the matter, and the latter states: "'But imagine . . . a group of people, a cult, all thinking the same thoughts, worshipping the same imaginary figure. What might not happen, if their fanaticism were such that they thought and felt deeply? A physical manifestation, alien to those of us who did not believe . . .'" (198). This is not exactly a Lovecraftian idea, but consider the following, as the two protagonists explore a wood where some mysterious creature or force is causing widespread death:

> I think that the human mind, far from being a curse, is the most merciful thing in the world. We live on a quiet, sheltered island of ignorance, and from the single current flowing by our shores we visualize the vastness of the black seas around us, and see—simplicity and safety. And yet, if only a portion of the cross-currents and whirling vortices of mystery and chaos would be revealed to our consciousness, we should immediately go insane. (203)

This is a crude and blundering mimicry of the first paragraph of "The Call of Cthulhu." When the mysterious force spreads death and disease in an ever-widening arc around the woods, killing all the vegetation in its path ("Fifty, a hundred or two hundred feet in a night the circle spread; trees that one day were fresh and alive, sprouting with shoots of green, were the next day harsh and yellow" [209]), we can hardly fail to think of "The Colour out of Space." A few pages later occurs another subtle borrowing: "There are vocal qualities peculiar to men, and vocal qualities peculiar to beasts; but nowhere this side of the pit of hell itself can be heard the raucous cries that issued from their straining throats as we grasped our tapers and raced toward them" (212). Recall "The Call of Cthulhu": "There are vocal qualities peculiar to men, and vocal qualities peculiar to beasts; and it is terrible to hear the one when the source should yield the other" (*DH* 137).

It cannot properly be said that "The House of the Worm" is a "Cthulhu Mythos story": it is merely a tale loosely based on Lovecraftian conceptions and lifting actual phrases out of a Lovecraft story. The most bizarre parallel is surely accidental: the title of the tale exactly matches the title of a novel that Lovecraft claimed to be working on in 1920 (*SL* 1.295, 304), although probably he never began it. The "worm" in Prout's story is merely the graveworm, symbolising death. In spite of certain crudities, the tale is not ineffective in its suggestions of cosmicism and its development of cumulative horror.

Lovecraft and his colleagues took immediate note of Prout's borrowings. Lovecraft himself remarked to Clark Ashton Smith:

> Finished the new W.T. last night, and would say it's about an average issue—saved from utter mediocrity by the excellent items of yours and Two-Gun's and Mearle Prout's. This latter is a newcomer, but to me his story seems to have a singularly authentic quality despite certain touches of naivete. It has a certain atmosphere and sense of brooding evil—things which most pulp contributors totally lack. Prout will be worth watching if the commercial bug doesn't get him![10]

Elsewhere Lovecraft notes: "Yes—I thought I saw touches of my own style here & there,"[11] making it clear that he was well aware of Prout's borrowings from himself.

We need not linger long on Richard F. Searight's "The Sealed Casket" (*Weird Tales*, March 1935), for its sole point of interest—the epigraph from the Eltdown Shards—has already been noted. The tale itself is highly conventional and cannot be said to utilise Lovecraftian elements to any great extent. The epigraph itself refers to an entity named Avaloth—clearly an adaptation of Azathoth, although this creature is nothing but some kind of ice demon. The story tells of a sealed casket, "the ancient coffer of Alu-Tor" (9), bequeathed to a man named Wesson Clark by his old friend, Martucci. Given that Clark had been having an affair with Martucci's wife, the story's supernatural revenge motif becomes immediately predictable: after great effort Clark manages to open the casket, whereupon he feels an "icy gust" (10). He is later found with every bone in his body broken and entirely drained of blood. (One would think a more effective ending would be to have Clark found frozen to death, in spite of the fact that his house has burned down.) The persistent rumours that Lovecraft helped to write either the epigraph or the story itself can be mercifully ended by consulting Lovecraft's correspondence with Searight, which conclusively establishes that he provided Searight no assistance on the work.

The veteran pulpsmith Hugh B. Cave (1910–2004) wrote at least two stories that utilise Lovecraftian elements. "The Isle of Dark Magic" (*Weird Tales*, August 1934) is set on an island in the South Pacific and attempts to mingle Lovecraft's focus on the "forbidden book" with local magic. The protagonist, Peter Mace, offers prayers to various Lovecraftian gods in an attempt to bring a marble statue of his dead beloved, Maureen Kennedy, to life. The statue in fact comes to life, but the incantation has unwittingly revived the actual corpse of Maureen, who comes to the island; in the end the marble statue kills both Maureen and Mace.

This rambling and long-winded tale would by now have been forgotten if not for its Lovecraftian references—indeed, it apparently *has* been forgotten, for not even the diligent efforts of Robert M. Price have caused it to be reprinted, and it is cited only by the indefatigable Chris Jarocha-Ernst. We first find that Mace has a predictable supply of "forbidden books"—specifically, "*Black Cults* of Von Heller," "the unexpurgated edition of what is now *The Veil Unseen*," and "the missing portion of that perilous treatise, *Le Culte des Morts*, of whose missing portion only four copies are reputed to exist!" (187). This passage shows that the "forbidden book" topos had become hackneyed even before Lovecraft's death. The first title is manifestly a variation of von

Junzt's *Nameless Cults* (also called the Black Book), while the third is an adaptation of M. le Comte d'Erlette's *Cultes des Goules*.

Mace's incantation is a bit lengthy, but the relevant parts are these:

> "This is the night, O Bethmoora. . . . Hear me, while I walk by the black lake of Hali, O Nyarlathotep. . . . Hear me . . . heaven in art . . . heaven in art . . . and the Yellow Sign is burning on the altar of my desire, that She may open her eyes and be mine again. Who father our name, thy be hallowed! Words for you, O Yuggoth, O Yian, O Hastur, O Prince of Evil! . . . Give her to my arms, O Yuggoth! Hear me, O Lord of Lords, O Nyarlathotep!" (194)

It can readily be seen that every single term (aside from the generic "Prince of Evil") has been borrowed from the notorious list of Mythos terms in "The Whisperer in Darkness" (*DH* 223). Indeed, it becomes evident that Cave has cited these entities without any real understanding of their origin or significance, since he apparently envisions Bethmoora to be a person or god (it is a city in Lord Dunsany's story "Bethmoora" [1910]), and perhaps Yuggoth also, although surely no one who has read "The Whisperer in Darkness" could come to such a conclusion. The vivification of an inanimate object has no connexion to Lovecraft's pseudomythology, although Cave attempts to manufacture a connexion by noting, "Those horrors of outer darkness had given her the power of life!" (201). Lovecraft remarked charitably that Cave's story was "not offensively crude," going on to say: "he uses our own evil pantheon in a way which plays the deuce with the 'style-sheet.'"[12] I don't suppose the term "style-sheet" is of much significance here: Lovecraft is simply noting that Cave's use of the pseudomythological terms do not in fact tally well with that found in previously published stories.

A few years after Lovecraft's death, Cave wrote another tale, "The Death Watch" (*Weird Tales*, June/July 1939), on very much the same theme as "The Isle of Dark Magic." Here a woman, Elaine Ingram, attempts to revive her dead husband by an incantation: "'Hear me, O Mighty Nyarlathotep!' she was incanting. 'You who walk in the farthest shadows by the black lakes of Hali, listen to me, I entreat you! And you, O Hastur, O Prince of Evil! Send him back to me, for my own god has failed me. Give him to me as he promised to return . . .'" (28). This story is perhaps minimally better than its predecessor, but only by virtue of its being shorter. Lovecraft and Cave had corresponded briefly and somewhat acrimoniously in the early 1930s; evidently Cave took offence at Lovecraft's anti-commercial attitude and felt that cheap pulp hacks like himself should only be engaged in making as much money as possible from the manufacturing of quasi-literary products for the delectation of an ignorant public. He certainly fulfilled his own aesthetic principles to the letter.

Henry Hasse's "The Guardian of the Book" (*Weird Tales*, March 1937) was published in the very month of Lovecraft's death, but it can scarcely be said to form a fitting tribute to him. The story cites the usual array of "forbidden" books, including the *Necronomicon,* but it says preposterously of another book that it is "the most damnable book in the universe" (262). This proves to be an apparently untitled work in which one Tlaviir of Vhoorl speaks of a friend, Kathulhn (evidently reflecting the widely erroneous pronunciation of Cthulhu), who learns of the existence of certain gods or creatures called the Outer Ones, who are "pure *evil*" (272). At this point the usual array of entities—Cthulhu (spelled *Kthulhu*), Tsathoggua (spelled *Tsathoqquah*), Yog-Sothoth (spelled *Yok-Zothoth*), and the like (276)—are cited. But of course the world is saved in the nick of time.

A later story by Hasse, "Horror at Vecra" (*Acolyte*, Fall 1943), isn't much better. Here we are introduced to the community of Vecra, a small town in Massachusetts where the denizens speak the backwoods English of "The Dunwich Horror." We also learn of the existence of a book called *Monsters and Their Kynde,* which conveniently tells of such creatures as "B'Moth and Ftakhar, Lloigor and Kathuln and ye others" (81). The novelty that Hasse introduces in this story is the notion that whoever is attracted to these evil gods becomes a part of them, so that in the end the protagonist, emptying his revolver into some alien creature he encounters in a tomb, sees his friend's face within the flabby folds of the creature's mass.

I daresay we need not waste much time with Manly Wade Wellman's "The Terrible Parchment" (*Weird Tales*, August 1937), a story that was apparently meant as a kind of affectionate tribute to the lately deceased Lovecraft, and deals with a character who stumbles upon the *Necronomicon*—but then destroys it with holy water. Did Wellman know that Lovecraft was an atheist and would have been appalled (or, perhaps more likely, amused) at this bit of religious conventionality? It is impossible to know; but Wellman's story deserves nothing but oblivion.

Of a very different and radically superior order is Robert Barbour Johnson's "Far Below" (*Weird Tales,* June/July 1939). Little is known of Johnson (b. 1909?), who published a few stories in *Weird Tales* beginning as early as 1936 and continued to publish tales in scattered fan and semi-pro markets up to the later 1960s, after which he disappears. But he deserves to be remembered on the basis of this single story. Dealing with a nebulous monster (or group of monsters) in the New York subways, the tale is a long monologue by Gordon Craig, who had been appointed as head of a secret security operation to guard the unsuspecting inhabitants of the city from these loathsome entities.

The first hint of Lovecraftian influence in "Far Below" comes in Craig's memorable phrase, "the charnel horrors of this mad Nyarlathotep-world far underneath" (16). Lovecraft himself is explicitly mentioned a bit later:

> "And then the modern writers—Lord! There's a whole library of them on the subject. One of them, a great student of the subject, had almost as much data on Them from his reading as I'd gleaned from my years of study down here. Oh, yes; I learned a lot from Lovecaft—and he got a lot from me, too! That's where the—well, what you might call the *authenticity* came from in some of his yarns that attracted the most attention!" (17)

The reference would seem to be to "Pickman's Model," although of course that is set in Boston and makes allusions to the Boston subway system. For the entities that Craig is combating are nothing other than ghouls, and toward the end he gives some idea of what he is up against:

> "And yet the thing interests me, I'll admit; it interests me scientifically, even though it horrifies my very soul, even though it damns me for ever. For it shows how They may have come about—*must* have come about, in fact, in the world's dim dawn; perhaps never quite human, of course, perhaps never Neanderthal or even Piltdown; something even lower, closer linked to the primeval beast, but that when driven underground, into caves and then beneath them by Man's coming, retrograded century by uncounted century down to the worm-haunted darkness—just as we poor devils are retrograding

down here from very contact with them—until at last none of us will
ever be able again to walk above in the blessed sunlit air among our
fellow men—" (21–22)

Those final words suggest the true horror of the tale: after twenty-five
years of close contact with the ghouls, Craig is gradually becoming one
himself. . . .

It is difficult to summarise the extraordinary subtlety of the cumulative horror of "Far Below." Every word, every sentence, every paragraph
contributes to the inexorable but stunning denouement, which reveals
the simultaneous influence of "Pickman's Model," "The Lurking Fear,"
and "The Shadow over Innsmouth." Whether this is properly a "Cthulhu
Mythos" tale may be debatable; but that it most emphatically draws upon
some central tenets of the Lovecraft Mythos—especially the notion of an
entire civilisation (of a sort) dwelling on the underside of human society,
awaiting the proper moment to overwhelm our race in an orgy of cataclysmic horror—can scarcely be denied.

And now we come to the curious case of A. Merritt (1884–1943).
Merritt had, of course, established himself as a major figure in hor-
ror/fantasy fiction some years before Lovecraft, and to the end of his
life Lovecraft retained a fondness for Merritt's powerful novella "The
Moon Pool" (*All-Story*, June 22, 1918), later reworked into the much
inferior novel *The Moon Pool* (1919). That story could be said to have
been a minor influence on "The Call of Cthulhu," as it takes place on
or near the Pacific island of Ponape, in the Carolines, and speaks of a
"moon-door" that, when tilted, leads the characters into a lower region
of wonder and horror—similar, perhaps, to the enormous door that the
sailors of the *Emma* inadvertently open to release Cthulhu.

The question is: Did Merritt return the favour? Did he, in other
words, imitate Lovecraft in his late novel *Dwellers in the Mirage* (1932)?
Will Murray makes a strong case for it.[13] The novel concerns the quest
for Khalk'ru the Kraken, an octopoid creature supposedly cited in
Norse legend. This description, not to mention the very name, brings
Cthulhu to mind. At one point a character states:

"Don't you know what this is? It is the Kraken—that super-wise, malignant, and mythical sea-monster of the old Norsemen. . . . It symbol-
ized the principle that is inimical to Life—not Death precisely, more
accurately annihilation. The Kraken—and here in Mongolia! . . . And

the ancient legend of the South Seas told of the Great Octopus, dozing on and biding his time till he felt like destroying the world and all its life. And three miles up in the air the Black Octopus is cut into the cliffs of the Andes! And the same symbol—here!"[14]

Khalk'ru does not, however, reside under the sea, but rather in another dimension—in this sense resembling the Yog-Sothoth of "The Dunwich Horror." Numerous other details in the novel evoke Lovecraftian conceptions and entities, to such an extent that Murray concludes, "All in all, *Dwellers in the Mirage* is so riddled with uniquely Lovecraftian concepts that it beggars belief to think they weren't drawn directly from H.P.L.'s stories."[15] Lovecraft did read *Dwellers in the Mirage* but made no specific reference to its possible borrowings from his own work; this is, however, not surprising, given Lovecraft's customary humility and the considerable respect with which he regarded Merritt.

It can be seen from the above that, aside from Robert Bloch and Fritz Leiber, several of the younger authors working in the Lovecraftian idiom during and just after Lovecraft's lifetime were wittingly or unwittingly adopting the Derleth Mythos in their purported imitations. With rare exceptions, these stories are inferior works as stories, all apart from their departures from Lovecraft's conceptions or philosophical orientation. August Derleth himself was laying the groundwork for the Derleth Mythos even in Lovecraft's lifetime, and it is to that heroic task of literary misconstrual that we now turn our attention.

VI.

The Derleth Mythos

A UGUST DERLETH (1909–1971) wrote to H. P. Lovecraft in the summer of 1926, after having received Lovecraft's address from Farnsworth Wright of *Weird Tales*. This resulted in an extensive eleven-year correspondence, comprising nearly 400 letters on Lovecraft's side (only about 50 of Derleth's letters to Lovecraft survive). Their recent publication[1] allows us to gain as intimate a glimpse of the literary and personal relations of these two writers as we are likely to get. I have already cited these letters on numerous occasions and will continue to do so, especially in this chapter.

There is no doubt that Derleth had tremendous admiration for Lovecraft, both as a writer and as a person. In their correspondence, however, Derleth chided Lovecraft on his reluctance to submit his work to pulp markets, his sensitivity to rejection (in this sense anticipating L. Sprague de Camp's criticism of Lovecraft's "unprofessional" literary stance), and other perceived "flaws" in his character. Indeed, it becomes evident that, for all the mutual respect that the two figures had for each other, they were nearly antipodal in temperament: Lovecraft the archaic, gentlemanly, diffident, self-consciously "amateur" writer; Derleth the modern, aggressive, overly self-confident professional writer who spread his work far and wide in both pulp and mainstream markets. In several other ways they were far apart, as the correspondence reveals: Derleth was rather slipshod in his writing, preferring quantity production to the meticulous crafting of any single item, as was Lovecraft's wont; he was a strong believer in occultism, telepathy, spiritualism, and other forms of charlatanry whose truth-claims Lovecraft habitually shot down; he was religiously orthodox (a Catholic), whereas Lovecraft was an avowed atheist; and in his taste for weird fiction Derleth tended to prefer relatively conventional ghostly tales to the innovative "cosmic" work of such writers as William Hope Hodgson, Donald Wandrei, and Lovecraft himself. This last trait—which Lovecraft recognised when he dismissively referred to Derleth as a "self-blinded earth-gazer" (*SL* 3.295)—may have had considerable influence on Derleth's misconstruals of the Lovecraft Mythos.

For it is by now evident—as Lovecraft scholarship beginning in the 1970s (for which see Chapter VIII) has overwhemingly established—that Derleth did misinterpret Lovecraft's pseudomythology in an egregious fashion. In hindsight, it becomes astounding how Derleth could have developed so erroneous a view of the Lovecraft Mythos and propounded it for so long; and yet, with few exceptions, nearly every reader, critic, and writer accepted the Derlethian point of view to the extent that subsequent contributors to the Mythos ended up writing unwitting pastiches of Derleth rather than of Lovecraft.

It did not take Derleth long to begin his work. The little-known article "H. P. Lovecraft, Outsider," published in a little magazine called *River* in June, 1937, and clearly written shortly after Lovecraft's death, is a dubious landmark in this regard.[2] The central passage in this article is as follows:

> After a time there became apparent in his tales a curious coherence, a myth-pattern so convincing that after its early appearance, the readers of Lovecraft's stories began to explore libraries and museums for certain imaginary titles of Lovecraft's own creation, so powerful that many another writer, with Lovecraft's permission, availed himself of facets of the mythos for his own use. Bit by bit it grew, and finally its outlines became distinct, and it was given a name: the Cthulhu Mythology: because it was in *The Call of Cthulhu* that the myth-pattern first became apparent. It is possible to trace the original inception of this mythology back through Robert W. Chambers' little-known *The King in Yellow* to Poe's *Narrative of A. Gordon Pym* and Bierce's *An Inhabitant of Carcosa;* but in these stories only the barest hints of something *outside* had appeared, and it was Lovecraft who constructed the myth-pattern in its final form. In his stories then he merged fantasy with terror, and even his poetry took on certain symbols of the mythos, so that presently he was writing: ". . . all my stories, unconnected as they may be, are based on the fundamental lore or legend that this world was inhabited at one time by another race who, in practising black magic, lost their foothold and were expelled, yet live on outside ever ready to take possession of this earth again . . .", a formula remarkable for the fact

that, though it sprang from the mind of a professed religious unbeliever, it is basically similar to the Christian mythos, particularly in regard to the expulsion of Satan from Eden and the power of evil.

This passage has so many errors and fallacies that it is difficult to enumerate them. It may be simplest to break down these errors in a sequence for convenience of discussion:

1. The Mythos had its "inception" in the work of Poe, Chambers, and Bierce.
2. Lovecraft gave the Mythos its name.
3. Lovecraft gave his "permission" to other writers to write Cthulhu Mythos stories.
4. The Mythos is "basically similar" to the Christian mythos.

Let us discuss each of these points in turn.

1. The fact that Lovecraft drew elements—usually innocuous proper names and terms—from earlier writers and incorporated them into his own mythos does not suggest that the Mythos "originated" in the work of these earlier writers. This would suggest that the Mythos was somehow an independent entity or pre-existing myth-pattern that Lovecraft himself, along with these earlier writers, was drawing upon, when of course it was Lovecraft who invented the Mythos and sought to suggest that earlier writers were drawing upon it.

2. This point is related to the above. Derleth's use of the passive voice ("it was given a name") cannot conceal the fact that it was Derleth himself who, in this article, first gave the Mythos its name. Lovecraft, as we have seen, tossed around the terms "Cthulhuism," "Yog-Sothothery," and "the Arkham cycle" in letters, and it is by no means clear what Lovecraft meant by these terms or what stories were included in them. Indeed, as early as 1931 Derleth had written to Lovecraft with the suggestion that the Mythos be called "The Mythology of Hastur," to which Lovecraft replied:

> It's not a bad idea to call this Cthulhuism & Yog-Sothothery of mine "The Mythology of Hastur"—although it was really from Machen & Dunsany & others, rather than through the Bierce-Chambers line, that I picked up my gradually developing hash of theogony—or daimonogony. Come to think of it, I guess I sling this stuff more as Chambers does than as Machen & Dunsany do—though I had written a good deal of it before I ever suspected that Chambers ever wrote a weird story![3]

3. It has already become apparent, in the discussion of Lovecraft's contemporaries, that Lovecraft had very little control over the Mythos "additions" of his fellow writers. He was not telling them what to do, and he gave no one his "permission" (nor denied his permission) to do so. Even his apparent enthusiasm over individual contributions by his colleagues cannot be construed as tantamount to Lovecraft's "welcoming" additions to his myth-cycle, since Lovecraft was temperamentally disinclined to criticise the work of his fellow-authors or to dictate what they could or could not write. Once again, Derleth has apparently misinterpreted a critical passage from one of Lovecraft's letters to him. This passage was written in response to Farnsworth Wright's rejection of "The Horror from the Depths" (then called "The Horror from the Lake") in July 1931, only a few months after the "Hastur" discussion above. Lovecraft, expressing sympathy with Derleth, wrote as follows:

> Of all the Boeotian blundering & irrelevancy! And what pointless censure of the introduction of Cthulhu & Yog-Sothoth—as if their use constituted any "infringement" on my stuff! Hades! The more these synthetic daemons are mutually written up by different authors, the better they become as general background-material! I *like* to have others use my Azathoths & Nyarlathoteps—& in return I shall use Klarkash-Ton's Tsathoggua, your monk Clithanus, & Howard's Bran.[4]

It would seem that Derleth understood this passage as giving him—as well as others—"permission" to "use" Lovecraft's conceptions in their own stories. Certainly, no other passage in a letter to Derleth or to anyone else could ever have led anyone to assume such a thing.

Robert M. Price has come to Derleth's defence on this point, stating that the various "additions" to Lovecraft's Mythos by his contemporaries (and, by implication, later writers) ought to be accepted because "Lovecraft had explicitly blessed such additions as his letters to Kuttner, Derleth and others reveal."[5] Exactly how Lovecraft did so is by no means clear. Price goes on to deride those critics (including myself) who have ridiculed this idea of "blessing" others' additions: "Again a critic may reply, and some have, that Lovecraft was simply being polite. In other words, again, he was just kidding. And how do we know when he was kidding?"[6] "Being polite" is not the same as "kidding"; and we can infer that Lovecraft was being polite by the tone of his letters—as when he tells Henry Kuttner that "some time I'll quote darkly from your *Book of Iod*" (*SL* 5.226) but never did so, and surely never intended to do so.

4. We are now reaching the heart of Derleth's misconstruals. There is no way that anyone could have believed that the Lovecraft Mythos was "basically similar" to the Christian mythos—in other words, that it embodied the battle between "good" and "evil," with the ultimate triumph of the former—except by the interposition of the Elder Gods, which were entirely Derleth's invention and which he introduced as a countervailing force of "good" against the "evil" Old Ones—Cthulhu, Yog-Sothoth, and the rest. Derleth outlines this schema in his widely reprinted essay, "The Cthulhu Mythos" (1969):

> As Lovecraft conceived the deities or forces of his Mythos, there were, initially, the Elder Gods, none of whom save Nodens, Lord of the Great Abyss, is ever identified by name; these Elder Gods were benign deities, representing the forces of good, and existed peacefully at or near Betelgeuze in the constellation Orion, very rarely stirring forth to intervene in the unceasing struggle between the powers of evil and the races of Earth. These powers of evil were variously known as the Great Old Ones or the Ancient Ones, though the latter term is most often applied in the fiction to the manifestation of one of the Great Old Ones on Earth. The Great Old Ones, unlike the Elder Gods, are named, and make frightening appearances in certain of the tales.[7]

Derleth goes on to name the usual gods. In response to those defenders of Derleth who claim that Derleth was within his rights to write "Cthulhu Mythos" stories of his own using his own schema, even if it represented a departure from Lovecraft, it should be made clear that the above passage unequivocally attributes the "Derleth Mythos" to Lovecraft himself. I repeat that there are no Elder Gods in Lovecraft, and I have already mentioned that Derleth appears to have derived them from a misunderstanding of certain passages in "The Strange High House in the Mist" and *The Dream-Quest of Unknown Kadath* (the only two stories that cite Nodens)—stories that Derleth then declared were not "part" of the Cthulhu Mythos! A quick check of an index to Lovecraft's fiction and poetry[8] establishes that Betelgeuze is never mentioned by Lovecraft—but it *is* mentioned by Derleth repeatedly, first in "The Return of Hastur."

Derleth's interpretation of the Mythos was of course strongly bolstered by his citation of the "All my stories . . ." quotation, which he first published in "H. P. Lovecraft, Outsider." With this statement apparently coming right from Lovecraft's mouth, the idea that the "evil" Old Ones were "expelled" from rulership of earth does indeed make the Lovecraft Mythos sound as if it is unwittingly parallel to the Christian mythos. Unfortunately (as I shall explain in Chapter VIII), the quotation is spurious. However, it is not, as was believed for a time, an actual fabrication by Derleth; instead, Derleth found it in a letter to him from Lovecraft's correspondent Harold S. Farnese. Derleth, indeed, believed the quotation to be genuine, so to that extent his misconstrual of the Lovecraft Mythos might be said to be largely the result of a mere misunderstanding of Lovecraft's conceptions rather than a sinister plot to twist those conceptions in a manner more suitable to his conventional imagination.

The passage from "H. P. Lovecraft, Outsider" makes it plain that Derleth well knew of Lovecraft's atheistic stance; to that extent, the spurious quotation was for him quite literally a godsend, for it allowed Derleth (a devout Catholic) to assert that Lovecraft was in fact an *anima naturaliter Christiana* in spite of himself. The passage, of course, is almost antipodally at variance with the celebrated passage in Lovecraft's letter to Farnsworth Wright when resubmitting "The Call of Cthulhu" in July 1927. Let us read that passage again:

> Now all my tales are based on the fundamental premise that common human laws and interests and emotions have no validity or significance in the vast cosmos-at-large. To me there is nothing but puerility in a tale in which the human form—and the local human passions and conditions and standards—are depicted as native to other words or other universes. To achieve the essence of real externality, whether of time or space or dimension, one must forget that such things as organic life, good and evil, love and hate, and all such local attributes of a negligible and temporary race called mankind, have any existence at all. Only the human scenes and characters must have human qualities. These must be handled with unsparing *realism*, (*not* catch-penny *romanticism*) but when we cross the line to the boundless and hideous unknown—the shadow-haunted *Outside*—we must remember to leave our humanity and terrestrialism at the threshold. (*SL* 2.150)

It cannot be asserted that Derleth was unfamiliar with this passage, or that he misquoted it in coming up with the spurious "All my stories . . ." quotation. Another article, "A Master of the Macabre," published in *Reading and Collecting* in August 1937 but begun during Lovecraft's own lifetime,[9] not only cites the spurious "All my stories . . ." quotation but the above quotation as well—but not all of it. Derleth quotes the first sentence, then skips the next two, resuming with "Only the human scenes . . ." In this way, the extreme contradiction between the Derlethian idea of the "power of evil" embodied in the Old Ones and the repudiation of the idea of "good and evil" in fiction-writing as espoused by Lovecraft could be partially concealed.

Some defenders of Derleth have stated that there are rudiments in Lovecraft's own work of the good-vs.-evil idea, or at least the idea of cosmic battles between extraterrestrial forces, that parallel Derleth's Elder Gods-vs.-Old Ones dichotomy. Robert M. Price has written:

> Was Derleth's use of the rubric "Elder Gods" so alien to Lovecraft's in *At the Mountains of Madness?* Perhaps not. In fact, this very story, along with some hints from "The Shadow over Innsmouth," provides the key to the origin of the "Derleth Mythos." For in *At the Mountains of Madness* we find the history of a conflict between two interstellar races (among others): the Elder Ones and the Cthulhu-spawn. . . . So here we have a primordial conflict between a group of "Elder Ones" (so called earlier in the story) and another race, the minions of Cthulhu.[10]

But Price is ignoring the numerous differences between the Derlethian battle of Elder Gods and Old Ones and Lovecraft's depictions of the battles of the Old Ones and the Cthulhu spawn. In particular, Lovecraft places no *moral emphasis* on the battle: it is simply one of numerous struggles between extraterrestrial entities that the earth has witnessed. Neither group is called either "good" or "evil." Even more significantly, the battle does not take place *for the sake of the human race*. Whereas Derleth's Elder Gods are battling specifically for the welfare of humanity, the conflict of Old Ones and Cthulhu spawn in *At the Mountains of Madness* has no relevance to the fate of human beings, who are in any case merely an insignificant and accidental creation of the Old Ones. In "The Shadow over Innsmouth" Lovecraft suggests that this battle is still continuing, but again humanity is almost a bystander as these two groups struggle to gain control of the earth.

One of Derleth's other conceptions in regard to the Old Ones—that they are elementals—should be addressed. In "The Cthulhu Mythos" Derleth, after naming the principal deities in Lovecraft's tales (including "Hastur the Unspeakable, who occupies the air and interstellar spaces, half-brother to Cthulhu"), writes: "Parallels in macabre fiction are immediately apparent, for Nyarlathotep corresponds to an earth-elemental, Cthulhu to a water-elemental, Hastur to an air-elemental, and Shub-Niggurath is the Lovecraftian conception of the god of fertility."[11] In the introduction to *The Dunwich Horror and Others* (1963)—a revision of chapter 3 of *H. P. L.: A Memoir* (1945)—Derleth adds that "I myself added Cthugha, corresponding to the fire elemental Lovecraft failed to provide."[12]

The number of absurdities in these passages is, again, difficult to enumerate. Even putting aside the fact that Hastur is not a Lovecraftian "god" but (as depicted here) entirely an invention of Derleth, the idea that any of the Lovecraftian entities—who are explicitly depicted as extraterrestrial—could correspond to "elements" probably found only on earth would seem inherently preposterous. The idea that Cthulhu is a water elemental has been roundly ridiculed by Dirk W. Mosig and others, who pointed out that Cthulhu was *imprisoned* in his city of R'lyeh when it sunk under the Pacific, making it extremely unlikely that water was his natural element. Many have failed to observe Lovecraft's own comment, in *At the Mountains of Madness*, that "Another race—a *land* [my emphasis] race of beings shaped like octopi and probably corresponding to the fabulous pre-human spawn of Cthulhu—soon began filtering down from cosmic infinity . . ." (*M* 66). How Nyarlathotep is an earth-elemental is similarly mysterious. And if, as Derleth repeatedly maintained, Lovecraft was systematically working on the Cthulhu Mythos for the last decade of his life, how could he have been so foolish as to neglect to invent a fire-elemental, forcing Derleth to come to the rescue with Cthugha?

And yet, even this absurd idea of the Old Ones as elementals has found its defenders. Robert M. Price, ignoring the passage I have just quoted from *At the Mountains of Madness*, claims that "Derleth is more nearly right than Mosig, since after all Cthulhu is described as having the head of an octopus and to be served by the ichthyic Deep Ones!" Price goes on to say that the basic notion [of elementals] appears not to be so utterly foreign to Lovecraft at all. In Lovecraft's stories it is clear that the monstrous elder races *do* symbolize certain geographic areas or particular landscapes which Lovecraft found potently evocative. . . . When he created the crinoid Old Ones in the ice-fields of Antarctica, or the crustacean Outer Ones of the domed Vermont hills, isn't it obvious that these entities were in fact intended as incarnations of the sheer strangeness of nature in these places?[13]

It is, I fear, far from obvious—at least in the sense that Price means. If Price somehow thinks that the Old Ones are a kind of "snow elemental" because they dwelt in Antarctica, he ignores the fact that Antarctica was not a frozen wasteland at the time of their settlement there, and that they had numerous other colonies all around the world. Similarly, the fungi from Yuggoth have established bases all over the world, and the fact that Henry Akeley stumbles upon them in Vermont is purely fortuitous. Most significantly, the notion of elementals is a very precise idea derived from mediaeval philosophy, and cannot be usefully extended in the way Price suggests.

I have laid stress on Derleth's articles on Lovecraft published in the years after Lovecraft's death, but what is remarkable is that Derleth, as a fiction writer, began his mutilation of the Lovecraft Mythos during Lovecraft's lifetime. The chief documents on this point are "The Horror from the Depths," "The Lair of the Star-Spawn" (both of them nominally cowritten with Mark Schorer, but clearly almost entirely the work of Derleth), and "The Return of Hastur."

"The Horror from the Depths," originally titled "The Horror from the Lake," was apparently written in the summer of 1931. Sent to Farnsworth Wright, it was rejected, inspiring Lovecraft's comment that "I *like* to have others use by Azathoths & Nyarlathoteps . . ." Wright rejected the story again in July 1932, and it did not see print until it appeared in *Strange Stories* for October 1940. In this story we learn of a fossil dug up from the depths of Lake Michigan, which ultimately comes to life. This idea itself may have been borrowed from *At the Mountains of Madness*, the typescript of which Lovecraft had completed on May 1 and which Derleth read later that month.[14] It is stated, in relation to the creature in question, that "the beast from the depths was not fundamentally of earth" (234). A passage from the *Necronomicon* is paraphrased, as the protagonist, Professor Jordan Holmes, notes that

> he had stumbled upon the lost and terrible legend of Hastur, the Unspeakable, upon evil as old as, older than the universe, upon those ancient genii of evil—Hastur, Cthulhu, Yog-Sothoth, Lloigor, Zhar, and others. It was then that he had his first vague knowledge of the Elder Gods, the Ancient Ones, and of those others, mad genii of evil who inhabited outer space before the world was born. It was they who descended to ravage Earth and were vanquished by the Elder Gods, and banished to the bottom of the sea. . . .
>
> It was in the *Necronomicon* that these long-dead tales were brought together. From this book, Professor Holmes finally drew a consecutive and logical story of the age-long struggle between the forces of cosmic evil and the Elder Gods—the final defeat of the Evil Ones, and their ultimate banishment into the far corners of the earth. (245)

This passage—if it is identical to what Derleth had written in 1931—is the first encapsulated utterance of the Derleth Mythos. Let me be clear on what my objections to this passage are. It is not Derleth's deviation from Lovecraft's conceptions that is at fault here; it is (as in his articles) Derleth's attribution of *his own* mythic conceptions to Lovecraft, and also the aesthetic and imaginative impoverishment implicit in Derleth's misconstrual of the Lovecraft Mythos. To speak of "cosmic evil" without defining how, exactly, the entities in question are evil (as Derleth never does), aside from their putative harm to the human race, is to set up a kind of cowboys-and-Indians kind of story in which we are axiomatically to root for the "good guys" (human beings and the Elder Gods who presumably defend them) and hate and despise the "bad guys" (Old Ones). I am reminded of an early letter by Lovecraft, in which he whimsically declares:

> Our philosophy is all childishly *subjective*—we imagine that the welfare of our race is the paramount consideration, when as a matter of fact the very existence of the race may be an obstacle to the predestined course of the aggregated universes of infinity! How do we know that that form of atomic and molecular motion called "life" is the highest of all forms? Perhaps the dominant creature—the most rational and God-like of all beings—is an invisible gas! Or perhaps it is a flaming and effulgent mass of molten star-dust. (*SL* 1.24)

Such a conception would, of course, be anathema to the "earth-gazer" Derleth.

Another problem with Derleth's conception of the "evil" Old Ones "imprisoned" by the "good" Elder Gods is exactly how the former can cause any ruckus. Derleth realised this dilemma and came up with what he no doubt thought was an ingenious solution: star-stones. These are the five-pointed stone figures that crop up repeatedly in Derleth's fiction. They appear in "The Horror from the Depths," as the monk Clithanus writes that the Old Ones are "held down by the power of the blessed stars laid out over the water in the form of one great star, the five points marking the directions of the earth and the secret place beyond the earth from which the things of Evil had first come" (240), whatever that is supposed to mean. But, conveniently, these star-stones, lying at the bottom of Lake Michigan and keeping the horrible monster at bay, have been dislodged by an excavation, allowing the creature to wreak havoc until our valiant protagonists find a cache of them and trap the entity once again. Not only that, but the Elder Gods themselves lend a hand: "It was the Elder Gods, sweeping down with the wind from the north, avenging mankind, destroying forever the brood of Cthulhu, the horror from the depths!" (252). Bravo!

Where did Derleth get the idea for these star-stones? Clearly from *At the Mountains of Madness*, but there they are merely objects found among the frozen remains of the Old Ones. The explorer Lake states:

> Have found peculiar soapstone fragment about six inches across and an inch and a half thick, wholly unlike any visible local formation. Greenish, but no evidences to place its period. Has curious smoothness and regularity. Shaped like five-pointed star with tips broken off, and signs of other cleavage at inward angles and in centre of surface. Small, smooth depression in centre of unbroken surface. Arouses much curiosity as to source and weathering. Probably some freak of water action. Carroll, with magnifier, thinks he can make out additional markings of geologic significance. Groups of tiny dots in regular patterns. (19–20)

The objects are mentioned several times throughout the story, but Lovecraft never elucidates their purpose. One thing we can be certain of, however: Lovecraft certainly did not envision them as (in Mosig's memorable words) "ridiculous star-stone amulets which played the role of garlic and the crucifix in the hackneyed vampire tale."[15]

"The Horror from the Depths," as I have mentioned, was rejected by Farnsworth Wright of *Weird Tales*. His letter of rejection survives and is of consuming interest:

> THE HORROR FROM THE LAKE is obviously inspired by Long's story, THE HORROR FROM THE HILLS, and some of the early scenes in your story parallel Long's. This in itself would be sufficient objection to bar the story from Weird Tales. Also, your story does not have the distinction of style which is one of the charms of Long's story.
>
> But a more serious objection to this story is the fact that you have lifted whole phrases from Lovecraft's works, as for instance "the frightful *Necronomicon* of the mad Arab Abdul Alhazred," "the sunken kingdom of R'lyeh," "the accursed spawn of Cthulhu," "the frozen and shunned Plateau of Leng," etc. Also you have taken the legends of Cthulhu and the Ancient Ones directly out of Lovecraft. This is unfair to Lovecraft. Robert Louis Stevenson once said that in the days of his apprenticeship to the writing craft he "had played the sedulous ape" to different authors in turn. But you have not merely aped Lovecraft in this story—you have even lifted his wording. My admiration for Lovecraft's writing amounts almost to idolatry, and I cannot allow such imitation in Weird Tales. It is all right to use the legends as Howard and Smith have used them—a mere allusion to them; but your usage oversteps the bounds of propriety.[16]

There is much truth to this. In particular, Wright was correct in detecting that Derleth was "playing the sedulous ape" to Lovecraft. Derleth, indeed, was an inveterate imitator. By this time he had already begun writing his Solar Pons stories in blatant imitation of Conan Doyle's Sherlock Holmes, and, aside from his numerous Lovecraft pastiches, he would even attempt to mimic Edgar Lee Masters's *Spoon River Anthology* in some of his poetry. One begins to wonder whether Derleth ever had anything of his own to say in fiction. Moreover, Wright is entirely on target in distinguishing this Derleth story from the tales of Smith and Howard that only glancingly allude to Lovecraftian terms and conceptions—what Lovecraft himself, in his letter to Derleth responding to Wright's comments, refers to as "general background-material." Derleth never used the components of the Lovecraft Mythos as "background-material," but as foreground material, and in so doing he not only perverted Lovecraft's conceptions but created the Derleth Mythos.

And yet, Wright belied his promise not to "allow" such blatant imitations of Lovecraft in *Weird Tales*, for he accepted "The Lair of the Star-Spawn" (the title of which was supplied by Lovecraft) and published it in the issue for August 1932. It is in this story that Derleth introduces the Tcho-Tcho people—a "weird race of little people" who live "near or on the Plateau of Sung" (62), apparently in Burma. A Chinese doctor, Fo-Lan, who has become the servant of the Tcho-Tchos tells the explorer Eric Marsh that "long before the time of man, strange beings from the stars—from Rigel, Betelgeuze—the stars in Orion, lived here. And some of them—*live here yet!*" (69). Fo-Lan proceeds to name these beings: "Lloigor and Zhar, ancient evil ones, and their minions await the day when they can once more sweep over the earth to bring death and destruction and incredible age-old evil!" (69). Later the doctor adds that these horrible creatures "are working for the destruction of all that is good in the world" (70), but neglects to specify exactly what this "good" is. It is a bit odd that these "evil" creatures also come from Betelgeuse, which is where Derleth specified his Elder Gods originated; indeed, in this story he refers to these bad entities as "Elder Ones"—

> "the evil followers of Cthulhu, Hastur the Unspeakable, Lloigor and Zhar, the twin Obscenities, and others. The Great Old Ones fought these evil beings for possession of the earth, and after many centuries, they conquered. Hastur was exiled to Hali in the Hyades, Cthulhu was banished to the lost sea kingdom of R'lyeh, while Lloigor and Zhar were buried alive deep in the inner fastnesses of Asia—beneath the accursed Plateau of Sung!" (70)

Here is more confusion, for what Derleth here calls the "Great Old Ones" (the term Lovecraft used in "The Call of Cthulhu" to refer to the spawn of Cthulhu) are now equivalent to the Elder Gods, a term in fact used elsewhere in the story as well (see 70, 79).

Why Farnsworth Wright thought this story any less of a co-opting of Lovecraft's conceptions than "The Horror from the Depths" is not apparent; but he did draw the line when Derleth submitted "The Return of Hastur." This story was apparently conceived as early as February 1932,[17] but Derleth seemed to make no headway on it until January 1933, when he announces to Lovecraft:

I am finally at work on THE RETURN OF HASTUR. In connexion

with this ms., I am using this line from THE CALL OF CTHULHU—
"Ph'nglui mglw'nafh Cthulhu R'lyeh wgah'nagl fhtagn"—though my
line reads "Ph'nglui mglw'nafh Hastur Be'elgs wgah'nagl fhtagn"—or,
rather in line with your translation of the cult line, In his house at
Be'elgs (Betelgeuse) banished Hastur waits dream—later I want to bring
in your line for comparison to clinch a point in the narrative. I may also
quote from THE CALL, THE WHISPERER IN DARKNESS, and
perhaps even from THE SHADOW OVER INNSMOUTH—with due
indication of origin, of course.[18]

There is much of interest here, and I shall address it presently. Derleth
apparently put off writing or finishing the story until just after Lovecraft's death, and it was published in *Weird Tales* for March 1939. Evidently Farnsworth Wright felt that, with Lovecraft's death, there was
not likely to be any additional Cthulhu Mythos stories from his pen (although Wright had twice rejected "The Shadow over Innsmouth" during Lovecraft's lifetime), so that he might as well publish this purported
imitation in an attempt to satisfy those many fans who were still thirst-
ing for Lovecraft material.

"The Return of Hastur"—at least in its published form—is about
as exhaustive an exposition of the Derleth Mythos as anyone could
want. It is set in Arkham, has the now customary citation of "forbidden" books (including Derleth's own contribution, the *R'lyeh Text*), and
includes a "brief outline of the mythology," in which it is stated that
there are beings "of two natures, and two only: the Old or Ancient
Ones, the Elder Gods, of *cosmic good,* and those of *cosmic evil,* bearing
many names, and themselves of different groups, as if associated with
the elements and yet transcending them" (11)—whereupon the usual
array of evil gods, now arranged as elementals, are cited. We now find,
however, that "among the Evil Ones there is apparently often conflict,
as among lesser beings. The Water Beings oppose those of Air; the Fire
Beings oppose Earth Beings, but nevertheless, they together hate and
fear the Elder Gods and hope always to defeat them in some future
time" (11–12).

It is here, of course, that Hastur—which, let us recall, was not specified as an entity in Lovecraft—is deemed the "half-brother of Cthulhu"
(26). How this could be is never explained by Derleth. Who was the
common father (or mother) of these two baleful entities? Perhaps Der-

leth did not at this time have access to the genealogical chart of the Old Ones that Lovecraft had drawn up in a letter to James F. Morton, in which it is plainly indicated that Cthulhu is the offspring of Nug (*SL* 4.183)—no mother indicated, assuming for the sake of argument that Nug is male. Possibly Derleth is adapting the *Necronomicon* passage in "The Dunwich Horror" where Alhazred says that Cthulhu is the "cousin" of the Old Ones (*DH* 170). In any case, the whole of "The Return of Hastur" is devoted to a valiant human being's ultimately successful efforts to prevent Hastur's return. The entire story is concerned with this matter; there is no broader symbolism or message implicit in the tale. Even as a weird tale it is unimaginative, unbelievable, and shallow; as a purported contribution to literature it is a nonentity.

Let us return to Derleth's discussion of the story in his 1933 letter to Lovecraft. He does in fact quote the "Ph'nglui" line from "The Call of Cthulhu" in the story, and indeed mentions the story and Lovecraft by name (15); but he mercifully does not cite the altered line about Hastur and "Be'elgs." Lovecraft had told Derleth that Betelgeuse was merely an Arabic name for the star in question, so that it would be unlikely that an extraterrestrial language would come up with a similar name for that star. Derleth instead merely has a character say, "And Cthulhu and Hastur struggle here for the haven while Great Orion strides above the horizon, with Betelgeuse where the Elder Gods are, who alone can block the evil designs of these hellish spawn!" (27)—although it is by no means clear how this person has come by this information.

The completion of "The Return of Hastur" in April 1937 incited an intensely interesting correspondence exchange between Derleth and Clark Ashton Smith, to whom Derleth had sent the story.[19] If Derleth was assuming that Smith would praise him for his signal contribution to the Cthulhu Mythos, he was destined to be rudely awakened. Derleth's letter of April 10, 1937 initiates the exchange, as he asks Smith to "put down for me all you know of the Cthulhu mythology, particularly in regard to your own contributions." In this letter Derleth already outlines his theory of the Mythos gods (whom he calls "the Evil Ones") as elementals: "[Robert] Bloch divides them as water-beings, lurkers beyond Time, survivals on earth; which seems to me pretty good, but I myself have always considered them as divided elementally; Beings of water (Cthulhu), air (Azathoth), etc. I can see where that would be erroneous in view of the fact that Azathoth, Hastur, etc. 'stalk the star-spaces,' etc." This passage should put to rest the frequent conjecture that it was Francis T. Laney (in "The Cthulhu Mythology: A Glossary" [1942]) who originated the idea of the Old Ones as elementals and that Derleth borrowed the concept from him. Curiously, however, Derleth never cites Azathoth as an "air elemental" in any of his published writings.

Smith immediately challenged this entire line of reasoning in a letter of April 13, 1937:

> As to classifying the Old Ones, I suppose that Cthulhu can be classed both as a survival on earth and a water-dweller; and Tsathoggua is a subterranean survival. Azathoth, referred to somewhere as "the primal nuclear chaos", is the ancestor of the whole crew but still dwells in outer and ultra-dimensional space, together with Yog-Sothoth, and the demon piper Nyarlathotep, who attends the throne of Azathoth. I shouldn't class any of the Old Ones as *evil:* they are plainly beyond all limitary human conceptions of either ill or good.

But these words of sanity were entirely ignored by Derleth, who was convinced that he and he alone had the goods on the Mythos.

In a non-extant letter dating to mid-April 1937, Derleth must have outlined his broader view of the Mythos as parallel to the Christian mythos, for it elicited a reply by Smith in a letter of April 21:

> A deduction relating the Cthulhu mythos to the Christian mythos would indeed be interesting; and of course the *unconscious* element in such creation is really the all-important one. However, there seems to be no reference to *expulsion* of Cthulhu and his companions in "The Call". According to the testimony given by the cult-member, De Castro [*sic*], Cthulhu and the other Old Ones "died" or were thrown into a state of suspended animation "when the stars were wrong." When the stars were "right," some outside force would serve to liberate and resurrect them. This would seem to indicate the action of cosmic laws rather than a battle between good and evil deities. However, the passage that you quote from the letter to Farnese would seem to give the problem another complexion. However, if the "expulsion" was accomplished by animate agencies or gods, it is strange that they are not referred to in the stories.

This, in a nutshell, is Smith's exposure of the "Derleth Mythos." It shows that Derleth had already, by this time, come upon Farnese's spurious "All my stories . . ." quotation and was using it to buttress his own misconception of the Lovecraft Mythos.

It was at this point that Derleth, in white-hot haste, entirely rewrote "The Return of Hastur" from its incomplete draft of 1933; but he was irked that Farnsworth Wright promptly rejected it, so he sent it on to Smith to read. Smith's reaction, recorded in a letter of April 28, 1937, is highly illuminating. Although praising the story somewhat formulaically ("it is a remarkable production"), Smith goes on to remark that "I do not find the tale very satisfactory." He elaborates his concerns:

> One reaction, confirmed rather than diminished by the second read-
> ing, is that you have tried to work in too much of the Lovecraft my-
> thology and have not assimilated it into the natural body of the story.
> For my taste, the tale would gain in unity and power if the interest
> were centered wholly about the mysterious and "unspeakable" Hastur.
> Cthulhu and the sea-things of Innsmouth, though designed to afford
> an element and interest *of conflict*, impress me rather as a source of con-
> fusion. I believe a tremendous effect of vague menacing atmosphere
> and eerily growing tension could be developed around Hastur, who
> has the advantage of being a virtually unknown demon.

Although Derleth, in his reply of May 3, 1937, makes the routine remark, "Yes, I think all the points you make in re The Return of Hastur
are very well taken indeed," it is clear that Derleth never bothered to
revise the tale, nor took any notice of Smith's criticisms of Derleth's
preposterous kitchen-sink approach to the Mythos, whereby in story
after story an entire litany of Mythos beings and terms is dumped into
the narrative, serving only to bolster Derleth's increasingly erroneous
view of Lovecraft's conceptions.

Derleth's other Cthulhu Mythos stories aren't much better than
"The Return of Hastur." Indeed, not a single one of them can qualify
as a success, on purely literary terms. "Spawn of the Maelstrom" (*Weird
Tales*, September 1939; nominally cowritten with Schorer) takes us to an
island off Norway, where a shape-shifting creature—"a thing of cosmic
evil in the shape of a man" (29)—dwells. But the star-stones come to
the rescue again. This also happens in "Something from Out There"
(*Weird Tales*, January 1951), where it is stated that the star-stones give
off "a kind of benign strength" (586); indeed, one such stone actually
has an inscription by the pious St. Augustine!

Two early stories, "The Thing That Walked on the Wind" (*Weird Tales*, January 1933) and "Ithaqua" (*Strange Stories*, February 1941), exhaustively treat the elemental idea. In the former, the entity Ithaqua is explicitly called an "air elemental" (98)—and, later, "the wind-walking elemental" (99). Both these stories are virtual ripoffs of Algernon Blackwood's "The Wendigo," as Derleth has borrowed many features from this tale, ranging from the setting in the wilds of Canada to the use of footprints to indicate the presence of a gigantic entity (Lovecraft himself borrowed this feature from Blackwood in "The Dunwich Horror"). Both Blackwood and Lovecraft are mentioned by name in the story (101–2). It is never clarified exactly how (or whether) Ithaqua is related to the Old Ones, or how he manages to roam free while the other evil entities are "imprisoned" by the Elder Gods.

"Ithaqua" was the story that Derleth was writing in the 1930s under the title "The Snow-Thing." He explicitly states that it is "patterned closely after THE THING THAT WALKED ON THE WIND, though it is not quite as good, being a little less definite."[20] He apparently did not finish the story before Lovecraft's death. In this tale Ithaqua is now referred to as "the Snow-Thing" (105) and as "a strange god of the great white silence" (105). This is probably a borrowing from Blackwood's "The Glamour of the Snow," which features an entity that could plausibly be called a snow-elemental. It now appears that Hastur controls "the spirits of the elements and subdue[s] them to his will" (112), so evidently these elementals (or at least Ithaqua and others like him) are subordinate to the Old Ones. But how can this be, if the Old Ones themselves are elementals? Well, no matter. The protagonist of this story attempts to convince a colleague of the truth of all this gibberish by stating, "After all, have we not our own Biblical legend of the struggle between elemental Good and Evil as personified by our deity and the forces of Satan in the pre-dawn era of our earth?" (112). Quite so.

Derleth included eleven of his Mythos stories in *The Mask of Cthulhu* (1958) and *The Trail of Cthulhu* (1962), although two of them had appeared in his first horror collection, *Someone in the Dark* (1941). It would be too painful to treat these stories in detail, but we can touch upon a few low points. In "The Whippoorwills in the Hills" (*Weird Tales*, September 1948) whippoorwills are seen as harbingers of death— a transparent ripoff of "The Dunwich Horror," which unsurprisingly remained Derleth's favourite Lovecraft story. In this tale he further borrows from that story in an attempt at backwoods New England dialect. "The House in the Valley" (*Weird Tales*, July 1953) is a tissue of ripoffs of "The Dunwich Horror," "The Call of Cthulhu," and "The Shadow over Innsmouth." "Something in Wood" (*Weird Tales*, March 1948) has the novelty of featuring Clark Ashton Smith as a quasi-character. "The Sandwin Compact" (*Weird Tales*, November 1940) borrows heavily from "The Shadow over Innsmouth."

The Trail of Cthulhu is a purportedly linked series of five tales—although they were published over an eight-year period, 1944–52—in which the valiant Dr. Laban Shrewsbury continually battles the Old Ones on behalf of the Elder Gods and humanity; in the final tale, "The Black Island" (*Weird Tales*, January 1952), nuclear weapons are used against Cthulhu. Shrewsbury, it transpires, is the author of a learned treatise, *An Investigation into the Myth-Patterns of Latterday Primitives With Especial Reference to the R'lyeh Text* (4). In "The House on Curwen Street" (*Weird Tales*, March 1944) Shrewsbury disappears for three years—then suddenly returns. During his absence he actually ventured (somehow) to the star Celaeno, "in that great library of ancient monolithic stones with their books and hieroglyphs stolen from the Elder Gods" (43). His purpose becomes clear:

> . . . Dr. Shrewsbury had set himself upon the trail of great Cthulhu, intent upon closing all avenues to the Outside. . . . And he had learned how to utilize the strange creatures from other, alien dimensions out of time and space, in his pursuit of Cthulhu, intent upon saving the world he knew from enslavement to a ghastly era of aeon-old evil completely beyond the comprehension of mankind! (45)

Hear, hear! Bully for you! It is not entirely clear why Shrewsbury's efforts are even necessary, given that Cthulhu is presumably "imprisoned" under water by the Elder Gods; but it appears that the minions of the Old Ones have a nasty way of escaping the Elder Gods' star-stones and other such protections. In "The Watcher from the Sky" (*Weird Tales*, July 1945) this hypothesis is actually put forth: ". . . the Great Old Ones . . . have their minions, their secret followers among men and beasts, whose task it is to prepare the way for their second coming, for it is their evil intention to come again and rule the universe as once they did after their breaking away and escape from the domain of the Ancient Ones" (68). This story is nothing but a retelling of "The Shadow over Innsmouth," just as "The Gorge Beyond Salapunco" (*Weird Tales*, March 1949) is a retelling of "The Call of Cthulhu."

Probably the greatest of Derleth's derelictions (pardon the pun) is his writing of sixteen "posthumous collaborations" with Lovecraft. It is of significance that only two of these sixteen (which includes the unfinished novel *The Watchers out of Time*) appeared in magazines prior to their collection into books: Derleth clearly had difficulty selling these inferior works, so that he was forced to publish them himself. Four appeared in Derleth's own anthologies published by Arkham House, while others appeared in two collections—*The Survivor and Others* (1957) and *The Shadow out of Time and Other Tales of Horror* (Gollancz, 1968)— before being gathered in *The Watchers out of Time and Others* (1974).

A charitable interpretation might assert that Derleth was attempting to keep Lovecraft's name before the public during a period—the 1950s and early 1960s—when his own tales had in some cases fallen out of print: Derleth was, after all, careful to place Lovecraft's name before his own. But the deceitfulness of the practice is all too patent, for of course these mediocre tales had the unintended effect of dragging Lovecraft's reputation down several notches in the estimation of those who admired Lovecraft's own work. I distinctly remember, as a teenager, striving to find more work by Lovecraft and coming upon the Ballantine paperback edition of *The Shuttered Room and Other Tales of Terror* (1971), but being severely disappointed at the inferior quality of the tales. Lovecraft must have written these on a bad day!

But of course, Lovecraft wrote none of them; even in the two or three in which Derleth admitted that he had used extensive plot notes left behind by Lovecraft, the execution and development of the tales was entirely Derleth's, and the end result was probably very far from what Lovecraft intended. Chief among these departures is the fact that nearly every one of the tales is a "Cthulhu Mythos" story. Derleth actually claimed that "The unfinished novel, *The Lurker at the Threshold*, which I completed and saw published in 1945, is also part of the Mythos."[21] But of course Lovecraft left behind no "unfinished novel"; as Derleth had already acknowledged, *The Lurker at the Threshold* (1945), a novel of some 50,000 words, was based on two very small fragments by

Lovecraft, amounting to no more than 1200 words, and it is very unlikely that Lovecraft regarded these as fitting into a single work, although Derleth stated that "they appealed to me as manifestly related and as possible to connect." He went on to say that "out of them I constructed and wrote *The Lurker at the Threshold,* which had nowhere been laid out, planned, or plotted by Lovecraft, but was evoked from his fragments and notes."[22]

Derleth reproduces the notes—found on a newspaper clipping—that he wrote up as "The Survivor." They mostly relate to the life-dates of the protagonist, Jean-François Charrière. Otherwise, Derleth based his claim of Lovecraftian "collaboration" on the fact that he devised the stories based on plot-germs (if they can be called that) in Lovecraft's commonplace book. When he printed the commonplace book in *The Shuttered Room and Other Pieces* (1959) he conveniently identified the items that were the basis of the "posthumous collaborations" written up to that time. We can add to that tabulation to arrive at a full exhibition of the Lovecraftian content of the other fourteen works (excluding *The Lurker at the Threshold* and "The Survivor," already discussed). I derive the text of the commonplace book from my corrected edition in *Miscellaneous Writings.*

"Wentworth's Day" (1957): Entry 8: "Hor. Sto.: Man makes appt. with old enemy. Dies—body keeps appt."

"The Peabody Heritage" (1957): Entry 142: "Members of witch-cult were buried face downward. Man investigates ancestor in family tomb and finds disquieting condition."

"The Gable Window" (1957): Entry 195: "Pane of peculiar-looking glass from a ruined monastery reputed to have harboured devil-worship set up in modern house at edge of wild country. Landscape looks vaguely and unplaceably *wrong* through it. It has some unknown time-distorting quality, and comes from a primal, lost civilisation. Finally, hideous things in other world seen through it."

"The Ancestor" (1957): Derived from "A List of Certain Basic Underlying Horrors Effectively Used in Weird Fiction": "Man tries to recapture *all* of his past, aided by drugs and music acting on memory. Extends process to *hereditary* memory—even to pre-human days. These ancestral memories figure in dreams. Plans stupendous recovery of primal past—but becomes sub-human, develops a hideous primal odour, takes to the woods, and is killed by own dog" (*CE* 2.173).

"The Shadow out of Space" (1957): Entry 157: "Vague lights, geometrical figures, &c., seen on retina when eyes are closed. Caus'd by rays from *other dimensions* acting on optick nerve? From *other planets?* Connected with a life or phase of being in which person could live if he only knew how to get there? *Man afraid to shut eyes*—he has been somewhere on a terrible pilgrimage and this fearsome seeing faculty remains."

"The Lamp of Alhazred" (1957): Entry 146: "Ancient lamp found in tomb—when filled and used, its light reveals strange world."

"The Shuttered Room" (1959): Entry 162: "Ultimate horror—grandfather returns from strange trip—mystery in house—wind and darkness—grandf. and mother engulfed—questions forbidden—somnolence—investigation—cataclysms—screams overheard—"

"The Fisherman of Falcon Point" (1959): Entry 60: "Fisherman casts his net into the sea by moonlight—what he finds."

"Witches' Hollow" (1962): Entry 130: "N. E. region call'd 'Witches' Hollow'—along course of a river. Rumours of witches' sabbaths and Indian powwows on a broad mound rising out of the level where some old hemlocks and beeches formed a dark grove or daemon-temple. Legends hard to account for. Holmes—*Guardian Angel.*" Also entry 134: "Witches' Hollow novel? Man hired as teacher in private school misses road on first trip—encounters dark hollow with unnaturally swollen trees and small cottage (light in window?). Reaches school and hears that boys are forbidden to visit hollow. One boy is strange—teacher sees him visit hollow—odd doings—mysterious disappearance or hideous fate."

"The Shadow in the Attic" (1964): Unknown; possibly entry 117: "A secret living thing kept and fed in an old house."

"The Dark Brotherhood" (1966): Possibly entry 212: "Strange human being (or beings) living in some ancient house or ruins far from populous district (either old N. E. or far exotic land). Suspicion (based on shape and habits) that it is not *all* human."

"The Horror from the Middle Span" (1967): Entry 217: "Ancient (Roman? prehistoric?) stone bridge washed away by a (sudden and curious?) storm. *Something* liberated which had been sealed up in the masonry thousands of years ago. Things happen."

"Innsmouth Clay" (1971): Entry 216: "Man idly shapes a queer image—some power impels him to make it queerer than he understands. Throws it away in disgust—but something is abroad in the night."

The Watchers out of Time (written 1971, published 1974): Based on a Lovecraft fragment published under the title "The Rose Window" (*CE* 5.253–54).

It can be seen from this that *none* of the plot-germs (most of which are really more like random images to be incorporated into a weird tale) has anything to do with the Lovecraft Mythos, much less the Cthulhu Mythos. Indeed, probably only a single entry in the commonplace book *does* have any relation to his Mythos—entry 61: "A terrible pilgrimage to seek the nighted throne of the far daemon-sultan *Azathoth*" (*MW* 90). (Lovecraft probably used this idea as the basis of *The Dream-Quest of Unknown Kadath,* substituting Nyarlathotep for Azathoth.) And yet, nearly every one of the "posthumous collaborations" is explicitly a Mythos tale.

Even the most substantial of them, *The Lurker at the Threshold,* is seriously flawed. This short novel is really a novelette idea stretched and padded well beyond its proper bounds. It is, by necessity, set in New England because the two fragments Derleth used are clearly relate to bizarre happenings in early New England times. The first of its three lengthy sections is effective, but it quickly gets bogged down in verbosity and over-explanation. We are here concerned with one Ambrose Dewart, who is attempting to find out information about his great-great-grandfather, Abijah Billington, and his ancestors. He calls in his cousin, Stephen Bates, "an authority on early Massachusetts history" (52), to assist him. As in nearly all Derleth's other Mythos tales, we have tedious catalogues of Mythos gods and entities, as if the mere recitation of their names could evoke horror. It turns out that Ambrose, apparently under the spell of the Old Ones, has resurrected an Indian guide, Quamis (presumably identical to the "Misquamacus" in one of the Lovecraft fragments). At this point, Bates goes to Dr. Seneca Lapham, who acts as a Laban Shrewsbury figure (Shrewsbury is actually mentioned in passing [138]) and puts the monsters to rout. We once again have a long account of the Elder Gods' battles against the Old Ones, narrated in a manner that Lovecraft condemned as a "schoolroom effect" (*SL* 4.175–76)—a comment he made when reading E.

Hoffmann Price's original sequel to "The Silver Key." But the worst flaw in *The Lurker at the Threshold* is its preposterously anticlimatic denouement: the world is saved merely by the shooting of Dewart and Quamis and the restoration of the "Elder Sign." It is almost as an afterthought that we learn that the titular "lurker at the threshold" is Yog-Sothoth. The conclusion of the story, in which Quamis shouts out the name of Yog-Sothoth, is another ripoff of "The Dunwich Horror."

The curious thing about the other "posthumous collaborations" is that many of them, even though presented as Cthulhu Mythos tales, involve ghosts, revenants, and other relatively conventional supernatural manifestations. "The Survivor" is nothing but a story about abnormal longevity, and the Mythos paraphernalia that gets dragged in is entirely adventitious. "The Shadow in the Attic" is a routine ghost story, while "The Horror from the Middle Span" largely concerns reanimation of the dead.

What is particularly galling about many of these tales is the shameless way in which they steal elements—or entire plots—from some of Lovecraft's greatest stories. I have indicated that this is a persistent failing of many "additions" to Lovecraft's pseudomythology: in reality, such tales are not so much "additions" as merely variations or near-plagiarisms of Lovecraft's own core plots and themes, with no significant elaborations or developments of the idea. Consider "Wentworth's Day." It begins: "North of Dunwich lies an all but abandoned country, one which has returned in large part . . . to a state perilously close to the wild" (168). This is already close to a steal of the opening sentence of "The Dunwich Horror"; but we soon find that "There are areas of woodland in which no axe has ever fallen" (168)—a clear borrowing of the opening sentence of "The Colour out of Space." When a backwoods character croaks, "Storm ketched ye, eh?" (171), we are clearly reminded of the first statement of the preternaturally aged figure in "The Picture in the House": "Ketched in the rain, be ye?" (120). The use of whippoorwills, not to mention the character Clem Whateley, clearly echoes "The Dunwich Horror." Derleth is clearly conscious of these borrowings, and in fact expects his readers to understand them also: in this way he attempts to borrow the horrific atmosphere of the Lovecraft tales and graft them on to his own, without having to do the hard work of actually creating an atmosphere by actual manipulation of prose.

The pilfering continues in other tales. "The Peabody Heritage" features a curiously angled room, a Black Man, skulls and bones of children, a black cat as a familiar, and other elements that clearly borrow from "The Dreams in the Witch House"—but without its cosmic (and Mythos) elements. "The Shadow out of Space" is a clumsy ripoff of "The Shadow out of Time," and Derleth makes awkward attempts to engraft the Great Race into his conventional division between Elder Gods and Old Ones. The Great Race may themselves be "gods" (246). "The Dark Brotherhood" also borrows heavily from "The Shadow out of Time," and in this case attempts to portray the members of the Great Race as "evil" because they wish to take over the world—although apparently they will do so not through mind-transference but by "reproducing themselves in the shape of men!" (350). "The Fisherman of Falcon Point" and "Innsmouth Clay" borrow from "The Shadow over Innsmouth" but add nothing to its central ideas. The latter story is of interest in that it presents a condensed version of Zadok Allen's lengthy speech about the Deep Ones, here entrusted to one Seth Akins. When reading "The Shadow over Innsmouth" in typescript, Derleth himself had suggested that Lovecraft shorten the speech, to which Lovecraft had replied: "Zadok's story could probably be made shorter by a better writer, but not by me—since I arrived at the existing form only after long & repeated experimentation."[23] Derleth later suggested that he himself be allowed to revise the story for Lovecraft! Lovecraft tactfully declined, but decades later Derleth got his chance to write "The Shadow over Innsmouth" the way he apparently thought it should have been written. Whether anyone will think "Innsmouth Clay" a better story than Lovecraft's is an open question.

At this point I imagine it is well known that "The Ancestor" is an unintentional plagiarism of Leonard Cline's *The Dark Chamber* (1927). One would have thought that Derleth could have figured this out on his own, since by his own admission he had taken the plot-germ from "A List of Certain Basic Underlying Horrors *Effectively Used* [my emphasis] in Weird Fiction"; but in his haste he apparently thought the plot-germ was one of Lovecraft's own.

If there is any story among the "posthumous collaborations" that actually amounts to anything, it is "The Lamp of Alhazred." Let it pass that the basic plot had already been used (as Derleth well knew) in the poem "The Lamp" in *Fungi from Yuggoth*. Let it also pass that this story of New England renders a well-known locale in the Providence area, Neutaconkanut Hill, as Nentaconhaunt (249). (The matter is further confounded by the fact that local residents pronounce the name *Neutaconakut*.) Derleth has used one of Lovecraft's late letters, telling of his lengthy jaunt into this unspoiled rural enclave, as the basis of a touching story in which Lovecraft himself is clearly the central character; and at its conclusion he paints a portrait of Lovecraft, dying of cancer, recapturing his past that is genuinely moving: "The sunlight burst suddenly all about him. He felt shorn of his shackles, and he began to run lithely along the shore of the Seekonk to where, ahead of him, the scenes of his childhood waited and he could renew himself, beginning again, living once more the halcyon time when all the world was young . . ." (256). Even this is a borrowing from "The Silver Key," but it remains effective nonetheless. If nothing else, the story testifies to the deep bonds of friendship that Lovecraft and Derleth had created purely through correspondence, and the profound sorrow that Derleth felt when he heard of Lovecraft's unexpected passing.

"The Dweller in Darkness" (*Weird Tales*, November 1944) is perhaps Derleth's one relatively successful Mythos tale, in spite of the fact that the opening sentence once again rips off "The Dunwich Horror" ("Until recently, if a traveler in north central Wisconsin took the left fork at the junction of the Brule River highway and the Chequamegon pike on the way to Pashepaho, he would find himself in country so primitive that it would seem remote from all human contact" [116–17]) and the fact that the tale as a whole is heavily dependent on "The Whisperer in Darkness." Part of the reason for the story's success is its setting in Wisconsin, a terrain Derleth knew intimately by lifelong residence. His many other Mythos tales set in New England—a region he had visited only a few times—suffer from errors large and small in points of history and topography, as when, in "The Survivor," he envisions a seventeenth-century Quebec-style house existing on Benefit Street (149), when in fact there are no houses on Benefit Street dating earlier than 1750 and all are in the New England colonial style. But "The Dweller in Darkness" evokes rural Wisconsin vividly. Derleth, admittedly, drags in the usual paraphernalia of Mythos gods and properties, including the Elder Gods and the Old Ones as elementals; but the tale manages to develop an effective atmosphere of cumulative horror, as the dweller in darkness (Nyarlathotep) first appears as a "gigantic protoplasmic mass, a colossal being who towered upward toward the stars" (142), and then reshapes himself as Professor Upton Gardner.

An earlier story, "Beyond the Threshold" (*Weird Tales*, September 1941), is also set in Wisconsin, but is a less effective tale of Ithaqua.

It becomes evident that Derleth, in his Cthulhu Mythos writing, has entirely failed to grasp the "demythologising" of the Lovecraft Mythos that occurred in *At the Mountains of Madness* and "The Shadow out of Time," which is why elements from these stories rarely appear in Derleth's own, except in a curiously botched fashion. He was clearly intent on preserving the Old Ones as "gods," and particularly as "evil" gods, so that they could be a suitable counterweight to the "good" Elder Gods. Let me once again reiterate that Derleth, in his own fiction, was entirely at liberty to refashion the Lovecraft Mythos in any manner he saw fit; I simply assert that this refashioning was, from a purely aesthetic perspective, quite unsuccessful and resulted in stories that, even as contributions to weird literature, are weak and insubstantial. Furthermore, they are merely stories: they broach no broader concerns about human life and the cosmos, and there is no depth or substance in them that can be probed beyond their surface events. In many cases, they do not even constitute legitimate (or illegitimate) "additions" to the Lovecraft Mythos, but merely crude and clumsy retellings of Lovecraft's own stories.

Nevertheless, Derleth was within his rights to pen as many Cthulhu Mythos tales as he wished. But he was *not* within his rights to foist his interpretation of the Mythos on to Lovecraft, as he did repeatedly in article after article, and he was not within his rights to claim that his "posthumous collaborations" were anything but stories entirely conceived and written on his own and which widely departed from what Lovecraft himself would have done had he written them. For these and other failings, Derleth has been rightly condemned, and no attempts by some of his posthumous defenders to salvage his reputation can amount to anything but special pleading.

VII.

Interregnum

ERLETH WAS NOT THE ONLY WRITER generating Cthulhu My-thos tales in the years following Lovecraft's death; as we have seen, Robert Bloch and Fritz Leiber were doing their part, and tales vaguely related to Lovecraft's conceptions were being written by Manly Wade Wellman, Robert A. W. Lowndes (a late correspondent of Love-craft), and others, some of them appearing in the first Lovecraft-related fanzine, the *Acolyte* (1942–46). Most of these tales amount to little, and the more substantial ones continued to appear in *Weird Tales*.

Two of the most interesting stories were produced by the other-wise unknown writer C. Hall Thompson (1923–1991). Thompson pub-lished four stories in *Weird Tales* in the period 1946–48, two of which, "Spawn of the Green Abyss" (November 1946) and "The Will of Claude Asher" (July 1947), are clearly influenced by Lovecraft. Both are substantial works, especially the first.

"Spawn of the Green Abyss" is set in the town of Kalesmouth, in northern New Jersey, where the recluse Lazarus Heath lives in a house called Heath House. We are immediately triggered to a Lovecraft influe-nce when we learn that, according to one of his servants, Lazarus "got a funny smell about him . . . a dead smell, like dead fish washed up on the beach" (220). The bulk of the tale concerns Lazarus's daughter, Cassan-dra. She has summoned a physician, James Arkwright, to tend to her fa-ther, who seems gravely ill and at one point cries incoherently about some entity named "Zoth Syra" and "The Great Ones of The Green Abyss" (224). Lazarus dies, and Arkwright gradually falls in love with Cassandra. They marry and take up residence in Heath House. But Cas-sandra herself falls gravely ill, and upon examination Arkwright is horri-fied to see that she seems to be developing gills. At one point she cries out, "I come, O, Yoth Kala! Your bride has heard your call!" (235).

203

Cassandra is pregnant, but she later announces that the child is not Arkwright's: she is the bride of Yoth Kala, her "husband of the Green Void" (240). She then tells the story of her father, who in the 1920s had been shipwrecked on an island covered with green slime. Going underwater (he can apparently breathe with gills), he encounters an undersea city whose architecture was "all wrong" (248). This nod to "The Call of Cthulhu" is, in fact, the first *explicit* allusion to a Lovecraft tale, although it is fairly obvious that the earlier parts of the narrative were inspired by "The Shadow over Innsmouth." In any case, Lazarus encounters Zoth Syra, Empress of the Abyss, and she bears his child—Cassandra. As Cassandra is telling this story, the monstrous entity Yoth Kala comes to reclaim his bride:

> I cannot say the Thing in the cove walked; it moved inland rapidly, but with a seemingly gradual, amoebic motion. It expanded and ebbed, gelatinous tendrils creeping over the sand of the cove, spreading like a stain of ink, or black, poisonous blood. I saw no distinct form. I was conscious only of a monstrous, jelly-like mound, black and glistening with a slime-coated, nauseous putrescence. The Thing slobbered onward to Heath House, covering ground with frightening speed. And from this hellish creature, through the whiplash of the storm, shrilled the high, hypnotic voice of Yoth Kala, calling his bride. (252)

Later references to "slimy tentacles," "foul ichor," and "a tarry stickiness" (253)—that last two descriptives a direct echo of the demise of Wilbur Whateley in "The Dunwich Horror" ("The thing that lay half-bent on its side in a foetid pool of greenish-yellow ichor and tarry stickiness . . ." [DH 174])—make the Lovecraft influence pretty clear. When Yoth Kala approaches, Cassandra urges Arkwright to kill her: what if her child is like its father? Arkwright does so, and the monster withdraws.

"Spawn of the Green Abyss" is a more than respectable tale. Its true "addition" to the Lovecraft Mythos is not its invention of various monstrous creatures but, much more significantly, the fusion of Lovecraft's cosmic horror with the intimate domestic drama of the love affair between Cassandra Heath and James Arkwright. This is handled with genuine sensitivity and skill, and we feel profound emotion at the tragic denouement.

"The Will of Claude Asher" is a lesser tale, both as a story and as a pastiche of Lovecraft. The "will" in question refers not to a legal document but to the force of character of its central figure, a resident of Innswich, in New Jersey. A ferociously driven and vaguely evil figure, Claude announces his intention to pursue medicine at Miskatonic University, but he is later expelled. After spending years in the West Indies, where he has evidently studied voodoo, he returns home—this time with a bride, Gratia Thane. It becomes clear that he is engaged in experiments regarding personality exchange—this time in a reversal of "The Thing on the Doorstep," where Asenath Waite wished to possess the body of Edward Derby. Here, Claude Asher believes that a female body has its advantages, as he debates the matter with his brother, Richard, the narrator:

> "You can't," I said dully. "You can't do this to Gratia. She's lovely. She . . ."
> "That's just the point!" Claude's voice was a feverish whisper. "Lovely! She's the most beautiful creature I've ever seen. Think, Richard! Think what I could do with such loveliness. Think of a woman possessed of such beauty, and of my personality, my brain directing that beauty! A woman such as that could rule any man . . . a million men . . . an empire . . . a world!" (163)

But Claude's increasingly erratic behaviour causes him to be locked up in an asylum. His baleful work, however, is not over—for he gradually switches bodies with his own brother, who then tells his tale while imprisoned in the form of Claude Asher.

This story, although somewhat overwritten, is an ingenious riff on "The Thing on the Doorstep" in that it portrays the effects of body-exchange in the first person, as Richard Asher tells us exactly what it feels like to be exiled from his own body:

> The first conscious sensation was one of gnawing pain that seemed to pervade every inch of my body, eating at my flesh like some needle-fanged cannibalistic monster. With an exhausting effort, I opened my eyes. The lids felt oddly swollen, and I saw only mistily through narrow slits. The whiteness wavered before me again; I made out a white-washed ceiling and tall, colorless walls; pallid moonlight slanted through a window on my right. I blinked and tried to bring the ghostly rectangle of the casement into better focus. Then, the razor-edged knife of terror sliced into my brain. The moonlight that seeped

into that barren chamber was cut into segments by shadowy stripes; the window was reinforced—with steel bars! (174)

Robert Weinberg reports that August Derleth demanded that Thompson stop using elements from Lovecraft's stories in his own work, although Weinberg presents no documentary evidence to this effect.[1] However, it is by no means inconceivable: Derleth is on record as having stated, in the 1940s, that the Cthulhu Mythos (or some of its appurtenances) was under copyright by Arkham House,[2] so it is not unimaginable that he would have taken umbrage against a writer who had no direct connexion with Lovecraft and was not one of the anointed six (or eight) supposedly designated by Lovecraft (in reality by Derleth) to "contribute" to Lovecraft's mythos. At any rate, Thompson's two other *Weird Tales* stories—"The Pale Criminal" (September 1947) and "Clay" (May 1948)—have no Mythos or Lovecraftian allusions, and he disappeared from the scene soon thereafter. (Stefan Dziemianowicz, however, points out that Thompson published three western novels in the 1950s.[3])

The 1950s were a lean period for Lovecraft, for Arkham House, and for weird fiction in general. In 1954 *Weird Tales* finally ceased publication, so that the principal venue for the Lovecraft Mythos and the Cthulhu Mythos was finally withdrawn. Such writers as Robert Bloch and Fritz Leiber had moved on to other work: Bloch became quickly noted for his hard-boiled suspense writing, as in *The Scarf* (1947) and *Psycho* (1959), while Leiber shifted to science fiction and fantasy, becoming one of the most distinguished genre writers of his time, with a body of work as rich and substantial as Lovecraft's own. This left Derleth pretty largely alone, and Arkham House as the chief forum for the Cthulhu Mythos; but Arkham House itself published only fourteen books in the 1950s, including *The Survivor and Others* (1957) and *The Mask of Cthulhu* (1958). Clearly, a new generation of Mythos writers was needed.

One of that generation's first, and youngest, contributors was Ramsey Campbell (b. 1946), whose *The Inhabitant of the Lake and Less Welcome Tenants* (1964) astounded the Lovecraft community by the fact that it was written by an Englishman barely eighteen years of age. (We now know that some of the stories date to as early as Campbell's fourteenth year.) Campbell has gone on to become perhaps the greatest horror writer of his generation, and his first volume is therefore a bit of an embarrassment. Nevertheless, the stories, lurid and bombastic as they may be, are written with such vitality and enthusiasm as to be on the whole superior to the mechanical imitations of such purportedly mature authors as Brian Lumley and even Derleth himself.

Campbell began writing as early as the age of eleven, and produced an entire small volume entitled *Ghostly Tales* (1957/58). Consisting of sixteen stories—some very short, others relatively lengthy—the volume reveals a rather surprising diversity of tone and style, and Campbell need feel no embarrassment at the exhibition of his eleven-year-old juvenilia. Lovecraft is not the focus of this collection: it opens with a weird poem rather in the manner of Thomas Lovell Beddoes, and at one point M. R. James is cited by name (37). The one explicitly Lovecraftian reference is rather an amusement: coming upon the term "shoggoth," one character looks it up in the dictionary (!), where it is defined: "evil spirit or demon in the shape of a tree with mouths scattered over its trunk" (9). Lovecraft would, no doubt, be startled to read this definition, since his shoggoth is a fifteen-foot protoplasmic amoeba; but Campbell has mentioned to me that the definition is derived from Robert Bloch's "Notebook Found in a Deserted House." Nevertheless, by 1960–61, when the first of the tales to be included in *The Inhabitant of the Lake* were written, Campbell had grasped, and even begun very tentatively to go beyond, the Lovecraft influence.

"The Tomb-Herd" and "The Tower from Yuggoth" (both written 1960–61) testify to Campbell's desire, as he writes in the 1990 introduction to *Demons by Daylight*, "to sound as much like H. P. Lovecraft as I could."[4] The former is set in Lovecraft's Kingsport, the latter in Arkham; moreover, both seem to take place in Lovecraft's own era rather than in Campbell's: although the date of "The Tomb-Herd" is not specified, "The Tower from Yuggoth" is clearly set in 1929, and its hero is given the transparently Lovecraftian name of Edward Wingate Armitage. In terms of style, the opening of "The Tomb-Herd" says it all: "There are myriad unspeakable terrors in the cosmos in which our universe is but an atom; and the two gates of agony, life and death, gape to pour forth infinities of abominations. And the other gates which spew forth their broods are, thank God, little known to us" (3). It is just as well that neither of these stories were actually included in *The Inhabitant of the Lake*. The first of Campbell's stories that was included was "The Horror from the Bridge"; and it is in this story that Campbell introduces his British analogue for Lovecraft's mythical New England topography. In the course of his early stories Campbell (at the suggestion of August Derleth[5]) invented such towns as Severnford, Temphill, Brichester, Camside, Goatswood, and Clotton, all evidently set in the Severn valley and all conforming to Lovecraft's Arkham, Dunwich, Kingsport, and Innsmouth. But even "The Horror from the Bridge" is still set in 1931, as if Campbell were satisfied merely to transplant the Lovecraftian scenario to another continent.

Mechanically imitative as most of these early stories may be, some of them already betray signs that Campbell was seeking to find his own voice. "The Church in High Street" (written 1960–61) and "The Render of the Veils" (written 1962) contain considerably more dialogue than was Lovecraft's wont; the former tale, a revision of "The Tomb-Herd," is now set in Temphill. Other tales reveal a clever adaptation of Lovecraftian themes. "The Insects from Shaggai" utilises the notion of insects penetrating a man's brain, which, as Campbell admits,[6] was taken from a late entry in Lovecraft's commonplace book, as were the plots of a number of other early Campbell stories. "The Inhabitant of the Lake" resembles Lovecraft's "The Whisperer in Darkness" in its use of the documentary style—in this instance, correspondence between the two protagonists—to achieve narrative distancing and verisimilitude. And, of course, Campbell cannot resist concocting his own Lovecraftian god (Glaaki, first cited in "The Room in the Castle") and mythical book (*The Revelations of Glaaki,* first cited in "The Render of the Veils"). All these devices would be used to much greater effect in some of the stories in *Demons by Daylight* (1973), in which Campbell both abandoned an overtly Lovecraftian idiom and almost single-handedly initiated the contemporary horror movement.

Even before the publication of *The Inhabitant of the Lake,* however, Campbell was seeking to shed the Lovecraftian cloak he had donned. In 1963 he produced the first draft of "The Interloper," one of the more memorable tales in *Demons by Daylight;* "Before the Storm" (written 1965) is an exceptionally bizarre dream-fantasy, although it is still rooted in Lovecraft's Mythos:

> His flesh was crawling, but he dared not scratch. Sensation in his
> hand had subsided into a pounding ache. He fumbled with the pen and

tried to think, to select items from his memory that would help describe his plight. But other images crowded in, things he had seen, places he had visited: the colossi guarding black canals on Yuggoth—the whistling heads—the horn-notes which pursued through the forests of Tond— the giant eye which peered between trees—the face which mouthed in the gulf beyond the rim—the dead things in orbit around the worlds beyond Shaggai—the shuttered storehouses hidden in a dockland town— the last revelation by the lake of Glaaki—the sun-bleached buildings of a forgotten city whose walls throbbed a word T R A K and in whose corners white shapes shifted feebly— (187–88)

But if we are to look for any single story of Campbell's that truly marks his declaration of independence from Lovecraft, it is "The Cellars" (written 1965). Not only is this Campbell's first tale to be set in his native Liverpool, it is in other ways typical of his later work—in its focus on human relationships, its evocation of the squalor of urban decay, its oblique narration, and its nebulous, indirect, and nearly incomprehensible horrific climax.

Campbell has spoken frequently of Lovecraft's influence upon his work, most extensively in the introduction to *Cold Print* (1985), a collection of his Lovecraftian tales; but other remarks are also illuminating. In the 1990 introduction to *Demons by Daylight* he notes that in that collection he was striving to be as unlike Lovecraft as possible: "Having imitated Lovecraft, I rejected him with all the obstreperousness of a fanzine contributor determined to make a name for himself at the expense of his betters." His most insightful comment may be in the introduction to *The Height of the Scream:* "Lovecraft had rooted his horrors in recognizable settings; I wanted to root mine in recognizable human behavior, an altogether more universal thing."[7] This may not be entirely fair to Lovecraft—there is far more realism in Lovecraft than mere settings, and the absence of vivid characters or relationships in his work is a direct result of his portrayal of the brutal truth of humanity's inconsequence in an infinite and uncaring cosmos—but it adequately conveys not merely Campbell's own difference from Lovecraft but the overall tendency of all post-Lovecraftian weird fiction, a tendency that Campbell has simply exemplified more distinctively and powerfully than any of his contemporaries. This tendency may be very crudely defined as the shift from the cosmic to the human: when Campbell remarks that

Lovecraft's "minimal characterization and plot work because they are right for him,"[8] he is suggesting that it is not characters but phenomena that form the true heart of Lovecraft's fiction, whereas for Campbell (as for most other modern weird writers) the human characters become not merely the object of the reader's sympathy but the sole or prime focus of the horrific scenario. In Campbell, the focus on the human takes the form of an extremely intense concentration on individual psychology, to the degree that much of his work approaches stream-of-consciousness while yet retaining a sort of clinical detachment. As a result, Campbell's vision is distinctly lacking in Lovecraftian cosmicism, and even later tales in which he attempts to arouse a sense of cosmic fear ("The Tugging," "The Voice of the Beach" [for which see Chapter VIII]) seem half-hearted and unconvincing.

Two magnificent tales in which Campbell reveals himself to have fully assimilated the Lovecraft influence while at the same time speaking in his own voice are "Cold Print" (written 1966–67) and "The Franklyn Paragraphs" (written 1967). It is conceivable that the former—involving a man who ventures into a bookstore in a seedy area of Brichester in search of the fabled twelfth volume of the *Revelations of Glaaki*—was inspired by the opening sonnet of Lovecraft's *Fungi from Yuggoth:*

> The place was dark and dusty and half-lost
> In tangles of old alleys near the quays,
> Reeking of strange things brought in from the seas,
> And with queer curls of fog that west winds tossed.
> Small lozenge panes, obscured by smoke and frost,
> Just shewed the books, in piles like twisted trees,
> Rotting from floor to roof—congeries
> Of crumbling elder lore at little cost. (*AT* 64)

But the vividness of Campbell's Brichester, with its dismal slums and its inhabitants stunted and imaginationless from poverty and urban decay, is too evocatively etched to be the product of mere literary influence; Campbell's later admission that Brichester had by now become merely a metaphor for Liverpool ("My invented town of Brichester, originally intended as the Severn Valley equivalent of Lovecraft's Arkham, was Liverpool by now in all but name"[9]) only confirms what we suspected all along. Campbell's great innovation in this story was to revivify the stale concept of the mythical book of occult lore—which, even toward the end of Lovecraft's own career, had become more and more of a game or in-joke—by linking it to the world of violent pornography. Campbell's seedy narrator, entering a bookstore on the edge of town, is by no means "charmed" (as the narrator of Lovecraft's sonnet is) by his surroundings: he had come to find books analogous to those he has purchased elsewhere, *Miss Whippe, Old-Style Governess* and *Prefects and Fags* (199); but the *Revelations* prove more than he bargained for. It is exactly in such a place that the horror originally inspired by Lovecraft's *Necronomicon* can be re-created in the present day.

"The Franklyn Paragraphs" is Campbell's most the audacious attempt to mimic—and perhaps also to parody—Lovecraft's documentary style. Campbell himself appears as a character in the story, acting as narrator and engaging in a correspondence with the eccentric writer Errol Undercliffe. At one point Undercliffe criticises one of Campbell's own stories, "The Stocking" (elsewhere in *Demons by Daylight*), dismissing it as "elaborately pointless" (33): it is as if Undercliffe is a sort of maturer version of Campbell himself, one who can examine Campbell's work with the objectivity that greater years and greater experience as a writer bring. The story is written as if it were a critical article, with Lovecraft's own Mythos the subject of the commentary. Undercliffe discovers a strange volume by one Roland Franklyn, *We Pass from View;* Campbell (the narrator) claims that it "displays marked affinities with the Cthulhu Mythos in certain passages, [but] such Lovecraft scholars as Derleth, Lin Carter, Timothy d'Arch Smith and J. Vernon Shea can supply no information on the book" (31). Later Campbell reproduces the British National Bibliography entry for the book (his years spent working in a library were not spent in vain) and also the scornful *Times Literary Supplement* review of it.

But "The Franklyn Paragraphs" is more than a succession of playful in-jokes; it is one of the most insidiously horrific tales of Campbell's early period. Its power stems both from the subtlety and the indirection of its execution. As frequently in Lovecraft, narrative distance is taken almost to an extreme: at one point Campbell the narrator quotes a letter from Undercliffe who quotes a passage of Franklyn's book. In fact, there is an additional level of narrative distance here, since Campbell the author must be separated from the persona he has adopted as the narrator of the story. Moreover, the story, as frequently in his later work, probes the relationship between writing and reality. What happens if an actual horror descends upon the writer of supernatural fiction? Should he not be prepared for it, given his predisposition to the weird? Undercliffe concludes that the opposite is the case:

> Even the supernatural-story writer who believes what he writes (and I'm not saying I don't) isn't prepared for an actual confrontation. Quite the reverse, for every time he fabricates the supernatural in a story (unless based on experience) he clinches his skepticism; he knows such things can't be, because he wrote them. Thus for him a confrontation would be doubly upsetting. (42)

And when Franklyn's widow tells Undercliffe what would happen if he were to experience the supernatural ("'God! You'd never write about it, you'd never write about anything again'" [42]), we see the reason for the fragmentary and halting nature of Undercliffe's last letter. The genuinely supernatural obliterates writing, renders one speechless (a theme to be found also in T. E. D. Klein's "The Events at Poroth Farm"). But the tale is still more complex than this, and one of its most potent moments is when Errol Undercliffe, reading Franklyn's *We Pass from View*, sees words appearing of their own accord on the page:

> FEEL THEM COMING SLOWLY BURROWING WANT ME TO SUFFER CANT MOVE GET ME OUT SAVE ME SOMEWHERE IN BRICHESTER HELP ME (37)

We can think of this as a vast refinement of the Lovecraftian narrator's penchant for scribbling until the bitter end; but in reality it symbolises the writer's heroic effort to maintain his art in the face of the most overwhelming obstacles.

This richly textured story—with its complex network of narrative voices, its attempt to maintain a harried sobriety in the face of unthinkable horror, and its gradual build-up to a spectacularly powerful climax—is the summation of Campbell's Lovecraftian work, and remains one of the signal contributions to the Lovecraft Mythos. Undercliffe's final message—"No longer could I trust the surface of the world" (44)—is exactly the burden of Lovecraft's work, but is here expressed with a vividness that is Campbell's own.

Another powerful contribution to the Lovecraft Mythos, by another British writer, is a very different proposition indeed. When Colin Wilson (b. 1932) published *The Outsider* (1956), a probing sociological and intellectual study, at the age of twenty-four, one would never have thought that he would become, after a fashion, a disciple of Lovecraft. But by the time Wilson wrote the literary study *The Strength to Dream: Literature and the Imagination* (1961), he had stumbled upon Lovecraft's work. His reaction was, to put it mildly, bizarre. Accusing the mild-mannered Lovecraft of being "sick" and of "rejecting 'reality,'" and even comparing him to the mass-murderer Peter Kürten, Wilson condemned Lovecraft more severely than even his namesake Edmund Wilson had done years before. Wilson later admitted that Lovecraft's bleak, cosmic vision—which saw little place for an insignificant human race amidst the boundless vortices of space and time—was anathema to his own cheerful, optimistic view of humanity's future intellectual and psychological development.

The upshot was, however, that August Derleth was incensed when he read *The Strength to Dream* and, as Lovecraft's designated champion and defender, strongly rebutted Wilson in the introduction ("H. P. Lovecraft and His Work") to *The Dunwich Horror and Others* (1963). Derleth also got in touch with Wilson directly and challenged him to write a Lovecraftian tale. Wilson, who by this time had written several novels fusing his intellectual concerns with crime, suspense, and sex, obliged—and the result was *The Mind Parasites* (1967).

The novel purports to be the work of Professor Gilbert Austin, who disappeared in 2007. In 1997, Austin, an archaeologist, and Wolfgang Reich discover the remains of a city two miles underground in Turkey, far antedating any known civilisation. August Derleth (!) writes to Austin, pointing out the possible connexion between this city and some of Lovecraft's inventions. Austin and Reich read "The Shadow out of Time" and other works by Lovecraft, and journalists end up naming the underground city Kadath. Austin, however, later comes to realise that these excavations were "a red herring deliberately introduced by the mind parasites" (48).

Who, exactly, are the mind parasites? Karel Weissman, a psychologist and an old friend of Austin's who committed suicide, had written a treatise maintaining that the human race was being attacked "by a sort of mind-cancer" (49). These creatures attack the intelligent and creative person and "cause him to become an enemy of life and of the human race" (58). Austin and Reich become convinced of this theory, and they therefore begin a succession of mental experiments to confirm it. Austin finds that he is able to move or direct objects with his mind. They begin converting other intellectuals to the idea of the mind parasites. Austin is then suddenly attacked by the creatures, at a deeper level of consciousness than he can resist. He recovers, but twenty of his colleagues die. One who has survived, Georges Ribot, a writer on spiritualism, now tries to sabotage Austin's work by claiming that Austin and Reich had organised a suicide pact. Is Ribot controlled by the mind parasites? They confront Ribot in a hospital and probe his mind. But the parasites induce Ribot to commit suicide.

Austin and others now announce the dangers of the mind parasites at a press conference. The group goes into space to escape the parasites, who have made attempts (through other human beings) to kill them. The parasites are trying to induce a race war on earth. As Austin's group gets farther from the earth, the parasites become fearful; finally, they leave the earth. Ultimately, Austin ascertains the origin of the parasites: it is a "new" moon captured by the earth around 5000 B.C.E. Austin's group returns to the earth and manage to turn this moon around (purely by the force of their minds) so that the parasites' psychic energy is no longer turned toward the earth. They then release the moon from its orbit; the parasites are apparently defeated. But then Austin and his crew disappear on the spaceship *Pallas* on a voyage toward Pluto. The editor of the document believes that Austin had (in his own words) "'lost contact with the rest of the human race', and that the battle against the parasites had 'geared him to a faster rate of evolution'" (186).

It is difficult to describe the intellectual richness of *The Mind Parasites*—and, more significantly, its enthralling narrative pace, in spite (or perhaps because) of the fact that a great deal of the action in it takes place literally within the minds of the central characters. It can be seen from the synopsis that the Lovecraftian element is, in a sense, rather slight, even insignificant; but what Wilson has done is to use Lovecraftian conceptions and images—in particular, the suggestion of ancient alien civilisations far antedating human life—as a springboard for a novel that reflects Wilson's (not Lovecraft's) ideas regarding the future development of the human race. It might be said that the very idea of the mind parasites derives from such stories as "The Call of Cthulhu" (Cthulhu's power to influence dreams) and "The Shadow out of Time" (the Great Race's ability at mind-transference), but the parallels are slight and the conception remains largely Wilson's own.

It is, of course, of interest that Lovecraft becomes a minor character in the early stages of the novel—or, rather, that his work acts as a catalyst for Austin's development of his theories regarding the mind parasites:

> The study of Lovecraft was, in itself, an interesting and pleasant occupation. He was a man of remarkable imagination. Reading his works in chronological order, we observed a gradual change of viewpoint. The early stories tend to have a New England background, and deal with a fictional county [*sic*] called Arkham, with wild hills and sinister valleys. The inhabitants of Arkham seem to be mostly weird degenerates with a taste for forbidden pleasures and the conjuration of demons. Inevitably, a large number of them come to a violent end. But gradually, there is a change in the tone of Lovecraft's work. His imagination turns from the horrible to the awe-inspiring, to visions of tremendous aeons of time, of giant cities, of the conflict of monstrous and superhuman races. Except that he continues to write in the language of horror stories—no doubt with his market in mind—he might be considered one of the earliest and best exponents of science fiction. It was mostly with his latter 'science fiction period' that we were concerned . . . (43–44)

This is an accurate and perceptive analysis of the development of Lovecraft's work, and it has been echoed by several later scholars. It can be seen from this that Wilson is one of the few "Cthulhu Mythos" writers (assuming he can even be properly called such) to understand, and be influenced by, Lovecraft's later, cosmic narratives in which the early Mythos "gods" have been demythologised to become extraterrestrials.

Wilson's later novella, "The Return of the Lloigor," written for Derleth's *Tales of the Cthulhu Mythos* (1969), is somewhat of a disappointment, even though it is much more pronouncedly a "Cthulhu Mythos" tale than *The Mind Parasites*. Its protagonist is Paul Dunbar Lang, an Englishman who teaches at the University of Virginia. He is working on the Voynich manuscript—an actual work (now in the Beinecke Rare Book and Manuscript Library at Yale University) apparently composed in the fifteenth century and written in a still indecipherable script and language. Lang discovers that the text is actually in mediaeval Arabic and is in fact the *Necronomicon*. Lovecraft is again cited in the text, as is Arthur Machen. A Colonel Lionel Urqart tells Lang of the lost continent of Mu:

> The continent of Mu existed in the South Pacific between twenty thousand and twelve thousand years ago. It consisted of two races, one of which resembled present day man. The other consisted of Urquart's "invisible ones from the stars." These latter, he said, were definitely aliens on our earth, and the chief among them was called Ghatanathoa, the dark one. (226)

This is interesting in reflecting the influence of Lovecraft's revisions (in this case, "Out of the Aeons") on Wilson. In any case, these aliens are the Lloigor. They are the most profound pessimists the world has ever known—"They *lived* their pessimism" (228). They had come from the Andromeda nebula, but as they dwelt on earth they gradually weakened, and their "slaves"—the human race—supplanted them. Every now and then, however, the Lloigor erupt and wreak havoc on the earth's surface. As another character explains to Lang: "You see, this is their world anyway. We're a mistake. They want it back again" (250). Lang and Urquart disappear in a plane as they are going to Washington, D.C., to talk with a senator about their findings.

"The Return of the Lloigor" has provocative ideas but fails to develop them adequately. Lengthy as it is, it should have been a full-length novel to probe its ideas of optimism, pessimism, and the origin of human life. The notion that human beings are a "mistake" is clearly derived from *At the Mountains of Madness*, where the Old Ones created us as a "jest or mistake." Even so, Wilson has merely lifted this tidbit to underscore his own philosophy. Wilson has acknowledged his own optimistic view of humanity, so nothing could be more terrifying to him than a race of creatures that "*lived* their pessimism." Derleth was no doubt flattered that a writer of Wilson's stature would choose to elaborate upon one of his own creations, the Lloigor, but the end result is unsatisfactorily sketchy and insubstantial.

Wilson has written two further novels elaborating upon the conceptions in *The Mind Parasites*, both of which have Lovecraftian elements, although in very differing degrees. *The Philosopher's Stone* (1969) utilises these elements extensively—to such a degree, indeed, that Lin

Carter makes a good case that this novel, rather than *The Mind Parasites*, is Wilson's true "Cthulhu Mythos" novel. As with its predecessor, the "action" of *The Philosopher's Stone* is conducted almost entirely within the minds of the protagonists—but it is no less engrossing for that. It is the first-person account of Howard Lester who, in 1955, at the age of thirteen, meets the scientist Sir Alastair Lyell. Both are engaging in the quest for "wider consciousness" (43); indeed, at one point they come to the realisation that "if life is consciousness, then the prolonging of life should be the problem of increasing consciousness" (50). In a sense, this is Wilson's echo of Lovecraft's repeated literary and philosophical goal of overcoming the limitations of time: "The reason why *time* plays a great part in so many of my tales is that this element looms up in my mind as the most profoundly dramatic and grimly terrible thing in the universe. *Conflict with time* seems to me the most potent and fruitful theme in all human expression" ("Notes on Writing Weird Fiction" [*CE* 2.176]). Wilson's protagonists are engaged in an unusual quest for the philosopher's stone—the search for eternal life—and seem to have found it in purely mental activity.

Lyell dies, and Lester later comes under the influence of Sir Henry Littleway, another scientist who appears to be working on the same issues of ageing and consciousness. Further experiments convince Lester that he has solved the problem of ageing, at least from the mental standpoint; specifically, this involves a particular kind of stimulation of the prefrontal cortex of the brain. Lester seems to develop the ability to cast his imagination into the past, sometimes by merely touching or even looking at a particular ancient object. (In the course of this work, he incidentally ascertains to his satisfaction that Bacon wrote the plays of Shakespeare.) When holding one particular object, purportedly a Hittite figurine, Lester is convinced that it is far older—perhaps half a million years old. Later, when studying some Mayan artifacts, he concludes that Mayan priests had "a secret so terrible that the world might be destroyed if it was ever revealed" (205).

Lester and Littleway now perceive that certain "forces" are trying to block their further acquisition of information. Littleway's brother, Roger, tells them of Lovecraft and his concept of "elder races" (217). Unfortunately, the exposition here descends into Derlethianism: "According to Lovecraft, the Ancient Old Ones had come from the stars, and once

THE RISE AND FALL OF THE CTHULHU MYTHOS

dominated the earth, building immense cities of gigantic stone blocks. They had destroyed themselves through the practice of black magic, and were now 'sleeping' under the earth" (219). Lester wonders whether the Old Ones are the source of all human religion on the earth. There are later mentions of Ghatanathoa, Yig, and other Lovecraftian conceptions.

Lester now hears of Benjamino Evangelistica, the leader of a cult, who had written a long book, begun in 1906 and completed in 1926, which mentions a book called the *Necremicon* (253). Lester concludes at once that this is the origin of Lovecraft's *Necronomicon*. A librarian tells him about the Voynich manuscript and the work of Paul Dunbar Lang. Lester ascertains, however, that the Voynich manuscript is not the *Necronomicon* itself, but a commentary on it. He is also troubled by the conventional account of the Old Ones: ". . . the black magic explanation of their downfall made no sense. For surely black magic is a human invention, meaning the attempt by human beings to ally themselves with the Great Old Ones?" (274). Just so!

The conclusion of *The Philosopher's Stone* must be read to be fully appreciated. It tells a long, elaborate account of the fall of the Old Ones—how they had almost destroyed themselves six million years ago, how a high-priest on Mu named K'tholo (the origin of Lovecraft's Cthulhu) had become their immortal servant, and so on. The overriding question for Lester becomes: When will the Old Ones awake from the million-year sleep? And what will they find when they do so? For him, it is man who must change—no longer must he be the servant of the Old Ones, but rather their master. This ties in with Wilson's own philosophical quest for the evolution of the human mind to a new and higher level:

> Let me put this in the clearest possible way. Man should possess an infinite appetite for life. It should be self-evident to him, all the time, that life is superb, glorious, endlessly rich, infinitely desirable. At present, because he is in a midway position between the brute and the truly human, he is always getting bored, depressed, weary of life. He has become so top-heavy with civilisation that he cannot contact his springs of pure vitality.
>
> Control of the prefrontal cortex will change all this. He will cease to cast nostalgic glances towards the womb, for he will realise that death is no escape. Man is a creature of life and the daylight; his destiny lies in total objectivity. (317–18)

The Philosopher's Stone is a rambling, shambling hodge-podge of a novel, full of interesting but entirely extraneous digressions and diversions, and weakened by windy and pompous philosophising; but it retains interest throughout because of the compelling intellectual issues it raises. Much more so than *The Mind Parasites*, it utilises Lovecraft's conceptions in such a way as to express Wilson's (not Lovecraft's) philosophical outlook. In this sense, it is one of the finest homages Lovecraft has ever received.

The Space Vampires (1976)—filmed as *Lifeforce*—is a very different kettle of fish. As if suddenly weary of heavy philosophising, Wilson has here written a slim, action-packed science-fiction thriller on a much lower literary level. As such, it is considerably less compelling from an intellectual or aesthetic perspective, and its Lovecraftian elements are far more tangential. We are here concerned with an immense, fifty-mile-long alien spacecraft (to which the media give the name the *Stranger*) found in space by an earthly vessel, the *Hermes*. The year is 2080. The *Hermes'* captain, Olof Carlsen, finds a group of thirty humanoid creatures on the *Stranger*, apparently in a state of suspended animation; he brings three back to earth, but they quickly revive, chiefly by sucking the life out of any human beings with whom they come into contact—to such a degree that a twenty-year-old young man looks like a man of seventy when found dead after an encounter with one of the aliens. Carlsen and Hans Fallada, a criminologist, conclude that these creatures are "energy vampires," often using sex as a means to suck the life out of their prey.

The Lovecraftian elements—if they can be called that—are very late in appearing. A concluding scene with the aliens reveals that they are "of the Ubbo-Sathla" (186)—a phrase that doesn't make any particular sense, given that Ubbo-Sathla is, in Smith's story, a purely earthly creature. (Wilson presumably read Smith's "Ubbo-Sathla" in *Tales of the Cthulhu Mythos*.) In any case, it turns out that the aliens have the ability to project their minds into the bodies of other beings. This idea might have derived from "The Shadow out of Time," but the critical element that distinguishes that story—mind-transference *over time*—is missing. Eventually the aliens are banished and the earth is saved.

The Space Vampires is only intermittently compelling, and its very spareness and absence of philosophical speculation make it seem thin and uninspired. It can be readily seen, moreover, that, while it picks up on certain conceptions from Wilson's other two novels, it does not make very clever or profound use of them. Indeed, it cannot be said that the three novels are in any proper sense a "trilogy," as is sometimes maintained; it is simply that they all delve into the possibility of alien entities taking over the minds of other species. Again, "The Shadow out of Time" is probably the source of this idea, although there it is not necessarily presented as hostile or evil.

Colin Wilson, as a literary or intellectual phenomenon, is certainly a curious case. Much of his philosophical work was received with hostility when it first appeared—because, in Wilson's view, he had not received a university education but was entirely self-taught and therefore threatened the traditional British class and educational structure—but of late he has marginalised himself by taking the occult seriously and writing a succession of books that have destroyed whatever reputation as a philosopher he once had. One of his latest treatises is *Atlantis and the Kingdom of the Neanderthals* (2006), in which he proposes with apparent seriousness that the Neanderthals had colonised Atlantis, developed powers of telepathy, and so forth. But even if Wilson has now become an intellectual buffoon, the extraordinarily interesting use he made of Lovecraftian elements in *The Mind Parasites* and *The Philosopher's Stone* provide striking evidence of what can be done when a genuinely talented literary and intellectual figure chooses to draw upon the Lovecraft Mythos.

If the thought of a British intellectual like Colin Wilson adding to the Lovecraft Mythos was a surprise, still more of a surprise was the contribution of the American mainstream novelist and poet Fred Chappell (b. 1936), in his novel *Dagon* (1968). This work went almost entirely unnoticed by the Lovecraft community for years, even decades, until finally in the 1980s Chappell was embraced as having produced a signal contribution to neo-Lovecraftian literature. His appearance at the Lovecraft Centennial Conference in 1990 capped his emergence from obscurity (obscurity, I should add, only to Lovecraftians—he had long before established an enviable reputation as a leading Southern American writer), and he has since gone on to write several more Lovecraftian tales, which shall be studied in their place.

Dagon is the story of Peter Leland, a scholar who is writing a treatise on *Remnant Pagan Forces in American Puritanism*. In order to find the seclusion necessary to write the book, he comes to a farm in North Carolina previously owned by his grandparents. On this property is a crude tenant family—Morgan, Ina, and a teenage daughter, Mina. Our suspicions are immediately raised when we learn that there is "something undeniably fishlike" (30) about Mina's face. Peter, the minister of a Methodist church in North Carolina, becomes interested in the figure of Dagon, who he knows was widely cited—and perhaps worshipped—in colonial times.

Peter is disturbed to find a letter from his grandparents with such terms as "Nephreu," "Yogg Sothoth," "Ka nai Hadoth," and "Cthulhu" (47). ("Nephreu" is an error for "Nephren-Ka," cited in "The Outsider" and other stories.) He later has dreams of cosmic bizarrerie:

> A bitter sleep, immediately shot through with yellow sick dreaming. He was still himself, but somehow impersonally so, huge, monolithic. There was no one else, but there were momentary impressions of great deserted cities which flashed through his consciousness, gleaming white cities with geometrics so queer and dizzying as to cause nausea. And when the cities remained stationary they were immediately engulfed by a milky-white odorous ocean. This same smelly chalky sea water was attacking him also and he began to dissolve away; he was becoming transparent, he was a mere threadlike wraith, merely a long nerve, excruciatingly alive. Somehow he perceived a voice in the milky substance, talking clearly and with immense resonance: "Iä, iä. Yogg Sothoth. Nephreu. Cthulhu." (69–70)

In the end, Peter's relations with his wife, Sheila, deteriorate as a result of his obsession with Dagon. As the narrative becomes increasingly surreal and dreamlike, there is a suggestion that he has killed her.

Peter moves in with the Morgan family, making love to Mina. They leave in Peter's car, settling in a house in a town called Gordon. At this point—if we believe the narrative voice—the god Dagon himself appears:

> The god Dagon was less than three feet long. Fat and rounded, like the belly of a crocodile. He couldn't see the mouth hidden away under the body, but he knew it: a wirelike grin like a rattlesnake's; double rows of venomous needles in the maw. On this side a nictitating eye,

but he thought that on the other side there would be no eye, but merely a filmy blind spot, an instrument to peer into the marrow of things. The visible eye gray, almost white. A body grayish-pink like powdery ashes. Chipped and broken scales covered it, tightly overlapped. It breathed and this took a long time. The froglike belly distended, contracted.—The reptilian shape was immobile; there was no way for it to move upon the earth.

He recognized the god Dagon.

An idiot. The god was omnipotent but did not possess intelligence. Dagon embodied a naked will uncontrollable. The omnipotent god was merely stupid. (177–78)

Peter Leland kills himself.

This strange, rather unpleasant novel is nonetheless a masterwork of psychological terror. It would seem that Dagon is meant largely as a symbol for unbridled sexuality. Dagon's appearance to Peter at the end of the novel is only the capstone to the portrayal of the increasingly uncontrollable sexual urges that possess Peter, particularly as they are directed toward the ignorant peasant girl Mina and away from Peter's own wife. The depiction of Dagon as both "omnipotent" and "stupid" may recollect Lovecraft's conventional description of Azathoth as a "blind idiot god," but in context it is clearly Peter's sexuality that is both omnipotent and mindless. The influence of "The Shadow over Innsmouth" is nonetheless present, but transmuted to convey a message about the human psyche rather than about the incursion of alien forces. The fact that, at the outset, Peter is a scholar in the best traditions of the Lovecraftian narrator makes his decline into something akin to barbarism and bestiality that much more powerful.

Another riff on "The Shadow over Innsmouth" is James Wade's "The Deep Ones," also written for Derleth's *Tales of the Cthulhu Mythos* (1969). Set in northern California, this substantial novelette tells of the studies of dolphins being conducted by Dr. Frederick Wilhelm. His assistant, Josephine Gilman (the last name will make any Lovecraftian perk up with interest), reveals a remarkable affinity to dolphins. Wilhelm's work is, however, being protested by hippies outside his laboratory; their leader, Alonzo Waite (another significant last name), warns Wilhelm that he should stop his research: he believes the dolphins are "evil, strong and evil" (172). It does not surprise us to learn later that Josephine is from Innsmouth. Waite, for his part, is working against groups seeking the return of the Old Ones. The dolphins are in fact allied to Cthulhu. Josephine later discovers that she is pregnant, and at the end of the tale she rides out to sea on a dolphin's back.

"The Deep Ones" perhaps does not broach any new features in the Lovecraftian mythology of the sea-creatures allied to Dagon and Cthulhu, but the telling of the tale is skilful and deft. Wade has apparently been ridiculed for bringing in the hippies as characters, but in fact this helps to give the story a sociological depth that raises it somewhat above mere shudder-mongering. An early passage describing Los Angeles has something of the feel of a hard-boiled crime novel:

> The impression had not been allayed by my arrival via plane in gritty, galvanic Los Angeles, or by a stroll through that tiny downtown park where predatory homosexuals, drug derelicts, and demented fanatics of all kinds congregate under the bloated, twisted palms, like so many patients in the garden of Dr. Caligari's madhouse. To some, Gothic battlements or New England backwaters represent the apex of spiritual horror and decay; for me, the neon-lit, screaming depravity of Los Angeles filled the bill. (163)

In terms of the Cthulhu Mythos, "The Deep Ones" might be said to advance a sort of modified Derlethianism:

> "These books tell of an ancient secret society or cult that believes the earth and all the known universe were once ruled by vast alien invaders from outside space and time, long before man evolved on this planet. These entities were so completely foreign to molecular matter and protoplasmic life that for all intents and purposes they were supernatural—supernatural and evil. . . .
> "At some point," the bearded *guru* continued, "these usurpers were defeated and banished by even stronger cosmic opponents who, at least from our limited viewpoint, would appear benevolent. However, the defeated Old Ones could not be killed, nor even permanently thwarted. They live on, imprisoned, but always seeking to return and resume their sway over the space-time universe, pursuing their immemorial and completely unknowable purposes." (191–92)

Here, at any rate, it is suggested that the "evil" nature of the Old Ones is merely a matter of perspective (since they are really so "foreign" in essence that human beings cannot truly understand them), and that the scope of the Old Ones' activities is the entire universe rather than the minuscule territory of the earth. Wade, like Wilson and even the youthful Campbell, was too talented a writer to swallow the Derleth Mythos in its entirety, and this novelette shows his tentative attempts to break free of its unimaginative and confining shackles. Wade went on to write several more Mythos tales over the next decade or two, but they are not substantial enough for individual discussion.

Derleth's *Tales of the Cthulhu Mythos* represents a kind of pinnacle of the Derleth Mythos. In two years he would be dead, and the year after that Lin Carter would publish his *Look Behind the "Cthulhu Mythos";* but from that point onward, advances in scholarship would destroy the flimsy edifice Derleth had erected over Lovecraft's work, so that readers and critics would be given the tools for a proper understanding of Lovecraft's philosophical thought and its influence upon his creative work. It would, however, take considerably longer for would-be imitators of the Cthulhu Mythos to grasp the new revelations, and many of them would remain unwitting Derlethians to the end.

VIII.

The Scholarly Revolution

L IN CARTER BEGAN WRITING *Lovecraft: A Look Behind the "Cthulhu Mythos"* in March 1971, unaware that the Mythos's true founder and patron, August Derleth, would die suddenly and unexpectedly on July 4 of that year. Carter's book was published in February 1972, and it would be only a few months later that the entire Derleth-Carter edifice of the Cthulhu Mythos would come tumbling down—largely as a result of a one-page essay by Richard L. Tierney, "The Derleth Mythos," published in an amateur collection of essays and stories edited by Meade and Penny Frierson, titled simply *HPL.*

It would be difficult to underestimate the revolutionary effect of this 500-word essay, which begins with devastating simplicity: "The 'Cthulhu Mythos' is largely the invention of, not H. P. Lovecraft, but August Derleth."[1] Tierney goes on to destroy the notion of the Elder Gods vs. the Old Ones, the parallels between the Cthulhu Mythos and the Christian mythos, and the idea of the Old Ones as elementals—or, rather, he shows that these are entirely Derleth's inventions, not Lovecraft's.

It was not long before Tierney's essay took root. It was written just at the time when a new generation of literary critics and scholars were directing their attention to Lovecraft with a keenness and lack of preconceptions that earlier "fan" critics could scarcely imagine. Although some valuable work had been done on Lovecraft from the 1940s to the 1960s, especially in the work of George T. Wetzel, Fritz Leiber, and Matthew H. Onderdonk, most of the discussion of Lovecraft, whether in the fan press or (rare as it was) in the mainstream or academic press, was painfully crude and ill-informed. Ironically, Derleth's publication of Lovecraft's *Selected Letters,* for all the errors and abridgments it contained, materially fostered the development of Lovecraft scholarship, for it revealed Lovecraft's own philosophical vision and the means by which he chose to express it in weird fiction.

Tierney's essay was followed by Dirk W. Mosig's "H. P. Lovecraft: Myth-Maker," first published in the *Miskatonic* (a journal for the Esoteric Order of Dagon, an amateur press association devoted to Lovecraft) for February 1976. It later received wider distribution in the semiprofessional magazine *Whispers* (December 1976). Mosig had by this time become the spearhead of the new Lovecraft scholarship movement, garnering such disciples as Donald R. Burleson, Peter Cannon, David E. Schultz, and myself. Mosig's essay was largely a follow-up and expansion of Tierney's, emphasising Lovecraft's mechanistic and atheistic philosophy and showing how a proper understanding of that philosophy required a rejection of the central tenets of the Derleth Mythos.

But in a sense, this scholarly revolution was incomplete because it had not come to terms with the infamous "black magic" quotation that Derleth had, beginning in April 1937, used as the principal justification for his interpretation of the Mythos. Mosig in his article addressed the point. Remarking that the quotation "doesn't sound like Lovecraft at all," he went on to note: ". . . when R. L. Tierney requested that Derleth produce the Lovecraft letter containing such [a] paragraph, the latter became angry and refused." Mosig reported that L. Sprague de Camp, then working on his biography of Lovecraft, "arrived at the conclusion that the famous paragraph simply *did not exist* in any of Lovecraft's letters to Derleth, or in any of the Lovecraft letters at the John Hay Lovecraft collection." Mosig was inclined to believe that the quotation "was a hoax, a fabrication by his ardent but misguided disciple."[2]

There the matter stood for another decade. Tempting as it was for anti-Derlethians to assume that Derleth had merely forged the evidently spurious quotation, it would have been more satisfactory if the actual origin of the quotation could be ascertained. This was finally done by David E. Schultz, who, in consulting the August Derleth Papers at the State Historical Society of Wisconsin in Madison, stumbled upon letters by Harold S. Farnese to Lovecraft and to Derleth. Farnese was a musical composer in Los Angeles who had briefly corresponded with Lovecraft in the 1930s and had set two of Lovecraft's *Fungi from Yuggoth* sonnets to music. Farnese seemed fascinated with Lovecraft's stories, but he evidently misunderstood their import, in spite of Lovecraft's detailed expositions of his metaphysical and aesthetic theories in his own letters to Farnese. As Derleth was collecting letters by Lovecraft from the latter's many correspondents, he got in touch with Farnese, who in a letter of April 11, 1937, wrote as follows:

> Upon congratulating HPL upon his work, he answered: *"You will, of course, realize that all my stories, unconnected as they may be, are based on one fundamental lore or legend: that this world was inhabited at one time by another race, who in practising black magic, lost their foothold and were expelled, yet live on outside, ever ready to take possession of this earth again."* "The Elders," he called them. [Emphasis by Farnese]

So here is the passage at last! And yet, Farnese is claiming that it is a direct quotation from a Lovecraft letter—so could the quotation be Lovecraft's after all? But if the entire correspondence between Derleth and Farnese (as well as between Farnese and Lovecraft) is read carefully, it can be seen that Farnese *did not have access to his letters from Lovecraft at the time he wrote this letter to Derleth*—he had already sent them to Derleth for transcription. Moreover, in other letters to Derleth, Farnese made manifest misquotations from Lovecraft's letters and fabricated quotations that simply did not exist in the letters. In any event, the quotation does not appear in the extant letters by Lovecraft to Farnese, which Derleth transcribed for the *Selected Letters* project. It is, therefore, highly plausible to believe that Farnese has once again fabricated a quotation—one that Derleth used to bolster his conception of the Mythos for more than thirty years.[3]

Lest we now blame Farnese for the long, sordid history of the Derleth Mythos, let us recall that Derleth had already envisioned the central elements of that Mythos in his stories of the early 1930s. Farnese's spurious quotation was merely a providential godsend to Derleth, confirming in his own mind that he was on the right track in attributing his own myopic and unimaginative Mythos to Lovecraft. As we have seen, Clark Ashton Smith had already been taken aback by this quotation when Derleth sprung it on him in April 1937, so it is not surprising that many others were similarly been deceived—and that Derleth, with the passage of decades, forgot where the quotation had come from and was unable to produce it.

The work of Mosig, Burleson, Schultz, and others was quickly dis-
seminated, and in such works as my *H. P. Lovecraft: Four Decades of Criticism* (1980) and Burleson's *H. P. Lovecraft: A Critical Study* (1983) it quickly
became the foundation of a new and unadulterated view of Lovecraft
and his Mythos. Much of the new scholarship appeared in my journal
Lovecraft Studies (1979f.). As we have seen, Robert M. Price, while fostering important scholarship of his own in his journal *Crypt of Cthulhu*
(1981f.), has of late been attempting to challenge the new orthodoxy, believing that Mosig and others (including myself) have gone too far in be-
rating Derleth and in taking a dim view of some of Lovecraft's own work
(such as "The Dunwich Horror") that fails to measure up to Lovecraft's
own professed ideals of weird fiction. I believe, however, that, for all the
valuable work he has done in illuminating numerous facets of the Mythos
from his perspective as a New Testament scholar, much of Price's defence of Derleth is unconvincing, and is largely the product of his personal fondness for the Mythos in all its forms irrespective of the aesthetic
merits of the material in question.

It was not to be expected, of course, that the new view of the
Lovecraft Mythos would have any pronounced or immediate effect
upon those writers who chose to imitate Lovecraft: the Derleth Mythos
had become too ingrained in publishing and in popular culture to be
overturned lightly. Indeed, the 1970s were a time when Lovecraft's
work first achieved a mass audience. As a result of revenue from the
early film adaptations of Lovecraft's stories, Derleth's Arkham House
had reprinted Lovecraft's fiction in three volumes in the early 1960s.
These editions in turn served as the basis for paperback editions from
Lancer Books in the mid-1960s and then, beginning in 1969, from Beagle (later Ballantine) Books. It is, however, symptomatic that the so-
called Arkham Edition of the Works of H. P. Lovecraft, published in
eleven volumes by Beagle/Ballantine in 1969–71, included only four
volumes consisting entirely of Lovecraft's own work. One volume consisted of selected "revisions," two other volumes were filled with the
Derleth "posthumous collaborations," two more with Derleth's *Tales of
the Cthulhu Mythos*, and—most egregiously—two others reprinted Derleth's *Mask of Cthulhu* and *Trail of Cthulhu*. No wonder so many readers
and writers latched on to Derleth's ideas as if they were Lovecraft's!

One of those who did so most vigorously was the other member of the "British invasion" of the later 1960s, Brian Lumley. Lumley (b. 1937) was probably the last major Mythos writer to have come into direct contact with Derleth before the latter's death. His first story was published in the *Arkham Collector* (Summer 1968), and he had two quite dreadful stories in *Tales of the Cthulhu Mythos* (1969). A story collection, *The Caller of the Black,* appeared from Arkham House in 1971, followed by a novel, *Beneath the Moors* (1974). At this point, Lumley began publishing in wider venues, and his Mythos work includes a succession of novels: *The Burrowers Beneath* (1974), *The Transition of Titus Crow* (1975), *The Clock of Dreams* (1978), *Spawn of the Winds* (1978), *In the Moons of Borea* (1979), and *Elysia: The Coming of Cthulhu* (1989). There have been a great many short stories and novellas as well.

It would be too painful to treat Lumley's work in detail; a few items can speak for the whole. One of Lumley's purported innovations is to fuse Lovecraft's "Mythos" and "dreamworld" realms, but often the result is confusion and bathos. Consider *Beneath the Moors*. Here we have the story of Professor Ewart Masters, an archaeologist who comes upon the sculpture of a reptilian "god" newly excavated in England. He connects it with another professor's conjectures of the ancient city of Lh-yib, lying beneath the moors of Yorkshire. In a work called the *Brick Cylinders of Kadatheron* he finds mention of the inhabitants of Ib, which readers will recollect from Lovecraft's early tale "The Doom That Came to Sarnath" (1920). Masters finds a statement by one Robert Krug, who reports that he has travelled to such sites as the Nameless City, Sarnath, and Ib itself. Lh-yib is Ib's sister city, whatever that is supposed to mean. (Lumley has here incorporated into his novel the novella "The Sister City," from *Tales of the Cthulhu Mythos*.) Masters, descending into a region called the Devil's Pool (where Krug had apparently plunged to his "death"), finds himself beneath the moors—and meets Bokrug, the water-lizard! (This is also from "The Doom That Came to Sarnath.") What is more, Bokrug speaks to Masters, delivering a history of his race. In fact, the inhabitants of Ib had come from the stars, settling in Ib and Lh-yib. Masters is later captured by creatures that he refers to as Thuun'ha:

> The Thuun'ha were hideous, and no other word could adequately fit them. Perhaps four and one-half feet tall, green as Yorkshire beer

> bottles, bulge-eyed with flabbily hanging, wattled lips and strangely tapering, furred ears—*hideous!* And their touch was soft, their movements sure, and their telepathic songs were unutterably foreboding as they bore me to that incredible cavity wherein stood the Sister City. (358–59)

Masters also senses the presence of a shoggoth. He later vanishes.

It is difficult to describe, short of profanity, the extreme incompetence of *Beneath the Moors*. Not only does it borrow heavily—right down to points of phraseology—from several of Lovecraft's poorer stories (notably "The Doom That Came to Sarnath" and "The Nameless City"), but, in spite of its attempt to mimic the verisimilitude of Lovecraft's documentary style, it presents events so preposterously unbelievable that the sense of realism and plausibility is entirely absent. The friendly chat that Masters has with Bokrug under the earth is a particularly delectable piece of buffoonery.

The Burrowers Beneath begins a six-book series featuring Titus Crow, a brave Mythos combatant. As this novel opens sometime in the 1960s, Crow has heard of a mining inspector who has found evidence of tunnels artificially dug somewhere in northern England; there are octopus drawings on the walls, and the inspector hears chanting in the distance. Crow peremptorily summons his colleague, Henri-Laurent de Marigny (evidently a descendant of Etienne-Laurent de Marigny, Randolph Carter's friend in "Through the Gates of the Silver Key"). Crow tells Marigny that the chantings are similar to those he has found in the *Cthaat Aquadingen*, which he believes to be "part of the *Necronomicon*" (26). I neither know nor care whether this is the first mention of Lumley's addition to the Lovecraftian library; all I can say is that this ungainly title, with its queer Latin-German compound ("aqua" = water; "dingen" = "things"), is pretty much on a par with his other "additions."

Crow, it transpires, is psychic, and he provides his background: he has been investigating the Old Ones since the 1930s, using both his psychic powers and his researches into obscure tomes. It is unsurprising that Crow presents the Derleth Mythos in all its absurdity:

> I had learned, somewhat skeptically, of the forces or deities of the unthinkably ancient mythology; of the benign Elder Gods, peacefully placed in Orion but ever aware of the struggle between the races of Earth and the Forces of Evil; of those evil deities themselves, the

Great Old Ones, ruled over (created by, originating from?) the blind idiot god Azathoth, "the Bubbler at the Hub," an amorphous blight of nethermost, nuclear confusion from which all infinity radiates; of Yog-Sothoth, "the all-in-one and one-in-all," coexistent with all time and coterminous in [*sic*] all space; of Nyarlathotep the Messenger; of Great Cthulhu, "dweller in the Depths" in his House at R'lyeh; of Hastur the Unspeakable, a prime elemental of interstellar space and air, half-brother to Cthulhu; and of Shug-Niggurath, "the black goat of the woods with a thousand young," fertility symbol in the cycle. (28–29)

"The Bubbler at the Hub" is brilliant parody—too bad it isn't intended as such.

But to continue. The archaeologist Amery Wendy-Smith has found the city of G'harne (discussed in the *G'harne Fragments*), the dwelling-place of the dreadful creature Shudde-M'ell, who, "hiding deep in the honey-combed ground, plots the dissemination of evil and madness throughout the world and plans the resurrection of other, even worse abominations!" (37). Yes, the exclamation mark is Lumley's. Shudde is apparently trying to recover the eggs that Wendy-Smith took from G'harne, but Crow now has them. What makes the matter urgent is that the spells of the Elder Gods are wearing off, which can mean only one thing: "that Cthulhu and all the others must likewise be free to roam and kill and . . ." (60). Well, it is too unpleasant to think about. It turns out, by the way, that these spells worked on the *minds* of the Old Ones—"The magic of the Elder Gods was a sort of psychiatric science" (63). Crow mails the eggs to various colleagues in order to prevent Shudde from getting them. He then comes into contact with Wingate Peaslee (the son of Nathaniel Wingate Peaslee, as cited in "The Shadow out of Time"), who heads the Wilmarth Foun-dation—a band of 500 men devoted to protecting humanity from the Old Ones! Well, I feel much better now. In the end, of course, these CCD (Cthulhu Cycle Deities) are banished from the United Kingdom. But certain of them appear indestructible, so no doubt they will be back later, causing trouble. . . .

The problem with *The Transition of Titus Crow* and all its successors, aside from the sheer bad writing that riddles them, is that Lumley has attempted to take Lovecraft's cosmic conceptions and make an action-adventure plot out of them. The effort is doomed to failure; for, as I have observed earlier, the true horror in Lovecraft's work is the mere *knowledge* that the Old Ones exist. This psychological devastation in the face of human insignificance makes any actions on the part of the "gods" or monsters seem utterly insignificant. But to a figure like Titus Crow, the CCD (!!!) are merely stand-ins for gangsters or thugs or other "villains" that have to be defeated somehow, whether with psychic powers or star-stones or some other ridiculous method.

However, let us proceed with *The Transition of Titus Crow*. Here we are introduced to Cthylla, the "Secret Seed of Cthulhu" (196). It appears that Cthulhu wishes to reincarnate himself in Cthylla's womb, evidently as a way of escaping from his imprisonment in R'lyeh. Crow, for his part, is "lost in time" (208)—he had, like Randolph Carter at the end of "Through the Gates of the Silver Key," gone through a magical clock to escape Ithaqua. Through psychic means, Marigny helps Crow return to earth. Crow tells of how he travelled backward and forward in time, meeting such inimical creatures as the Hounds of Tindalos and the Great Race. He finally reached the planet Elysia, home of the Elder Gods; he learned that the CCD were actually Elder Gods themselves who had turned "evil" (335), forcing the "good" Elder Gods to banish or imprison them. In any event, Crow and Marigny take up the battle against Cthylla, and of course they prevail. But Arthur D. Meyer of the Wilmarth Foundation warns his colleagues: "Always remember, Cthulhu lives and dreams on, yet seeking to rule the minds of men; and through them all of space and time—*and I say to you that already he has gained certain victories!*" (347). And so the saga continues.

In *The Clock of Dreams* Marigny has used the time-clock to follow Crow to Elysia, where he meets "Kthanid the [Elder God] Eminence and cousin to Great Cthulhu" (19). Crow has fallen in love with an "incredible girl-goddess" (17), Tiania, but they are trapped in earth's dreamlands—Marigny must bring them back to Elysia. At this point Lumley begins shamelessly ripping off *The Dream-Quest of Unknown Kadath*, including the Enchanted Wood, Zak, Sona-Nyl, and so on and so forth. For it seems that Cthulhu has caused his "inhuman concepts" (28) to infiltrate the dreamworld, and this must not be allowed to stand. Marigny rescues Crow and Tiania in Dylath-Leen—but a night-gaunt snatches Tiania. Not to worry: she is later rescued. They all go to Ilek-Vad and meet Randolph Carter. The novel culminates in a confrontation of Nyarlathotep and Kthanid, in which of course the latter wins.

Spawn of the Winds tells of one Hank Silberhutte, who joins the Wilmarth Foundation to hunt down Ithaqua in Canada; but Hank disappears. Ithaqua has taken him and others to the planet of Borea—he wants Hank's sister to bear his children! But star-stones come to the rescue and he is defeated. In *In the Moons of Borea* Silberhutte has now become a warlord on Borea. Marigny comes through the time-clock, pursued by the Hounds of Tindalos. At this point he loses the clock, and it falls into the hands of Ithaqua, who takes it and puts it in one of the moons of Borea. Silberutte and Marigny get the clock back and manage to trap Ithaqua under one of Borea's moons. Hank, by the way, has married Armandra, Ithaqua's daughter (!). In *Elysia*, Marigny, on Borea, wants to meet up with Crow on Elysia. Kthanid tells Crow that the stars are coming right—the Old Ones might get free! The Elder Gods have now forgotten that they had imprisoned the Old Ones! After a trip through the dreamlands, Marigny uses the clock to get to Elysia. The Old Ones follow him through—but this is a trap by the Elder Gods to subdue them. But of course, they can't be killed, so presumably there is the possibility of more adventures . . .

Mercifully, Lumley has to date written no more Mythos novels, instead switching to writing equally ridiculous space-vampire works in the Necroscope series. One can only hope that this talentless hack will permanently abandon his unwitting parodies of Lovecraft's themes and conceptions.

As Brian Lumley was churning out novel after novel paying unwitting homage to August Derleth, a few writers were attempting to draw upon the genuine sources of horror in Lovecraft's own work. One of these was veteran weirdist Karl Edward Wagner (1945–1994), whose devotion to the sword-and-sorcery work of Robert E. Howard and Fritz Leiber is well known. His best-known Lovecraftian tale, "Sticks" (*Whispers*, March 1974), is simultaneously a tribute to Lovecraft and to the artist Lee Brown Coye, whose cover illustrations to the Arkham House Lovecraft editions of the 1960s—not to mention the lavishly illustrated *Three Tales of Horror* (1967)—won him widespread recognition. Set in 1942, "Sticks" tells the story of the artist Colin Leverett, whose artwork becomes excessively gruesome after he encounters an apparently animated corpse in a farmhouse. Twenty-five years later he is asked by Gothic House (an obvious stand-in for Arkham House) to illustrate the work of horror writer H. Kenneth Allard. The publisher is later killed. A nephew of Allard, Dana Allard, comes to Leverett with a stack of Allard's unpublished stories that he wishes Leverett to illustrate. The artist, who had been fascinated by the stick-lattice work that he saw at the old farmhouse, undertakes the task, only to learn that these lattices are glyphs designed to aid in the summoning of the Great Old Ones. Dana Allard is, in fact, H. Kenneth Allard himself.

This recounting of the plot of "Sticks" cannot begin to convey the extraordinary skill in its execution. After a time the omnipresence of the stick-lattice figures (something Lee Brown Coye actually used in his Lovecraft illustrations) becomes oppressive and hideous, and the tale is a masterwork of slowly cumulative horror. In the end, the story perhaps has no broader message to convey, and to that extent it can be considered nothing but a clever horror tale; but as such it ranks high, both in the canon of modern supernatural fiction and in the very slim canon of competent Lovecraft pastiches.

Competence is not a word we can use for Basil Copper's *The Great White Space* (1974). One of the first novels of the Cthulhu Mythos since Derleth's *The Lurker at the Threshold* (1945), it is a fiasco from beginning to end. What led prolific British author Copper (b. 1924) to write this work, aside from a desire to capitalise on Lovecraft's new-found popularity, is difficult to fathom. Set in 1933, the novel is narrated by one Frederick Seldon Plowright, a photographer who is asked by the explorer Clark Ashton Scarsdale (!!!) to accompany him and three others—Cornelius Van Damm, a geologist and electrical engineer; Norman Holden, an historian and radio expert; and Geoffrey Prescott, a linguist and Egyptologist—to a region somewhere in Asia to find some region called the "great white space." Scarsdale tells Plowright about this peculiar area:

> . . . it was an area which the Old Ones particularly regarded with awe and which they had always formally referred to, in their primeval writings as The Great White Space. This was a sacred belt of the cosmos through which beings could come and go, as through an astral door, and which was the means of conquering dizzying billions of miles of distance which would have taken even the Old Ones themselves thousands of years to traverse. (31)

Scarsdale has learned about this region from (you guessed it) consulting various "blasphemous old books and forbidden treatises" (30), including something called *The Ethics of Ygor.*

To make a long, tedious, boring story short, the explorers find the great white space, not long after they come upon an underground gallery on either side of which is a row of large jars containing the remains of hideous creatures and an immense city full of strange geometries (this is the "ancient city of Croth" [127]). Of course, the great white space has horrible creatures of its own:

> It was a colossal height which accounted for the vast doors through which we had ourselves passed on our way to this abode of abomination. The thing made a squelching, slopping noise as it progressed in a series of hopping jerks and with the noise came the stench, borne to our nostrils by the warmly acrid wind which blew as out of the vastnesses of primeval space. . . . The head of the thing, which appeared to change shape as it hopped along, was something like a gigantic snail or slug, while vague, lobster-like claws depended from its middle. In general form it appeared to be monadelphous; that is, a number of filament-like particles made up what we should call a body, uniting into one bundle from which depended the claw-members. (153–54)

(Copper seems proud of his discovery of the recondite word "monadelphous," as he uses it repeatedly in the latter portions of the novel; it perhaps makes up for his repeated misspelling of "hieroglyph" as "heiroglyph.") In spite of the valiant attempts by the explorers to destroy these creatures with hand grenades and other weapons, three of the five explorers are devoured. Apparently a worse fate is in store for Scarsdale, for Plowright encounters him toward the end strangely changed: he has become converted to the side of the aliens and wants Plowright to join him. But Plowright flees, eventually making his way back to civilisation; and at the very end he reserves the worst horror for last: Scarsdale was no longer himself, but wearing a waxen mask.

The myriad confusions and difficulties in the plot of *The Great White Space,* along with its transparent ripoffs from key Lovecraft stories, make it a textbook of how not to write a Lovecraftian tale. The borrowings from Lovecraft are exceedingly obvious—"The Nameless City" (the underground gallery lined with the coffins of monsters), *At the Mountains of Madness* (the immense underground city of Croth), "The Call of Cthulhu" (the strange geometry of Croth), and "The Whisperer in Darkness" (the mask motif)—and Copper has done nothing to develop or elaborate upon these conceptions. What conceptions he has added of his own are either inchoate or confused. What exactly is *The Ethics of Ygor* (a most unfortunate name), and how has it obtained its information about "the great white space"? We never learn. Most important of all, if this "great white space" has always existed as a conduit for the Old Ones to enter our realm, why have they not already taken over the world, as they could so easily do? Copper supplies no rationale for why Scarsdale (whose name goes beyond "unfortunate" and enters the realm of the grotesquely ludicrous) is so intent on coming upon this region now, as opposed to any other time. Nor does Plowright explain his purpose in issuing his warning about this "space." Exactly what can human beings do to close this "space" and prevent the Old Ones from entering? And since the expedition was so obviously a failure, why is it that we are not already overrun by these evil entities?

It is almost inconceivable that the slipshod writer of *The Great White Space* could have written so moving and elegant a story as "Shaft Number 247," in Ramsey Campbell's *New Tales of the Cthulhu Mythos* (1980). In this science fiction tale, it appears that humanity is now confined to underground chambers, or perhaps under water. Shaft no. 247 leaks—because something is turning the bolts *from the other side.* Is something trying to lure human beings to come out? Wainewright, one of the guardians of the shaft system, becomes increasingly attracted at the thought of going through the shaft—and perhaps to freedom.

Subtle, moving, and powerful as "Shaft Number 247" is, it is really not a Cthulhu Mythos story—not merely because it does not use any Mythos terminology (that would be a superficial means of classification, which would have the effect of excluding "The Colour out of Space" and other works by Lovecraft and others from consideration), but because it does not even constitute an adaptation or development of Lovecraft's core ideas. The story may well have been inspired by the phrase from a Lovecraft letter that Copper quotes as an epigraph—"The process of delving into the black abyss is to me the keenest form of fascination"—but this conception is not exclusive to Lovecraft and cannot be said to comprise a central element in his own Mythos tales.

More central to the Mythos is the work of Walter C. DeBill, Jr., who did some noteworthy work in the 1970s—mostly for such small-press venues as *From Beyond the Dark Gateway* and *Nyctalops*—and whose Mythos tales have now finally been gathered in *The Black Sutra* (2006). De-Bill's work is very uneven, and some of his tales fall woefully flat, but a few of them are skilfully told. The best of them are set in the Southwest, an area Lovecraft attempted to exploit (through second-hand knowledge) in "The Curse of Yig" and "The Mound." The first of these appears to be "What Lurks among the Dunes" (*Etchings and Odysseys*, 1973), an otherwise undistinguished work that makes use of a new entity or deity, Yidhra, an alluring female figure introduced in DeBill's story "Predator" (in Meade and Penny Frierson's *HPL* [1972]). Far and away DeBill's best tale is "Where Yidhra Walks," in Edward P. Berglund's *The Disciples of Cthulhu* (1976). This richly textured narrative evokes the barren and sparsely populated Southwest in a masterful manner. A local resident tells of Yidhra and her cult: "'. . . Yidhra doesn't much care about spreading the cult. She's part of life and death and the earth itself; domination means nothing to her. She takes only what she needs. She was born with life itself on this planet and as life grew she grew, as life changed so she changed. And like all life she must change to live'" (111). The protagonist's research into various esoteric books (including the *Black Sutra* of U Pao) fills in the background in Yidhra and her cult, and it is scarcely surprising that the attractive young woman Yolanda whom the protagonist meets proves to be Yidhra herself. The story perhaps does not broach anything notably new or original, but the working of the Lovecraftian material in this new topographical setting is deft.

Gary Myers's *The House of the Worm* (1975) might be said to constitute the first significant Lovecraftian work of fiction that draws upon the new scholarship. In many ways its most interesting feature is its brief introduction, in which Myers bluntly declares that he is engaging in "an interesting heresy" (vii) by departing from Derleth's conception of the battle between the "evil" Great Old Ones and the "benign" Elder Gods. Myers flatly states that "the Elder Gods, with the exception of Nodens, are entirely the creation of August Derleth" (vii). In this sense, Myers's only "heresy" is in ditching the Derleth Mythos to return to the purity of Lovecraft's own vision.

But perhaps Myers engages in a milder heresy of a different sort. His express purpose is to exploit Lovecraft's "Dunsanian" fantasies, where he recognises that "Elder Ones" (not Elder Gods) exist, but that these are merely the mild gods of earth as opposed to the redoubtable (but not necessarily "evil") Other Gods. In the first story in the collection, "The House of the Worm," Myers actually uses the term Elder Gods to designate the former entities, but he refers to them as "the gods who love men, and to whom they prayed at evening," and also as "those weak little gods" (11). This is orthodox enough, but Myers is intent on incorporating the Lovecraftian deities from the real world into his dreamworld. He recognises that "This is all very far . . . from the Cthulhu Mythos" (viii), i.e., the Lovecraft Mythos, because it essentially reverses the progression of Lovecraft's own writing, which abandoned the Dunsanian dreamworld for the real-world horrors of Cthulhu and Yog-Sothoth. In fact, however, the gods themselves play little role in Myers's tales, except as sinister presences in the background.

The ten stories in *The House of the Worm* are engaging enough—they are presented as chapters of a (very short) novel, but there is no particular interconnexion between them, and they are all self-standing tales—and draw upon not only Lovecraft's "Dunsanian" tales but those of Dunsany also. I do not find them as charming or as compelling as either of their originals: Myers's imagination does not extend beyond utilising such relatively conventional conceptions from Lovecraft and Dunsany as thieves getting their fitting comeuppance, dreadful dooms on ill-fated cities, and the like. The whole book is merely an exercise in pastiche in the strictest sense: how closely can a writer echo his originals? Myers writes skilfully enough, but precisely because he fails to introduce any new elements or ideas his work inevitably suffers from comparison with its distinguished originals.

Myers is, indeed, a rather curious case. Since the publication of his book, he has written virtually nothing, and the sum total of his more than thirty years of writing is the slim volume *Dark Wisdom* (2007), all of 140 pages. While there is something refreshing in this eschewing of quantity production, one wishes that his pen flowed a little more freely.

As the 1970s progressed, several veteran Lovecraftians took up their pens to write vivid new stories and novels that represented genuine expansions of Lovecraftian conceptions. It should be noted that the 1970s constituted the beginning of a two- or three-decade horror "boom" that caused both supernatural and non-supernatural fiction to achieve a mass audience for the first time. Powered by best-selling writers like Stephen King, Peter Straub, and (later) Clive Barker and Anne Rice, the horror "boom" resulted in a vast array of work in both the commercial press and the small press; as with all such phenomena, however, the great majority of work produced during this time was aesthetically inferior, both as concerns Lovecraftian writing and horror writing as a whole.

Fritz Leiber finally broke down and produced an avowed Lovecraftian pastiche, writing "The Terror from the Depths" when invited by Edward P. Berglund to contribute to his anthology, *The Disciples of Cthulhu* (1976). The result is an extraordinarily rich and complex novelette that, as Bruce Byfield has shown,[4] is a model for Leiber's incorporation of the mythic theories of Jung and Joseph Campbell in his later work. On a superficial level, "The Terror from the Depths" can be read as a vast in-joke: it would require a lengthy commentary to pinpoint all the tips of the hat to works by Lovecraft scattered through this story, including something so insignificant as the cry "Merciful Creator!" (301), borrowed from "Pickman's Model" (*DH* 22). More interestingly, Leiber has written a loose sequel to some of Lovecraft's most celebrated later tales, especially "The Whisperer in Darkness," whose protagonist Albert N. Wilmarth plays a major role in the story. Wilmarth, amusingly enough, bears a striking physical resemblance to Lovecraft himself. Although Leiber of course never met Lovecraft, he had by this time read enough about Lovecraft's life and mannerisms to capture some of his characteristic behaviour-patterns:

> He [was] . . . a tall young man, cadaverously thin, always moving about with nervous rapidity, his shoulders hunched. He'd had a long jaw and a pale complexion, with dark-circled eyes which gave him a haunted look, as if he were constantly under some great strain to which he never alluded. . . . He'd seemed incredibly well read and had had a lot to do with stimulating and deepening my interest in poetry. (290)

The narrator, Georg Reuter Fischer, even remarks to Wilmarth at one point: "'You know, . . . I had the craziest idea—that somehow you and he [Lovecraft] were the same person'" (310). Lovecraft himself, indeed, plays a minor role in the tale. Conversely, Fischer (whose first and last names are derived from Leiber's friends Georg Mann and Harry O. Fischer, and whose middle name is Leiber's own) is clearly modelled on

Leiber himself, so that the story's scenario—in which Wilmarth acts as a sort of mentor to Fischer in the pursuit of arcane knowledge—echoes Lovecraft's own brief tutorship to the young Leiber.

More than mere imitation, however, "The Terror from the Depths" strives both to recapture some of the textural richness of Lovecraft's best stories and, perhaps, to show that profound portrayals of human character are not incompatible with the general "cosmic" orientation of Lovecraft's work. To put it very crudely, Fischer finds himself simultaneously attracted and repelled by the cosmic forces dwelling under his Southern California home; and his first-person narrative reveals, entirely unbeknownst to himself, the degree to which these forces have throughout his entire life affected his mind and guided his actions to the final cataclysmic conclusion. Leiber here has drawn from many of Lovecraft's tales: Cthulhu's control of dreams ("The Call of Cthulhu"); the possible attractions of yielding to the non-human ("The Shadow over Innsmouth"); the compelling quest for scientific knowledge in the face of personal danger ("The Whisperer in Darkness," *At the Mountains of Madness*). And yet, the result is a story that features considerably more psychological analysis than Lovecraft ever included in his own work.

Accordingly, "The Terror from the Depths" can on one level be seen as Leiber's attempt to "rewrite" "The Whisperer in Darkness" so that it has more to say about the "real world" and "real people." Recall that one of Leiber's criticisms of Lovecraft's tale is that Wilmarth is presented as excessively gullible—a comment that may point to Leiber's dissatisfaction with the portrayal of character in Lovecraft's work generally. The same cannot be said of "The Terror from the Depths," where the slow absorption of both Fischer and Wilmarth into the physical and mental grasp of the cosmic entities is depicted with subtlety and psychological insight. In Lovecraft's tale Wilmarth is also momentarily attracted by the prospect of cosmic insights that might be made available to him: "To shake off the maddening and wearying limitations of time and space and natural law—to be linked with the vast *outside*—to come close to the nighted and abysmal secrets of the infinite and the ultimate—surely such a thing was worth the risk of one's life, soul, and sanity!" (*DH* 243). But in the end he draws back and flees to the safety of the human world. Leiber's scenario shows that the mere option to yield or not to yield to the non-human has become a moot point, since Fischer's mind has long ago been captured by the cosmic beings. What Leiber has done here—and, really, throughout his work—is to break down the simple dichotomy of external horror and internal horror, showing that both can be, and usually are, fused into an enigmatic and chilling union.

Another colleague of Lovecraft, Robert Bloch, returned to the Mythos in the novel *Strange Eons* (1978), which constitutes Bloch's most extended tribute to Lovecraft. No one is likely to think it a masterwork of literature, but it may be among Bloch's more successful later novels and is certainly a delight to the Lovecraftian.

The premise of *Strange Eons* is simple: Lovecraft was writing truth, not fiction. This is, of course, the premise under which many occultist groups function; some asserting, with added implausibility, that Lovecraft himself was unaware of the literal truth of his work. This view was already prevalent among a few in Lovecraft's own lifetime; note his amused comment on the beliefs of the mystical William Lumley: "We [the Lovecraft circle] may *think* we're writing fiction, and may even (absurd thought!) disbelieve what we write, but at bottom we are telling the truth in spite of ourselves—serving unwittingly as mouthpieces of Tsathoggua, Crom, Cthulhu, and other pleasant Outside gentry" (*SL* 4.271).

Bloch actually renders the idea half-believable by the gradualness of his exposition and by his suggestion that Lovecraft was in fact aware of what he was writing and was trying to utter a warning of some kind. The novel opens with an individual discovering a painting that seems strikingly similar to one ascribed to Richard Upton Pickman in "Pickman's Model"; later it is discovered that the painting is in fact by one Richard Upton, who was in touch with Lovecraft and had shown him some spectacular canvases in Boston. As *Strange Eons* progresses, various events seem uncannily to mimic those found in Lovecraft's stories—"The Lurking Fear," "The Statement of Randolph Carter" (*"You fool—Beckman is dead!"* [25]), "The Whisperer in Darkness," and so on.

The focus of the novel is, as might be expected, Nyarlathotep—here embodied in the person of Reverend Nye, a black man who leads the Starry Wisdom sect, seemingly just another of the harmless cults found so bountifully in southern California. But very quickly it becomes clear that Nye and his cult are far from harmless, as character after character dies off after learning too much about them. Drawing upon the prose-poem "Nyarlathotep," Bloch sees in the figure of Nyarlathotep nothing less than a symbol for—and, indeed, the actual engenderer of—a cataclysmic chaos that could destroy the world and perhaps the universe.

Strange Eons is a grand synthesis of Lovecraftian tales and themes. Bloch fuses elements from the Lovecraft Mythos into a convincing unity: Nyarlathotep prepares for the emergence of Cthulhu from the depths of the Pacific; the mind-exchange that Asenath Waite practised in "The Thing on the Doorstep" allows a Starry Wisdom member to deceive an opponent at a critical juncture, just as the mimicry that tricked Wilmarth at the conclusion of "The Whisperer in Darkness" does so at an earlier point in the novel; and the female protagonist serves, like Lavinia Whateley in "The Dunwich Horror," as the unwilling mate in a sexual union with one of the Great Old Ones. Throughout *Strange Eons*, all the characters attempting to thwart Nyarlathotep—including a powerful secret branch of the U.S. government—are themselves thwarted by Nyarlathotep and his minions; and the conclusion offers no reassurance.

The final section of *Strange Eons*, a harrowing account of a severe earthquake that causes the submersion of a large part of California sometime in the near future, is narrated in a hypnotic, quasi-stream-of-consciousness manner that is as potently effective as the most incantatory Lovecraftian prose. Here the resemblance to the prose-poem "Nyarlathotep" is very marked, as all civilisation seems to be cracking at the foundations. It is quite possible that Bloch was thinking not only of the prose-poem but of the passage (which he had already quoted in "The Shadow from the Steeple") in the sonnet "Nyarlathotep" in *Fungi from Yuggoth*:

> Soon from the sea a noxious birth began;
> Forgotten lands with weedy spires of gold;
> The ground was cleft, and mad auroras rolled
> Down on the quaking citadels of man.
> Then, crushing what he chanced to mould in play,
> The idiot Chaos blew Earth's dust away. (*AT* 73)

That "noxious birth" is, in Bloch's conception, nothing less than the emergence of Cthulhu, and the novel ends grimly and apocalyptically:

> That is not dead which can eternal lie, and the time of strange eons had arrived. The stars were right, the gates were open, the seas swarmed with immortal multitudes and the earth gave up its undead.
>
> Soon the winged ones from Yuggoth would swoop down from the void and now the Old Ones would return—Azazoth [*sic*] and Yog-Sothoth, whose priest he [Nyarlathotep] was, would come to lightless Leng and old Kadath in the risen continents which were transformed as he was transformed. . . .
>
> He rose, and mountains trembled, sinking into the sea.
>
> Time stopped.
>
> Death died.
>
> And Great Cthulhu went forth into the world to begin his eternal reign. (194)

Such a cheerless ending would be unthinkable to many modern weird writers, who feel obligated to restore bourgeois normality at the end regardless of the havoc their monsters have caused; but Bloch is true to Lovecraft's vision here, for he knew that that vision was a bleak one that saw little place for mankind in a boundless universe in which it was an infinitesimal atom. This is what makes *Strange Eons* the true homage that it is.

In the same year that *Strange Eons* was published, Stephen King (b. 1947)—the best-selling horror writer of his generation, whose generally favourable views of Lovecraft (found in his informal treatise on horror fiction, *Danse Macabre*, 1981) can now be found as blurbs on recent editions of Lovecraft's work—produced his own Lovecraft pastiche in "Jerusalem's Lot," first published in his story collection *Night Shift* (1978). Here we find ourselves in the year 1850 in an unspecified New England town, where one Charles Boone has moved into a house belonging to his deceased cousin. He is intrigued by a deserted village nearby called Jerusalem's Lot. Its church proves to be full of satanic paraphernalia, among which is a copy of the book *De Vermis Mysteriis*. It turns out that an ancestor, Philip Boone, had secured a copy of the work in 1789. Charles later comes upon an immense worm underneath the church: it appears that his touching of the book activated the creature.

"Jerusalem's Lot" (which of course has nothing to do with King's earlier vampire novel, 'Salem's Lot [1975]) is a competent enough tale, but it is really nothing more than a story about a giant worm. It probes no deeper issues and is not executed with notable skill. It is, moreover, plainly an adaptation of the central plot of "The Haunter of the Dark," where Robert Blake's inadvertent closing of the Shining Trapezohedron releases the avatar of Nyarlathotep from the Starry Wisdom church. King's protagonist at one point screams, "Gyyagin vardar! . . . Servant of Yogsoggoth, the Nameless One!" (498), evidently making a deliberate error for "Yog-Sothoth" or introducing a new entity to the Mythos.

Ramsey Campbell reentered the ranks of Lovecraftian writers with several tales in the 1970s; but none of them can take rank with his two early masterpieces, "Cold Print" and "The Franklyn Paragraphs." "The Tugging" was written for *The Disciples of Cthulhu* (1976), while "The Faces at Pine Dunes" was included in Campbell's own anthology, *New Tales of the Cthulhu Mythos* (1980). Both stories attempt to fuse Campbell's patented "internal" horror—based on a meticulous examination of abnormal psychology—with Lovecraftian cosmicism, but with only indifferent results. "The Tugging" is a long and rather confused story about a reporter, Ingels, who remembers the cosmic dreams he had as a child, relating to the rising of Atlantis—an event that (as in "The Call of Cthulhu") might signal the destruction of the human race. Campbell attempts to relate these dreams to the appearance of Ghroth, a celestial body that is apparently passing close to the earth's orbit. In "The Faces at Pine Dunes" a young man named Michael suspects that his parents are involved in a witch cult, but his investigation of their property— which includes notes from such works as "*necro, Revelations Glaaki, Garimiaz, Vermis, Theobald*" (242)—indicates that their involvement is considerably more sinister.

Campbell has declared "The Voice of the Beach" (*Fantasy Tales,* Summer 1982) to be a Lovecraftian story, remarking that it "was my attempt to return to Lovecraft's first principles, to see how close I could get to his aims without the encumbrances of the mythos . . . For my part, I believe it's the most successful of these stories [in *Cold Print*]."[5] There is reason to question this judgment. To be sure, Campbell is correct in believing that too many imitators of Lovecraft are content merely to create a new god or book without attempting to capture the intensity of vision that animates the best of Lovecraft; and "The Voice of the Beach" is certainly refreshing in the total absence of the now hackneyed citations of the *Necronomicon* or Yog-Sothoth or what have you. But in its use of the equally hackneyed device of the harried narrator and his frequent ruminations of the "had-I-but-known" sort, the story falls into a different kind of cliché. Here again Campbell attempts to unite an intense focus on individual psychology with Lovecraftian cosmicism, but the former seems to work against the latter, which comes off sounding contrived and unconvincing: "I seemed to be observing myself, a figure tiny and trivial as an insect, making a timid hysterical attempt to join in the dance of the teeming beach" (497). Nor are we ever given a true indication of what the cosmic force on the beach is or how it is planning to overwhelm the world.

Campbell actually approaches Lovecraftian cosmicism more successfully in tales that are less explicitly Lovecraftian. One such example is "Snakes and Ladders" (written 1974; *Twilight Zone*, April 1982), an early version of "Playing the Game." To my mind, the earlier version is superior to its rewrite, as it deals with a reporter who investigates a possibly fraudulent worker of magic in a seedy part of town and, after expressing scepticism, is pursued by some nameless force. Here Campbell deftly combines natural and supernatural horror (pursuit by hostile individuals in a suspect milieu and the suspicion of some vast entity just out of sight) and expresses as keen a sense of the cosmic as anywhere in his work. Is it possible, the story suggests, that we are all merely the playthings of appalling cosmic entities that toy with us as if we are pieces of some inscrutable puzzle? If this is the message of the story, then it is more genuinely Lovecraftian than many of Campbell's explicitly Lovecraftian tales.

"The Pattern" (written 1975; first published in Campbell's anthology *Superhorror* [1976]), although somewhat prolix, is powerfully cosmic in its presentation of a very bizarre horrific conception. A young couple, Tony and Di, move into what appears to be an idyllic rural milieu, only to be disturbed by strange screams that sound curiously like echoes. In true Lovecraftian fashion, Tony consults an obscure volume, *Legendry and Customs of the Severn Valley*, to examine the history of the region, finding it to have been "dogged by ill luck and tragedy" (145) from remotest times. But what could be causing the screams? In a reprise of Lovecraft's fascination with the complexities and paradoxes of time, Tony learns that the screams are a kind of reverse echo of a tragedy from the future—the tragedy of Tony's own death: "He knew the pattern had reached its completion, and he was afraid. He had to close his eyes before he could turn, for he could still hear the scream he was about to utter" (150). This story is in no sense a Lovecraft imitation, but it is a good example of how the Lovecraftian influence has been absorbed so as to lend substance to Campbell's own imagination.

"Dolls" (written 1974; first published in Michel Parry's *The Fourth Mayflower Book of Black Magic Stories* [1976]) is perhaps worth mentioning here. This historical tale of a witch coven that meets in the woods near Camside seems similar in tone to Lovecraft's evocations of the atmosphere of seventeenth-century New England Puritanism in such tales as "The Festival" and "The Dreams in the Witch House." Its sexual explicitness, of course, is very far from what the prudish Lovecraft could have imagined.

The best story in *New Tales of the Cthulhu Mythos* is probably T. E. D. Klein's "Black Man with a Horn." Klein (b. 1947) is a Lovecraftian of long standing. As a student at Brown University he wrote an honours thesis in 1969 comparing Lovecraft and Lord Dunsany—a work that was eventually condensed into the substantial introduction to the corrected edition of *Dagon and Other Macabre Tales* (1986). Although such of Klein's works as "The Events at Poroth Farm" (1972) and *The Ceremonies* (1984) have vague Lovecraftian echoes, only "Black Man with a Horn" is a full-fledged Mythos tale. On one level it is nothing more than an affectionate portrait of Lovecraft and his best friend, Frank Belknap Long, who is without doubt the original of the first-person protagonist of the tale. But on another level the tale brilliantly elaborates upon some central Lovecraftian themes. The narrator comes across a display of ancient Malayan figures to which the catalogue applies the term "Tcho-tcho." The narrator knows of the term only through Lovecraft's reference to "the wholly abominable Tcho-Tchos" in "The Shadow out of Time" (*DH* 395), and had always fancied that Lovecraft had invented the term in a spirit of fun. (Klein, or his narrator, is apparently unaware that the term was actually invented by August Derleth and borrowed by Lovecraft.) Now he finds that the entities to which the term refers are, in some sense, real. "I'd been put in the uncomfortable position of living out another man's horror stories" (164). A later passage, in which a Malay boy is interviewed by a filmmaker, is quietly potent:

> INT: This Malay youth has sketched a picture of a demon he calls Sho Goron. (To Boy) I wonder if you can tell me something about the instrument he's blowing out of it. It looks like the Jewish *shofar,* or ram's horn. (Again to Boy) That's all right. No need to be frightened.
> BOY: He not blow out. Blow in.
> INT: I see—he drews air in through the horn, is that right?
> BOY: No horn. Is no horn. (Weeps) Is *him.* (175)

The whole tale is an extraordinarily subtle account of words turning insidiously into reality: what was thought to be fiction is in fact all too real, and the narrator vainly strives to convince the world that they are facing imminent danger at the hands (or appendages) of entities that do not exist merely on the printed page.

In the 1970s and 1980s, several horror writers sought to capitalise on the popularity of both the best-selling genre of supernatural fiction and the resurgence of interest in Lovecraft, as testified by proliferating paperback editions, film and television adaptations, role-playing games, and the like.

First on the agenda is British writer Graham Masterton (b. 1946), whose first novel, *The Manitou* (1975), created a sensation—for reasons that are quite inexplicable to me, for this is as trashy and contrived a popular novel as anyone could ask for. We know we are in trouble when we see an epigraph from "H. P. Lovecraft" that is in fact taken from *The Lurker at the Threshold*—although by dumb luck Masterton has hit upon a section of the 1200 words written by Lovecraft and not the 49,000 words written by Derleth. The passage in question concerns the Indian wonder-worker Misquamacus. The novel is narrated in the first person (aside from the "Prelude") by Harry Erskine, an acknowledged charlatan who poses as a clairvoyant in New York, finding a rich lode of chicanery telling false fortunes to wealthy widows and such. One person who comes to him is a young woman, Karen Tandy, who has a curious growth on her neck, for which she is about to undergo an operation (conducted by Dr. J. H. Hughes, who although he is only thirty-three years old has somehow managed to become the world's leading authority on tumours). Erskine can make nothing of the matter; and Hughes, for his part, finds that the "tumour" has become so imbedded with Karen's vital parts that it cannot be removed. It grows remarkably fast, becoming an immense goitre or sac on the back of her neck.

Erskine and others conduct a séance, during which a face like "a cigar-store Indian" (75) emerges in the very fabric of the wooden table. He later emerges from Karen's body and announces himself as Misquamacus. He in turn wishes to summon a "Star Beast" (163) who—as a contemporary Indian shaman, Singing Rock, informs us—is a "Great Old One" (176). This creature finally appears and is described by a cameraman—somewhat in the manner of one of the townspeople of Dunwich who had grabbed a telescope to look at the Dunwich horror—as follows:

> "It swam, it was swimming, it came swimming across the room and through the room at the same time and I caught a glimpse of just the edge of it like a sort of squid, like a squid, with waving arms, all waving, but it was big as well, I can't say how big it was, I was so frightened there was something inside my head like my whole brain was stolen. Only a glimpse, though, only a glimpse." (200–201)

But never fear: Singing Rock is here. He lets us know that every object in the world, including manmade ones, have a "manitou" (spirit) that can be summoned. Misquamacus and his creature are eventually dispatched by summoning up the spirit of a computer, which is "Christian [!!!] and God-fearing and dedicated to the cause of law and order" (189)—in spite of the fact that, much earlier, Singing Rock had declared, "These demons have nothing to do with Christianity at all. You can fight Christian demons with crucifixes and holy water, but these demons will just laugh at you" (118).

It would seem, based on this synopsis, that *The Manitou* is a pretty clear pastiche of Lovecraft (and/or Derleth), but the details of the depiction of the various supernatural creatures make this a much more problematical matter. The Great Old One is presented not as a Lovecraftian entity (except in his physical manifestation as a squidlike creature) but as an Indian spirit. As Singing Rock explains:

> "He is the equivalent to your Satan, or Devil. Gitche Manitou is the great spirit of life and Red Indian creation, but the Great Old One

is his constant enemy. There are many accounts of the Great Old One in ancient Indian writings, although none of them agree what he looked like, or how he could be summoned. Some say he looked like a huge toad, the size of several pigs, and othes say he looked like a cloud with a face made of snakes." (176)

Possibly the parallel to Satan is meant to evoke the Derlethian notion of the Old Ones and their battles with the Elder Gods, but the similarity is imprecise.

Whatever the case, *The Manitou* is a wretched piece of hash that was clearly meant to capitalise on the popularity of *The Exorcist* and other blockbusters. In the short run it succeeded in its goal, as it was made into a big-budget film in 1978 and spawned two sequels by Masterton, *The Revenge of the Manitou* (1979) and *Burial* (1992), which I have not had the masochism to read.

Still more tangentially Lovecraftian is *The Keep* (1981) by F. Paul Wilson (b. 1946), which was also turned into a lavish film. We are taken to an obscure corner of Romania in 1941, where the Nazis are occupying a small castle or keep that guards a critical pass in the mountains. Some mysterious entity is killing the Nazis one by one, and the army commander, Captain Claus Woermann, and an SS officer, Erich Kaempffer, reluctantly call in a Romanian Jewish scholar, Theodor Cuza (accompanied by his fetching daughter, Magda), to solve the riddle. Curious books have been discovered in a secret compartment of the keep:

> She [Magda] picked up a random volume. Its title was in English: *The Book of Eibon.* It startled her. It couldn't be . . . it was a joke! . . .
>
> Magda stopped and gingerly lifted two [other books]. One was *De Vermis Mysteriis* by Ludwig [*sic*] Prinn; the other, *Cultes des Goules* by Comte d'Erlette. . . . (128)

And so on. In all, we find such titles as the Pnakotic Manuscripts, *The Seven Cryptical Books of Hsan, Unaussprechlichen Kulten,* and even the *Necronomicon*—in fact, "the *Al Azif* in the original Arabic" (130), even though Lovecraft in "History of the *Necronomicon*" says that no copies of the Arabic original are in existence (*MW* 53).

Well, this seems promising, but the development of the novel is singularly un-Lovecraftian. The baleful entity causing all the ruckus is one Viscount Radu Molasar, apparently a colleague of Vlad Tepes. Is he, then, a vampire? It seems so, but a shadowy figure who calls himself Glenn, who has providentially arrived on the scene, informs us that he is of much older ancestry: he is actually a creature called Rasalom (Molasar backwards) deriving from a prehuman era called the "First Age," and he wants more than just blood: "He draws strength from human pain, misery, and madness" (359). Glenn is himself a member of an ancient species called the Glaeken, who has vowed to stop Rasalom's depredations. At the end he predictably does so, getting the girl (Magda) in true bestseller fashion.

But what of those books discovered in the keep? They figure singularly little in the narrative, and Wilson is even at a loss to account for their presence there; all Glenn can say, at the end, is that he himself (who built the keep in order to imprison Rasalom in it) put the books there: "They can be dangerous in the wrong hands, but I couldn't let them be destroyed. Knowledge of any kind—especially of evil—must be destroyed" (373). In the final analysis, the Lovecraftian tomes are merely thrown in as a sort of in-joke, and they have no bearing on the course of the story. *The Keep* is certainly superior to *The Manitou*, but it too is nothing more than a popular potboiler, with stereotypical characters, liberal doses of grisly murder and sex, and all the other elements that caused the horror "boom" to die of inanition and mediocrity. I am willing to believe that Wilson went on to better things, but solely on the basis of *The Keep* he would not deserve to be remembered.

Still less worthy of remembrance is Michael Shea's early novel *The Color out of Time* (1984). Even August Derleth did not have the temerity to elaborate upon "The Colour out of Space," but this has not stopped Shea from stepping into the breach. The novel concerns a curious wave of sickness that first comes to two park rangers at a New England woodland resort (clearly based upon the Quabbin Reservoir, where Lovecraft's story is set). Two professors, Ernst Carlsberg and Gerald Sternbruck, team up with the sister of one of the dead rangers, Sharon Harms (no relation, one hopes, to Lovecraft scholar Daniel Harms), to battle the entity.

From the first, Shea commits the catastrophic error of destroying the moral ambiguity in Lovecraft's tale by unequivocally deeming the entity "evil." The professors see the peculiar colour in the woods and immediately detect a "feel of *evil*" (10)—and again, "I glimpsed the hazed form of an Evil so consummate, a predation so total and remorseless, that thought might sooner abdicate than contemplate its face" (31). This entity seems endowed with "a cold and hungering hate" (33).

It turns out that Sharon Harms had actually been a correspondent and disciple of H. P. Lovecraft, who had based "The Colour out of Space" upon an actual case—a farm family named Simes. At this point Shea undertakes essentially a Cliff Notes synopsis of the Lovecraft story, with meteor, professors analysing the material, and so forth. The entity is actually referred to throughout the story as "the Enemy," and this view is attributed to Lovecraft himself by Sharon: "there are Enemies Outside, Enemies that know a different space and time, and yet can feed on men, and lust to feed on men" (89).

Things go from bad to worse, in Lovecraftian terms. Shea unearths the dreaded star-stones of Derlethian coinage, which he refers to as "talismans," "amulets," or the "Elder Sign"—and which, it appears, Lovecraft himself had given to Sharon! Clearly, Shea has not read Tierney's "The Derleth Mythos" or Mosig's "H. P. Lovecraft: Myth-Maker." Sure enough, in spite of the entity's destruction of a few dozen hapless tourists, the star-stones do the trick and banish the entity from the earth: the professors dive underwater (since the well of the Simes farm is now beneath the waters of the reservoir) and hurl a star-stone into the well, causing the entity to shoot up into space—just as in the original story. But here nothing is left behind to corrupt the planet: "This earth is free of it at last" (190).

The Color out of Time soils and ruins a masterful Lovecraft story by depriving it of all its subtlety and nuance. In the original tale, the very motivations of the entity (entities?) cannot be ascertained, because it is so far outside the realm of "common human laws and interests and emotions" (*SL* 2.150) that its psychological attributes cannot be determined. But Shea sweeps this all aside, making the creature unequivocally "evil" (presumably from the human perspective) and endowed with the commonplace human motives of hatred and revenge. And instead of lingering insidiously in the ground to taint the earth for succeeding generations, the entity is banished in a neat and tidy resolution that requires only the eventual marriage of Sharon and Sternbruck to put the seal on this happy ending (let it pass that Carlsberg bit the dust in the final cataclysmic scene). *The Color out of Time* is a sorry excuse for a novel, and one only hopes that Shea (b. 1946) has done better work in the past two decades. It would be hard to do worse.

We now come to "The Madness out of Space" by Peter Cannon (b. 1951). Cannon's accomplishments as a Lovecraft scholar speak for themselves: his bracing monograph *H. P. Lovecraft* (1989) for Twayne's United States Authors series, his superlative collection of Lovecraft memoirs, *Lovecraft Remembered* (1998), and his numerous critical essays. Cannon has also written several noteworthy works of fiction that fall just outside the scope of this volume: the entertaining *Pulptime* (1984), a tale in which Lovecraft, Frank Belknap Long, and others team up with the ageing Sherlock Holmes to solve a case in New York in 1925; numerous whimsies and parodies, now gathered in *Forever Azathoth and Other Horrors* (1999); and, preeminently, *The Lovecraft Chronicles* (2004), perhaps the finest depiction of Lovecraft as an historical character.

"The Madness out of Space" was serialised in *Eldritch Tales* in 1982–83, and, although its author apparently regards it as an indiscretion of his youth, it is a far more substantial and creditable piece than that genuine and truly dreadful indiscretion of the seventeen-year-old S. T. Joshi, "The Recurring Doom." We are introduced to Howard Wentworth Annable, a freshman at Miskatonic University, who in some regards is clearly a stand-in for Lovecraft. But, in radical deviation from Lovecraft, he hates cats and ice cream and loves seafood! All this is great fun, but the work takes a more serious turn when Annable comes upon evidence of a nineteenth-century cult that seeks to call down a "madness out of space" (372) at a location called Satan's Ledge. Annable and the narrator, E. Phillips Winsor, meet an old member of the cult, Jay Harper, who tells them more about the cult. Eventually Annable finds himself drawn into the cult himself; the cult begins to reenact a hideous ceremony that might summon the madness out of space, but it is interrupted by Winsor. Annable is spirited away by a hideous white entity.

On one level, "The Madness out of Space" is nothing more than a vast in-joke—or, rather, a series of in-jokes. One could hold a contest to see how many obscure references to Lovecraft's life and work a given reader can detect—including such delights as "the shocking *Goblin Tower* by Frank Belknap Long" (384). But the self-parodic whimsy eventually gives way to an enthralling and compelling narrative, in which Cannon is careful to note that the entities in question are not "evil" but indifferent, as Annable explains:

> "This goes infinitely beyond man's feeble morality. We're no more significant than the least bacterial scum in the larger scheme of the universe. The Old Ones have spared us worthless wretches so far because we count for so little. They may appear 'malign' to certain self-blinded earth-gazers, but are in fact indifferent—except to the occasional exceptional individual, to whom They may give the opportunity for the realization of and *participation* in the awesome secrets of time and space." (391)

There is a certain element of self-parody here too (as the phrase "self-blinded earth-gazers" betrays), but Cannon has nonetheless faithfully echoed the essence of the Lovecraft Mythos here.

Whether the relative success of "The Madness out of Space" as opposed to the mediocrity (or worse) of the novels of Masterton, Wilson, and Shea bespeak the consistent superiority of small-press horror work over that of the blockbuster bestseller is an unanswered question. All that we can say for certain is that the Cthulhu Mythos, in the past two decades, has become even more of a popular phenomenon than ever before, as an increasing number of writers seek to cash in on its appeal in an attempt to line their coffers. As with the horror field in general, the amount of truly meritorious work appears to be in precisely inverse proportion to its quantity, but in the next chapter we shall nevertheless seek to probe some of the high spots while passing over in merciful silence the numerous depths and nadirs.

IX.

Recrudescence

In the summer of 1990 the H. P. Lovecraft Centennial Conference was held in Providence. It was, in effect, the culmination of two decades of work by leading scholars to establish Lovecraft as an unassailable literary figure, and it attracted participants and an audience from around the world. Around the time of Lovecraft's centennial there appeared a flurry of volumes that continued to draw upon recent scholarship and make it available to a wider academic public—such works as Peter Cannon's *H. P. Lovecraft* (1989) for Twayne's United States Authors series; my philosophical work, *H. P. Lovecraft: The Decline of the West* (1990); Donald R. Burleson's challenging deconstructionist study *Lovecraft: Disturbing the Universe* (1990); and numerous others. Some years later, my biography, *H. P. Lovecraft: A Life* (1996), appeared. As the 1990s progressed, Lovecraft continued to ascend in critical esteem, as testified by my three annotated editions for Penguin Classics (1999, 2001, 2004), a Modern Library edition of *At the Mountains of Madness* (2005), and, as a capstone, the Library of America edition of Lovecraft's *Tales* (2005), which received wide notice in reviews (not uniformly complimentary, however) and sold a remarkable 25,000 copies within the first few months of publication. By this date it could safely be said that Lovecraft had been firmly lodged in the canon of American and world literature.

But Lovecraft's popular appeal remained vigorous, as exemplified by the continuing sales of mass-market and trade paperback editions of Lovecraft's tales by Ballantine and, preeminently, by a remarkable proliferation of Cthulhu Mythos writing. Much of this writing was spurred by Robert M. Price's determination to assemble as many volumes as possible for Chaosium, the California-based publishing company that issued the widely popular Call of Cthulhu role-playing game. Beginning in 1993, with *The Hastur Cycle*, Price compiled more than a dozen "cycles" of

Cthulhu Mythos tales, along with single-author collections by Lin Carter and Henry Kuttner. Chaosium also issued a revised version of Berglund's *Disciples of Cthulhu* along with a follow-up volume, and it has gone on to publish such esoteric books as a tribute to Ramsey Campbell's early Mythos fiction (*Made in Goatswood*) and Stephen Mark Rainey's *Song of Cthulhu* (2001), a volume of Mythos stories about artists and musicians.

Other publishers got into the act. Tor published Robert Weinberg and Martin H. Greenberg's *Lovecraft's Legacy* (1990). Arkham House commemorated both Lovecraft's centennial and its own sixtieth birthday (1989) with the issuance of a revised edition of Derleth's *Tales of the Cthulhu Mythos* (1990), silently edited by James Turner, who tactfully omitted some of the poorer tales (although also omitting the worthy "The Deep Ones" by James Wade) and including several more recent items, such as Stephen King's "Jerusalem's Lot." Turner went on to edit *Cthulhu 2000* (1995), which he appears to have envisioned as an example of the kind of sophisticated Lovecraftian fiction he would like to see in the future. After leaving Arkham House, Turner assembled *Eternal Lovecraft* (1998) for the Golden Gryphon Press. Fedogan & Bremer issued Stephen Jones's *Shadows over Innsmouth* (1994) and *Weird Shadows over Innsmouth* (2005) and Robert M. Price's *Tales of the Lovecraft Mythos* (1992), *The New Lovecraft Circle* (1996), and *Acolytes of Cthulhu* (2000). Martin H. Greenberg and Robert Weinberg's *Miskatonic University* (1996) was a paperback anthology from DAW, while John Pelan and Benjamin Adams's *The Children of Cthulhu* (2002) was published by Ballantine/Del Rey. David Wynn's Mythos Books, which began as a bookselling operation, began publishing books around 1996, and it continues to issue collections of Mythos tales by select authors. This is, I daresay, an incomplete list, and a diligent bibliographer would have to expend considerable effort to update Chris Jarocha-Ernst's *Cthulhu Mythos Bibliography and Concordance* (1999). Indeed, there seems to be a considerable quantity of foreign Mythos writing, especially in French, Italian, and Spanish. It is of interest that this writing is being issued not merely by small presses but by mainstream publishers as well, as they clearly see a market not only in the name "Lovecraft" but in that magical and esoteric term "Cthulhu Mythos," which has definitively taken on a life of its own.

It can be seen from the above that a substantial number of Lovecraft pastiches have been written in the modes of the short story or novelette—understandably so, since Lovecraft himself worked in those modes and since it is a perennial problem for writers to sustain the emotion of horror over the length of a novel. And yet, it is a sad fact that very few contributions to any of the Mythos anthologies listed above amount to much as independent aesthetic entities. F. Paul Wilson's novella "The Barrens" (in *Lovecraft's Legacy*) appears to have its defenders, but it is ultimately disappointing. The story is narrated by Kathy McKelston, who had had a love affair as a college student with the rather peculiar Jim Creighton. After college, Jim went into the field of clinical psychology, with a side-interest in anthropology, as he was attempting to discover what is "real"; as he confesses to Kathy when meeting up with her years later: "I don't know—really *know*—what reality is. Nobody does" (273). This doesn't sound very promising, but let it pass. Jim now thinks that he can somehow find out what is "real" by exploring the Pine Barrens—an immense area of overgrown vegetation in southern New Jersey. He asks for Kathy's help, as her family comes from there. Jim is writing a book on the so-called Jersey Devil, and at one point he and Kathy see a strange cascade of lights descending upon them; one of them goes into Jim, and he describes the sensation as one of "cold" and "burning" (307)—clearly reminiscent of Nahum Gardner's fragmented utterance, "cold an' wet, but it burns" (*DH* 71), in "The Colour out of Space." That story is evoked still more clearly when Jim says he is "looking for a place where nothing grows" (315)—an echo of the blasted heath. The light appears to have infected Jim so that he eventually becomes a hideous monster while he undauntedly continues his quest for the "real."

There are moments of effectiveness in "The Barrens," and also moments of Lovecraftian fun, as in passing references to "the Pickman prints" (271) and the *Liber Damnatus* (325) from *The Case of Charles Dexter Ward*. But Wilson is attempting to write in a cosmic vein that is apparently foreign to his temperament, and the effort fails to convince. Toward the end Kathy maintains that she has caught a glimpse from beyond the veil—

> I looked around and knew that everything I saw was a sham, an elaborate illusion. Why? Why was the veil there? To protect us from harm? Or to shield us from madness? The truth had brought me no peace. Who could find comfort in the knowledge that huge,

immeasurable forces beyond our comprehension were out there, moving about us, beyond the reach of our senses? (331)

But, in spite of the length of the tale, the reader has not truly been prepared for this conclusion, and the actual glimpse from beyond the veil is too fleeting and imprecise to carry any emotive impact. In a note following the tale, Wilson frankly admits that "The style is mine, but the Cosmic Horror is Lovecraft's" (334), unwittingly testifying to the unconvincingness of his narrative.

There is not much else that is of merit in *Lovecraft's Legacy*, in spite of the distinguished stable of writers who contributed to it. Brian McNaughton's "Meryphillia" is an engaging tale of ghouls (the author would later on write an entire volume of stories on the subject, *The Throne of Bones*, 1997), but the ghoul theme is only tangentially related to the Mythos. Gahan Wilson's "H. P. L." is a dreadful tale using Lovecraft as a character. Gene Wolfe's "Lord of the Land" is a moderately effective tale in which it is conjectured that An-uat, apparently an Egyptian god of death, may be alive and well in Appalachia.

It is perhaps no accident that Stephen Jones has been able to assemble two volumes of pastiches of "The Shadow over Innsmouth," as this richly atmospheric tale is in many ways a perfect encapsulation of both the Lovecraft Mythos and the Cthulhu Mythos—in its vivid portrayal of an imaginary New England backwater, its display of hideous hybrid entities from the sea, its use of secret cults on the underside of normal society, and so forth. And yet, *Shadows over Innsmouth* contains its share of disappointments as well. The longest tale in the volume, Basil Copper's "Beyond the Reef," is exactly as long as Lovecraft's own story—but there the resemblance ends. It is simply one more rewriting of the story, with nothing new or innovative added, and its lifeless prose and clumsy development make it a painful reading experience. Not much more can be said of some of the other lengthier tales in the book, among them Brian Mooney's "The Tomb of Priscus," Michael Marshall Smith's "To See the Sea," or Brian Lumley's laughable "Dagon's Bell."

Only a few stories stand out. Brian Stableford's "The Innsmouth Heritage" is probably the most innovative tale in the volume. It avoids the pitfalls of most pastiches by being a genuine extension of the idea contained in the original. Stableford takes the basic premise of Lovecraft's story—the mating of human beings and amphibians and the loathsome hybrids that result—and refashions it: the physical abnormalities of the town's denizens ("the Innsmouth look") are now interpreted as a genetic mutation. This is familiar ground for Stableford, whose *Sexual Chemistry: Sardonic Tales of the Genetic Revolution* (1991) also broached this theme; but here, I fear, the exposition is a trifle too clinical to carry much punch. Lovecraft, for all the pseudo-science of his later tales, never failed to tell a rousing story—a narrative that achieved an almost unbearable cumulative effect by the steady augmenting of tension and suspense. Stableford's story appeals too exclusively to the intellect, and what emotional resonances it has derive largely from its allusions to Lovecraft's tale.

David Langford's "Deepnet" is also cleverly innovative. Langford is primarily a science fiction writer and, like Stableford, ingeniously takes the "Innsmouth heritage" of disease and decay into the disturbingly near future: what would happen if the Innsmouth folk entered the computer age and began marketing video games and computer programs? Although, like Stableford's story, this tale lacks any overt climax or any real action to speak of, it manages to create an unnerving effect in its quiet way. Neil Gaiman's "Only the End of the World" involves a werewolf who disrupts the Deep Ones' ceremony that will presumably summon Cthulhu. This bald synopsis makes the tale sound ludicrous, but Gaiman's scintillating and intensely visual style and imagery allow him to pull it off. Nor can we overlook Nicholas Royle's "The Homecoming," a grim narrative set in post-Ceausescu Romania, in which several of the incidents in Lovecraft's tale (the bus ride into town, the narrator's stay at a seedy hotel, and the like) are employed to convey a sense of horror and decay—but in this case, a product not of unwholesome inbreeding but of political savagery and economic blight. Nothing supernatural occurs in the tale, but it may be the most frightening of the volume.

As for *Weird Shadows over Innsmouth,* we can note a few interesting specimens. Caitlín R. Kiernan's "From Cabinet 34, Drawer 6" cleverly links Innsmouth with the horror film industry, suggesting that the producers of *Creature from the Black Lagoon* derived their inspiration from the hybrid creatures in the decaying seaport. The tale is skilfully told, but it does not seem to introduce any truly innovative conceptions.

Kiernan (b. 1964), who has done outstanding work in the short story in recent years and may be close to the pinnacle of contemporary horror writing, has made no secret of her indebtedness to Lovecraft, Blackwood, and other classic writers; and her background in science, especially that of palaeontology, is frequently put to good use to create exactly the sort of scientific verisimilitude that Lovecraft employed. Kiernan's recent novel *Daughter of Hounds* (2007) makes some use of Lovecraftian themes, notably the ghoul theme.

One of the most remarkable figures in recent Lovecraftian fiction, as in weird literature as a whole, is Thomas Ligotti (b. 1953), who made his debut almost as a thief in the night with the small-press volume *Songs of a Dead Dreamer* (1986). Ligotti has been content to work chiefly in the small press and chiefly in the short story form—he has stated not only that he himself is incapable of writing a "horror novel," but that the very concept may involve a paradox or contradiction, as such works all too often devolve into mystery or suspense tales with horrific or supernatural interludes—and as a result his reputation has grown largely by word-of-mouth. Ligotti is as far from the image of the popular bestselling author as can be imagined, and his complex, at times tortuous style and extraordinarily bizarre conceptions make little accommodation to the lazy or unengaged reader.[1]

Ligotti is one of the most interesting and articulate spokesmen for the horror tale, and his frequent comments on it—and, specifically, on Lovecraft—might be a good place to begin our brief study of his Lovecraftian work. Ligotti has remarked: "I hope my stories are in the Lovecraftian tradition in that they may evoke a sense of terror whose source is something nightmarishly unreal, the implications of which are disturbingly weird and, in the magical sense, charming."[2] But in explaining why he does not often use the framework and nomenclature of Lovecraft's myth-cycle, Ligotti adds that "Lovecraft's universe . . . is a very specific model of reality, one whose portrayal demands a more realistic approach to fiction writing than mine is."[3] Ligotti has flatly declared that he is most attracted to Lovecraft's early tales,[4] in which the dream element is more prevalent and the supernatural elements not always satisfactorily accounted for; he has remarked of the later work that "I find Lovecraft's fastidious attempts at creating a documentary style 'reality' an obstacle to appreciating his work."[5] Two stories by Ligotti are markedly Lovecraftian. "The Sect of the Idiot" appears to be influenced chiefly by "The Music of Erich Zann" and "The Festival." "The Last Feast of Harlequin," dedicated "To the memory of H. P. Lovecraft" (45), does indeed draw upon Lovecraft's late tale "The Shadow over Innsmouth" (although more perhaps upon "The Festival," an earlier working out of the same idea), but this story is an anomaly in Ligotti's fiction. In any event, a very crude distinction between Lovecraft and Ligotti might be enunciated as follows: whereas Lovecraft tries to make the unreal (i.e., the supernatural) real, Ligotti tries to make the real unreal (i.e., everything is "supernatural," or at any rate unnatural and monstrous).

Ligotti's emphasis on language has led him, like Lovecraft, to be very prodigal in the inventing of mythical books. *Vastarien, Cynothoglys, The Noctuary of Tine*—these are only a few of the cryptic volumes in the Ligottian library. The author has remarked: "I have some notes about the 'forbidden book,' in the Lovecraftian sense, that is, a kind of metaphysical obscenity, an offense against all conception of order. I think my conclusion was that the forbidden book would require the forbidden author to write it, though it might be a work of imagination and not, like the *Necronomicon*, a book of genuine revelation."[6] Imagination as opposed to revelation: here again is a critical distinction between the Ligottian and the Lovecraftian universe. Lovecraft's tomes reveal loathsome truths about the real world; Ligotti's transport one to the unreal.

"Vastarien" is Ligotti's most searching exploration of the forbidden book theme. The plot of this richly atmospheric tale—which stands with "The Last Feast of Harlequin" at the pinnacle of his achievement—is deceptively simple: a man finds a book and it drives him mad. But what a wealth of dense imagery is created by means of this seemingly hackneyed device! Victor Keirion searches for a book to transport him out of this world, but most of the "forbidden" books he finds are insufficient for the task; they are all "sodden with an obscene reality, falsely hermetic ventures which consisted of circling the same absurd landscape. The other worlds portrayed in these books inevitably served as annexes of this one; they were impostors of the authentic unreality which was the only realm of redemption, however gruesome it might appear" (264–65). But *Vastarien* is different: it is "'not *about* something, but actually is that something'" (267). This is a piquant conception, and a very neat resolution of the inveterate problem of the relation between the signifier and the signified—here they are one! But what sort of book is *Vastarien?* "To all appearances it seemed he had discovered the summit or abyss of the unreal, that paradise of exhaustion, confusion, and debris where reality ends and where one may dwell among its ruins" (271).

Another extraordinarily powerful tale, "Nethescurial," strikes me as a very subtle—and perhaps unconscious—adaptation of "The Call of Cthulhu." This is not to deny the essential originality of Ligotti's story, nor to suggest that it in any way incorporates the hackneyed "Cthulhu Mythos" in the manner of an August Derleth or a Brian Lumley, but I believe that the basic framework of the two tales is strikingly similar. Lovecraft's tale is divided into three sections. In the first, a man discovers papers left by his grand-uncle attesting to the existence of a cult worshipping a hideous god, Cthulhu, and the possible existence of that entity itself; the second section narrates a policeman's discovery of this cult and its beliefs; the third finally reveals—although again through a document—the actual existence of Cthulhu as he attacks the hapless crew of a derelict ship.

It can be seen that the basic pattern in "The Call of Cthulhu" is the gradual transformation of words into reality: whereas at the outset we only read of Cthulhu from the narrator's paraphrase of documents, at the end we vicariously experience the proximity of the nameless creature. Ligotti adapts this pattern and in a sense even surpasses it. "Nethescurial" is presented as a letter written by one friend to another; it begins: "I have uncovered a rather wonderful manuscript" (69). This manuscript tells of a man who comes to a mysterious island named Nethescurial and, in the course of discussions with a Dr. N——, learns of an "omnipresent evil in the living world" (71), "an absolute evil whose reality is mitigated only by our blindness to it" (75). Suggestive as this is, the horrors remain curiously abstract. The letter writer even remarks that the "words of this peculiar manuscript seem rather weak in this regard"—i.e., in the matter of actually conveying the bizarrerie of the situation. Thus ends the first section of the tale.

In the second section the letter writer has experienced a disturbing dream in which he is in a room poring over maps, all of which feature some island named Nethescurial. In the room is an altar with an idol on it. When a weird band of worshippers comes to pray before it, one of the worshippers loathsomely melds with the idol.

The third section of the tale opens with the remark: "Well, it seems this letter has mutated into a chronicle of my adventures Nethescurialian" (81). The writer speaks more truly than he knows, for as this section proceeds we learn that the writer's own words are insidiously being mutated by Nethescurial (whatever it may be), as he unwittingly begins to duplicate the expressions of the manuscript he had so desultorily examined at the outset. The relations to Lovecraft's story are obscure but significant—Nethescurial as a parallel for the sunken island of R'lyeh; worshippers praying before an entity whose true nature they themselves may not understand; Cthulhu's influence of dreams mirrored by the narrator's loss of control over his own language. And Ligotti brings home the reality of the weird phenomenon in a way that perhaps even exceeds Lovecraft: the letter writer can only conclude with a pitiable denial of the true state of affairs—"I am not dying in a nightmare" (84).

Incredibly, "The Last Feast of Harlequin" (*Fantasy and Science Fiction*, April 1990) is a relatively early tale of Ligotti's,[7] and yet it is leagues away from the nightmarish unreality of the rest of his work. I trust it is not simply my bias toward supernatural realism that makes me rank this tale as his among his best. If nothing else, it may perhaps be the best homage to Lovecraft ever written. To call it a mere pastiche would be to do it an injustice.

The story follows traditional Lovecraftian lines: an anthropologist interested in exploring the "significance of the clown figure in diverse cultural contexts" (3) reads an article by a former professor of his, Dr. Raymond Thoss (who, I take it, is not the same as the Dr. Thoss of "The Troubles of Dr. Thoss"), about a festival that takes place every year in December in the Midwestern town of Mirocaw. He visits the town in the summer and thinks he sees Dr. Thoss there, although he appears transformed into an inarticulate derelict. This compels him actually to go to the town during the festival. He insinuates himself into the goings-on, dresses up as one of the many derelicts who seem to serve some cryptic ritual function, and is led by them into an underground chamber where horrors of various sorts transpire.

This superficial and incomplete synopsis cannot even begin to suggest the tale's richness of texture, density of atmosphere, psychological and topographical realism, and—the most Lovecraftian feature of all—the notion of ancient and loathsome rituals surviving into the present day, related to and perhaps the origin of the most ancient human myth cycles. If there is any complaint to be made of this story, it is that it appears to lack the cosmicism of Lovecraft's most representative work. The bulk of the story is very likely derived from "The Festival" (1923), with a brief nod to "The Shadow over Innsmouth" at the end. The horror of the story seems to affect only random individuals rather than, as in the later Lovecraft, the entire race or the entire cosmos. Nevertheless, "The Last Feast of Harlequin" clearly demonstrates that Ligotti can write the sort of documentary realism he appears to scorn without losing the individuality of his own voice.[8]

Fred Chappell, perhaps gaining inspiration from the word-of-mouth reputation that his 1968 novel *Dagon* was gradually achieving among Lovecraftians (it was reprinted in 1987), returned to horror fiction in several short stories in the 1980s and 1990s, some collected in *More Shapes Than One* (1991). Two stories stand out. "Weird Tales" (*Texas Review*, Summer 1984) is an engaging but error-sprinkled non-supernatural tale using Lovecraft as a character and focusing upon Lovecraft's encounter with Hart Crane in Cleveland in 1922. Much more relevant to our present purposes is "The Adder" (*Deathrealm*, 1989). Here the narrator's uncle tells him that he has a handwritten copy of Alhazred's *Al Azif*. But when the book comes into contact with a copy of Milton's poems, the latter's text is subtly but significantly altered (and Chappell, a noted poet himself, is convincing in presenting actual examples of the changed text). Even other copies of Milton, not physically touched by *Al Azif*, are affected. Presently, Alhazred's text is translating itself into English, and the pages of the Milton volume suddenly go blank. The protagonists manage to reverse the effect and save literature—but a fly that had landed on the page of Milton carries the poison out the window. This brilliant tale restores to the hackneyed idea of the "forbidden book" its original notions of apocalyptic danger and evil, for its corrupting influence has the potential to destroy our most cherished cultural artifacts.

Another veteran who has constantly returned to the Lovecraftian mode is Ramsey Campbell. In 1995 he published "The Horror under Warrendown" in a volume of imitations of his own early Lovecraftian

work, *Made in Goatswood.* This tale may well be among the most successful of Campbell's pastiches of Lovecraft—although, in a sense, that
success is obtained at the price of Campbell's partial suppression of his
own individuality. The story is quite similar in tone to some of Lovecraft's early tales, with their obsessive concern with the sensations of a
first-person narrator (a rare usage in Campbell) as he is slowly drawn
into the folds of an appalling horror. We are introduced to Warrendown, a "new" town in Campbell's Severn Valley. Graham Crawley
persuades the narrator to take him there because he has evidently im-
pregnated a woman and wishes to see how she and her child are doing.
The narrator is at first repulsed by the overwhelming "vegetable smell"
(256) of the place, whose humble cottages seem almost deserted; but as
he becomes unwillingly enmeshed into his friend's plight, he finds himself pursuing Crawley into a seemingly abandoned church, descending a
cavity at the altar (exactly reminiscent of a scene in "The Festival"), and
witnessing a hideous rite of worship:

> At first the dimness, together with shock or the torpor which had over-
> come my brain, allowed me to avoid seeing too much; only a horde of
> unclothed figures hopping and leaping and twisting in the air around an
> idol, which towered from the moist earth, an idol not unlike a greenish
> Easter Island statue overgrown almost to featurelessness, its apex lost
> in the darkness overhead. Then I saw that one of the worshipping
> horde was Crawley, and began to make out faces less able to pass for
> human than his, their great eyes bulging in the dimness, their bestial
> teeth gleaming in misshapen mouths. . . . The earth around the idol
> swarmed with their young, a scuttling mass of countless bodies which
> nothing human could have acknowledged as offspring. (266–67)

This is very good pseudo-Lovecraft, as the narrator comes to realise that
Crawley (whose very name symbolises a descent upon the evolutionary
scale) has mingled with creatures who have so renounced their humanity
as to become not merely bestial but half-vegetable. The conclusion—in
which the narrator, in a now hackneyed Lovecraftian convention, dis-
tractedly ponders whether there may be more cults like this one around
the world—is, if I may be pardoned a pun, a little too pulpish.

Campbell's contribution to *Weird Shadows over Innsmouth,* "Raised by
the Moon," is certainly more clearly written in his own voice and much
less of a straightforward pastiche, but it is unsatisfactory in other ways.

Dealing with a British seaside town called Baiting that contains Innsmouth-like features and inhabitants, the tale is heavy on mood (especially in its attempt to convey the stench of fish pervading the town) but weak on plot and motivation. Evidently the progress of civilisation has destroyed the formerly abundant fishing in the town, so that all that is left is the hideous hybrid entities who emerge from the deep and make off with the hapless protagonist. The whole tale is sketchily developed and lacks focus.

Campbell finally came close to working in the Lovecraftian mode in a novel in 2002, when he published *The Darkest Part of the Woods*. Here Campbell returns to the setting of some of his earliest tales—the imaginary town of Brichester, nestled within the Severn Valley. But this Brichester, far from being the implausibly archaic nexus of Lovecraftian horror that it was in the *Inhabitant of the Lake* stories, is a town fully enmeshed in the modern world, with its computers, cellphones, and televisions. And yet, Lovecraft is perhaps not far from Campbell's vision in this richly complex, meticulously crafted, and chillingly terrifying work.

We learn that Heather Price, struggling to support herself and her adult son, Sam, as a librarian, is the daughter of Lennox Price, a man confined in the Arbour, a nearby mental hospital. Lennox, the author of a scholarly work, *The Mechanics of Delusion*, has himself become unhealthily fascinated with the dense woods that surround Brichester, and on occasion he leads other inmates in conducting anomalous rituals in a clearing deep in the heart of the woods. He refuses to explain what he is searching for aside from uttering the curious name "Selcouth."

Matters are precipitated when Heather's long-lost younger sister, Sylvia, returns to Brichester after many years in America. Later she announces that she is pregnant, but refuses to reveal the father of the child. Sam, meanwhile, a man in his early twenties, finds himself unhealthily attracted to his young aunt.

The name Selcouth is finally elucidated (initially by an Internet site) as one Nathaniel Selcouth, a sixteenth-century magician who built a dwelling in the Brichester woods and sought to "create a messenger or servant that would mediate between him and the limits of the universe, both physical and spiritual" (163). It is here that the Lovecraft influence manifests itself, and even more so when Sylvia discovers Selcouth's journal in an underground cavity deep in the woods. The echoes of *The Case of Charles Dexter*

Ward, with Ward's discovery of Curwen's journal, are evident, and Campbell makes no secret of it: Curwen, it appears, "is known to have visited England in search of Selcouth's journals but failed to locate them" (163). What follows are some of the most terrifying passages in all Campbell's work, as successive characters brave the depths of the woods either to carry out or to thwart the sinister plans of the ancient mage.

The Darkest Part of the Woods is, however, far from merely an exercise in shudder-coining. Campbell, at the height of his form in fluidity of prose, sensitivity in character depiction, and mastery of narrative pacing, has produced a novel that continuously and lovingly shapes his characters as on a potter's wheel; every statement, every gesture, even every moment of silence contributes to the etching of each distinctive personality. At the same time, the evocation of the terrors of the natural landscape, and the horrors that can emerge from the centuried past, supply a backdrop of cosmic horror against which the characters appear to struggle in vain. It is remarkable, in a novel of this length, to find not a single wasted word, not a single sentence or passage that does not in some way contribute to that "unity of effect" which Poe believed was solely the province of the short story.

One of the most interesting writers in the modern Cthulhu Mythos tradition is Stanley C. Sargent. Although his first collection of Mythos tales, *Ancient Exhumations* (1999), contains relatively conventional items, his next collection, *The Taint of Lovecraft* (2002), features some extremely ingenious tales. Chief among these is "The Black Brat of Dunwich" (1997), one of the cleverest deconstructions of "The Dunwich Horror" on record. Here we learn from Abe Galvin, who had stayed with the Whateleys for a time as a tutor for Wilbur, that Henry Armitage, far from being the saviour of the human race, was in fact in league with Wizard Whateley in an attempt to let in Yog-Sothoth, and that Wilbur was in opposition to these two. It was Armitage who had allowed Wilbur's twin to escape under the earth during his apparent confrontation with him on Sentinel Hill; after this, Armitage returned to his home—in Innsmouth. It is difficult to describe one's emotions in reading "The Black Brat of Dunwich," where each succeeding revelation turns the Lovecraft story on its head and destroys the naïve "good-vs.-evil" dichotomy that appears to be inherent in that tale.

Nearly as clever but less well executed is "Their Love of Craft" (*Crypt of Cthulhu*, Hallowmas 1995), a science fiction tale taking place on "Experimental Planet 903" (1). The story puts forth the idea of OBs— "Organic Builders," clearly derived from the shoggoths. These creatures take up telepathic suggestions from their masters for building purposes—but if so, why are hideous creatures populating the planet? It turns out that some of the human explorers are reading Lovecraft, and the OBs are fashioning the monsters that the men are reading about! This, as I say, is extraordinarily clever, but such gaucheries as "General Clark Asmith" (5) and a prose style that is excessively florid and histrionic mar the overall conception.

The most seemingly impressive tale in *The Taint of Lovecraft* is the novella "Nyarlatophis, a Fable of Ancient Egypt," but it is not a strong item. The tale concerns the discovery of a manuscript apparently written around 2000 B.C.E. by Amenemhat, the grand vizier of the pharaoh Menuhotep IV, dealing with his battles with Nyarlatophis. The suffix *-ophis*, as the scholars who have translated the document explain, is identical in meaning with *-hotep*, "the former being of Greek derivation" (77)—but in that case, it is not clear why an ancient Egyptian would refer to Nyarlathotep using a Greek suffix that would not be in existence for at least another thousand years. But no matter. The "underlying theme of the document," as the scholars explain, "is concerned with the age-old struggle between good and evil" (72), and sure enough, Amenemhat struggles valiantly against the evil Nyarlatophis, even when the Hounds of Thindahloos capture Menuhotep and take him to Nyarlatophis's tower. Amenemhat burns the tower down; Nyarlatophis emerges in the shape of an immense lion; but eventually Amenemhat prevails. This long-winded, slow-moving tale does not represent Sargent at his best, nor do several of the other tales, some of which are mere flippant jokes (such as "An End to Worry," where the Lovecraft scholar Will Murray takes the stage as Will Worry), while others, even if less openly jokey, are scarcely less frivolous in overall theme (such as "Live Bait," in which a human fish manufacturer uses the flesh of the Deep Ones in his fish marketing business). But Sargent has one genuine and unalloyed triumph, "The Black Brat of Dunwich," to his credit, and that is far more than can be said of most of his predecessors and contemporaries.

Another highly promising Lovecraftian writer, who like Sargent has also made his name chiefly through the small press, is W. H. Pugmire (b. 1951), engagingly known at times as Captain Frogmarsh. Pugmire's volumes—ranging from *Tales of Sesqua Valley* (1997) to *Dreams of Lovecraftian Horror* (1999) to *Sesqua Valley and Other Haunts* (2003) to *The Fungal Stain and Other Dreams* (2006)—contain some of the richest veins of neo-Lovecraftian horror seen in recent years, although he has been writing since the early 1970s. Pugmire himself is a larger-than-life figure whose flamboyant ventures into punk rock and other avant-garde venues of popular culture are about as far from the stiff decorum advocated by the staid Lovecraft could possibly be; and yet, he acknowledges a genuine admiration for the works of the Providence writer and strives to duplicate their effects, but in a distinctly modern idiom. He makes no secret of his debt to Lovecraft and other authors, writing: "I wear my influences openly. Indeed, the foremost reason I write is to be *identified* with my literary heroes, Shakespeare and Wilde and Lovecraft."[9] Pugmire is one of those rare authors who can channel their literary influences while at the same time remaining profoundly original. Perhaps it would be more accurate to say that, since Pugmire's own literary goals and aspirations are so much in tune with those of his avowed influences, he can almost unconsciously allow those influences to mould his work in such a way as to convey the effects he independently wishes to achieve.

Consider "The Hands That Reek and Smoke." On the surface it would seem that this story is nothing more than a retelling of Lovecraft's prose-poem "Nyarlathotep," but its display of a female protagonist, its extensive use of dialogue, and its distinctively original prose-poetry make it substantially more than a pastiche. A single paragraph might suggest Pugmire's simultaneous ability to evoke Lovecraft and to convey his own literary essence:

> "You must see Nyarlathotep." Her strong clear voice echoed from above. "He is wonderful, and dreadful. He will show you prophecies of the cold bleak abysses between the stars, those places where dead gods fumble in dream-infested slumber. The great ones were. They are. They shall be." (153)

The first two sentences spoken by the character are echoes, not of the prose-poem itself, but of the letter of late 1920 in which Lovecraft recounts the dream that inspired it—a dream in which Samuel Loveman said to Lovecraft: "Don't fail to see Nyarlathotep if he comes to Providence. He is horrible—horrible beyond anything you can imagine—but wonderful."[10] The next sentence is Pugmire's own, although significantly influenced by the Lovecraft idiom. The remaining sentences are deliberate evocations of the celebrated passage from the *Necronomicon* in "The Dunwich Horror" ("The One Ones were, the Old Ones are, and the Old Ones shall be" [*DH* 170]).

Consider, too, the prose-poem "Necronomicon," which contains one of the most poignant reflexions on the psychological effects of the "forbidden book" that any contemporary Mythos writer has produced:

> The book is before me. I can smell the wormy pages whereon the words are found, those signals that reach beyond the void to where the One-in-All pulses in eternal corruption. As these plucked eyes stain my palms, I heard the nameless beating of wings. I hear unthinkable voices whisper my name above the storm. Yuggoth damn my puny soul! I stagger to my feet, and scream to darkness the unhallowed name. I feel shapeless paws grip under my arms and raise me upward. I limp beyond reason to that void of no return where lives no masquerade of human hope. (38)

In this passage is a simultaneous conveyance of cosmic and psychological horror that Lovecraft himself only rarely achieved.

"The Sign That Sets the Darkness Free" is a powerful prose-poem evoking memories of several Lovecraft poems, notably "The Messenger" and several of the *Fungi from Yuggoth* sonnets, but nonetheless remaining original by virtue of its emphasis on the weird power of music. The title is of course derived from a line in "The Messenger" about the Elder Sign, "That sets the fumbling forms of darkness free" (*AT* 64), but the tale's citation of the hideous church of St. Toad's, its passing mention of the "ancient bridge that crossed the filthy canal" (35) (recalling the *Fungi* sonnet "The Canal"), and other passages make this work a vivid fusion of Lovecraftian echoes.

It would, however, be unfair to Pugmire to suggest that his tales do nothing more than seek to recall Lovecraftian originals. The above tales are relative rarities in his work for their direct relations to specific Lovecraft works. A story such as "A Phantom of Beguilement" is a beautiful rumination on the Lovecraftian town of Kingsport; aside from random recollections of "The Terrible Old Man," it remains a strikingly original work. Pugmire has even brought distinction to some of the lesser Lovecraft imitators by revivifying their stale conceptions. "The Imp of Aether" (first published in *Tales of Sesqua Valley* and revised for *Sesqua Valley and Other Haunts*) performs the miracle of infusing August Derleth's fire elemental Cthugha with novelty and distinction. (The story is dedicated to Derleth.) A moving tale of a man who inexorably falls under Cthugha's sway, it concludes cataclysmically:

> I watched, as the parchment in his hand darkened and turned black. In horror I watched as the hand that held it darkened also and turned into a thing of ash. Oh, how his flesh crumbled and separated. Ah, the hot burning wind that came from nowhere, that encircled Wilus and the thing to which he was conjoined. A cyclone of ash rose toward the ceiling, and from within the mania of storm I could see the lustrous eyes of an ageless daemon. It raised an amorphous face and opened wide an expanse of mouth, an orifice that puckered and exhaled. A flake of ash sailed from out the tempest, drifted to me and floated into my heaving mouth. (125)

This single story is superior to the entire corpus of Derleth's ill-conceived Mythos work.

Pugmire has gained celebrity for his creation of the Sesqua Valley. It would be both facile and inaccurate to say that this is nothing more than a transference of Lovecraft's Arkham country to the Pacific Northwest, Pugmire's native land. In fact, no cities or towns are specified in the Sesqua Valley, which remains a largely rural or rustic realm. In spite of the relative absence of specific landmarks (a Mt. Selta is frequently mentioned), Pugmire's numerous tales of this vale of deep woods and supernatural forces manage to build it up into a strange reality analogous to Lovecraft's New England topography or the Severn Valley locale of Ramsey Campbell's stories. As one character pregnantly asks in "The Darkest Star": "What strange enchantment lingers in this darksome valley?" (75). Pugmire's first tale of Sesqua Valley was "O, Christmas Tree," written in 1974 and published in 1979. With the passing of years and the growth of his aesthetic compass, Pugmire has written tales that do far more than merely evoke Lovecraftian themes in a new setting; such a tale as "Beneath an Autumn Moon," which concludes *Sesqua Valley and Other Haunts*, owes little to Lovecraft and presages Pugmire's independent development as a writer who need not stand upon the shoulders of his illustrious predecessors.

If there is any flaw in Pugmire's work, it is that a fair number of his stories seem to lack focus and direction. Plotting is not a strong point, and his tendency toward prose-poetry makes many of his tales some-what rambling and confused. In this sense, his most aesthetically satis-factory volume may remain *Dreams of Lovecraftian Horror,* a collection of prose-poems whose delicacy and subtlety defy the clumsy analysis of the literary critic.

Much less impressive is the relatively recent writer Jeffrey Thomas. Thomas began his career in the late 1980s with a succession of short sto-ries set in the futuristic city of Punktown (the slang name for the town of Paxton), set on the planet Oasis and inhabited both by human beings and by a succession of quasi-human alien entities and species of a very differ-ent sort. It is discouraging to see Thomas—who is otherwise an occa-sionally effective writer—wholeheartedly espouse the Derleth Mythos with its conventional and imaginatively stultifying dichotomy of Elder Gods and Old Ones. Consider "The Bones of the Old Ones" (1995), a story in his collection of Lovecraftian tales, *Unholy Dimensions* (2005):

> "They're known as the Old Ones, the Great Old Ones, the Outsiders. . . . They once ruled everything . . . long before us. They may have seeded humans throughout many systems, like [*sic*] we'd plant crops. . . . Anyway, I think the Old Ones also might have seeded us because they wanted us around to help them come back through if they ever got locked out. Because that's exactly what happened. Another powerful amalgamation of beings—the Elder Gods—came up and overpowered them. Locked them up, locked them out." (10–11)

And yet, other stories reveal some minimal discomfort with this schema. Although, in "The Avatars of the Old Ones" (1999), it is stated that "The Old Ones are trying to come through again" (41), one char-acter expresses a certain scepticism about the Elder Gods: "Some peo-ple say that another race of beings, called Elder Gods, originally beat them down, locked them out of our dimension . . . but other people disagree about that, and claim there is no bad race/good race war, cor-responding with Christian devils and mysteries" (42). Finally, in "The Young of the Old Ones" (2003), Thomas states that the Elder Gods may merely be "rivals" (67) of the Old Ones.

The introduction of the Elder Gods would not be fatal to Thomas's stories if they were more compelling in other ways; but they are not. The majority of them devolve into shoot-'em-up stories in which various characters undertake to battle the Old Ones or their spawn by means of various high-tech weaponry. As in the work of Brian Lumley, this fusion of Lovecraftian cosmicism with an action-adventure plot is rarely successful. Other stories by Thomas simply devolve into the absurd, as in "Through Obscure Glass," where gugs (from *The Dream-Quest of Unknown Kadath*) make an incursion into W. H. Pugmire's Sesqua Valley, or "Out of the Belly of Sheol," where it turns out the the biblical Jonah was swallowed, not by a whale, but by Cthulhu.

Many of the worst flaws in Thomas's Lovecraftian work are on full display in his first novel, *Monstrocity* (2003). Here one Christopher Ruby stumbles upon a plot by various figures to facilitate the Old Ones' return by the use of the *Necronomicon*, which although still rare is now available in computerised form. Thomas makes his own additions to the Mythos library in the form of Wadoor's *The Atlas of Chaos* and Skretuu's *The Veins of the Old Ones* (38), whatever that might refer to. The novel focuses around the attempts by various cults to awaken a creature named Ugghiutu, but Ruby and a valiant band of heterogeneous colleagues manage to foil the plans—for now. The disappointing feature of the novel is that no real attempt is made to specify exactly what the *Necronomicon* is aside from a book of spells (as Ruby once remarks, "I spend this morning casting spells to protect me from evil" [144]), or to specify the nature of the various "gods" or "spawn" of gods, aside from their possession of tentacles and other repulsive physical characteristics. Even the futuristic setting, for which Thomas has apparently won praise, is really nothing more than a watered-down and intellectually unchallenging version of the dystopias of J. G. Ballard and Philip K. Dick.

The one minimally original element in the novel is Ruby's disappointment when he sees that his valiant efforts do not seem to have changed the supersexed, superviolent nature of his society:

> I had hoped to see the opposite. A decrease in crime, in mental illness, in murder and rape. I had hoped the disruption in Ugghiutu's plan would lessen his influence. That he might fall deeper into slumber, and the poisonous tendrils he inserts into our minds would withdraw. Either he is too powerful to be greatly inconvenienced by

my efforts, or else I have overestimated his strength and the hold he has over our city. Perhaps even if I had killed that powerful being, dreaming in some overlapping dimension, the people here would be just as hateful, just as dangerous, just as poisoned. Maybe a god can't be blamed for their actions. Maybe all together, they dwarf the corruption of all of the Old Ones combined. (227–28)

Other works by Thomas—the story collection *Punktown* (2005) and the novels *Everybody Scream!* (2004) and *Deadstock* (2007)—have considerably fewer Lovecraftian elements, so they need not be treated here.

Several other recent writers have produced full-scale Cthulhu Mythos novels, but with indifferent success. Remarkably, one of the poorest of them is *The House of the Toad* (1993) by Richard L. Tierney—the very writer who exposed the "Derleth Mythos" so trenchantly in his brief 1972 essay. Twenty years later, he himself attempted an extended fictional treatment of the Mythos—but with disastrous results.

The novel focuses on James A. Kerrick, a hunter of ancient artifacts who stumbles upon mysterious bronze-coloured hemispheres in the jungles of Mexico and brings them back (illegally) to sell to a wealthy collector in Illinois, J. Cornelius Wassermann. Kerrick has been plagued by dreams in which he seems to be participating in a ritual sacrifice to a god named Ghanta. Wassermann, living in an immense, pentacle-shaped mansion near the town of Riverton, tells him that he has amassed such globes from all corners of the world, and that they have been found in nearly all ancient civilisations. Wassermann, an occultist, has written a book called *The Occult Foundation* in which he expounds his views:

> The sufferings of sentient beings provide the banquet of the gods. For this reason alone did those Primal Ones design the universe and the natural laws that govern it, in order that its congealing clouds of elements might condense to form stars and planets and, over the ages, evolve beings of greater and greater complexity, beings possessing a greater and greater capacity for suffering. The nervous system is the generator of pain, and pain is the energy that feeds the Primal Ones. (15)

It happens that the Primal Ones are looking forward to the "Great Dying, which is soon to come," during which "the Primal Gods shall feast upon this earth as never before . . ." (16).

This theme is of some small interest, in that it seems to connect with a rather piquant strain of misanthropy evident in Tierney's other work, especially his poetry. Consider some stanzas of the poem "To the Hydrogen Bomb":

> O Mushroom-cloud unfolding o'er the world,
>   No terrors in *my* soul do you inspire;
> Within this breast a dreadful hate lies furled,
>   Hotter by far than your atomic fire.
>
> . . .
>
> Within the whiteness of your fiery core
>   The dawning of a brighter age I see—
> When, in the crescendo of all-ending War,
>   Mankind shall all be gathered unto thee.[11]

But in *The House of the Toad* Tierney conventionally takes the side of a valiant humanity against the awful Primal Ones, and the results are sad to witness. For it becomes quickly evident that Wassermann is an agent of the Primal Ones and is attempting to bring about the Great Dying by various rituals, in which he envisions Kerrick himself to take part.

But never fear! Humanity has allies on its side, specifically in the form of Professor Ralph Duncan, a professor of ornithology at the local university (his scientific expertise comes into play because Wassermann has enlisted the aid of owls and bats as spies and agents in his nefarious plans) and one Bill Holgrave, a member of some shadowy quasi-governmental agency devoted to foiling the Primal Ones. Holgrave, in fact, is aware that such writers as Lovecraft have written about these creatures, and he expounds Lovecraft's views of them:

> "He wrote about the Great Old Ones who lurk beyond cosmic space, forever plotting to burst forth from other dimensions when 'the stars became right' in order to conquer our universe. And he also wrote that a few sensitive dreamers—artists, madmen and the like—could sense in their nightmares the imminent 'breakthrough' of these evil [*sic!*] beings into our own region of space-time." (151)

How low are the mighty fallen! Here was the critic who, in "The Derleth Mythos," specifically criticised Derleth for devising the conflict between the Old Ones and the Elder Gods, "making it a struggle between 'good' and 'evil' from an anthropomorphic point of view,"[12] but who in his own fiction does exactly the same thing! It is even more surprising to see Tierney adopt the "all are welcome" attitude toward the Mythos found in such critics as Lin Carter and Robert M. Price, when he writes that Lovecraft "influenced a subsequent generation of writers whose innate sensitivities predisposed them to further explore the dark chambers he had unlocked, notably Derleth [!], Long, Bloch, Campbell, Lumley [!!], Klein, Ligotti" (151). The ultimate degradation is reached when Holgrave and some other characters use the infamous star-stones as protective amulets. Say it ain't so! But there it is in black and white: "the object that emerged from the neck of her blouse was of dark, greenish stone carved in the shape of a five-pointed star. In its center gleamed a greenish-yellow gem suggestive of a candle flame in shape" (181). It is an insignificant matter that Tierney does not literally introduce the Elder Gods themselves into the scenario; for how could these star-stones have the power they have if they were not the product of some countervailing force of "good"? Sure enough, the amulets come into play in an action-packed climactic scene, when Kerrick and his cohorts interrupt a ceremony in which Wassermann is presumably planning to introduce the god Ghanta (which, we are informed, is identical to the Ghatanathoa of "Out of the Aeons") into the world. Indeed, that god in fact appears—a "vague, moving blackness, studded with eyes that glowed like a thousand dim, vindictive points of light" (234)—but somehow our stalwart band escape him and kill Wassermann with a convenient Uzi, thereby (temporarily) ending the threat to the world.

The House of the Toad is a dismal failure in every way. It is, quite frankly, not the work of a professional writer but the work of an amateur, a fan. Its characters are stiff and mechanical, its action clumsy and predictable, its prose wooden and uninspired, and its attempt to endow the contrived action-adventure plot with philosophical meaning is catastrophically inadequate. Tierney's adoption of the "Derleth Mythos" is the least of its difficulties.

We are in a very different territory in *Résumé with Monsters* (1995) by William Browning Spencer (b. 1946), one of the most innovative works ever written in the Lovecraftian vein. The plot of this lengthy and substantial novel is complex and needs to be expounded in detail for the novel's merits to be exhibited. It largely concerns Philip Kenan, a forty-five-year-old typesetter in Austin, Texas, who believes he is cursed by the Old Ones, especially during the years he had spent with a firm called MicroMeg, in Fairfax, Virginia; for it was here that "the ancient, implacable curse that his father had called the System or sometimes, Yog-Sothoth or simply the Great Old Ones, had torn them asunder" (12). "Them" is Philip and his estranged girlfriend, Amelia. At this point the details become a little fuzzy, for, as Philip tells his therapist, Lily Metcalf, "hideous, cone-shaped creatures from outer space are going to leap, telepathically, across six hundred million years and destroy human civilization" (26). These are, of course, the members of the Great Race, not the Old Ones, and they flourished one hundred and fifty million years ago, not six hundred million years ago, and (in "The Shadow out of Time," at any rate) they have no desire to destroy the human race. But these are small matters. The reference to Philip's father is significant, for we soon learn that his father had been a Lovecraft devotee—not only had he read *Weird Tales*, but he had read Lovecraft stories to his son.

We seem, therefore, at this moment concerned with a man who, through his father's influence, has become so psychologically damaged that he is obsessing about Lovecraft's creations as if they were real. This impression is augmented when we later learn that Philip's father had committed suicide; Philip himself believes that the Old Ones, and he himself, are jointly responsible ("His father is dead because his father's son, yes, Philip Kenan, has prayed to the System that it be so" [117]).

The novel takes a much darker turn when a coworker at Philip's office, Monica, becomes inflamed with jealousy and attacks him. In a scuffle she dies. Philip is astounded when his boss, Ralph Pederson, attempts to resurrect Monica—by the use of the *Necronomicon*. Does this mean that the boss is himself afflicted with the same psychological malady as Philip himself? What, then, do we make of this scene?

> As Philip watched, Monica raised one of her arms, and Pederson, heartened by this success, spoke yet more rapidly, the abhorred words ripping from between his teeth like viscous bubbles in molten lead.
> *Rift.*
> The hole in the ceiling widened; its radiance filled Philip's head with strange voices, voices grotesque and terrible but also—dear God—familiar.

They were trying to come through. Pederson, that fool, was summoning them. (186–87)

This, really, is the first indication that the supernatural—and the Mythos as such—is coming into play. Philip interrupts the ceremony and foils Pederson's attempt to revive Monica.

Philip, although still confusing the Great Race with the Old Ones, believes that Lovecraft is in error on one point. "The Old Ones are taking a telepathic leap from pre-Pleistocene times. The Pnakotic manuscripts suggested that they would leap beyond the reign of man, into sentient crustaceanlike beings, the next dominant life form on the planet. I think Lovecraft was mistaken on this. I think they are coming into our world, what you could loosely call 'now'" (214–15). The reference is to the "hardy coleopterous species [i.e., beetles] immediately following mankind, to which the Great Race was someday to transfer its keenest minds en masse in the face of horrible peril" (*DH* 395).

Philip now finds himself bouncing back and forth in time, going back to when he first worked at MicroMeg. At one point, he stumbles upon a sub-basement where MicroMeg's chairman, Alastair Stern, and other workers are summoning the Old Ones by the use of machinery:

YOG-SOTHOTH! the crowd screamed. YOG-SOTHOTH! YOG-SOTHOTH! There was a collective shivering, an undulating frenzy that seemed to travel through the crowd, each member convulsing as though part of some fused chain, electrified and then released, the air thick and silver. And in the liquid-mercury air, hidden by its reflective properties, things moved. And without seeing their true form, Philip knew their terror and otherworldliness. The Old Ones. (269–70)

But the effort fails. Philip tries to escape, but he is caught and taken to an immense workroom, where he sees a shoggoth. He manages to destroy the MicroMeg office before the Old Ones can get through.

In the present time, Amelia, believing that Philip's psychological maladies are beyond cure, has become engaged to another man. Philip himself is temping at an office called Pelidyne, where Amelia works. At one point he sees a horrible ghoul-like old man coming out of a vent; he thinks that an entire subculture of degenerate office-workers is living there. Philip is presently captured and taken to see a Mr. Melrose, at which point he appears to catch a glimpse of Azathoth: "'A sort of blue octopus the size of a football field with human heads on the ends of its tentacles. Parts of the creature appeared to be semi-liquid, like blue Jell-O, and human sexual organs, a stew of vaginas and penises, floated in the liquid—like rats'" (390). This does not seem quite like the imposing figure who blasphemes and bubbles at the centre of chaos, but let it pass. Philip is now fearful that Amelia is going to be taken to Yuggoth. He breaks into Ralph Pederson's office, takes the *Necronomicon*, goes to Pelidyne, summons Azathoth, and sends him back into the void, rescuing Amelia in the process.

It is difficult to convey in a bald plot synopsis the dynamism and vibrancy of *Résumé with Monsters*. The transition from psychological to supernatural horror is handled with masterful skill and subtlety, and is especially impressive in what appears to be Spencer's second published novel (following *Maybe I'll Call Anna* [1990]). Its lively, smooth-flowing prose makes no attempt to imitate Lovecraft's richly textured style, and yet it nevertheless develops a cumulative power through the accumulation of deft supernatural touches and the careful delineation of character, whereby each figure stands out sharply and distinctly. Spencer has accomplished the remarkable feat of fusing external and internal horror exactly as Lovecraft has done in some of his greatest tales, notably "The Shadow over Innsmouth" and "The Shadow out of Time." In addition, there is a keen social commentary generally absent from Lovecraft's writings, as Spencer pungently evokes the tedium, drudgery, and lifelessness of office work. Spencer does not seem to have returned to the Lovecraftian idiom in his subsequent works, although there appears to be at least one Lovecraft-inspired story in his recent story collection, *The Ocean and All Its Devices* (2006).

Quite a bit different in quality—surprisingly so from such a skilled veteran in the horror/suspense field—but surprisingly similar in certain fundamentals is *Mr. X* (1999) by Peter Straub (b. 1943). Straub, who edited the Library of America edition of Lovecraft's *Tales* (2005), has here written a kind of take-off of "The Dunwich Horror," but it cannot be considered a success. The novel is narrated by Ned Dunstan, who has returned to his hometown of Edgerton, Illinois, to be with his mother, who appears to be dying. Ned's first-person narrative is interrupted at moments by journal entries (à la Wilbur Whateley?) by a character identified only as Mr. X, who appears to be obsessed with Lovecraft and his creations, referring to the former constantly as the "Providence Master" (8); at one point Mr. X elaborates: "You who read the words I here inscribe . . . already know the significance of the ruined house to Your Great Race. It was within its sacred enclosure that the Great Old Ones imbued my early torments and humiliations with the salvific Spendor of Preparation. An Elder God spoke, and I learned All" (58). It appears that Mr. X regards the Great Race, the Great Old Ones, and the Elder Gods as alternate names for the same group of entities.

While in the Army in 1941, Mr. X reads a copy of *The Dunwich Horror.* Straub knows that such a book did not exist at the time, but he appears unaware that a book entitled *The Dunwich Horror and Other Weird Tales* was published by the Editions for the Armed Services around 1945, making it likely (barring the conflict of dates) that this is the volume Mr. X read. In any event, he realises that throughout his life he has been plagued by an adversary—his own son. We know by this time that this son is Ned Dunstan, who was born when his mother, Star, slept with an unidentified man in college.

At this point, as in the Spencer novel, we appear to be dealing with psychological suspense with a Lovecraftian tinge: Mr. X seeks to kill Ned out of fear that he will be killed by him. Much of the novel remains on this psychological level. Ned, for his part, seeks to learn more about his unknown father; on her deathbed, Star tells him that his name is Edward Rinehart. Ned soon finds a copy of a book of Lovecraftian short stories, *From Beyond,* written by Rinehart and published in 1957. It received very few notices, but among them was a highly negative review in *Weird Tales* (191). (Too bad *Weird Tales* had ceased publication three years earlier!) Ned also learns that Star had apparently been carrying twins at the time he was born—so what happened to his twin? This twin's name is Robert, and he eventually appears—a coarser, more unpredictable version of Ned. The two of them discover two properties purchased in 1950 by, respectively, Charles Dexter Ward and Wilbur Whateley (263). Ned, who has been reading Lovecraft, quickly identifies these as Lovecraft characters and deduces that Rinehart purchased them under pseudonyms. In one of these properties and makes a startling discovery:

> There were thousands of books in that room. I looked at the spines: H. P. Lovecraft, H. P. Lovecraft, H. P. Lovecraft. I moved to the ladder and went up a couple of rungs. Multiple copies of every edition of

each of Lovecraft's books lined the shelves, followed by their translations into what looked like every possible foreign language. First editions, paperbacks, trade paperbacks, collections, library editions. (364)

Very impressive! Ned also reads "The Dunwich Horror" and finds that the name of the caretaker of these houses, Earl Sawyer, is a character in that story; he concludes that Sawyer is none other than Rinehart himself. So why did Rinehart not kill him when Ned was in the house with him? Robert believes that Rinehart knows he must kill both twins to be safe. Eventually it is discovered that Rinehart is in fact one Cordwainer Hatch, the illegitimate son of Ned's grandfather, Howard Dunstan, and Ellie Hatch, scion of an illustrious family in town.

The novel is not entirely lacking in supernaturalism, however. At one point, Cordwainer kills a fellow soldier through apparently extraordinary means ("knowing for the first time since my experiments in the ruined house that I could freeze a human heart, [I] sent an icicle into his. . . . Fletcher tumbled dead to the floor" [66]). Ned, in turn, has developed (somehow) the power to go back and forth through time, and in a climactic scene he takes Cordwainer back in time and dispatches him there.

Mr. X is a tiresome, long-winded, staggeringly verbose novel that lacks the tight plotting of such notable Straub novels as *Ghost Story* (1979) and *The Throat* (1993). Its riff on "The Dunwich Horror," notably the use of the journal entries and the idea of twins with supernatural powers, is buried under a mountain of verbiage and irrelevancy, especially a long subplot about the financial shenanigans of Stewart Hatch, who is himself attempting to do away with Ned because Ned would stand to inherit millions of dollars of the Hatch fortune if Stewart were sent to jail. The supernatural elements of the novel are unconvincing and distracting, and the novel would have been better if it had been a straight work of suspense. For all the frequent references to Lovecraft and his creations, *Mr. X* cannot perhaps be termed a Cthulhu Mythos novel, for of course none of the Mythos "gods" come into play, and the supernatural manifestations have nothing to do with Lovecraft.

We may take brief note of Stephen King's *The Dark Half* (1989). This novel also makes use of the notion of twins, although in this case King, in his portrayal of the writer Thad Beaumont and his pseudonym, George Stark, who comes to life, is providing a supernaturalised version of the "outing" of King's own pseudonym, Richard Bachman. But

King explicitly makes use of the idea of birds as psychopomps, a deliberate nod to "The Dunwich Horror." But whereas Lovecraft's whippoorwills merely attempt to catch the souls of the dying, King's sparrows are rather more formidable:

> The sparrows were eating George Stark alive. His eyes were gone; where they had been only vast dark sockets remained. His nose had been reduced to a bleeding flap. His forehead and most of his hair had been struck away, revealing the mucus-bleared surface of his skull. The collar of his shirt still ringed his neck, but the rest was gone. Ribs poked out of his skin in white lumps. The birds had opened his belly. A drove of sparrows sat on his feet and looked up with bright attention and squabbled for his guts as they fell out in dripping, shredded chunks. (421)

On the whole, *The Dark Half* is one of King's more successful novels, and its subtle but emphatic Lovecraftian undercurrent adds to its effectiveness.

One of the most superficially imposing Cthulhu Mythos novels is Joseph S. Pulver, Sr.'s *Nightmare's Disciple* (1999), a gargantuan 400-page epic. We are here concerned with one Gregory Bradshaw Marsh, a resident of Schenectady, N.Y., who becomes a serial killer as a means of reintroducing into the world the dreaded entity Kassogtha, evidently some relative or former spouse of Cthulhu. The mingling of the serial killer novel with the Cthulhu Mythos is a potentially interesting idea, especially as we are held in suspense throughout the novel as to whether, as with Straub's Mr. X and the father of Philip Kenan, Marsh is merely a lunatic who has become so fascinated with Lovecraftian fiction that he now believes it to be fact, or whether there actually is such an entity named Kassogtha whose return he will effect. I am giving away nothing by saying that the latter hypothesis proves to be correct.

What cripples *Nightmare's Disciple*, however, is its unrelenting, appalling prolixity. The one thing a novel of this sort needs is narrative drive and pacing; and it is the one thing it lacks. It begins finely, but rapidly gets so bogged down in tedious and windy expositions of the Mythos by various characters (in particular a self-styled expert named Cosmo who runs a horror bookshop) that the core of the plot—Marsh's successive murders and the efforts of a police detective, Chris Stewart, to solve them—is frequently all but forgotten. This is not a work of the Cthulhu Mythos, or even the Derleth Mythos, but the Kitchen Sink Mythos: every Mythos name that could possibly be thrown in is thrown in, as in the following catechism that Marsh undergoes in his youth: "Can you name the three mates of Cthulhu? Which one is dead? Which was abandoned on Xoth? Do you know of the ancient priests Tchotghtguerele, Hnas-ry-Gij, Kreuhn, Ankh-f-n-Khonsu, or Varnsenda-Rasu? Have you read Clithanus' *Confessions,* the *Celaeno Fragments,* or the *Occultus of Hierarchus?"* (185).

It is of interest that Pulver resolutely adheres to the Elder Gods/Great Old Ones dichotomy in this novel. His character Cosmo initially attributes this view to Lovecraft; later he grudgingly acknowledges that there actually is no battle between Elder Gods and Great Old Ones in Lovecraft, although he can't bring himself to admit that there are in fact *no* Elder Gods in Lovecraft at all, but that they were entirely an invention of Derleth. The rationale for preserving this dichotomy is of some interest. Chris says at one point: "I sure hope the school of the Mythos you told me about, the one that throws out Derleth's war between the Elder Gods and the GOO [*sic*], is wrong. I'd hate to be some puny little human facing these monsters without hope of divine intervention, or without the Elder Sign" (195). In this, Pulver exactly echoes Derleth's own motivations for inventing the Elder Gods: he could not endure Lovecraft's unflinchingly bleak vision of the universe, so he had to introduce a radical alteration into it to make it more palatable.

Once again, I emphasise that I do not criticise Pulver merely for writing about the Elder Gods, or introducing any other revision of Lovecraft's Mythos. All I say is that the result is a little less than scintillating. Is it more compelling to envision us "puny" humans as the helpless pawns of immensely greater forces who care nothing for us, or as the centre of a cowboys-and-Indians struggle between one set of morally "good" entities and another set of morally "evil" entities? Which one accords more with the actual state of the universe rather than the vain hopes and wish-fulfilment fantasies of the great mass of humanity?

And yet, Pulver is a good writer. When not riding his Mythos hobby-horse, he can produce such passages of quiet eloquence as this, describing his ageing police detective: "Thirty-two somehow became forty-three as he watched the years pass—some in the bottle, all in pain—leaving few dreams and no illusions. Now the files and photos spread across the desk in his den were fast removing what little remained of his battered belief in human decency" (10). Pulver's more recent work (much of it regrettably unpublished) is very much along these same lines; in particular, he has found much inspiration in Robert W. Chambers's *The King in Yellow* and has written several tales that bring some of Chambers's inventions into the gritty, crime-laden world of the present. It is hoped that this newer, richer writing by Pulver can soon find print so that his considerable talents as a writer can be displayed to the public.

Heroic (in size) as Pulver's novel is, it is dwarfed to insignificance by an even more weighty tome, Donald Tyson's *Alhazred: Author of the Necronomicon* (2006). Tyson, of whom I know nothing, appears to be an occultist of some kind, as he has previously written books on the tarot, "sexual alchemy," and such esoteric matters. He began his Lovecraftian career with an ill-advised attempt to write the *Necronomicon*, entitled *Necronomicon: The Wanderings of Alhazred* (2004). Possibly this was just a dry run for *Alhazred*, but whatever the case, Tyson has written a remarkable historical/supernatural novel—fully 677 pages in length, and yet as compelling as a modern-day thriller.

In essence, Tyson has attempted to flesh out the very skeletal and tantalising information on Abdul Alhazred that Lovecraft supplied in "History of the *Necronomicon*," specifically the fact that he was "a mad poet in Sanaá, in Yemen," that he "visited the ruins of Babylon and the subterranean secrets of Memphis and spent ten years alone in the great southern desert of Arabia," and that "in his last days Alhazred dwelt in Damascus, where the *Necronomicon* (*Al Azif*) was written" (*MW* 52). Tyson's novel opens when Alhazred is nineteen years old. He had been brought to the court of King Huban of Yemen at the age of twelve, to be a poet/singer. His early remark "I cared nothing for God or the Caliph" (6) is an echo of Lovecraft's comment that "He was only an indifferent Moslem" (*MW* 52). Because he is (rightly) accused of dallying with the Princess Narisa, he suffers punishment too hideous to describe here and is exiled to the "Empty Space." It is here, in an underground cavern, that he comes upon a "god" who, we eventually learn, is Nyarlathotep.

Alhazred spends a long time in (or under) Irem, the City of Pillars, where he encounters an ancient witch, I'thakuah. Why Tyson would choose a name so reminiscent of Ithaqua, the snow-creature invented by Derleth, is unclear. At any rate, it is from her that he learns something about Nyarlathotep and the Old Ones, and their battles with the unspecified "Elder Things" (108). Alhazred later makes his way to Suez, where he falls in with a group called the Order of the Sphinx, who worship Nyarlathotep. They are involved in making the "essential salts" (248) of various human and other bodies. Oddly enough, Alhazred here learns of Yig, "the supreme god of Khem, the black land" (324), as well as of Tsathoggua. At one point Alhazred is attacked by a reanimated corpse—and killed.

But we are only halfway through the book, so clearly this is not the end. He is revived by a young woman named Martala, who has become his colleague and companion. She takes him to Alexandria, where he acquires many books of necromantic lore. At considerable trouble and expense he copies a scroll written in the language of the Old Ones. Moving on to Babylon, Alhazred and Martala encounter a horrible "Beast" with multiple heads of the human beings it has absorbed. Its mother is Shub-Niggurath. Later Alhazred joins a caravan that worships Shub-Niggurath, and he sees a carven image of her:

> The polished black limbs of the stone idol within the shrine were frozen in the posture of dance. She stood upon her pedestal on one foot, the other upraised, her arms askew, her eyes staring with insane glee, her thick lips writhed away from her ivory teeth and her tongue extended in a silent scream of ecstay. In the middle of her forehead a third eye glared. An ivory necklace of exquisitely carved human skulls hung from her naked torso below the level of her full breasts. Her hairless and obscenely exposed vulva had been shaped by the artist in complete detail. Inset between its lips glowed a rounded emerald of the deepest green. Her vulva seemed to gape as though about to give birth to the jewel, and this same impression of pregnancy was conveyed by the dome of her belly. (605)

But Alhazred is quick to point out that "The images of Shub-Niggurath that I had come across in my studies and my wandering did not resemble this dancing pregnant woman" (606). At the end of the novel Alhazred is in Damascus, although presumably he is only twenty-one or twenty-two years old, so he still has many years to live before being "seized by an invisible monster in broad daylight and devoured horribly before a large number of fright-frozen witnesses" (*MW* 52), as Lovecraft has it.

The passage on Shub-Niggurath encapsulates a curious problem with *Alhazred*. In an exact reversal of the situation with Pulver's *Nightmare's Disciple*, this novel, in spite of its tremendous length, offers too *little* information regarding the Old Ones, and the Cthulhu (or Lovecraft) Mythos in general, to be fully satisfying. It is impeccably written, with convincing historical background and a prose style of quiet elegance and dignity, with no attempt at either pseudo-Lovecraftian floridity or juvenile humour; but the work is more an adventure story than a supernatural novel. In spite of the fact that Lovecraft himself says that Alhazred worshipped "unknown entities whom he called Yog-Sothoth and Cthulhu" (*MW* 52), we learn little of Alhazred's relations with these creatures. Early on Alhazred is told that "Yog-Sothoth is the way" (51), but this entity otherwise figures almost nowhere in the novel. Even the figure of Nyarlathotep, who hovers balefully over the entire narrative as a "black man," is never precisely defined, nor is Alhazred's relation to him clarified. Toward the end Alhazred infiltrates a sect called the Order of the Sons of Sirius, which is opposed to Nyarlathotep, and encounters a hideous monster confined in an iron cage in the cellar of the order's monastery—a creature deemed a "spawn of Cthulhu" (548); but little is made of this matter.

Paradoxically, for all the novel's length, Tyson may have erred by exercising too much restraint in mimicking or elaborating upon Lovecraft's conceptions. The long section about Alhazred's ventures in Irem brings some features of "The Nameless City" to mind, but Tyson wisely avoids merely rewriting the story. Ghouls figure here and there (Alhazred himself becomes one during his long exile in the "Empty Space"), and Alhazred spends plenty of time escaping sundry assassins, one of whom in particular is attempting to retrieve that scroll of the Old Ones that Alhazred has copied; but, typically, we never learn what that scroll contains.

Given that Alhazred is still a relatively young man by the time he reaches Damascus at the end of *Alhazred*, one wonders whether Tyson is envisioning the writing of some kind of sequel in which the mad Arab's life in that city is elaborated, and his encounters with Cthulhu, Yog-Sothoth, and others is expounded in greater detail. I for one would welcome such a work. *Alhazred* itself is an entirely engrossing historical/adventure novel without a single false note. Its central character comes to vivid life in its pages, and several of the subsidiary characters are similarly alive and distinctive. In spite of its almost coy refusal to elaborate upon the Mythos elements it is purportedly dealing with, it remains one of the most striking and compelling works of the Lovecraft Mythos written since the heyday of Lovecraft himself.

It should be evident that the influence of the Cthulhu Mythos—to say nothing of Lovecraft's overall influence—is now so wide-ranging that no single volume could encompass it. Such works as Roger Zelazny's *A Night in the Lonesome October* (1993), Charles Stross's *The Atrocity Archives* (2004), and numerous others contain significant Lovecraftian echoes. John Langan has written of Laird Barron's *The Imago Sequence and Other Stories* (2007):

> Barron's vision of a godlike intelligence trapped in the gravity of its own matter is consonant with Lovecraft's Azathoth, while the character of Anselm Thornton, in "The Imago Sequence," seems a type of Nyarlathotep. Nor do the comparisons stop there: the Choate family of "Hallucigenia" calls to mind the Whateleys of "The Dunwich Horror"; the human-seeming predators of "Proboscis" invoke the population of Innsmouth; the photographs of "The Imago Sequence" find their echoes in the paintings of "Pickman's Model."[13]

Even such a work as Thomas Pynchon's *Against the Day* (2006) features several references to Lovecraft, especially to *At the Mountains of Madness*. Indeed, one scholar has made the plausible claim that Pynchon's early novel *The Crying of Lot 49* (1966) was significantly influenced by "The Call of Cthulhu."[14] The Mythos influence extends also to poetry, as seen in such works as Lin Carter's creditable *Dreams from R'lyeh* (1971) to Ann K. Schwader's superlative *The Worms Remember* (2001). W. H. Pugmire has produced some admirable Lovecraftian sonnets in "The Songs of Sesqua Valley."

It is safe to say, then, that Lovecraftian and Cthulhu Mythos themes have, amidst a plethora of unimaginative and derivative hackwork, seen a number of capable treatments in recent decades, and there is no reason to believe that the trend will not continue into the future.

Epilogue

IT SHOULD BE EVIDENT by now that the somewhat supercilious title of this book does not accurately reflect my understanding of the progression of the Lovecraft (or even the Cthulhu) Mythos from 1917 to the present day. Even the assumption that the Mythos "rose" during Lovecraft's lifetime and "fell" after his death would be misleading, for it is not only clear that the Lovecraft Mythos had its ups ("The Call of Cthulhu," "The Colour out of Space," "The Whisperer in Darkness," *At the Mountains of Madness,* "The Shadow over Innsmouth," "The Shadow out of Time") and downs ("The Dunwich Horror," "The Dreams in the Witch House," "The Thing on the Doorstep") even when Lovecraft was alive, but that similar fluctuations in quality and distinctiveness have occurred in the seven decades following Lovecraft's passing. If the Cthulhu Mythos "fell" dramatically, both in quality and in conception, when August Derleth gave it birth in the early 1930s, it rose again sporadically in the hands of such writers as Robert Bloch, Fritz Leiber, C. Hall Thompson, Karl Edward Wagner, Ramsey Campbell, Colin Wilson, Fred Chappell, T. E. D. Klein, Thomas Ligotti, W. H. Pugmire, Stanley C. Sargent, William Browning Spencer, Donald Tyson, and several others. Each of these writers, it should be noted, consciously bypassed the Derleth Mythos to return to Lovecraftian fundamentals, several of them doing so even before the revolution in scholarship in the 1970s made it transparently obvious that Derleth had seriously disfigured the cosmic awe of the Lovecraft Mythos and replaced it with his own fraudulent and aesthetically unimaginative knock-off.

It is also evident that certain core elements of the Lovecraft (and Cthulhu) Mythos have exercised an unusual fascination for writers following in Lovecraft's wake, notably the forbidden book, outlandish "gods," the scholarly narrator, and an imaginary New England topography (or its adaptations and permutations into other locales). There is no

reason to wonder at this, for it is these elements that are the most superficially obvious features of Lovecraft's stories and the ones most amenable to imitation. That the great majority of such imitations are
stereotyped and mechanical does not militate against their distinctiveness
and vitality in Lovecraft's own work and in the work of those few who
have elaborated upon them in an ingenious and profound manner. But it
is telling that the true aesthetic and philosophical essence of the Lovecraft Mythos—cosmicism—has found few effective imitators. Lovecraft
himself was aware that cosmicism was a relatively rare trait in writers, as
in human beings generally, and he expatiated on the matter frequently. In
his rather aggressive defence of cosmicism in the *In Defence of Dagon* essays of 1921, he wrote:

> I could not write about "ordinary people" because I am not in the
> least interested in them. Without interest there can be no art. Man's re
> lations to man do not captivate my fancy. It is man's relations to the
> cosmos—to the unknown—which alone arouses in me the spark of
> creative imagination. The humanocentric pose is impossible to me, for
> I cannot acquire the primitive myopia which magnifies the earth and
> ignores the background. (*MW* 155)

In 1930 he expressed the same idea somewhat more broadly:

> The true function of phantasy is to give the imagination a ground for
> limitless expansion, & to satisfy aesthetically the sincere & burning cu
> riosity & sense of awe which a sensitive minority of mankind feel to
> ward the alluring & provocative abysses of unplumbed space &
> unguessed entity which press in upon the known world from un
> known infinities & in unknown relationships of time, space, matter,
> force, dimensionality, & consciousness. This curiosity & sense of awe,
> I believe, are quite basic amongst the sensitive minority in question; &
> I see no reason to think that they will decline in the future . . . But the
> truly sensitive will never be more than a minority, because most per
> sons—even those of the keenest possible intellect & aesthetic ability—
> simply have not the psychological equipment or adjustment to feel
> that way. . . . It is not every macabre writer who feels poignantly & al
> most intolerably the pressure of cryptic & unbounded outer space. (*SL*
> 3.196)

Either you feel the "cosmic quality" or you don't; and we have seen how
a number of writers have attempted to duplicate Lovecraft's cosmicism

but failed, because it did not arise naturally from their own temperament. There will always be "self-blinded earth-gazers" among us.

What this means is that the very essence of the Lovecraft Mythos is not amenable to "imitation" in any obvious or superficial sense because it must have already found lodgment in the author's aesthetic and philosophical compass. Imitations of the Lovecraft (or even the Cthulhu) Mythos can be effective without the cosmic quality, but there will always be a sense that something vital is lacking. The "forbidden book" topos, for example, can be used to create powerful effects on a purely mundane level (as it does in Fred Chappell's *Dagon*), but, as Lovecraft evolved it in his later tales, it always carries with it the implication of apocalyptic glimpses into a cosmos that contains immense forces just beyond sight and the derisive insignificance of a human race whose fate is of utter inconsequence to the progression of an infinite and timeless universe.

I trust that my discussion has adequately conveyed my awareness that Lovecraftian and Mythos themes have in fact been utilised with relative effectiveness in a good many works over the past century; indeed, I will frankly admit that the number of such works is larger than I had initially suspected. I need not reiterate that I have deliberately passed over in merciful silence the great majority of inferior, inadequate, and incompetent treatments of the Lovecraft and Cthulhu Mythos; their number is legion, and they scarcely deserve even the dubious eminence of condemnation. And I have little doubt that, in my necessarily incomplete canvassing of Cthulhu Mythos writing, I have overlooked any number of meritorious works that should have been brought to the reader's attention. What should be apparent is that working in the Lovecraft vein is by no means a recipe for aesthetic disaster. In the youthful writer, sedulous imitation can serve as a valuable stepping-stone to the development of literary skills that can be put to better use elsewhere; for the experienced writer who seeks to mine Lovecraftian conceptions in a work purporting to have independent aesthetic value, the exercise can result in an augmentation of power and distinctiveness if those conceptions are used within the framework of the author's own aesthetic vision. Samuel Johnson's blunt axiom, "No man ever became great by imitation," remains true more than two centuries after its utterance. But those writers who do something more than *mere* imitation of Lovecraft have a chance to produce work that will live, and deserve to live.

Notes

Introduction

1. Stanley C. Sargent, "Author's Preface & Acknowledgements," in *The Taint of Lovecraft* (Poplar Bluff, MO: Mythos Books, 2002), p. vii.
2. C. L. Moore to HPL, 30 January 1936 (ms., JHL).
3. David E. Schultz, "Who Needs the 'Cthulhu Mythos'?," *Lovecraft Studies* No. 13 (Fall 1986): 51.
4. John Haefele, "A Look Behind the Derleth Mythos," *Hesperia* 14, No. 2 (Summer 2007): 8 (Esoteric Order of Dagon mailing 139).
5. R. Boerem, "Lovecraft and the tradition of the Gentleman Narrator," in *An Epicure in the Terrible: A Centennial Anthology of Essays in Honor of H. P. Lovecraft*, ed. David E. Schultz and S. T. Joshi (Rutherford, NJ: Fairleigh Dickinson University Press, 1991), pp. 257–72.
6. Schultz, "Who Needs the 'Cthulhu Mythos'?," p. 48.
7. Dirk W. Mosig, "H. P. Lovecraft: Myth-Maker," in *H. P. Lovecraft: Four Decades of Criticism*, ed. S. T. Joshi (Athens: Ohio University Press, 1980), p. 110.
8. David E. Schultz. "From Microcosm to Macrocosm: The Growth of Lovecraft's Cosmic Vision," in *An Epicure in the Terrible*, p. 212.
9. Ibid., p. 213.
10. See, e.g., *A Subtler Magick: The Writings and Philosophy of H. P. Lovecraft* (1996) and *H. P. Lovecraft: The Decline of the West* (1990).
11. HPL to August Derleth, 3 August 1931; *Essential Solitude: The Letters of H. P. Lovecraft and August Derleth*, ed. David E. Schultz and S. T. Joshi (New York: Hippocampus Press, 2007), p. 353.
12. Maurice Lévy, *Lovecraft: A Study in the Fantastic*, tr. S. T. Joshi (Detroit: Wayne State University Press, 1988), p. 110.
13. Steven J. Mariconda, "Toward a Reader-Response Approach to the Lovecraft Mythos," in Mariconda's *On the Emergence of "Cthulhu" and Other Observations* (West Warwick, RI: Necronomicon Press, 1995), pp. 29–44.

I. *Anticipations (1917–1926)*

1. "'Dagon''s author [is killed] by the very monster he had seen. It had apparently followed him back stateside." Robert M. Price, "'Dagon' and 'The Madness from the Sea,'" *Crypt of Cthulhu* No. 9 (Hallowmas 1982): 11 (as by "Joachim Feery"). Cf. HPL to Rheinhart Kleiner, 27 August 1917: "Both ['The Tomb' and 'Dagon'] are analyses of strange monomania, involving hallucinations of the most hideous sort." *Letters to Rheinhart Kleiner,* ed. S. T. Joshi and David E. Schultz (New York: Hippocampus Press, 2005), p. 112. A later letter states: "In 'Dagon' I shewed a horror that *may appear,* but that has not yet made any effort to do so." HPL to Clark Ashton Smith, 7 November 1930 (*SL* 3.213).

2. David E. Schultz, "From Microcosm to Macrocosm: The Growth of Lovecraft's Cosmic Vision," in *An Epicure in the Terrible: A Centennial Anthology of Essays in Honor of H. P. Lovecraft,* ed. David E. Schultz and S. T. Joshi (Rutherford, NJ: Fairleigh Dickinson University Press, 1991), p. 211.

3. Matthew H. Onderdonk, "The Lord of R'lyeh" (1945), rpt. *Lovecraft Studies* No. 7 (Fall 1982): 14.

4. George T. Wetzel, "The Cthulhu Mythos: A Study" (1972), in *H. P. Lovecraft: Four Decades of Criticism,* ed. S. T. Joshi (Athens: Ohio University Press, 1980), p. 82.

5. See my article "Lovecraft and the *Regnum Congo,*" in *Primal Sources: Essays on H. P. Lovecraft* (New York: Hippocampus Press, 2003).

6. HPL to Robert E. Howard (16 January 1932); cited in S. T. Joshi, *H. P. Lovecraft: A Life* (West Warwick, RI: Necronomicon Press, 1996), p. 19.

7. See n. 4.

8. Joan C. Stanley, *Ex Libris Miskatonici* (West Warwick, RI: Necronomicon Press, 1993), p. 53.

9. Price, "The Figure in the Flying Carpet," in *The Necronomicon,* ed. Robert M. Price (Oakland, CA: Chaosium, 1996), p. x.

10. See Donald R. Burleson, "H. P. Lovecraft: The Hawthorne Influence," *Extrapolation* 25 (Fall 1984): 267.

11. Poe, *Tales and Sketches,* ed. Thomas Ollive Mabbott (Cambridge, MA: Harvard University Press, 1978), 1:408–9.

12. Ibid., 1:419n15.
13. Ibid., 1:413.
14. See Robert Marten, "Arkham Country: In Rescue of the Lost Searchers," *Lovecraft Studies* No. 39 (Summer 1998): 1–20.
15. Ibid., p. 15.
16. Ibid.
17. See Donovan K. Loucks, "Antique Dreams: Marblehead and Lovecraft's Kingsport," *Lovecraft Studies* Nos. 42/43 (Autumn 2001): 47.
18. Letter to Rheinhart Kleiner, 14 December 1920; *Letters to Rheinhart Kleiner*, p. 200. The letter is misdated (14 December 1921) in *SL.*
19. HPL to R. H. Barlow, [1 December 1934]; *O Fortunate Floridian: H. P. Lovecraft's Letters to R. H. Barlow*, ed. S. T. Joshi and David E. Schultz (Tampa: University of Tampa Press, 2007), p. 191.
20. "Azathoth—Nyarlathotep was based on a dream-name." Barlow, "[Memories of Lovecraft (1934)]," in *O Fortunate Floridian*, p. 404. The use of the singular "was" is a bit puzzling, but perhaps Barlow was regarding the two terms as somehow a unity.
21. See the letter to Frank Belknap Long (9 June 1922) quoted in Joshi, *H. P. Lovecraft: A Life*, p. 286.
22. Wetzel, "The Cthulhu Mythos: A Study," p. 79.

II. *The Lovecraft Mythos: Phase I (1926–1930)*

1. Lovecraft, *Letters from New York*, ed. S. T. Joshi and David E. Schultz (San Francisco: Night Shade Books, 2005), p. 172.
2. Robert M. Price, "The Lovecraft-Derleth Connection," in Price's *H. P. Lovecraft and the Cthulhu Mythos* (Mercer Island, WA: Starmont House, 1990), p. 97.
3. Arthur Machen, "The Great God Pan," in *The Three Impostors and Other Stories* (Oakland, CA: Chaosium, 2001), p. 49.
4. Maurice Lévy, *Lovecraft: A Study in the Fantastic*, trans. S. T. Joshi (Detroit: Wayne State University Press, 1988), p. 105.
5. HPL to August Derleth, [15 April 1927]; *Essential Solitude:*, p. 83.
6. I offer reasons for Lovecraft's error in "Lovecraft, Regner Lodbrog, and Olaus Wormius," in *Primal Sources*, pp. 145–53.
7. See Will Murray, "On the Natures of Nug and Yeb," *Lovecraft Studies* No. 9 (Fall 1984): 52–59.

8. Donald R. Burleson, "The Mythic Hero Archetype in 'The Dunwich Horror,'" *Lovecraft Studies* No. 4 (Spring 1981): 9.

9. HPL to August Derleth, [27 September 1928]; *Essential Solitude*, p. 158.

10. Robert M. Price, "Dunwich Homecoming," in *Tales out of Dunwich* (New York: Hippocampus Press, 2005), p. 9.

11. Robert M. Price, "Introduction" to *Tales of the Lovecraft Mythos* (Minneapolis, MN: Fedogan & Bremer, 1992), p. xiv.

12. *Crypt of Cthulhu* No. 102 (Lammas 1999): 13–21.

13. See Peter Cannon, "Dunwich Daydreams," *Crypt of Cthulhu* No. 82 (Hallowmas 1992): 9.

14. Burleson, "Humour beneath Horror: Some Sources for 'The Dunwich Horror' and 'The Whisperer in Darkness,'" *Lovecraft Studies* No. 2 (Spring 1980): 5–8.

15. See *Lovecraft Studies* No. 33 (Fall 1995): back cover, for a transcription of the map. See also Will Murray's article "Where Was Foxfield?" in the same issue (pp. 18–23).

16. Price, "Genres in the Lovecraftian Library," *Crypt of Cthulhu* No. 3 (Candlemas 1982): 14–17.

17. Found on the typescript of "The Mound" (John Hay Library, Brown University); quoted in S. T. Joshi, "Lovecraft's Revisions: How Much of Them Did He Write?," in *Selected Papers on Lovecraft* (West Warwick, RI: Necronomicon Press, 1989), p. 50.

18. Steven J. Mariconda, "Tightening the Coil: The Revision of 'The Whisperer in Darkness,'" *Lovecraft Studies* No. 32 (Spring 1995): 12–17.

19. Mariconda and Price believe that Lovecraft made an error in the "waxen mask" passage because the face and hands are manifestly the actual face and hands of Akeley, not a mask or imitation; but I believe that Lovecraft was merely intending to convey the fact that Nyarlathotep would appear later in the story in disguise. In any case, Wilmarth, when examining these objects, states: "I hope . . . they were the waxen products of a master artist, despite what my inmost fears tell me" (*DH* 271), a clear allusion to the "waxen mask" phrase.

20. Sam Gafford, "Who Was 'The Whisperer in Darkness'?," *Damned Thing* No. 4 (Winter 1992–93): 22–28.

21. Price, "The Criticism of Azathoth," *Crypt of Cthulhu* No. 80 (Eastertide 1991): 8–9.

22. See Robert W. Chambers, *The Yellow Sign and Other Stories* (Oakland, CA: Chaosium, 2000), pp. 16, 73.

23. Will Murray, "An Uncompromising Look at the Cthulhu Mythos," *Lovecraft Studies* No. 12 (Spring 1986): 31.

III. *The Lovecraft Mythos: Phase II (1931–36)*

1. Robert M. Price, "Demythologizing Cthulhu," in *H. P. Lovecraft and the Cthulhu Mythos*, pp. 76–84.
2. Price, "The Last Vestige of the Derleth Mythos," *Lovecraft Studies* No. 24 (Spring 1991): 20–21.
3. Will Murray, "The Trouble with Shoggoths," *Crypt of Cthulhu* No. 32 (St. John's Eve 1985): 35–38, 41.
4. See HPL to August Derleth, 24 March [1931]; *Essential Solitude*, p. 325.
5. Steven J. Mariconda, "Lovecraft's Cosmic Imagery," in *An Epicure in the Terrible*, p. 192.
6. See Robert M. Price, "The Revision Mythos," in *H. P. Lovecraft and the Cthulhu Mythos*, pp. 103–12.
7. See Duane Rimel, "A History of the Chronicle of Nath," *Etchings and Odysseys* No. 9 (1986): 80.
8. For this draft see *Crypt of Cthulhu* No. 10 (1982): 21–25.
9. It was first printed in *Crypt of Cthulhu* No. 10 (1982): 47–56.
10. See the Hippocampus Press edition of 2001, deriving from the autograph manuscript that surfaced in 1994. All citations to this text derive from this edition.
11. See Robert M. Price, "Lovecraft's Cosmic History," *Crypt of Cthulhu* No. 37 (Candlemas 1986): 18–24.
12. See *Letters to Robert Bloch*, ed. S. T. Joshi and David E. Schultz (West Warwick, RI: Necronomicon Press, 1993), p. 67.

IV. *Contemporaries (I)*

1. Cited in David E. Schultz, "Notes toward a History of the Cthulhu Mythos," *Crypt of Cthulhu* No. 92 (Eastertide 1996): 33.
2. Derleth, "H. P. Lovecraft: The Making of a Literary Reputation," *Books at Brown* 25 (1977): 16–17.
3. HPL to August Derleth, [c. February 1930]; *Essential Solitude*, p. 248.

4. See Donald Sidney-Fryer, "On the Alleged Influence of Lord Dunsany on Clark Ashton Smith," *Amra* No. 23 (January 1963); rpt. *Klarkash-Ton* No. 1 (June 1988): 9–13, 15.

5. See HPL to August Derleth, 3 August 1931; *Essential Solitude*, p. 353.

6. Clark Ashton Smith to HPL, 9 January 1930; *Selected Letters of Clark Ashton Smith*, ed. David E. Schultz and Scott Connors (Sauk City, WI: Arkham House, 2003), p. 108.

7. Clark Ashton Smith to August Derleth, 26 July 1944; *Selected Letters of Clark Ashton Smith*, p. 344.

8. Clark Ashton Smith to August Derleth, 13 April 1937; *Selected Letters of Clark Ashton Smith*, p. 287.

9. See n. 7.

10. Clark Ashton Smith to August Derleth, 4 January 1933 (ms., State Historical Society of Wisconsin).

11. See n. 7.

12. Robert E. Howard to H. P. Lovecraft, [c. August 1930]; *Selected Letters 1923–1930*, ed. Rusty Burke et al. (West Warwick, RI: Necronomicon Press, 1989), p. 56.

13. N. J. O'Neail, letter to "The Eyrie" (March 1930); *H. P. Lovecraft in 'The Eyrie,'* ed. S. T. Joshi and Marc A. Michaud (West Warwick, RI: Necronomicon Press, 1979), p. 31.

14. See n. 12.

15. *H. P. Lovecraft in 'The Eyrie,'* pp. 27–28.

16. HPL to August Derleth, 3 August 1931; *Essential Solitude*, p. 353.

17. *Selected Letters 1923–1930*, p. 60.

18. See Mariconda, "Tightening the Coil," p. 13.

19. Lin Carter, ed., *The Spawn of Cthulhu* (New York: Ballantine, 1971), p. 169.

20. *Letters to Robert Bloch*, p. 23.

21. See Robert M. Price, "Gol-Goroth, a Forgotten Old One," *Crypt of Cthulhu* No. 3 (Candlemas 1982): 12–13, 17.

22. Arthur Machen, *The Three Impostors* (London: John Lane; Boston: Roberts Brothers, 1895), p. 146.

23. Donald Wandrei to H. P. Lovecraft, 20 December 1926; *Mysteries of Time and Spirit: The Letters of H. P. Lovecraft and Donald Wandrei*, ed. S. T. Joshi and David E. Schultz (San Francisco: Night Shade Books, 2002), p. 5.

24. HPL to Duane W. Rimel, 30 October 1934; cited in *Mysteries of Time and Spirit*, p. 5n2.
25. HPL to Donald Wandrei, 25 September 1931; *Mysteries of Time and Spirit*, p. 286.
26. It will appear in my edition of *Dead Titans, Waken! and Invisible Sun* (forthcoming from Fedogan & Bremer).
27. Donald Wandrei to HPL, 9 September 1929; *Mysteries of Time and Spirit*, pp. 240–41.
28. Donald Wandrei to HPL, 26 June 1930; *Mysteries of Time and Spirit*, pp. 251–52.
29. See HPL to Donald Wandrei, [31 July 1931]: "I am gratified to hear that the monstrous antarctic chronicle did not bore you." *Mysteries of Time and Spirit*, p. 283.

V. *Contemporaries (II)*

1. See Lovecraft, *Letters to Robert Bloch: Supplement* (West Warwick, RI: Necronomicon Press, 1993), p. 11.
2. This is the name of the character as given in the *Weird Tales* appearance of the story. Subsequent appearances (beginning with *The Opener of the Way* [1945]) give the name as Carnoti. Stugatche is clearly Bloch's original name for this character, and it is mentioned in several letters by Lovecraft. Bloch remarks of it: "The name comes from a group of imaginary characters who—believe it or not—were invented to serve as players on teams in a card-game called 'Baseball'— the invention of my friends Herb Williams and Harold Gauer. . . . I later used the name for a central character in my story, 'The Faceless God'" (*LB* 70n205). Perhaps August Derleth advised Bloch to change the name for the book appearance.
3. Bloch, introductory note to "Satan's Servants," in Lovecraft's *Something about Cats and Other Pieces* (Sauk City, WI: Arkham House, 1949), pp. 118–19.
4. HPL to Henry Kuttner, 12 March 1936; *Letters to Henry Kuttner*, ed. S. T. Joshi and David E. Schultz (West Warwick, RI: Necronomicon Press, 1990), p. 9.
5. Ibid.
6. Ibid.

7. Cited in Bruce Byfield, *Witches of the Mind: A Critical Study of Fritz Leiber* (West Warwick, RI: Necronomicon Press, 1991), p. 11.

8. Leiber, "Fafhrd and Me" (1975), in *Fafhrd and Me: A Collection of Essays* (Newark, NJ: Wildside Press, 1990), p. 15.

9. Stefan Dziemianowicz, "Dead Ringers: The Leiber-Lovecraft Connection," *Crypt of Cthulhu* No. 76 (Hallowmas 1990): 8–13.

10. HPL to Clark Ashton Smith, 3 October 1933 (ms., JHL); quoted in Will Murray, "Mearle Prout and 'The House of the Worm,'" *Crypt of Cthulhu* No. 18 (Yuletide 1983): 29–30, 39.

11. HPL to Alfred Galpin, 25 October [1933]; *Letters to Alfred Galpin*, ed. S. T. Joshi and David E. Schultz (New York: Hippocampus Press, 2003), p. 194.

12. HPL to R. H. Barlow, [14 August 1934]; *O Fortunate Floridian*, p. 163.

13. See Will Murray, "The Call of Khalk'ru and Other Speculations," *Nyctalops* 4, No. 1 (April 1991): 72–76.

14. Cited in Murray, p. 73.

15. Murray, p. 75.

VI. *The Derleth Mythos*

1. See *Essential Solitude: The Letters of H. P. Lovecraft and August Derleth*, ed. David E. Schultz and S. T. Joshi (New York: Hippocampus Press, 2007; 2 vols.).

2. August Derleth, "H. P. Lovecraft, Outsider," *River* 1, No. 3 (June 1937): 88–89.

3. HPL to August Derleth, 16 May 1931; *Essential Solitude*, p. 336.

4. HPL to August Derleth, 3 August 1931; *Essential Solitude*, p. 353.

5. Price, "Introduction" to *Tales of the Lovecraft Mythos*, p. xiv.

6. Ibid.

7. Derleth, "The Cthulhu Mythos," in *Tales of the Cthulhu Mythos*, ed. August Derleth (1969; rpt. New York: Ballantine Books, 1971), p. viii.

8. S. T Joshi, *An Index to the Fiction and Poetry of H. P. Lovecraft* (West Warwick, RI: Necronomicon Press, 1992).

9. Derleth, "A Master of the Macabre," *Reading and Collecting* 1, No. 9 (August 1937): 9.

10. Robert M. Price, "The Lovecraft-Derleth Connection," in *H. P. Lovecraft and the Cthulhu Mythos*, p. 98.

11. See n. 7.

12. Derleth, "H. P. Lovecraft and His Work," in *The Dunwich Horror and Others* (Sauk City, WI: Arkham House, 1963), p. xiv.

13. Price, "Introduction" to *Tales of the Lovecraft Mythos*, p. xiii.

14. See *Essential Solitude*, p. 335.

15. Dirk W. Mosig, "H. P. Lovecraft: Myth-Maker" (1976), in *H. P. Lovecraft: Four Decades of Criticism*, p. 108.

16. Quoted in *Essential Solitude*, p. 355n2.

17. "I shall be eager to see your new tales—especially 'The Return of Hastur . . .'" HPL to August Derleth, 19 February 1932; *Essential Solitude*, p. 455.

18. Derleth to HPL, 27 January [1933]; *Essential Solitude*, p. 538.

19. Smith's letters to Derleth are printed in Smith's *Letters to H. P. Lovecraft*, ed. Steve Behrends (West Warwick, RI: Necronomicon Press, 1987), pp. 58–67. Derleth's letters to Smith survive in ms. in the Clark Ashton Smith Papers at the John Hay Library, Brown University.

20. Derleth to HPL, 14 August 1933; *Essential Solitude*, p. 601.

21. Derleth, "The Cthulhu Mythos," p. xi.

22. Derleth, "Final Notes" (1959), in Lovecraft's *The Dark Brotherhood and Other Pieces*, ed. August Derleth (Sauk City, WI: Arkham House, 1966), p. 308.

23. HPL to August Derleth, [28 January 1932]; *Essential Solitude*, p. 445.

VII. *Interregnum*

1. Robert Weinberg, *The Weird Tales Story* (1977), quoted in Stefan Dziemianowicz, "C. Hall Thompson: The First Neo-Lovecraftian?," *Crypt of Cthulhu* No. 75 (Michaelmas 1990): 14.

2. See Schultz, "Notes toward a History of the Cthulhu Mythos," p. 30 (item 55).

3. See Dziemianowicz, p. 3.

4. Campbell, "Introduction" to *Demons by Daylight* (New York: Carroll & Graf, 1990), n.p.

5. Campbell, "Introduction" to *Cold Print* (1985; rpt. New York; Tor, 1987), p. 4.
6. Ibid., pp. 5–6.
7. Campbell, "Introduction" to *The Height of the Scream* (Sauk City, WI: Arkham House, 1976), p. xi.
8. Ibid., pp. x–xi.
9. Campbell, "At the Back of My Mind: A Guided Tour," in *The Face That Must Die* (Santa Cruz, CA: Scream/Press, 1983), p. xxi.

VIII. The Scholarly Revolution

1. Richard L. Tierney, "The Derleth Mythos" (1972), in *Discovering H. P. Lovecraft*, ed. Darrell Schweitzer (Holicong, PA: Wildside Press, 2001), p. 52.
2. Dirk W. Mosig, "H. P. Lovecraft: Myth-Maker" (1976), in *H. P. Lovecraft: Four Decades of Criticism*, pp. 109–10.
3. See David E. Schultz, "The Origin of Lovecraft's 'Black Magic' Quote," *Crypt of Cthulhu* No. 48 (St. John's Eve 1987): 9–13.
4. See Byfield (ch. 5, n. 7), pp. 57–58.
5. Campbell, "Chasing the Unknown," in *Cold Print* (London: Headline, 1993), p. 18.

VIII. The Scholarly Revolution

1. Richard L. Tierney, "The Derleth Mythos" (1972), in *Discovering H. P. Lovecraft*, ed. Darrell Schweitzer (Holicong, PA: Wildside Press, 2001), p. 52.
2. Dirk W. Mosig, "H. P. Lovecraft: Myth-Maker" (1976), in *H. P. Lovecraft: Four Decades of Criticism*, pp. 109–10.
3. See David E. Schultz, "The Origin of Lovecraft's 'Black Magic' Quote," *Crypt of Cthulhu* No. 48 (St. John's Eve 1987): 9–13.
4. See Byfield (ch. 5, n. 7), pp. 57–58.
5. Campbell, "Chasing the Unknown," in *Cold Print* (London: Headline, 1993), p. 18.

IX. Recrudescence

1. Many of my following remarks are derived from my study of Ligotti in *The Modern Weird Tale* (Jefferson, NC: McFarland, 2001). For an in-

teresting—but, to my mind, not entirely convincing—qualification of or rebuttal to my comments, see Matt Cardin, "The Master's Eyes Shining with Secrets: H. P. Lovecraft's Influence on Thomas Ligotti," *Lovecraft Annual* 1 (2007): 94–125.

2. Shawn Ramsey, "A Graveside Chat: Interview with Thomas Ligotti," *Deathrealm* No. 8 (Spring 1989): 21.

3. Ibid.

4. See Carl T. Ford, "Notes on the Writing of Horror: An Interview with Thomas Ligotti," *Dagon* Nos. 22/23 (September–December 1988): 34.

5. Ibid., p. 33.

6. Stefan Dziemianowicz and Michael A. Morrison, "The Language of Dread: An Interview with Thomas Ligotti," in *Science Fiction & Fantasy Review Annual 1990*, ed. Robert A. Collins and Robert Latham (Westport, CT: Greenwood Press, 1991), p. 116.

7. See Ford, p. 34.

8. For a more detailed study of the story, with extensive discussion of Lovecraft's influence upon it, see John Langan, "Thomas Ligotti's Metafictional Mapping: The Allegory of 'The Last Feast of Harlequin,'" *Lovecraft Annual* 1 (2007): 126–44.

9. W. H. Pugmire, "Afterword" to "The Songs of Sesqua Valley," in *Sesqua Valley and Other Haunts* (North Webster, IN: Delirium Books, 2003), p. 99.

10. See Ch. II, n. 18.

11. Richard L. Tierney, "To the Hydrogen Bomb," *Collected Poems* (Sauk City, WI: Arkham House, 1981), p. 82.

12. Tierney, "The Derleth Mythos," p. 52.

13. John Langan, "Domination of Black" (review of Laird Barron's *The Imago Sequence and Other Stories*), *Dead Reckonings* No. 2 (Fall 2007): 37–38.

14. See J. L. Meikle, "Other Frequencies: The Parallel Worlds of Thomas Pynchon and H. P. Lovecraft," *Modern Fiction Studies* 27, No. 2 (Summer 1981): 287–94.

Bibliography

A. *Works by H. P. Lovecraft*

The Ancient Track: Complete Poetical Works. Ed. S. T. Joshi. San Francisco: Night Shade Books, 2001.

At the Mountains of Madness and Other Novels. Ed. S. T. Joshi. Sauk City, WI: Arkham House, [1985].

Collected Essays. Ed. S. T. Joshi. New York: Hippocampus Press, 2004–06. 5 vols.

Dagon and Other Macabre Tales. Ed. S. T. Joshi. Sauk City, WI: Arkham House, [1986].

The Dunwich Horror and Others. Ed. S. T. Joshi. Sauk City, WI: Arkham House, [1984].

Essential Solitude: The Letters of H. P. Lovecraft and August Derleth. Ed. David E. Schultz and S. T. Joshi. New York: Hippocampus Press, 2007. 2 vols. (numbered consecutively).

Miscellaneous Writings. Ed. S. T. Joshi. Sauk City, WI: Arkham House, 1995.

Selected Letters. Ed. August Derleth, Donald Wandrei, and James Turner. Sauk City, WI: Arkham House, 1965–76. 5 vols.

The Shadow out of Time. Ed. S. T. Joshi and David E. Schultz. New York: Hippocampus Press, 2001.

B. *Works by Others*

Bloch, Robert. "Black Bargain." In *Flowers from the Moon and Other Lunacies*. Ed. Robert M. Price. Sauk City, WI: Arkham House, 1998.

———. *Mysteries of the Worm*. 2nd ed. Ed. Robert M. Price. Oakland, CA: Chaosium, 1993. [Includes "The Brood of Bubastis," "The Dark Demon," "The Faceless God," "Fane of the Black Pharaoh," "The Grinning Ghoul," "The Secret of Sebek," "The Shadow from the

Steeple," "The Sorcerer's Jewel," "The Suicide in the Study," "Terror in Cut-Throat Cave," "The Unspeakable Betrothal."]

———. *Strange Eons*. Chapel Hill, NC: Whispers Press, 1978.

Campbell, Ramsey. *Cold Print*. London: Headline, 1993. [Includes "Before the Storm," "Cold Print," "The Voice of the Beach."]

———. "Dolls." In *Scared Stiff: Tales of Sex and Death*. Los Angeles: Scream/Press, 1986.

———. "The Faces at Pine Dunes." In *New Tales of the Cthulhu Mythos*, ed. Ramsey Campbell. Sauk City, WI: Arkham House, 1980, pp. 223–53.

———. "The Franklyn Paragraphs." In *Demons by Daylight*. Sauk City, WI: Arkham House, 1973.

———. *Ghostly Tales*. Mount Olive, NC: Cryptic Publications, 1987.

———. "The Horror under Warrendown." In *Made in Goatswood*, ed. Scott David Aniolowski. Oakland, CA: Chaosium, 1995, pp. 255–68.

———. "The Pattern." In *Dark Companions*. New York: Macmillan, 1982.

———. "Raised by the Moon." In *Weird Shadows over Innsmouth*, ed. Stephen Jones. Minneapolis, MN: Fedogan & Bremer, 2005, pp. 196–209.

———. "Snakes and Ladders." In *Inconsequential Tales*. New York: Hippocampus Press, 2007, pp. 230–37.

———. "The Tomb-Herd." In *The Tomb-Herd and Others*. Mount Olive, NC: Cryptic Publications, 1986, pp. 3–9.

Cannon, Peter. "The Madness out of Space." In *The New Lovecraft Circle*, ed. Robert M. Price. Minneapolis, MN: Fedogan & Bremer, 1996, pp. 364–99.

Cave, Hugh B. "The Death Watch." In *Cthulhu's Heirs*, ed. Thomas M. K. Stratman. Oakland, CA: Chaosium, 1994, pp. 23–34.

———. "The Isle of Dark Magic." *Weird Tales* 24, no. 4 (October 1934): 185–203.

Chappell, Fred. *Dagon*. 1968. New York: St. Martin's Press, 1987.

———. *More Shapes Than One*. New York: St. Martin's Press, 1991. [Contains "The Adder," "Weird Tales."]

Copper, Basil. *The Great White Space*. 1974. New York: Manor Books, 1976.

———. "Shaft Number 247." In *New Tales of the Cthulhu Mythos*, ed. Ramsey Campbell. Sauk City, WI: Arkham House, 1980, pp. 115–43.

Derleth, August. "The Dweller in Darkness." In *Tales of the Cthulhu Mythos*, ed. August Derleth (rev. James Turner). Sauk City, WI: Arkham House, 1990, pp. 116–52.

———. *The Mask of Cthulhu*. 1958. Rpt. New York: Beagle Books, 1971. [Contains "The Return of Hastur" and "The Whippoorwills in the Hills."]

———. "Something from Out There." In *Weird Tales: 32 Unearthed Terrors*, ed. Stefan R. Dziemianowicz, Robert Weinberg, and Martin H. Greenberg. New York: Bonanza Books, 1988, pp. 584–94.

———. "The Thing That Walked on the Wind." In *Tales of the Lovecraft Mythos*, ed. Robert M. Price. Minneapolis, MN: Fedogan & Bremer, 1992, pp. 94–104.

———. *The Trail of Cthulhu*. 1962. New York; Beagle Books, 1971.

———. *The Watchers out of Time and Others*. As by "H. P. Lovecraft and August Derleth." Sauk City, WI: Arkham House, 1974.

Derleth, August, and Mark Schorer. *Colonel Markesan and Less Pleasant People*. Sauk City, WI: Arkham House, 1966. [Contains "The Horror from the Depths," "The Lair of the Star-Spawn," "Spawn of the Maelstrom."]

DeBill, Walter C., Jr. "Where Yidhra Walks." In *The Disciples of Cthulhu*, ed. Edward P. Berglund. New York: DAW Books, 1976, pp. 101–29.

Gaiman, Neil. "Only the End of the World Again." In *Shadows over Innsmouth*, ed. Stephen Jones. Minneapolis, MN: Fedogan & Bremer, 1994, pp. 316–29.

Hasse, Henry. "The Guardian of the Book." In *Tales of the Lovecraft Mythos*, ed. Robert M. Price. Minneapolis, MN: Fedogan & Bremer, 1992, pp. 258–83.

———. "Horror at Vecra." In *The Acolytes of Cthulhu*, ed. Robert M. Price. Minneapolis, MN: Fedogan & Bremer, 2000, pp. 67–87.

Howard, Robert E. "The Children of the Night." In *The Spawn of Cthulhu*, ed. Lin Carter. New York: Ballantine, 1971, pp. 171–89.

———. *Cthulhu: The Mythos and Kindred Horrors*. New York: Baen, 1987. [Contains "The Black Stone," "Dig Me No Grave," "The Thing on the Roof," "Worms of the Earth."]

———. *Skull-Face and Others*. Sauk City, WI: Arkham House, 1946. [Contains "The Fire of Asshurbanipal," "The Scarlet Citadel."]

Johnson, Robert Barbour. "Far Below." In *Far Below and other Horrors*, ed. Robert Weinberg. West Linn, OR: FAX, 1974, pp. 11–22.

Kiernan, Caitlín R. "From Cabinet 34, Drawer 6." In *Weird Shadows over Innsmouth*, ed. Stephen Jones. Minneapolis, MN: Fedogan & Bremer, 2005, pp. 169–95.

King, Stephen. *The Dark Half*. New York: Viking, 1989.

———. "Jerusalem's Lot." In *Tales of the Cthulhu Mythos*, ed. August Derleth (rev. James Turner). Sauk City, WI: Arkham House, 1990, pp. 468–502.

Klein, T. E. D. "Black Man with a Horn." In *New Tales of the Cthulhu Mythos*, ed. Ramsey Campbell. Sauk City, WI: Arkham House, 1980, pp. 145–85.

Kuttner, Henry. *The Book of Iod*. Ed. Robert M. Price. Oakland, CA: Chaosium, 1995. [Contains "Bells of Horror," "The Hunt," "The Invaders," "The Salem Horror," "The Secret of Kralitz."]

Leiber, Fritz. *Fritz Leiber and H. P. Lovecraft: Writers of the Dark*. Ed. Ben J. S. Szumskyj and S. T. Joshi. Holicong, PA: Wildside Press, 2004. [Contains "Adept's Gambit," "A Bit of the Dark World," "Diary in the Snow," "The Dreams of Albert Moreland," "The Sunken Land."]

———. *Night's Black Agents*. 1947. Rpt. New York: Berkley, 1978. [Contains "The Automatic Pistol," "The Hill and the Hole," "The Hound," "Smoke Ghost."]

———. "The Terror from the Depths." In *Tales of the Cthulhu Mythos*, ed. August Derleth (rev. James Turner). Sauk City, WI: Arkham House, 1990, pp. 267–312.

Ligotti, Thomas. *Grimscribe*. New York: Carroll & Graf, 1991. [Contains "The Last Feast of Harlequin," "Nethescurial."]

———. *Songs of a Dead Dreamer*. 1986. Rev. ed. London: Robinson, 1989. [Contains "The Sect of the Idiot," "The Troubles of Dr. Thoss," "Vastarien."]

Langford, David. "Deepnet." In *Shadows over Innsmouth*, ed. Stephen Jones. Minneapolis, MN: Fedogan & Bremer, 1994, pp. 255–59.

Long, Frank Belknap. *The Horror from the Hills*. In *Odd Science Fiction*. New York: Belmont, 1964.

———. *The Hounds of Tindalos*. New York: Jove/HBJ, 1978. [Contains "The Hounds of Tindalos," "The Space-Eaters."]

Lumley, Brian. *Beneath the Moors*. 1974. In *Beneath the Moors and Darker Places*. New York: Tor, 2002.

———. *Titus Crow, Volume One: The Burrowers Beneath; The Transition of Titus Crow*. New York: Tor, 1997.

———. *Titus Crow, Volume Two: The Clock of Dreams; Spawn of the Winds*. New York: Tor, 1997.

———. *Titus Crow, Volume Three: In the Moons of Borea; Elysia*. New York: Tor, 1997.

Masterton, Graham. *The Manitou*. 1975. New York: Pinnacle Books, 1976.

Myers, Gary. *The House of the Worm*. Sauk City, WI: Arkham House, 1975.

Prout, Mearle. "The House of the Worm." In *Tales of the Lovecraft Mythos*, ed. Robert M. Price. Minneapolis, MN: Fedogan & Bremer, 1992, pp. 196–215.

Pugmire, W. H. "Necronomicon." In *Dreams of Lovecraftian Horror*. Poplar Bluff, MO: Mythos Books, 1999.

———. *Sesqua Valley and Other Haunts*. North Webster, IN: Delirium Books, 2003. [Contains "Beneath an Autumn Moon," "The Darkest Star," "The Hands That Reek and Smoke," "The Imp of Aether," "O, Christmas Tree," "The Songs of Sesqua Valley."]

———. "The Sign That Sets the Darkness Free." In *The Fungal Stain and Other Dreams*. New York: Hippocampus Press, 2006.

Pulver, Joseph S., Sr. *Nightmare's Disciple*. Oakland, CA: Chaosium, 1999.

Royle, Nicholas. "The Homecoming." In *Shadows over Innsmouth*, ed. Stephen Jones. Minneapolis, MN: Fedogan & Bremer, 1994, pp. 237–54.

Sargent, Stanley C. *Ancient Exhumations*. Poplar Bluff, MO: Mythos Books, 1999.

———. *The Taint of Lovecraft*. Poplar Bluff, MO: Mythos Books, 2002. [Contains "The Black Brat of Dunwich," "Their Love of Craft."]

Searight, Richard F. "The Sealed Casket." In *The Sealed Casket and Others*. West Warwick, RI: Necronomicon Press, 1996.

Shea, Michael. *The Color out of Time*. New York: DAW Books, 1984.

Smith, Clark Ashton. "The Door to Saturn." In *Lost Worlds*. 1944. St. Albans, UK: Panther, 1974 (Volume 2).

————. "The Nameless Offspring." In *The Abominations of Yondo*. 1960. St. Albans, UK: Panther, 1974.

————. *Out of Space and Time*. 1942. St. Albans, UK: Panther, 1974. [Volume 2 contains "The Return of the Sorcerer" and "Ubbo-Sathla."]

————. *A Rendezvous in Averoigne*. Sauk City, WI: Arkham House, 1988. [Contains "The Holiness of Azédarac," "The Seven Geases," and "The Tale of Satampra Zeiros."]

————. *Strange Shadows: The Uncollected Fiction and Essays of Clark Ashton Smith*. Ed. Steve Behrends, with Donald Sidney-Fryer and Rah Hoffman. Westport, CT: Greenwood Press, 1989. [Contains "The Beast of Averoigne," "The Coming of the White Worm."]

Spencer, William Browning. *Résumé with Monsters*. Clarkston, GA: White Wolf, 1995.

Straub, Peter. *Mr. X*. New York: Random House, 1999.

Thomas, Jeffrey. *Monstrocity*. Canton, OH: Prime Books, 2003.

————. *Unholy Dimensions*. Poplar Bluff, MO: Mythos Books, 2005. [Contains "The Avatars of the Old Ones," "The Bones of the Old Ones," "Out of the Belly of Sheol," "Through Obscure Glass," "The Young of the Old Ones."]

Thompson, C. Hall. "Spawn of the Green Abyss." In *Tales of the Lovecraft Mythos*, ed. Robert M. Price. Minneapolis, MN: Fedogan & Bremer, 1992, pp. 216–57.

————. "The Will of Claude Asher." In *The Acolytes of Cthulhu*, ed. Robert M. Price. Minneapolis, MN: Fedogan & Bremer, 2000, pp. 138–76.

Tierney, Richard L. *The House of the Toad*. Minneapolis, MN: Fedogan & Bremer, 1993.

Tyson, Donald. *Alhazred: Author of the* Necronomicon. Woodbury, MN: Llewellyn Publications, 2006.

————. *Necronomicon: The Wanderings of Alhazred*. Woodbury, MN: Llewellyn Publications, 2004.

Wade, James. "The Deep Ones." In *Tales of the Cthulhu Mythos*, ed. August Derleth. 1969. New York: Ballantine, 1971, Vol. 2, pp. 161–204.

Wagner, Karl Edward. "Sticks." In *Tales of the Cthulhu Mythos*, ed. August Derleth (rev. James Turner). Sauk City, WI: Arkham House, 1990, pp. 427–48.

Wandrei, Donald. *The Eye and the Finger.* Sauk City, WI: Arkham House, 1944. [Contains "The Tree-Men of M'bwa."]

———. *The Web of Easter Island.* Sauk City, WI: Arkham House, 1948.

Wellman, Many Wade. "The Terrible Parchment." In *Necronomicon,* ed. Robert M. Price. Oakland, CA: Chaosium, 1996, pp. 2–6.

Wilson, Colin. *The Mind Parasites.* 1967. Rpt. St Albans, UK: Panther, 1969.

———. *The Philosopher's Stone.* 1969. New York: Warner Books, 1974.

———. "The Return of the Lloigor." In *Tales of the Cthulhu Mythos,* ed. August Derleth. 1969. New York: Ballantine, 1971, Vol. 2, pp. 205–69.

———. *The Space Vampires.* 1976. New York: Pocket Books, 1977.

Wilson, F. Paul. "The Barrens." In *Lovecraft's Legacy,* ed. Robert E. Weinberg and Martin H. Greenberg. New York: Tor, 1990, pp. 269–334.

———. *The Keep.* 1981. New York: Berkley, 1982.

C. *Criticism*

Carter, Lin. Lovecraft: A Look Behind the "Cthulhu Mythos." New York: Ballantine, 1972.

Hall, Loay, Terry Dale, and Randall Larson. "A History of the Cthulhu Mythos." *Fandom Unlimited* No. 2 (Spring 1977): 21–28; No. 3 (Summer 1977): 8–14.

Harms, Daniel. *Encyclopedia Cthulhuiana.* Oakland, CA: Chaosium, 1994 (rev. ed. 1998).

Harms, Daniel, and John Wisdom Gonce III. *The Necronomicon Files.* Mountain View, CA: Night Shade Books, 1998.

Jarocha-Ernst, Chris. *A Cthulhu Mythos Bibliography and Concordance.* Seattle: Armitage House, 1999.

Joshi, S. T. *H. P. Lovecraft: A Life.* West Warwick, RI: Necronomicon Press, 1996.

———. *H. P. Lovecraft: The Decline of the West.* Mercer Island, WA: Starmont House, 1990.

———. *A Subtler Magick: The Writings and Philosophy of H. P. Lovecraft.* Mercer Island, WA: Starmont House, 1996.

Mariconda, Steven J. "Toward a Reader-Response Approach to the Lovecraft Mythos." In Mariconda's *On the Emergence of "Cthulhu" and*

Other Observations. West Warwick, RI: Necronomicon Press, 1995, pp. 29–44.

Mosig, Dirk W. "H. P. Lovecraft: Myth-Maker." In *H. P. Lovecraft: Four Decades of Criticism,* ed. S. T. Joshi. Athens: Ohio University Press, 1980, pp. 104–12.

Murray, Will. "An Uncompromising Look at the Cthulhu Mythos." *Lovecraft Studies* No. 12 (Spring 1986): 26–31.

Pearsall, Anthony. *The Lovecraft Lexicon.* Tempe, AZ: New Falcon Publications, 2005.

Price, Robert M. *H. P. Lovecraft and the Cthulhu Mythos.* Mercer Island, WA: Starmont House, 1990.

———. "Lovecraft's 'Artificial Mythology.'" In *An Epicure in the Terrible: A Centennial Anthology of Essays in Honor of H. P. Lovecraft,* ed. David E. Schultz and S. T. Joshi. Rutherford, NJ: Fairleigh Dickinson University Press, 1991, pp. 247–56.

Schultz, David E. "The Origin of Lovecraft's 'Black Magic' Quote." *Crypt of Cthulhu* No. 48 (St. John's Eve 1987): 9–13.

———. "Who Needs the Cthulhu Mythos?" *Lovecraft Studies* No. 13 (Fall 1986): 43–53.

———, ed. "Notes toward a History of the Cthulhu Mythos." *Crypt of Cthulhu* No. 92 (Eastertide 1996): 15–33.

Tierney, Richard L. "The Derleth Mythos." 1972. In *Discovering H. P. Lovecraft,* ed. Darrell Schweitzer. Holicong, PA: Wildside Press, 2001, pp. 52–53.

Index

LaVergne, TN USA
16 October 2009
161185LV00002B/14/P